GREATER
THAN
EVER

DANIEL L.
DOCTOROFF

GREATER
THAN
EVER

NEW YORK'S
BIG COMEBACK

PUBLICAFFAIRS
NEW YORK

Copyright © 2017 by Daniel L. Doctoroff.

Published by PublicAffairs™, an imprint of Perseus Books, LLC, a subsidiary of Hachette Book Group, Inc.

The Hachette Speakers Bureau provides a wide range of authors for speaking events. To find out more, go to hachettespeakersbureau.com or call 866-376-6591.

Book Design by Amy Quinn

Library of Congress Cataloging-in-Publication Data

Names: Doctoroff, Daniel L., author.
Title: Greater than ever : New York's big comeback / Daniel L. Doctoroff.
Description: First edition. | New York : PublicAffairs, [2017] | Includes index.
Identifiers: LCCN 2017017398 | ISBN 9781610396073 (hardcover)
Subjects: LCSH: Doctoroff, Daniel L. | New York (N.Y.). Office of the
Mayor--Officials and employees--Biography. | City managers--New York
(State)--New York. | Olympic host city selection--2012. | Economic
development--New York (State)--New York. | Urban renewal--New York
(State)--New York. | City planning--New York (State)--New York. | New York
(N.Y.)--Politics and government—1951–
Classification: LCC F128.54.D63 A3 2017 | DDC 974.7—dc23
LC record available at https://lccn.loc.gov/2017017398

ISBN 978-1-61039-607-3 (HC)

ISBN 978-1-61039-608-0 (EB)

First Edition

LSC-C

10 9 8 7 6 5 4 3 2 1

To Alisa, who made our
life in New York possible

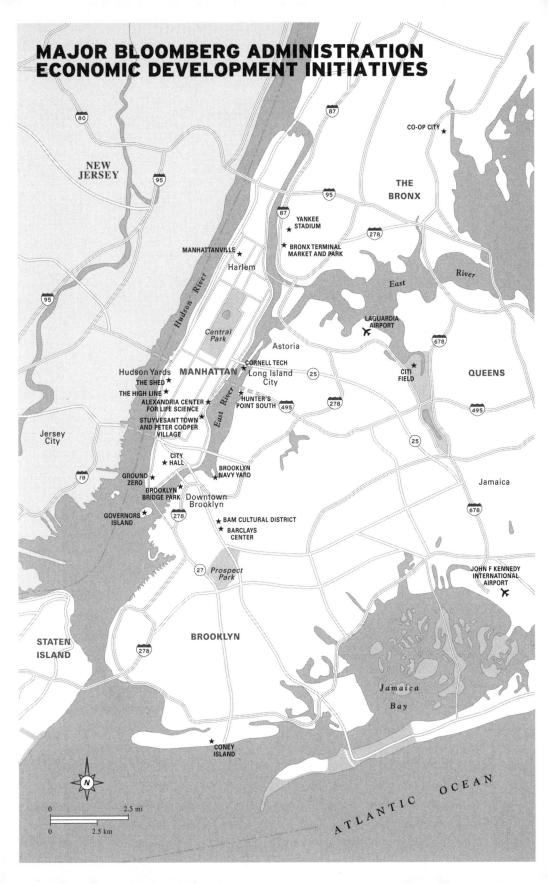

CONTENTS

PROLOGUE

I VIVIDLY REMEMBER my first visit to New York City; it was hate at first sight.

It was the summer of 1968, and I had just turned ten. A typical summer vacation for our family was a long car trip from our home in suburban Detroit to the East Coast. My parents packed my three younger brothers and me into our 1965 dark-blue Impala station wagon, and we headed first to Montreal to see Expo 1967, one year late, then down through Vermont and on to the obligatory stop in Boston, where our grandparents lived. Before heading home, Mom and Dad decided to visit my Dad's brother, Mike, and his family, who had just moved to Brookfield, Connecticut, about seventy miles from New York City.

On the spur of the moment, the adults decided it would be fun to go see the Ringling Brothers and Barnum & Bailey Circus at the then-new Madison Square Garden. Back into the station wagon we piled, and we headed for New York City for a day trip.

It was the kind of grayish, sweltering, August day that made the air above the road shimmer in waves. As we drove south on the highway, just past the sign that said "Entering New York City," I was in the backseat on the left side staring out the window when I suddenly saw in the distance what looked like an alien city. As we drove closer, the outlines of dozens of seemingly identical brown buildings piercing the sky grew clearer. They seemed to be replicating, with more anonymous clones under construction—a vast, bleak, spreading mass. In the foreground was a dump. My dad announced that this was Co-op City.

Co-op City was built in the 1960s and early 1970s as a new type of development for middle-income New Yorkers. An unprecedented endeavor, it is still the largest single residential development in the United States—thirty-seven towers plus garages, schools, and its own postal code.

I knew none of that as we drove by, but just that the uniform towers, alone in the distance, looked monstrous. They were the first image I had of New York. "I am never going to live in this city," I shouted out from the backseat.

Despite my resolution, on January 1, 2002, I stood on a ledge of a damaged skyscraper looking down on Ground Zero and realized that my fate was intertwined with the future of New York. At that moment, as I contemplated the twisted wreckage, I was overcome by my responsibility as the new Deputy Mayor for Economic Development and Rebuilding for the Michael Bloomberg Administration, not only to oversee the rebuilding of the World Trade Center site but also to consider New York City's place in the world.

In the wake of September 11, 2001, fundamental questions about the practicality of cities across the country—and indeed the entire free world—were raised. Were great cities still possible? Could millions of people live together safely and even thrive in a world that faced unprecedented economic, security, and even existential threats? New York had always stood alone among cities for its openness and ambition. Now people were questioning whether the very things that made the city so unique could continue.

Less than two months earlier, on November 11, 2001, the *New York Times* had run a front-page story outlining a bleak possible future: "The slowing economy, the collapse of the dot-com bubble and the impact of September 11 have raised the specter of the city's enduring another period of austerity, a return to the days of dirtier streets, legions of the homeless, an increase in the welfare population, a rise in crime, a plummet in the quality of life so sharp that people fled town."

The writers were right to be worried. On January 1, 2002, it was fair to question the very premise of New York. In the three months after the attack that spanned roughly seventeen minutes, New York City lost approximately 430,000 jobs and $2.8 billion in wages. Gross domestic product (GDP) for the city declined by an estimated $11.5 billion by the end of 2001, resulting in more than $2 billion in lost tax revenues. Approximately 18,000 small businesses were destroyed or displaced after the attacks. In some neighborhoods around Ground Zero, vacancy rates shot to over 40 percent.

Cornerstone businesses such as American Express and Lehman Brothers had to abandon their smoldering headquarters. In fact, New York City lost 25,000 of its 208,000 security-industry jobs in the month after the attacks.

For a city highly dependent on its financial services sector, this could have been a crippling blow by itself. It was made worse by the shattering of the city's second most important industry—tourism, which employed 263,000 people and generated $25 billion per year. The number of tourists plummeted by almost 50 percent, dropping hotel occupancy below 40 percent; 3,000 employees in the travel and tourism industry were laid off in a single week after the attack.

September 11 could have broken the city's back, forever associating New York with its most famous disaster. But New Yorkers, aided by people from around the world, took the challenge to heart. This book is the story of some of the people who rose to that challenge in, or in partnership with, the city's mayoral administration. By the time Mike Bloomberg completed his third term at the end of 2013, New York was in remarkable shape.

Although the financial rebound was spectacular, I suspect that when the legacy of this time is judged generations from now, the history books will focus not on the money but on what was built with it. The Bloomberg years changed the physical nature of the city in ways that will undergird prosperity for decades.

Back in 2001, there had been little physical change to the city for nearly a half century. There were many reasons for this, including the fact that New York had been too budget-strapped to invest and that trauma from development catastrophes in the 1960s, such as tearing down the original, extraordinary Pennsylvania Station, had left the city paralyzed.

In this suspended state, New York was rotting—literally. Vast swaths of riverfront property were decrepit and unusable. Neglected industrial buildings and railyards, relics of a bygone manufacturing era, marred the outskirts of all the boroughs. The transportation and energy infrastructure had not been changed in decades. The city's housing stock was woefully insufficient. And as a coastline city, we faced grave new threats from rising oceans and storms caused by global warming.

Against these odds came a group of city officials, most of whom had virtually no government experience or expertise in city policy. I brought zero experience in government to the task of reviving New York from its most serious financial, emotional, and existential crisis in modern history. And the only staff I could afford was young (average age: twenty-eight), with even less experience than I had. On paper, we were probably among the least-prepared administrations in history—at a time when the stakes had never been higher.

My friends are often curious about why I am writing this account only now, a decade after I've been out of office. The answer is that building big things takes time. And it is only now that the full sweep of what we were able to accomplish is becoming clear, and I can confidently evaluate all that has succeeded—and, of course, the areas in which we fell short.

From the street level, it is hard to absorb all the changes. In fact, many of our adjustments to make the city more financially secure and environmentally sustainable are invisible to the naked eye. It is hard to appreciate the fact that hundreds of thousands of jobs were created during the Bloomberg Administration, many of which were in industries that were the subject of targeted policy interventions, or that the air is healthier, the water is cleaner, the energy infrastructure has been upgraded, hundreds of playgrounds opened up, and a million trees were planted because of PlaNYC, the city's novel sustainability plan. Yet there is so much that you can see.

Imagine that you could come with me to one of my favorite places in New York, the Panorama at the Queens Museum. Originally built for Robert Moses's 1964 World's Fair, it features one huge room where you can hover just above a replica of the entire city, with all of its nearly one million buildings. In one quick turn of your head you can take in everything from the Harlem River in the Bronx to the north of the city to the Verrazano Bridge, which spans New York Harbor before it breaks into the Atlantic Ocean, to the south.

From high above the Bronx, you couldn't miss the new Yankee Stadium, but perhaps, without a guide, you wouldn't know that you were looking down on acres of new apartment buildings—just some of the astonishing 165,000 units we erected as part of a pathbreaking affordable-housing plan.

Dropping down over Queens, you would see another new stadium for the Mets, but here you would also spot the towers of Hunters Point and Long Island City—part of a sustained building boom we brought about by resuscitating an abandoned industrial waterfront and stimulating a new commercial district.

That plan also provided parkland along the East River extending well into Brooklyn. As your eyes traveled south along the Brooklyn waterfront, you would see hundreds of new buildings in Greenpoint and Williamsburg, neighborhoods rezoned to accommodate residential uses, which now contain perhaps the greatest concentration of hipsters in the world.

If you looked carefully enough, you could spot new industrial buildings in the Brooklyn Navy Yard, once the shipyard that launched many of the nation's most venerable naval vessels, now reinvented to accommodate new manufacturing uses appropriate for a twenty-first-century economy. Just a little farther south, you would see, just under the highway that separates elegant Brooklyn Heights and the waterfront, the new Brooklyn Bridge Park, a spectacular public space that has restored the views of Lower Manhattan after decades of their being blocked by unused pier heads.

From Brooklyn Bridge Park, if you looked just a short distance into the inner harbor, you would spot Governors Island, an abandoned military base transformed into a vast new park soaring against the skyline, with four glorious hills made partly out of the rubble of the old buildings torn down to make way for the hills. Off in the distance you would spy a revived Coney Island, where new attractions and amusements have drawn people back to the waterfront in South Brooklyn, beginning to stimulate new residential and commercial investment.

If you tore yourself away from this buzzing, beloved waterfront, you could move inland to the new towers of Downtown Brooklyn, nestled amid a reinvigorated arts district with new theaters and, yes, another arena there, home to the Brooklyn Nets and the New York Islanders. The Barclays Center brought professional sports back to a borough whose population would make it the fourth largest city in the United States for the first time since the beloved Brooklyn Dodgers relocated to Los Angeles in 1957.

Crossing the East River to the bottom of Manhattan Island, the ferries shuttle passengers around the curve of the borough and up the twist of the river, providing vital new arteries of transportation in the city. Far from being scarred forever by the attacks, Lower Manhattan is now on its way to being nearly completely rebuilt as a twenty-first-century, live-work-visit community, attracting internationally renowned companies to its commercial core; young families to its burgeoning network of housing, schools, and parks; and visitors from around the world to a deeply moving memorial to the events of 9/11.

Now we go up the Hudson to Manhattan's last undeveloped frontier, the Far West Side, which at its core was six blocks of active railyards and is now becoming—on top of those railyards—the country's largest-ever development, a glittering neighborhood of skyscrapers made easily accessible by a new subway stop and anchored by the world-renowned High Line Park. When the Bloomberg Administration entered office, the decaying, elevated line was slated to be destroyed; it quickly became the tenth most Instagrammed site in the world.

The road to these achievements, and many more, was never a smooth or simple one. Nothing in New York ever is. This is not to say that everything we tried was successful or that there weren't unintended consequences. We made enormous mistakes, but generally we learned and adapted. Along the way, we gained a far more nuanced understanding of New York's unique character—its assets and liabilities. From this understanding, we developed a guiding philosophy and a new set of tools for making plans and then executing them.

As Deputy Mayor for Economic Development and Rebuilding, my role was focused on the physical and financial recovery of New York. This is the story of that recovery. This story is not a comprehensive history of the Bloomberg Administration. Mike Bloomberg recruited and then led an extraordinarily talented group of public officials, many of whom remained in the Bloomberg Administration for all three four-year terms, in part because they believed in their city and because they were empowered by the Mayor to be bold and take risks.

The success we enjoyed on the economic and physical fronts rested, in the first place, on the foundation of the sound fiscal management by the Mayor, Deputy Mayor Marc Shaw, and Budget Director Mark Page and their teams in the immediate aftermath of 9/11, when huge budget deficits could have crippled the city. The economic rebound we experienced would not have been possible but for the dramatically safer city that Police Commissioner Ray Kelly and the New York Police Department (NYPD) provided at the same time they were ensuring that the city was protected from another terrorist attack; the growth that we experienced benefited from the Mayor's willingness to take over the school system along with Chancellors Joel Klein and Dennis Walcott's efforts to open hundreds of new schools, invest in old ones, and make teachers, principals, and administrators more accountable, leading to significant improvements in student performance. Improvements in quality of life—for all residents, businesses, and visitors—make a city worth living in, and with few exceptions Deputy Mayors, Commissioners, and their staffs bequeathed to their successors creative and responsive agencies committed to doing just that. Overseeing all of that was a Mayor—with First Deputy Mayor Patti Harris providing unassuming but indispensable support—who guided and supported his team, especially when things got very difficult.

Although this is my story and New York's story, I also think it is a tale that has broader applicability. All cities struggle with the same issues: sprawl, congestion, public safety, underused land, affordability, job growth, deteriorating water quality and shortages, derelict waterfronts, environmental sustainability, quality of life, and, maybe most important, how to stay dynamic and viable in an increasingly competitive world. I hope our path can be a guide and inspiration for others around the world, especially given New York's status as a beacon for other cities.

CHAPTER ONE

SETTLING (RELUCTANTLY) IN NEW YORK

A S MY WIFE, Alisa, and I were contemplating where to live after graduate
school, New York was the last place we expected to end up.

We had met at Harvard as freshmen and married at what now seems like
the shocking age of twenty-three. We decided to go to graduate school at the
University of Chicago, where she studied business and I pursued law.

Alisa's MBA program finished a year before mine, so she was going to
have to find a permanent job while I looked for something over the summer.
We agreed to focus our search on Boston or Philadelphia, nice East Coast
cities that were not New York. I had to choose first because the interviewing
season for law schools was in the fall, whereas business schools waited until
winter. I picked the top Philadelphia firm, Dechert Price and Rhoads.

Meanwhile, Alisa concluded that she really wanted to work in media. She
reached out to every television station, every newspaper, anything that resem-
bled a media company in Philadelphia. No luck.

Then she uttered the dreaded words: "I think I have to look in New York."
It was the media capital of the world. How could I argue? Alisa found a job
in the city at HBO, and we moved. I commuted that summer to Philadelphia
and arranged to take my final year of law school at New York University. We
expected to stay for only a couple of years.

A friend let us rent his spacious Gramercy Park apartment for about
$600 a month. Back then the park and the brownstones around it retained
their elegance, but the neighborhood around it was run down. Park Avenue

South was filled with prostitutes. Union Square was a haven for drug dealers. Somewhat reluctantly, I figured if I was going to be stuck in New York for the foreseeable future, I might as well explore it. I spent days wandering the city, taking the then-wretched subway to remote stations in the system just to see the neighborhoods above them. I began to play a game of guessing how many different nationalities there were among the passengers on the subway cars.

My other activity that year was trying to find a job. My summer in Philadelphia had helped me to understand what I wanted to do. I had been assigned to work on one of the largest attempted hostile takeover bids in history. Our job was the defense of Getty Oil from an attack by Pennzoil. One day I saw on a partner's desk a blue, Velo-bound book with "Goldman Sachs" stamped on it. I vaguely understood that Goldman Sachs was involved in the deal but didn't really know what an investment bank did. I asked to look at it, and the partner tossed it over to me. Later that evening, I started leafing through it. Filled with pages and pages of numbers, it analyzed the value of Getty Oil from dozens of different perspectives.

Right then and there I decided that I was going to be an investment banker. Never mind that I barely knew what that meant. I was convinced it was connected to an unlikely talent I had discovered in college: spotting stories in numbers. On a whim, I had taken a summer job between my junior and senior years with a political pollster and learned statistics. Until that point, I had been largely aimless and adrift at Harvard, unsure of my place. But as I dug into the polling numbers, I began seeing patterns. As my senior thesis, I developed an algorithm to predict congressional elections that correctly explained nearly all of the races I analyzed.

An unremarkable student my first three years, I worked harder than I ever had in my life. I ended up summa cum laude on the thesis, the highest grade of the more than one hundred seniors in the department. Surely, I could be an investment banker!

Salomon Brothers and Goldman Sachs briskly rejected me. I guess that having no relevant skills wasn't a plus. ("But I took Accounting for Lawyers," I protested to no avail.)

A friend from law school who already worked at Lehman Brothers helped me get an interview at that then-prestigious investment bank. Somehow I survived the first-round interrogation and was called back. I had no idea what to expect, but I was ushered into the plush partners' dining room and seated at the end of a huge, oval table. Two senior partners, Steve Fenster and Peter

Solomon, sat on either side of me. Two things were immediately apparent. First, the fact that I had attended Harvard was a huge plus for the two Harvard alums—for much of the interview that's all we talked about. The second was that they really didn't care for each other much and so spent the rest of the time bickering. As a result, they didn't have time to uncover just how ignorant I really was. A few days later, I was offered a position as an investment banking associate.

Investment banking came naturally to me, and I found that my law school training helped distinguish me from the other associates. I had learned to organize my thoughts logically, to articulate them, and to write. This allowed me to use the numbers I felt comfortable with to tell compelling stories in the service of selling companies or raising debt or equity. My timing in joining Lehman couldn't have been better. Between the time I accepted the offer and the time I actually started, the firm was acquired by Shearson, a large brokerage firm, which in turn was owned by American Express. The elite investment bankers at Lehman who had signed up for a small, prestigious partnership were deeply disappointed that they now worked for a huge company, briefly renamed Shearson Lehman American Express (or, unfortunately, SLAMEX), and, over the next two years, left in droves. Within months I was given responsibility I couldn't have imagined. In my first year there, I made more money than did my parents, a Michigan Court of Appeals judge and a psychologist, combined.

One of the great things to come out of my time at Lehman was that Peter Solomon took a real interest in me that has lasted to this day. He had started his career at Lehman and risen to be vice chair, but along the way he had served as Deputy Secretary of the US Treasury and as Deputy Mayor of Economic Policy and Development for Mayor Edward Koch. He was smart and irreverent. He said what he thought, which made him a controversial truth-teller within the firm. He also had a huge heart, and if he cared about you, he would really watch out for you. Later, when I asked him why he bothered to mentor me, he said he thought I had the right character. "Anyone can buy numbers people," he told me, "but investment banking is about interpersonal skills and relationships."

With Solomon's blessing, I chose to work in the merchant banking group. One of my first assignments was to structure an investment partnership between Lehman and Robert M. Bass, one of the Fort Worth–based Bass Brothers, one of the leading investors of that era. It was 1986, and the firm was on the cutting edge of a still-nascent field called private equity investing. After the partnership was set up, the founder of the partnership asked me to join. Solomon, who could have blocked me from leaving, let me go.

For the next fourteen years, I was a partner at what became known as Oak Hill Capital. By 1992, three partners and I were managing the firm. Fortunately, we rode the boom in the financial markets, and I achieved financial independence quickly. I worked hard and had little time for anything other than my job and family. So for my first eleven years in New York, I was, like most other residents, intently absorbed in my own narrow slice of life. Only very gradually did I begin to appreciate New York.

The first hint of that for me—when I first began to overcome my strong, negative, reflex reaction to the city—came within a month or so after I started at Lehman Brothers. I routinely worked sixteen- to eighteen-hour days as I labored to catch up to my MBA-educated peers. One early morning, I was riding back home from Lehman's Downtown offices after working all night. Slumped against my seat in exhaustion, I might have fallen asleep, my head swimming with details of spreadsheets. Instead, for some reason I glanced back. The rising stone towers of the Brooklyn Bridge were illuminated against the brightening sky, their reflections shimmering across the water, dancing off the New York Harbor and beyond. I had seen that view a thousand times in pictures, but this time I was completely stunned by how magical it seemed.

During that first decade in New York, our family grew to include our three children, Jacob, Ariel, and Jenna. When Alisa and I got engaged, I had volunteered to keep kosher and more or less observe the Jewish Sabbath (she came from a far more observant family than I did—I hadn't even been bar mitzvahed), which meant that I rarely worked on Saturdays. Instead, we went to synagogue regularly and spent much of the rest of our weekends in the playgrounds and pushing strollers around the Upper West Side neighborhood to which we had moved. I barely paid attention to the city around me. I no longer had time to randomly ride the subway. I never read the *New York Post* or the *Daily News*. The Metro section of the *New York Times* was the last section of the paper I looked at, if I looked at it at all.

But there were signs that I was gradually stepping out of my bubble and becoming more of a New Yorker, for better or for worse. To my own astonishment, I started rooting for New York sports teams, earning the never-ending condemnation of my brothers, who viewed it as an act of treason to our beloved Detroit Tigers, Pistons, Lions, and Red Wings.

Very gradually, almost imperceptibly, when I would fly back into LaGuardia or Newark Airport from a business trip, it began to feel like coming home. I looked forward to our routines around the neighborhood. Our kids' school began to feel like a community. Some of my partners at work became my closest friends. Eventually, Alisa and I couldn't imagine wanting to live anywhere else.

As New York started to feel more and more like home, I also started to notice and care more about my surroundings. The grime, the homelessness, and the prostitutes who patrolled the streets not far from our apartments, first near Gramercy Park and then on the Upper West Side, began to agitate me more after we had children and started to feel more invested in the city. I also became more and more aware of the racial tensions rising in the city in the late 1980s and early 1990s.

The 1989 Spike Lee movie, *Do the Right Thing*, captured those tensions brilliantly. In the movie, a set of seemingly minor incidents sets off a chain reaction of misunderstandings, igniting the underlying distrust between blacks and whites, culminating in a riot. I had my own mini-*Do-the-Right-Thing* moment one Sunday evening in the summer of 1992.

After a weekend on Long Island, I dropped off Alisa and the kids at our Upper West Side apartment building and then went to return the rental car. The light turned green at 90th Street and Amsterdam, a block from our apartment, and I started through the intersection. Almost immediately, I was lightly bumped by a car that had run the red light. I leapt out of the car, furious. "What the hell were you thinking?" I yelled at the driver.

The other driver, a middle-aged African American woman, got out and shouted that I had run the red light. As we argued, a crowd materialized, seemingly out of nowhere. I was stunned to realize that the growing crowd divided completely along racial lines, with the whites yelling that she was guilty and the blacks and Latinos screaming back that I had caused the accident. I doubt any of them had actually seen it. There wasn't much damage to my car and none to hers, so I apologized and the incident ended without escalation, but the point was not lost on me.

I voted for David Dinkins, the first African American Mayor of New York, in 1989, but given the decline in quality of life and the racial divisiveness that plagued the city during his mayoralty, I switched to Rudy Giuliani, the hard-charging former prosecutor, in 1993. He was the first Republican for whom I had ever voted, in any election. The fact that I was prepared to switch my vote for the first time was a sign that the city—its future well-being and prospects—had gotten its hooks into me. I had voted out of concern for its best future, not out of party loyalty. I had, without acknowledging it to myself, started to care enough to believe in the possibility of a better city.

But it took a sporting event that I couldn't have cared less about to turn me into one of New York's biggest boosters.

CHAPTER TWO

OLYMPIC BID TO DEPUTY MAYOR

NEW YORKERS GENERALLY straddle a strange line, taking comfort in the presence of countless strangers while simultaneously ignoring them. But sports obliterate barriers, resulting in enthusiastic eye contact on the subway, high-fiving strangers, and collective spontaneous singing. The connections, usually latent, become explicit and electrified, giving the vast city a small-town sense of intimacy. For New Yorkers, there was no time like June 1994. Both the Knicks and the Rangers made it to the finals of their league championships, and a friend and I attended nearly every home game of both series (the Knicks lost, but the Rangers won their first Stanley Cup since 1940).

The next month the World Cup came to the United States, and because we were on a roll, this friend, Andy Nathanson, tried to convince me to trek out to Giants Stadium with him on a hot July afternoon to watch the semifinal game. I had never been to a soccer match before, but based on the few times I'd glimpsed a game on television I had a clear opinion of the sport: it was terrible. Nobody scored. Nothing happened. The clock made no sense. It was boring. But I figured that it would be the only time in my lifetime the World Cup would be held in the United States. So, reluctantly, I agreed to go.

I regretted it almost instantly. The bus ride from Manhattan to Giants Stadium in New Jersey might be only eight miles, but we became mired in gridlock and it took more than an hour. We stepped out into a sweltering afternoon and trudged through the heat toward the stadium, immediately sweating. I gave Nathanson a look. What had we been thinking?

Then I walked into the stadium and stopped. Something was different—just standing there was electrifying. The game pitted Italy against Bulgaria, and Giants Stadium overflowed its capacity of nearly eighty thousand. The stands were teeming with roaring Italian Americans and Bulgarian Americans (and Italians and Bulgarians) standing, chanting, and singing, brandishing flags and painted bodies that screamed their national colors of white, red, and green.

No one sat down the entire game. Even after I had seen the Rangers and the Knicks the month before, that soccer game was the most spectacular sporting event I had ever attended. Period. As I stood there engulfed by sound, the stadium shaking as fans shrieked and danced at every feint, pass, and hurtling player, I realized something even more astounding: as incredible as this was, you could play that game in the New York area with almost any two countries in the world, and the emotion in the stands would be exactly the same.

I didn't know at that time that nearly 40 percent of New Yorkers are born outside the United States and that another 25 percent have at least one parent who is an immigrant, or that nearly every nation in the world is represented in the New York City public school system. Although I had been casually counting nationalities on the subway for years, there was something about the crowd in the stands that day that made me appreciate the utterly unique scale of the diversity of my adopted city.

Standing there, I fatefully began to ask myself why the most diverse city on the planet had never hosted the most international sporting event in the world, the Olympics. I had loved the Olympics since 1968, when glued to a new black-and-white television, my brother Mark and I first watched our Detroit Tigers win in the World Series and then the Olympics in Mexico City.

Those Olympics were filled with political and athletic drama. The pageantry of the Opening Ceremony, with almost every nation marching into the Olympic Stadium and then collecting on the infield, impressed us as a stunning display of international togetherness, especially during an era when images of Vietnam were on the news every night. We watched as John Carlos and Tommie Smith raised their gloved fists in a Black Power salute. We were thrilled by Dick Fosbury's over-the-top flop. We cheered on George Foreman as he won the heavyweight boxing gold medal and Al Oerter as he won his fourth gold medal in the discus.

The highlight of the Olympics for us, though, was Bob Beamon's record-setting long jump. Neither of us has ever forgotten the distance—29.2

feet—eclipsing the world record holder by more than 2 feet; so far that the equipment of the day was inadequate to capture it, and a measuring tape had to be brought to the field. Mark and I were so excited that we immediately began practicing long jumps between our twin beds.

So, I left Giants Stadium after the World Cup game with the vague notion that New York should host the Olympics. I had no idea what that actually meant—or what it would take. But what started as just a crazy idea grew in my mind into an increasingly intense calling.

At first, the only person I told about my idea was Alisa, who supplied the quiet, supportive confidence she brought to all of my craziest ideas. Alisa, the consummately practical person, had always indulged my leaps into unreality, such as going from being a lawyer to investment banker without any knowledge of a balance sheet. But I knew that if I was going to convince anyone else I had to know more than anyone about everything—about the economics of hosting the Games, the physical and other requirements, the bidding process, and every other detail. The upcoming 1996 Olympics in Atlanta were in the news frequently, so I read every possible source of information I could find about them. I also began doing research on past Games, especially those in Barcelona, Tokyo, and Los Angeles. This was before the rise of the Internet, but as a judge, my dad had unlimited access to an online service called Lexis-Nexis. Every night after the kids were asleep, I logged on and found newspaper articles from across the country, scholarly reports analyzing the impact of the Olympics on host cities, and comparisons of Atlanta and previous Games. I became obsessed. I quickly discovered that one of the first objections anyone raises to proposed Olympic Games is that they will make traffic unbearable. But I had a faint memory of reading somewhere that for Los Angeles in 1984 just the opposite happened. After much searching of Lexis-Nexis, I found an academic paper comparing the incidence rates of traffic jams during seventeen days of the Olympics in 1984 with rates during the exact seventeen days a year earlier. The study showed that it had actually declined—by 95 percent during the first few days of the Games (on subsequent days, as people saw that traffic wasn't a problem and ventured out, the declines were less). I must have repeated that statistic a thousand times over the next ten years.

The most important insight I gained from the research was that the biggest benefit from hosting the Olympics wasn't really about the actual Games at all. It came from the deadlines and international attention that forced cities to propose bold projects and then be accountable in the most public way possible. The prospect of being shamed around the world is a powerful motivator. When done effectively, hosting became a catalyst for getting things done that would be deemed politically or financially impossible under normal circumstances.

In 1964, Tokyo had leveraged hosting the Games to rapidly build its subway system. Barcelona had used the 1992 Olympics as an opportunity to shrug off decades of neglect under Franco to rebuild infrastructure and reconceive its waterfront. Largely as a result of hosting the Olympics, it is now one of the most visited cities in Europe. In 1996 Atlanta used hosting the Games to build affordable housing and to develop a downtown core that continues to make it more attractive to corporations and to residents twenty years later.

As I began to better understand both New York and the dynamics of hosting the Games, I began to conclude not only that New York could host the Olympics but also that it desperately *needed* to host the Games. New York had never really recovered from the 1970s, when white flight to the suburbs, a recession, and excessive spending had led the city to the brink of bankruptcy. Even after the city had been put on more solid financial footing, the late 1980s and early 1990s followed with a crack epidemic and soaring crime rates.

In 1994, Rudy Giuliani took office as the first Republican Mayor in more than two decades of a city in which more than a million New Yorkers that year had relied on welfare and about two thousand people had been murdered. A few months into his term, Mayor Giuliani's commitment to safety and improving quality of life were already having an impact. When Alisa and I bought an abandoned townhouse on West 91st in February 1994, there were homeless people sleeping on our stoop and crack vials in the tree pit in front of our house. By the time we moved in more than a year later, they were gone.

But there still hadn't been time or money to address basic infrastructure, and the terrible toll of neglect was still apparent everywhere. As I studied hosting the Olympics, I began to see the city through the eyes of a visitor. The frames on the bus stop shelters were rusting and appeared like ugly brown hulks on every other block. The medians on Broadway were choked with weeds and trash. The subways, despite significant investment, were scarred with graffiti.

I also started following the newspapers more closely and reading more about the city's history, and I discovered that New York was still saddled with land-use policies better suited to a bygone industrial and shipping era than to the final years of the twentieth century.

The result was huge swaths of land across the city filled with abandoned factories, wharves, and warehouses, many of them littered along the 520 miles of the city's waterfront. The potentially beautiful edge along the Hudson River was marred by rotting and abandoned piers. Railyards and rail lines on the West Side of Manhattan, in Downtown Brooklyn, and in Long Island City in Queens were inhospitable to any form of development.

Despite the obvious need for action, the city had been paralyzed by a virtual development freeze for more than thirty years. Part of the problem was nostalgia for New York's manufacturing past. Maybe more powerful was the lingering trauma of three development projects that had left local preservation groups well mobilized and city officials deeply conflicted and fearful. One was the notorious attempt by Robert Moses to build a highway through SoHo, stopped by Jane Jacobs, which only exacerbated the anti-Moses sentiment engendered by his urban renewal plans, only half of which were approved. A second was the destruction of the magnificent, marbled Pennsylvania Station, razed to make way for the thoroughly graceless Madison Square Garden. Finally, in the 1980s the city had tried to tackle the waterfront divide with its most ambitious development project in decades and was defeated. The Westway project would have eliminated the dilapidated West Side Highway and replaced it with public parks built over a tunnel, reconnecting neighborhoods along Manhattan's West Side to the river. The plan was defeated in 1985 in federal court because of its impact (or the failure to disclose its impact) on the striped bass.

When I left Giants Stadium after the World Cup, I had no idea of any of this, but eighteen months later I had done enough work to convince myself that hosting the Olympics could be the antidote to New York's development phobia and that the project could be funded privately from ticket sales, sponsorship revenues, television rights, and other revenues, just as had been done in Los Angeles and Atlanta (even though I still had no idea where any of the forty or so sports would go).

Now I was ready to test the idea on others. The first person I approached was my good friend, Oak Hill Capital's general counsel, John Monsky. Monsky is the perfect lawyer. He never fails to see the opportunities in a situation and to find a way around the obstacles. But he also wasn't afraid to tell me when I was wrong. I knew he would listen carefully and then wouldn't hold back in expressing his opinion.

Monsky was more than supportive; he was excited. He said we needed help and immediately volunteered that he knew whom to bring in. Monsky had taken an urban planning course at Yale and through a connection there had gotten the name of an adjunct architecture professor named Alex Garvin. At the time, Garvin was also a member of the New York City Planning Commission. And as it turned out, he had recently published his book *The American City: What Works and What Doesn't*.

Barnes and Noble was around the corner. I ran out and grabbed a copy. What shone through was Garvin's optimism. As a reviewer in the *New York Times* wrote:

> Basically, everything you've previously noticed with irritation or with a sigh—too much decay or too much sameness, a deteriorating park or a sterile new convention center—takes on the appearance of a fixer-upper [in Garvin's eyes]. Something mendable, retrievable. A situation whose solution is, in fact, ready to hand. And in that moment there's another buzzing around your head; not black flies but the confident, cheerful, practical voices of Mr. Garvin's heroes, the men and women whose accomplishments are so proudly set forth in the pages of *The American City*.

Monsky called him and asked him if he would come in to see us. It was exactly what we needed. Garvin arrived at our offices wearing a bow tie and looking like he had just stepped out from behind an Ivy League lectern. His academic facade masked a playful personality. I asked him one question: Could New York find the venues to host the Olympics? Garvin, who knew nothing about sports and less about the Olympics, responded cheerily, "I don't see why not."

So we got to work. At the time Atlanta was in the final stages of preparing to host the summer Olympics of 1996, but the information the city leaders had used to win their bid was a closely guarded secret. Monsky used connections through used book dealers to search for the highly detailed bid books for Barcelona and Atlanta. A dealer wanted $800 just for the Atlanta book. It seemed like a rip-off, but we bought it anyway. It turned out to be a hugely valuable transaction. A few months later, we would meet with William "Billy" Payne, the charismatic leader who brought the Olympics to Atlanta, who would jokingly offer to sell us those very same books for $50,000.

Meanwhile, Garvin was beginning to understand the requirements for each of the venues as well as for transportation, hospitality, security, and other aspects of putting on the Games. He surveyed the city for possible sites, frequently bringing me along on scouting trips. We tramped to parts of New York that I had never seen (I now understood why Far Rockaway was named

Far Rockaway), and he helped me imagine what they could become. I initially scoffed when he suggested transforming a hulking, elevated freight line sneaking up the West Side of Manhattan into a private transportation system for Olympic athletes. We didn't end up putting the High Line to that use, but Garvin was one of the first to recognize its potential.

I kept my promise to Alisa to preserve Friday nights and Saturday for family, so during the week I worked at my actual job, slipping in Olympic meetings when I could and then continuing at night when I got home and the kids were asleep. I carved out Sunday mornings for field trips to potential Olympic venues. It mostly worked. Then my mom was diagnosed with cancer.

She had had a small tumor removed in 1981 but never told us. Then near the end of 1994 I was visiting my parents in Detroit. As we drove home from dinner one night, she told me about her previous bout and then delivered the bad news: they'd discovered another tumor. It was small, and she was planning to have it removed the following week.

By the winter of 1996, I was finally ready to reveal to someone outside my family, Monsky, and Garvin my idea that New York ought to bid to host the 2008 Olympic Games. I arranged to have breakfast at the old Drake Hotel with Bob Kiley, who ran the New York City Partnership (inexplicably, it is now called the Partnership for New York City), a coalition of New York City–based business leaders. Over breakfast, I laid out the vision for an Olympics in New York. Kiley, who had been Deputy Mayor of Boston and had played a major role in the turnaround of the Metropolitan Transportation Authority (MTA), immediately saw the potential, especially the role of Olympic deadlines in spurring development. He asked me to make a presentation to his board a few months later.

I'm not sure what Kiley expected, but naively I was determined to make that presentation so good that the idea of hosting the Olympics would be completely irresistible to what I assumed would be a group of skeptical executives. I expanded our little Olympics team, hired a design and production firm, and set to work. We set up camp in some unused offices at Oak Hill. For three months we worked on the presentation. John Monsky wrote the first draft. I rewrote it. Back and forth we went. We obsessed over every little detail, infuriating the production team.

The final version began with the opening scene from the musical *West Side Story*, which zooms in from the sky onto the Jets and Sharks, the rival gangs on their turf in the slums of the 1950s West Side of Manhattan. That scene dissolved into images of Lincoln Center, which had replaced those slums, and the neighborhood that boomed around it in the thirty years since. It then told similar stories about the creation of Central Park (fifteen years after it was completed, the land surrounding the park was worth nine times what it had been!) and the building of the United Nations (that site had been stockyards and slaughterhouses).

The presentation went on to describe, through cutting-edge video and other graphics, the catalytic impact that hosting the Olympics had achieved in other cities. It covered the financial aspects of hosting the Games and especially how Los Angeles and Atlanta had been financed completely privately. It raised and then deflected the most common objections, such as traffic, and explained why the International Olympic Committee (IOC) would find a New York bid compelling.

Most importantly, we presented a detailed plan for precisely where New York could host the Games. We had anticipated that everyone's second reaction (after the specter of traffic) was going to be, "How would you actually fit the Olympics into New York?" and we had to have a visionary, yet achievable, plan. So, we laid one out. The Olympic Village would be on new landfill to the north of Battery Park City, which itself was being constructed on landfill across from the World Trade Center. The Olympic Stadium would be on rail-yards on the Far West Side of Manhattan, a couple of miles to the north. The Village and the stadium, the two most important venues in the Olympics, would be connected by that old freight line, which would be refurbished. We scattered other venues for the sporting competitions along the waterfront and in all five boroughs, with a particular emphasis on neglected areas where nothing had happened in decades. Finally, we closed with a very emotional appeal to New Yorkers' pride. The final image was of a small girl waving an American flag while looking up at the Statue of Liberty. When we were finally done, we thought the message was clear—hosting the Olympics could spur New York's next big leap forward.

In early May I walked with Monsky to a Midtown office to give the presentation to the Partnership. About thirty members of the Executive Committee and staff were there, including the CEOs of the *New York Times*, Time Warner, Chase Manhattan Bank, along with several of the largest developers and investors in the city. I didn't know any of them. As I stepped into the room I was terrified, mostly because the presentation was on video, so I had to sync perfectly my twenty-eight minutes of live dialogue with the graphics. Even a few seconds of delay would have made me look ridiculous. I think I practiced more than one hundred times.

I was too scared to focus on the audience. But almost from the start I could tell people were engaged. They laughed at the scene with the Jets and the Sharks, and then, almost on cue, the laughter faded to knowing acknowledgment of the impact of building Lincoln Center. When the statistic on Central Park came up, I heard a collective gasp, and I knew we were on the right track. The lights were dimmed, but Monsky was watching the audience intently. He claimed afterward that the audience members never took their eyes off the big screen. When the last scene of the little girl standing in front of the Statue of Liberty appeared, he saw their eyes mist. When the lights came up, everyone in the room rose in a standing ovation.

Meanwhile, unbeknownst to me, the guy who actually had the job of Mayor had heard about the presentation. Around a week later, Giuliani's Deputy Mayor for Economic Development called to yell at me for not looping in the city leadership and summoned me to City Hall. I was such a neophyte I actually got lost on my way. As we sat down, I instantly and honestly claimed naiveté. My cluelessness was so clear that she believed me. We started discussing the proposal in earnest, and she asked me to come and make a presentation to the Mayor the next week.

When I arrived to meet the Mayor, his senior staff was assembled on the second floor in a room known as the Committee of the Whole (COW). It was one of City Hall's grandest rooms, with double-height ceilings and a big chandelier over an enormous round table. There were huge portraits of former Mayors and Revolutionary War–era generals. A few minutes later, the Mayor swept into the room, and the chattering stopped instantly.

It couldn't have been more intimidating, but this time I was not shaking. I knew I knew my lines. I had practiced a few dozen more times in the intervening week and pretty much had the script memorized. So this time, I was able to look up and watch the faces of Giuliani and his team. The entire team was focused on the screen. There was a lot of nodding and smiling. After I finished speaking, no one spoke until Giuliani did. "If we wanted to bid, what would we have to do?" he asked.

Afterward I was ushered downstairs to Giuliani's ornate private office, with a huge desk that had been used by Fiorello La Guardia. I felt like a young comedian on the *Tonight Show* who had pleased Johnny Carson, earning an invitation to sit on the couch for a few minutes and chat with the King of Late Night.

Giuliani, not generally known as a warm and fuzzy character, was encouraging, even avuncular. "Dan," he said, "I want to give you some advice.

This is New York. On any issue, if there are four New Yorkers discussing it, there are going to be five opinions. No matter how good an idea you have—and you have a great idea—some people are going to hate it. You can go into Times Square and start handing out one hundred dollar bills. Somebody will criticize you for it being too much. Somebody will criticize you for it being too little. And somebody will criticize you for not distributing it fairly. No matter how much you are criticized, stay true to what you believe in."

Giuliani's encouragement, combined with the enthusiasm of the business leaders, gave my little effort some momentum. Some of the executives requested follow-up meetings, which came to the attention of then Managing Editor of the *Daily News* Art Browne. Browne invited me to the paper to make the pitch to him and his news and op-ed teams. The Mayor's support made the difference. Browne deemed it a story.

On Sunday, June 23, 1996, the paper ran a banner headline, "Going for the Gold." There was a two-page spread outlining the entire plan and an editorial endorsing the idea: "The 2008 Olympics could be the catalyst for the creation of tens of thousands of New York jobs, for rebuilding the city's broken transit web and repairing its sagging infrastructure."

Suddenly, people were taking us seriously—that is, except one really important group. The article in the *Daily News* showed our newly designed NYC2008 logo, the Empire State Building with the Olympic rings floating down onto its spire as in a ring toss. The United States Olympic Committee (USOC) sent me a cease-and-desist order saying we had violated the Olympic trademark and disfigured the Olympic rings. Although our relationship with that organization would be characterized by dysfunction throughout much of our bid, in this case the USOC was completely correct. I was so clueless that I knew nothing about these legitimate concerns. The Olympic rings constitute one of the most valuable trademarks and corporate logos in the world—responsible for billions of dollars of sponsorship and other revenues. As such, the USOC protects it fiercely, and only certified candidate cities are allowed to use the image fully intact. After receiving the legal notice, we changed our logo.

Just as support for the bid was consolidating in the city—in polls during that period 75 percent of New Yorkers supported our bidding for the Olympics—the USOC was coming to the conclusion that it didn't make sense for the United States to bid for the 2008 Olympics. It was concerned that the IOC was unlikely to support another Games in the United States so soon after the Atlanta Games.

And so, in February 1997, the USOC announced that it would not submit a candidate to bid for 2008 and was likely to bid instead for 2012. I called President Bill Hybl of the USOC to complain. "Bill," I huffed, "2012 is fifteen years from now! Who will want to pursue this for fifteen years? By then, I'll be fifty-four!" "Dan," he replied tersely, "I'm fifty-six now." A few months later, the USOC officially made a decision to go for 2012 and set a deadline of August for interested cities to decide whether they wanted to pursue a bid for 2012. As the deadline approached, I had to decide whether to move forward.

I believed in the vision, but the costs and the frustrations of pursuing a bid for that long were steep. For starters, even though I had done some fundraising, I had already spent hundreds of thousands of dollars of my own money. After the *Daily News* story, I had hired a head of operations and a head of marketing. Garvin had hired two young planners to help him develop a real venue plan. After the USOC decision, I had to let them go, and they found other jobs. I also was spending a large portion of my office time on the bid, and some of my partners were starting to complain. I had neglected my family while traipsing around the five boroughs, and it turned out that my mother's cancer surgery and radiation hadn't been successful. Another tumor had been detected, and she was going to have to have surgery again and probably chemotherapy, so I needed to be in Detroit more.

My family and I were on vacation in Beijing a few days before the deadline for letting the USOC know. Our first night, I couldn't sleep. I had no idea what to do. Alisa was torn too. I lay in bed for hours, agonizing. Then, in the middle of the night, it came to me. I should call Bob Kiley, who had been so helpful to me the previous year.

I'm sure I sounded completely irrational when I reached him. "Bob," I ranted, "I don't know what to do!" I explained about the deadline and proceeded to tell him why I just didn't think I could go forward. "There's the money, my business, my parents. I lost my team!"

Kiley listened patiently and then simply asked, "What has really changed since last fall?" Then he addressed each of my concerns. "You can hire new people. The ones you had weren't with you for that long. Garvin's still available, right?" I couldn't disagree with him there. "You were prepared to spend the time away from your business last year. Why not now?" I couldn't really think of a reason. "The money? This is New York. You got people excited about the Olympics. You can raise the money," he confidently asserted.

"The one thing I can't answer for you is about your mother. But was she excited about what you were doing? Was she proud?" I had to admit she was.

"Why don't you ask her what she thinks?" In about five minutes he had dismantled every one of my arguments. He calmed me down. My anxiety faded, and I went back up to the room and fell soundly asleep.

In the morning, I told Alisa that I wanted to go forward. She was totally supportive. I called my mom to get her blessing, which she readily gave. I reached out to the Giuliani Administration to make sure its leaders were on board, which they were. A few days later, I let the USOC know we were in. So began NYC2012. The truth is, I was too hooked to ever really let it go.

Several months later, I formed a new team, with Garvin and one of his planners the only hold overs. I put it back in the same cramped office in Oak Hill's building. I started raising money. Garvin and his planners restarted the process of developing a venue plan. Garvin assembled a Facilities Advisory Board of some of the most experienced leaders of the development community in the city. The "plan" we had presented to the Partnership and to the Giuliani Administration had really just been an educated guess as to what we might do. Now we needed to turn it into a real plan. Over the next several months, we analyzed more than four hundred different sites across the New York metropolitan area as potential locations for venues.

We established a set of criteria by which we could evaluate individual sites and then, eventually, an overall plan. It became known as the 5 As. First, the plan had to be **Acceptable** politically. As Giuliani had warned, doing anything in New York is hard. We should try to satisfy as many constituents as possible by spreading around the benefits.

Second, it had to be **Accessible**. It was clear from studying previous Olympic host city decisions that the IOC increasingly wanted the spirit of the Games to thoroughly permeate the host city. A concentration of venues was critical to achieving that environment (of course, that didn't make it easy to satisfy the Acceptability test).

Third, it had to be **Affordable**. We were committed to the US model of privately financed Games, so we knew that our costs would be carefully scrutinized.

Fourth, the plan had to be **Achievable**. With a total of more than thirty venues for forty-plus sports in a city that hadn't developed much of anything for thirty years, we realized there would be a lot of skepticism about whether we could get one thing done, let alone forty. Fred Wilpon, a Facilities Advisory Board member, major developer, and owner of the New York Mets, advised us to "keep it simple. . . . Use existing facilities whenever you can. Do things temporarily if you can. Approvals will be easier. Only try to do a couple of things that are complicated. Have backups for everything, since neighbors are going to object to everything."

To some extent, Wilpon's "keep it simple" rule conflicted with the final A: **After-Olympics Legacy**. After all, the whole point of this effort was to use the Games as a catalyst to focus on the future of New York. It wasn't worth doing unless we could have a lasting impact.

After six months of research, Garvin and the board had identified dozens of locations that could realistically accommodate venues, ranked according to the 5 As. In some cases, they had construction firms do crude cost estimates. We had developed a rough sense of an overall budget, based on Atlanta, adjusted for the higher costs and revenue potential of New York, so we had at least some idea of what we could spend. What we didn't have was anything resembling a coherent concept that would be easy to explain to officials or the public. I felt strongly that we needed an organizing principle for our venue plan.

One late evening, I dropped into the NYC2012 office as I headed home for the night and saw on a yellow piece of draft paper an intriguing scheme. The idea was to place nearly every venue along one of two axes—the first ran north–south along the East and Harlem Rivers, and the second went east–west along the rail lines that extended from the Meadowlands out to Flushing Meadows in Queens. At the intersection of the two axes was the Olympic Village, the heart of any Games, which happened to be on a vacant site in Long Island City directly across the East River from the United Nations. Spectators would access the north–south venues on ferries and the east–west venues on the train lines. In what would prove a fateful decision, we decided to keep the proposed site for the stadium on the West Side, on the train axis, completely ignoring Wilpon's advice to keep it simple. I casually drew lines between the venues on each axis, and they formed a nearly perfect X (if you squinted). Thus was born the Olympic X plan.

Although I was keeping pace with Garvin on physical design, I knew that I had no skills to manage the local politics or the fundraising. I knew I needed someone who knew everyone in New York because I knew no one. It turned out that I needed Jay Kriegel, memorably described as "Brooklyn. Brilliant. Fearless. A little crazy. If schmoozing were an Olympic event, he would be the automatic gold medalist!" by the mutual friend who introduced us. Right out of Harvard Law School, he had become a top aide to John Lindsay when he became Mayor in 1966. Later in Kriegel's career he founded *American Lawyer* magazine, was a senior executive at CBS, saved the state and local tax deduction for New York when Ronald Reagan proposed to eliminate it, and was a partner in a communications firm.

I called him, introduced myself, and asked to meet with him. He had heard something about the Olympic bid and was intrigued enough to come to my office to hear what I was up to. I'm pretty sure no one has ever left that indelible a first impression on me.

In a book about the Lindsay Administration, Kriegel makes an appearance as a twenty-five-year-old, wild-eyed aide with flying hair who looks like he just stuck his finger in an electric socket. Now with shock-white hair, Kriegel still gave off an energy that made him seem like he was still twenty-five, not fifty-seven (eighteen years older than I was). His hair stood on end as he mumbled into two different phones at once and ushered me over to sit down (in my own office, of course). He hung up, smiled, and waved me impatiently into my narrative.

As I spoke, his eyes bored into me, assessing and weighing every statement. I could tell he was thinking deeply about the potential risks and rewards of such a scheme, and I eagerly wondered what his analysis, based on decades of experience and wisdom, would reveal. "So that's it," I said finally. "What do you think?" He didn't hesitate. "That is the stupidest fucking idea I've ever heard," he said.

I sensed he was testing me. I persisted. I started focusing on the catalytic impact of the Olympics, and then I knew he was intrigued. I showed him the venue plan. Kriegel, who had an encyclopedic knowledge of everything in New York, seemed to know the history of every site. In some cases, he had even dealt with them when he was in City Hall. He was frustrated that New York had been in a virtual development freeze. I was clearly winning him over. By the time he left, he agreed to advise me but only if I promised not to tell anyone he was working on it because, as he told me, "it was too fucking embarrassing." Not too long after, I managed to convince him to join NYC2012 almost full time as our Executive Director.

Kriegel had some brilliant but unconventional ideas for building support. The USOC kept no records of the current locations of Olympians, so Kriegel developed his own database of the athletes with connections to New York. After he had found them, he would reach out and get them to support our bid. Over time, our Circle of Olympians would grow to nearly two thousand athletes.

Some of these Olympians were living in poverty and long forgotten. Gertrude Ederle, a New Yorker who became the first woman to swim the

English Channel, had won one gold and two bronze medals at the 1924 Paris Olympics. In her day, Ederle was such an international celebrity that Calvin Coolidge called her "America's Best Girl" and she was given a ticker-tape parade.

In 1998, no one seemed to know where she was. Kriegel became obsessed with locating her. He finally discovered an old address for her out in Flushing, Queens. He went out there and discovered from a neighbor that she had moved to a nursing home. The neighbor had the contact information for her nephew, whom Kriegel called and persuaded to get his aunt to sign on to become the senior member (at ninety-two years old) of the Circle of Olympians. Only Kriegel would have ever thought of doing that.

We also began building our Olympic sports credibility. One of the big criticisms of New York we heard from people involved in the Olympic movement was that New Yorkers didn't care about Olympic events. So Kriegel, with his characteristic intensity, began to demonstrate the opposite. He arranged for the city to host the National Fencing Championships and Archery World Cup. Together we created the New York City Triathlon. We also won the right to host the World Championships of Wrestling (not the WWF kind!) at Madison Square Garden beginning on September 13, 2001.

Kriegel also introduced me to the arcane world of New York City politics and horse-trading. He educated me that the board of a nonprofit like ours was mostly valuable so people could feel included; it was basically a way to hand out favors and show respect. He patiently explained that we had to give all five Borough Presidents the right to appoint two seats on the board. That way, they would feel appreciated.

The board got very big very quickly. Under Kriegel's guidance, every labor union in town—the transit workers' union, the hotel workers' union, the garbage collectors' union—had a seat. When I expressed dismay that things were getting out of hand, he educated me: the more people who had a stake in our success, the better.

Kriegel was indefatigable. He would read about someone in the newspaper who seemed interesting and would just call him or her to have lunch. He or she always said yes because Kriegel had a reputation for being so interesting. He was also one of the kindest, most caring, low-ego people I have ever met. Kriegel loved introducing me to his friends, who included many of the city's most influential players. We estimated that we would have to raise $15 million or so just to bid to become the US candidate city; we needed money for staff, for events, and for lobbying the USOC members, who would vote on the candidacy. Kriegel introduced me to dozens of business leaders deeply invested in the long-term welfare of the city, including Jon Tisch, whose family owns the Loews Corporation and the New York Giants; Stephen Ross, one of the leading real-estate developers in the city; and David Komansky, then CEO of Merrill Lynch. Bronx-born Komansky was well known as a huge New York booster and Yankees fan. He was also a pin collector. Kriegel decided to make a special edition NYC2012 pin, beautifully mount and frame it, and then present it to Komansky when we made our pitch. We walked out with a $500,000 commitment.

One of the big New York personalities who contributed to the bid was a billionaire named Mike Bloomberg. Kriegel (naturally) knew Bloomberg and met with him (alone) at his office on Park Avenue in 1999, well before there were even whispers he would run for Mayor. Bloomberg, who by then was probably already New York's biggest philanthropist, wrote an almost obligatory check and agreed to put his name on our ever-expanding list of board members. He really didn't seem excited by the bid at all. Sometime later, I went by his office to thank him, but it was a brief, almost perfunctory, visit. Other than that visit, I saw Bloomberg rarely (he never showed up for a board meeting). When we were seated next to each other at one of the many dinners for charities that populate New York's fall and spring evenings, it was a struggle to make small talk.

On September 28, 1999, which also happened to be Ariel's ninth birthday, my mom finally succumbed to the neck cancer that had devastated her over the previous five years. At first the doctors had assured us that surgery successfully removed all the cancer. When it came back, they told us that more surgery and chemo would fix it. Despite these assurances, we had finally flown her to Memorial Sloan Kettering for another opinion from a different set of doctors, including one of the world's leading specialists on mucoepidermoid cancer.

He looked at the scans and back at us. There was no hope, he said. It was like a punch in the gut. My mother refused to accept the diagnosis. Through multiple surgeries that ultimately disfigured her face, through radiation, and through two years of chemo she desperately hoped would prolong her life, she never complained. She continued to see patients until just a few months before she died.

At her funeral, my three brothers and I each told one story that illustrated one of the four prime aspects of her life—wife, mother, psychologist, and friend. My story was about her as a mother. She loved being a mother of four boys, and she liked things as messy and chaotic as possible (perhaps explaining why I am obsessively neat). I told about her chasing us around the uninterrupted circuit on the first floor of our modest ranch house until we tired and she could catch us and smother us with kisses.

After the funeral, attended by nearly a thousand mourners, and at the shiva that followed, dozens of her patients—including friends I never knew had worked with her—came up to us and told us how she had profoundly affected them. In several cases, they said she had saved their lives.

Within weeks of my mom's death, my dad started to limp. Over the course of the next year, it grew more pronounced. By the time Alisa, my brother Tom, my dad, and I went to the Olympics in Sydney a year later, it was hard for my dad to keep up. Although distances between many of the venues were short, it quickly became clear that he needed a wheelchair. Shortly after he returned to Michigan, he was diagnosed with amyotrophic lateral sclerosis (ALS), also known as Lou Gehrig's disease. As we would quickly learn, for unknown reasons ALS causes motor neurons to die, weakening muscles and gradually immobilizing the body. The mind is unaffected but is trapped in a frozen prison of a body until breathing becomes impossible. The average life span after diagnosis is two to five years. The commuting back and forth between New York and Detroit resumed.

Throughout the rest of 2000 and into 2001, my life consisted of traveling back and forth to Detroit as my dad deteriorated. Back in New York, the Olympic bid remained widely popular. Nearly two-thirds of New Yorkers approved of hosting the Games, consistent across all ethnic groups, boroughs (a little lower in Manhattan), ages, and genders. In our Olympic materials we started calling New York "The World's Second Home" and "An Olympic Village Every Day."

Our Olympic X Plan was generally well received too, with a few notable exceptions. Queens borough President Claire Schulman vowed that the site we proposed for the Olympic Village would be used "over my dead body" because she was convinced that the entire site would be built well before 2012. Given the centrality of the site to our plan, we ignored her. The not-in-my-backyard oriented residents of Brooklyn Heights objected to using the abandoned piers as the home for the swimming and diving venue, fearing that somehow placing the pools there would end their dream of turning the piers into a park. (We moved the venue to the Williamsburg waterfront.) And, despite Garvin's and my pleas to the elders of the Jehovah's Witnesses to allow us to use their site for a gymnastics arena (we walked out of the meeting dutifully carrying stacks of conversion materials), we were shut out and shifted the sport to Madison Square Garden (and later, the Barclays Center).

By 2001, the biggest wild card for the bid's future was the upcoming mayoral election. Giuliani was term limited, and it seemed clear that City Hall would revert to a more traditional Democratic candidate. I hedged my bets and contributed to all four of the candidates. I assumed Bloomberg's run was just a vanity candidacy, although I did note with some interest that he had adopted some of the elements of the Olympic X Plan in his proposed economic development strategy, particularly the extension of the No. 7 subway train to a revitalized Far West Side.

September 11 was primary day in New York. As everyone in New York that day remembers, it was a perfect autumn day. No clouds. Warm but not hot. I voted early in the Democratic primary (I honestly can't remember for whom I voted; I've probably blocked it out) and got to the office about seven-thirty a.m. I was in a meeting when one of my colleagues at Oak Hill burst in and told us that a plane had hit the World Trade Center. We turned on a television in a conference room and didn't move for the next few hours.

Like everyone else I was gripped with the news, and at the same time I felt utterly helpless. To feel like I was doing something, anything, I went to the New York Blood Center to donate blood. But there were already hundreds of people in a line that stretched for a block (less than 1 percent of the blood donated in response to the 9/11 terrorist attacks was used to treat victims).

All I wanted was to be home with Alisa and the kids, but Kriegel and I had an immediate problem. The World Championships of Wrestling we had spent millions to attract to New York were slated to start in just two days. There was no choice: we canceled.

I suppose that Kriegel and I might have panicked and despaired that continuing the Olympic bid had become impossible. Instead 9/11 strengthened our resolve. The night of the attacks, Mayor Giuliani, in one of the many acts of remarkable leadership he displayed in the days and weeks after 9/11, declared that New York would rebuild and make the city greater than ever. His commitment set the tone for much of what was to follow. To Kriegel and me it was immensely moving and inspiring. Almost immediately we recognized that the whole purpose of hosting the Olympics—acting as a catalyst to get things done—had taken on an even greater importance.

A poll and focus groups we conducted a few months after 9/11 showed that New Yorkers still wanted the Olympics, not out of self-pity but out of pride. One particular story of selflessness illustrated this spirit. A few weeks after 9/11, Kriegel and I went to meet with Chief Executive Ken Chenault of American Express to seek his support. This would have been a difficult meeting under any circumstances. American Express is a quintessential New York company, but Visa, its competitor, was (and is) a TOP sponsor of the Olympics. Not only did Visa sponsor the Olympics but also it often used Olympic-related television ads to taunt American Express, a former sponsor.

After 9/11, American Express had been forced to move its Lower Manhattan headquarters (just to the west of Ground Zero) to New Jersey. With all other forms of transportation shut down, Kriegel and I took the ferry. Barely settled in his makeshift offices, Chenault couldn't have been more gracious. He not only gave us his corporate blessing but also made a large contribution on behalf of American Express. He had nothing to gain. It was just one of the many ways American Express gave back to New York after 9/11 (most importantly by being the first big company that had had to abandon Lower Manhattan to move back—just a couple of months after 9/11).

Even as the city was in the midst of coping with tragedy, the mayoral election was still moving forward. The primaries held on September 11 had been canceled and rescheduled for two weeks later (I voted a second time). In a measure of the anxiety that gripped the city, during this period Giuliani, who had shown such majestic leadership in the wake of the tragedy, proposed an unprecedented three-month extension of his term. The extension was blocked by Giuliani's nemesis in Albany, Sheldon Silver.

The only sure thing in my mind was who wouldn't win: Bloomberg. This opinion was shared by most, with the exception of my son Jacob, then fourteen. After watching the mayoral debate on TV, he announced that he thought Bloomberg would emerge victorious. "Why?" I asked in disbelief. "I watched the debate, and Mark Green was an idiot," Jacob said. "Bloomberg can manage the city's economy." I dismissed his analysis as ludicrous.

And then, in one of the dumbest decisions I have ever made—which I have never admitted to anyone other than my family—on Election Day I voted for a third time that fall—for Green. I think I just assumed that he was going to win and didn't want to have to feel like a total hypocrite when I dealt with him on the Olympic bid. Of course, Bloomberg was elected by a margin of thirty thousand votes, or less than 2 percent.

Ten days later, I got a call from Nat Leventhal. He had served as Deputy Mayor under Edward Koch and had just retired after seventeen years of running Lincoln Center. He had also served as a member of the NYC2012 Facilities Advisory Board, so he had watched the evolution of the bid. Because even Bloomberg hadn't really thought he would win, little planning had been done for the transition. Now Leventhal asked me two things: Would I sit on a transition team committee, and then, he slipped in almost as an after-thought, would I consider being Deputy Mayor for Economic Development and Reconstruction?

I said yes to the first but an emphatic no to the second. But even as I said no I got that little pang of excitement in my gut that I've gotten every other time I first heard of an opportunity that ended up in a career shift.

Still, for the moment, my head ruled over my gut. There was Oak Hill. Plus I was so invested in the Olympics, I couldn't see leaving the effort in someone else's hands, which I assumed would be a requirement of joining city government. And then, of course, there was my dad. It just didn't seem possible.

But Leventhal wasn't really asking. Later he told me that he had only one person on his list for the job—me. A week after I said no he called and suggested I just meet with Bloomberg. I agreed to that. The Mayor-elect's campaign office was across Park Avenue from my own office. I walked across the street assuming this would be a good opportunity to talk to him about the Olympic bid.

I took the elevator up, expecting to enter a dingy campaign office. That's not how he operated. There were fish tanks and snacks. For temporary offices, the furniture was nice. I was ushered into a glass-enclosed conference room. A few minutes later Bloomberg, Patti Harris, and Leventhal came in, and after a brief introduction from Leventhal describing how he had watched me build the Olympic bid, Bloomberg, in contrast to our previous, perfunctory meetings, turned on the charm—and the hard sell.

His opening line was "Why wouldn't you want to take this job? This is a historic time. You can be a key part of it." I stammered something about how I couldn't leave the Olympic bid. "Where better to get the things done in your plan than from City Hall?" he volleyed back. "What about my busi-ness?" I meekly retorted. "You can always make more money," he said. Easy for him to say. I told him about my dad. He told me how he had a friend from business school who died of ALS and then changed the subject quickly. I asked him about his management style. "My philosophy is to pick people smarter than me and let them do the job. My role is to support them."

We ended up talking for an hour and a half, but I pretty much knew I was going to take the job as soon as he gave the Olympic answer. He was right. I had become convinced that the real value of the Olympic bid was to change the face of New York, and now I would have a chance to do it from the inside. As I left, I told them that I was interested and would get back to Leventhal very soon.

I walked back to my office and called Alisa. She was excited for me, as were all three of my children when I got home that night. Over the next couple of days I must have talked to fifty friends and family members. That weekend, we flew to Detroit for one of our regular visits with my dad. I explained that I probably wouldn't be able to come out as much. He told me to do it.

I called Peter Solomon to get his advice. After all, he had had the job in the Koch Administration. He sent me an eight-page, handwritten letter telling me I would be stupid not to take the job, especially at a time when the city needed good people more than ever. And then he proceeded to tell me what agencies I would want reporting to me and how to organize them.

After the weekend, I called Leventhal back and told him I wanted to do it, although I was very firm about not giving up my post as Chair of NYC2012. I pushed so hard that he would later confess that I almost lost the job. Bloomberg had told him that if I brought up the Olympics one more time, he should move on to other candidates.

We eventually found a work-around. I could still oversee NYC2012 from City Hall but wouldn't have a formal position. After spending more than a month clearing conflicts, winding myself out of Oak Hill, and leaving my official role at NYC2012, I was announced as Bloomberg's Deputy Mayor of Economic Development and Rebuilding just three days before he was inaugurated as New York City's 108th Mayor. I had spent years, literally, planning for New York's future. Now I was on the cusp of having the opportunity to implement the vision.

CHAPTER THREE

BEGINNING TO REBUILD

AT NINE-THIRTY P.M. on December 31, 2001, a city-appointed car and driver picked up Alisa and me at our townhouse on the Upper West Side to take us to Times Square. As we got closer, the driver, Richie Corley, turned on the flashing lights and periodically blasted the siren as he skillfully and swiftly guided us past a half million revelers right into the heart of the Crossroads of the World. Alisa and I grinned at each other. I felt myself relax for the first time since saying yes.

I had taken the job knowing what I would sacrifice to become Deputy Mayor. It meant relinquishing some control over NYC2012, which made me feel like I was giving up one of my children. I was volunteering to work for one dollar a year (ninety-three cents after the city deducted payroll taxes, and then I had to pay for extra health care, so I actually wrote a check every month!). But the sacrifices paled when I considered the staggering challenges ahead.

I would be charged with protecting the city's economic future at one of the most perilous moments in its history. Since the terrorist attacks less than four months earlier, residents and businesses had fled Lower Manhattan. By the time we took office, tens of thousands of jobs had been lost, 13.4 million square feet of office space was destroyed, and the vacancy rate for apartments had soared. At Battery Park City, directly across the highway from the World Trade Center site, 40 percent of the residential units were abandoned in the months right after 9/11.

Despite an infusion of federal funds to help with recovery, the city's financial situation was dire, although as members of the new administration converged on Times Square, even we didn't know the extent of it. After we entered office, the scale of the financial disaster would quickly become clear: the city was on pace to lose $2.5 billion in tax revenues that fiscal year alone, according to the Comptroller's office. Things were only projected to get worse—much worse. In 2003, the first full fiscal year of our administration, we were looking at deficits of $5 billion on a budget of roughly $42 billion. By our second full year, the budget hole was projected to swell to nearly $6 billion.

That would have been bad enough. But I quickly learned that only about $15 billion of the overall budget was discretionary—the rest was mostly mandated federal and state payments that flow through the city's coffers. All my plans—the ones that had convinced me to accept the job in the first place—required major investments of funds the city no longer had.

Anyone could do these numbers and understand the bleakness of the city's situation. But I knew the situation was even worse than people thought. New York's long-term economic problems were deeper than 9/11. The city's concentration in financial services posed risks that were just not sustainable. Since starting the Olympic bid, I had read pretty much every book on the history of New York I could get my hands on. I began to focus on the impact of financial panics, busts, and crashes on the city since it became a financial center at the dawn of the nineteenth century. There had been twelve of them—in 1809, 1819, 1837, 1857, 1873, 1893, 1901, 1907, 1929 (the big one), the late 1960s, and 1987. Each one followed a similar pattern: some kind of innovation generated enormous enthusiasm among investors and created a speculative boom.

During the boom times, as a result of New York's status as the center of capital raising, money flowed through the city. During those periods the great arts and social service organizations were formed, making New York a cultural capital and, arguably, the most compassionate city in the country. For example, in the twenty years after the Civil War, the Metropolitan Museum of Art, the Museum of Natural History, and the Metropolitan Opera were all formed.

Inevitably, though, the boom times ended, and when they did the city would go through a painful period of retrenchment. The cycles of boom and bust left their marks on the city, almost like the cycles of the seasons leave rings in the trunk of a tree. We had to disrupt that cycle or condemn the city to an endless circle of soaring and collapsing.

Fixing any of this—restoring Lower Manhattan, diversifying industries, luring the Olympics and the widespread rebuilding and revitalization the bid would generate—would be impossible unless we could tackle something far less tangible: the city's image. After the terrorist attacks, New York became known as a devastated city. Every aftershock was reported widely around the world. Tourism plunged after 9/11. Surveys done of people around the country and around the world indicated that they thought the physical damage to the city was far more widespread than the terrible, but very localized, reality.

The local newspapers fed that perception. Stories of businesses' and residents' leaving the city abounded, contributing to the idea that New York was a deeply troubled place. The media speculated in hysterical tones about the city's future downfall. We understood that, unaddressed, perception becomes reality.

I had spent the four weeks between accepting the job and the inauguration in a frenzy, first untangling all of my complex business interests because everything I owned had to be put into a blind trust (I would have no knowledge of the status of any of my investments for the entire time I served in government), officially separating myself from any official position with NYC2012, preparing for the announcement of my appointment, and then in the final weekend before the inauguration beginning to build a team. Yet between the negotiations, fears over the future, and anxiety over leaving NYC2012, I hadn't considered what being Deputy Mayor would actually be like. When I found myself flying through Times Square on New Year's Eve, driven in an official car—one with a siren even—something else struck me. *Holy shit,* I thought. *This could be pretty amazing.*

We were driving into Times Square because, consistent with tradition, the new Mayor was to be sworn into office just moments after the ball dropped, right in the middle of the city's New Year's Eve festivities. The symbolism that year was especially powerful—the transfer of power in the middle of a massive celebration occurring just three and a half months after 9/11.

Mike Bloomberg had rented out ABC's *Good Morning America* studios, just steps away from the platform where he would take the oath of office, for a party for supporters and members of his new administration. Because I had nothing to do with the campaign and I hadn't been appointed until just a couple of days before the inauguration, I knew pretty much no one. Never having been good with cocktail party banter, it was slightly awkward for me.

Seconds after the ball dropped, Alisa and I stood on stage in the frigid air in front of hundreds of thousands and watched Bloomberg, surrounded by his ninety-two-year-old mother, two daughters, girlfriend, and ex-wife, promise that New York would remain the center of the world. Now we had to make it true.

As I walked into City Hall early on the morning of January 1, I got my second shock, this one not so pleasant. My "office" was going to be a five-foot-long desk in a converted hearing room with fifty other people. There was only a six-inch-high divider separating me from my neighbors. I was not in private equity land anymore—but there could be no complaining. Bloomberg, who was already there, was sitting about eight feet away in the center of the room.

A few hours later, the new Mayor was sworn in again, this time in a more formal ceremony on the plaza in front of City Hall. Despite the woolen blankets and hot chocolate Michael Bloomberg provided, it was freezing, and I couldn't wait for it to be over and to get to work. So, after a brief reception, I went back to my desk. At that point, my staff consisted of a single person, Sharon Greenberger.

When it became clear that I was going to take the Deputy Mayor post, I knew I was going to need a partner in City Hall, a chief of staff. I have always been more effective when I have someone I deeply respect to hear my ideas, to challenge me, and to manage the many details on which I tend to be less focused. Now that I was almost wholly unprepared for the path ahead, I knew that kind of partner would be essential. Senator Charles Schumer, who had become a friend after I did a fundraiser for him in 1998 for his first winning Senate campaign, was the first person I called. He immediately suggested Greenberger. "She is the smartest, most capable person I have ever worked with, and she understands Lower Manhattan, which has to be your top priority," he said.

Greenberger had worked for Schumer in 2000, when he put together the Group of 35 task force to analyze and advocate for the development of additional office space in new neighborhoods across New York City. She had taken a leave of absence from her job as Director of Economic Development for the Alliance for Downtown New York, which was the Lower Manhattan business improvement district (BID), to work for Schumer. I called her right away. We agreed to meet the next day at my Oak Hill Capital office, where I decided almost instantly that she was perfect. She had earned an advanced degree in urban planning from the Massachusetts Institute of Technology, worked in affordable housing, and possessed an intimate knowledge of Lower Manhattan, the area that would be fundamental to our success or failure. Most important, though, she exuded rare warmth that made me feel like I had known her forever. In fact, she epitomized the class of people who are among my favorite New Yorkers—midwestern immigrants to New York. I don't think I have ever met a midwesterner-raised-New-Yorker I haven't really liked. There is something about people who have the values and grounding typically associated with a midwestern upbringing, but who also have the drive and ambition to get up and try to make it in New York. Our first conversation revolved around growing up outside of New York, she from Kansas City and me from Detroit, and then coming to love the city.

What I hadn't known before we met in my office was that she had recently returned to work after nine months of treatments for, and six months of recovery from, Hodgkin's lymphoma. The cancer had been discovered two days after she had given birth to her second daughter. She finally came back to her job in August 2001. At 8:46 a.m. on September 11, she was riding the F train, which rises above ground as it clatters across the East River. Staring out the window, she saw the first plane veer toward the north tower and crash into the building ninety stories high. The train dipped back underground. Greenberger emerged into chaos at the Fulton subway stop and then walked back to her home in Brooklyn over the Brooklyn Bridge, coated in dust from the collapse of the towers.

Greenberger had worked for the Downtown Alliance for seven years, helping to make Lower Manhattan a more desirable place. She had played the key role in developing it into a technology hub. In moments it had been destroyed. Coming so close after her return from her illness, it could have been devastating, but in the months following the attack, she channeled her obvious energy into getting streets repaired, utilities reconnected, and businesses reopened. Clearly, she was as tough and determined as she was warm and smart. And no one better understood Lower Manhattan and many of the likely players in the rebuilding.

I knew I wanted her to take the job, but she wasn't sure she wanted to join me or deal with the intensity of the role. Our second conversation was a little harder. I met her at the Marriott in Brooklyn the next Sunday for breakfast. I wanted both to sell her on the prospect and to make sure we were in sync on my vision for the city. I asked her what she thought of the Olympic plan and the West Side Stadium.

She liked the idea of having the Olympics in New York; she understood the upside the deadlines that the process imposed could have. But she was very negative about the stadium. She thought it was stupid.

"Can't you do it somewhere else? Anywhere else?" she asked.

"There is nowhere else. The Mets don't want it in Flushing. There are no other sites. Plus it can be a real centerpiece for the entire area."

"Centerpiece? It's a huge building taking up space on the valuable waterfront!"

"What valuable waterfront?" I protested. "There's a railyard there. Nobody complains about the Javits Center taking up space on the waterfront."

"Even if I accepted that argument, you'll never get it done. The politicians over there are crazy."

I couldn't argue with that. The way she pushed back was just what I needed. We talked about whether if she came to work for me she would fully support the stadium, despite her reservations. She said she could. So right there I offered her the job as my Chief of Staff. She would be in charge of building and managing our team and developing the processes to move our entire agenda forward. She would need to be my alter ego so that it would be clear to everyone that she spoke and acted on my behalf. She took a day to think about it and then accepted. I can say today with the benefit of years of hindsight that it was the smartest decision I made in my time in City Hall.

That first morning after the Mayor's second swearing in, we stared at each other across the small partition between our desks. Our list of problems was almost limitless. I felt a little paralyzed. "Have you ever been to Ground Zero?" Greenberger asked me. "No," I admitted. "For a guy who has 'Rebuilding' in his title, don't you think it makes sense to go see it? How will it look if some reporter asks you whether you've been there, and you have to admit that you haven't?"

So on a cold, cloudy January afternoon, we walked the few blocks from City Hall to the site where nearly three thousand people had perished and where seven buildings had been destroyed. Entering the empty American Express building brought back a flood of memories. A year after I joined Lehman Brothers, that firm, owned by American Express, had moved into that building. Every day for two years I rode up the escalators to the sky lobby and then up the elevators to my shared office on the eighteenth floor. I had loved—and sometimes hated—coming into that building.

We were escorted onto a set-back roof about ten stories high, facing east, just a few floors below where my office had been, where we could look down upon Ground Zero. As we stared down across the West Side Highway at the mass of twisted wreckage, three and a half months after the attacks there was still a faint odor unlike anything I've ever smelled before. There were hundreds of ironworkers, welders, steelworkers, and other tradespeople on-site. The fires smoldering under the "Pile," as it was known, had been officially declared extinguished just weeks before.

Looking up, I saw a long, jagged piece of steel that had sliced through a window across the hall from my old office; metal ripped through the side of the building and protruded like a massive knife. Until that point, the task of rebuilding had seemed somewhat abstract. It was clearly first on the long list of projects I had on my to-do list. But visiting that site, looking down and seeing the devastation, and then looking up and seeing the steel cutting through the window on *my* floor—it suddenly felt very personal.

As Greenberger and I stood there staring out over the wreckage, a crater in the heart of Lower Manhattan spreading aftershocks throughout the world, we felt the weight of responsibility now on our shoulders. The prospect of rebuilding was overwhelming. It occurred to us that we really had no idea what our responsibilities were and who the other actors involved would be. I didn't even know who ran the Port Authority. It wasn't really clear that anyone else in our administration did either.

And yet that was just a fraction of what we needed to do, with the city's entire economy at risk. The decision by the United States Olympic Committee on its candidate city would be made in November. If we lost at that stage, the deadlines to achieve the vast agenda that came with the bid would be gone and with them any chance to enact my vision for the city's future.

With so much at stake, we were all running blind. I had no government experience, and neither did virtually anyone else—including the Mayor. Our "partners" in city government, the members of the City Council, were equally clueless. Because of recently enacted term limits, thirty-seven of the fifty-one Councilmembers, including the thirty-two-year-old Speaker, were new to their jobs. Meanwhile, because my appointment had not been announced until three days before the inauguration, I was way behind in hiring City Hall staff and most of the Commissioners who were going to report to me. All of this had to be done while I was going back and forth to Michigan to visit my dad, whose steady decline was continuing. By then, having lost the use of his legs and most function in his arms and hands, he was having difficulty breathing.

Nonetheless I felt energized; as we walked back, Greenberger and I began making lists of jobs we had to fill and of the people with whom we had to meet right away. We started to prioritize the many things we had to do. Our discussion continued until well into the night, just the two of us in a brightly lit conference room in an otherwise darkened City Hall. By the end of that day, we both felt that we had the outlines of an action plan.

Organization is good, but there are still only twenty-four hours in a day. Although I usually never remember my dreams, throughout the first year as Deputy Mayor I had a recurring one. In it I was swimming underwater, gasping for air, trying to reach the surface. Every time I got close, a big hand grabbed hold of my head and pushed me down.

Our first priority had to be hiring leadership for the agencies. They are the instruments by which anything gets done and in which anything can get bogged down—usually through interagency squabbles. Fortunately, Nat Leventhal, the transition head, had learned lessons from his years in city government and believed strongly that success or failure as an administration would largely rest on the structure of that administration. He felt that it was imperative for the Mayor to have strong Deputy Mayors, with clear areas of responsibility, who would each have a set of commissioners and agencies reporting to them. That way, the agenda would be driven by one person, and the conflicting resource and prioritization issues that come naturally with a sprawling bureaucracy would be minimized. (Of course, that didn't address how to get all of the agencies within a Deputy Mayor's territory to work together, not to mention how to address those issues in which agencies reporting to multiple Deputy Mayors were involved! But one step at a time.)

Leventhal and Bloomberg carved out five domains—Administration, Policy, Operations, Economic Development and Rebuilding, and Legal Affairs. In addition, Bloomberg had several key positions report to him directly: Police Commissioner, Fire Commissioner, Director of the Office of Management and Budget, Corporation Counsel, Schools Chancellor, and a Chief of Staff who would help to resolve the jurisdictional boundary disputes between Deputy Mayors.

Over time, I would come to understand just how brilliantly this structure would work. For the most part, although I would come to like them personally, I had relatively little substantive interaction with my fellow Deputy Mayors. That enabled me to move quickly on issues I was empowered to solve. Bloomberg encouraged us to work closely together when necessary, and he held twice- or thrice-weekly staff meetings with the top members of his administration to ensure that any issues could be resolved, but, in general, if we needed something to get done, we just walked over to Bloomberg in the bullpen and asked him. It was a true hub (Bloomberg) and spoke organization.

But the system almost broke down before it began, undermining my efforts. When I had interviewed with Bloomberg, one of the things that appealed to me most was that he said he was a great delegator. He promised me autonomy in being able to pick my own team, subject only to his final approval. Almost as soon as I agreed to the job, he revisited that commitment—with the two Commissioner positions I viewed as most vital to my success. As it turned out, it would be the only time in six years when he would not give me the freedom he promised—but at the time it was an immediate crisis.

As Deputy Mayor for Economic Development and Rebuilding, I was given fifteen agencies, boards, and commissions to manage. I believed that none was going to be more central to my vision than the Department of City Planning, and I knew exactly whom I wanted to run it: Alex Garvin. Not only was his enthusiasm for planning infectious and his knowledge of the city unmatched, but also, because of our work over the previous five years, I knew that with him at the helm my planning goals would be aligned perfectly with the Olympic bid.

But I quickly suspected that the Mayor had already promised the Commissioner of the City Planning Department job to one of his Upper East Side friends. He kept insisting that I interview Amanda Burden for the job.

I had met Burden when I was pitching the Olympic idea to Mark Green and was not impressed—she initially gave off the appearance of being little more than a dilettante. She was Green's appointed representative on the City Planning Commission, and I remembered her as being sarcastic and dismissive. I was worried she'd be exactly the wrong person to carry out my plans.

At the same time, Bloomberg threw me another curveball. Apparently Hugh Carey, the former Governor of New York, had supported Bloomberg's bid for Mayor, and Bloomberg felt that he owed him something. One of his sons, Michael Carey, was President of the city's Economic Development Corporation (EDC). Bloomberg was reluctant to replace him.

EDC was the key to many of my plans. It was originally established in 1966 as the Public Development Corporation to retain and create jobs and generate revenue for the city. Its scope broadened over the years to fostering economic development. As a separately chartered nonprofit, it technically existed outside of city government, although it was wholly owned by the city and reported to the Mayor. In the Bloomberg Administration it would report to me.

EDC has special powers. It owns real estate and can keep some of the proceeds outside of the normal city budgeting process when it disposes of the property. It has the capacity to issue tax-exempt, industrial-revenue bonds on behalf of private-sector borrowers and collect fees in exchange. So, it could generate money that could be used to develop and execute our plans. Most important, employees of EDC were not civil servants, so we could eliminate them without having to comply with the onerous civil-service rules. That was a huge benefit because EDC was an underperformer. I had dealt with it enough in my NYC2012 capacity to know that it was slow and not very creative. I had big plans for revamping the agency and turning it into a powerhouse. To do this though, I needed someone I could be confident really understood business and finance and was nimble and politic. And I had just the guy in mind.

Andy Alper, a partner at Goldman Sachs, and I had started as sparring partners when we spent two years in tortuous negotiations over the purchase and stabilization of some troubled insurance companies. Although we were on different sides of the deals, it became apparent that Alper was a financial problem solver whose calming presence could navigate incredibly complex and emotional terrain. He was great at seeing the ultimate objective and methodically moving the warring parties to a mutually satisfactory conclusion. Alper had earned my total respect and friendship. After our negotiation wrapped up, I even retained him to sell some of the companies in my firm's portfolio, at which I saw once again how effective he was. After we worked together, Alper became the Chief Operating Officer of the market-leading investment banking division of Goldman Sachs.

I thought Alper would be perfect to run EDC. He had financial and operational experience, and he would be a reassuring and persuasive voice to the business community, still fearful in the months after 9/11 and susceptible to fleeing to other locations. Although, like Bloomberg and me, he didn't have government experience, unlike Bloomberg and me he had great patience and was a wonderful listener, something I intuited would be necessary in the job.

In effect, I thought of City Planning as the brain and EDC as the muscle of our nascent economic development efforts. Yet before I even started the Mayor was gently, and then more forcefully, insisting on two candidates I didn't want and didn't think could get the job done. Back and forth we went. Bloomberg asked me to meet with Burden, which I did, but I still preferred Garvin. The pushing of Carey was less insistent, and because Alper hadn't told me that he was willing to take the job yet, I didn't push back as hard. Still, by the time Bloomberg was sworn in, we hadn't resolved the issue of who was going to run these two vital agencies.

Bloomberg insisted I meet a second time with Burden, so I did, this time at an Upper East Side coffee shop. She told me later that she prepared for weeks for the interview. The preparation was clearly worth it. I heard more about her background. Her mother was the legendary socialite Babe Paley, remarried to CBS founder Bill Paley. Professionally, Burden was much more accomplished than I had understood, having first obtained a degree in planning and then held planning positions of increasing responsibility, including Planning Director of Battery Park City, perhaps the only successful large-scale development in New York City in the previous thirty years. As we talked, it was clear that our views were not that different and that she was an incredibly hard worker. She made an impassioned plea for the job and agreed to support the elements of the Olympic plan.

I went back to Bloomberg and said I would hire her, but I was adamant that I had to be able to hire Alper. So we traded Burden for Alper. From this, I learned two valuable lessons: Bloomberg respects people who aren't pushovers, and to get anything done in government you have to trade.

If only the rest of the hiring had gone as smoothly. During the first few days of the administration, Greenberger and I did a tour of our agencies to familiarize ourselves with their workings and leadership. We were shocked by what we found. It was pretty clear that in the waning days of the Giuliani Administration, the management of many of them had deteriorated. When we made a surprise visit to one agency, we found the Commissioner sitting in her office watching a soap opera. She wasn't so easy to move out because she had come up through city government as a civil servant and had seniority. A "suitable" job for someone of her experience had to be found. Greenberger, who I quickly realized was a genius at managing bureaucracy, sort of like Radar on the 1970s TV show *M*A*S*H*, found her a high-ranking position at a small, mostly obsolete agency where she would have little responsibility.

We found similar situations elsewhere. Most agency employees were dispirited. It could have been the lingering impact of 9/11, but the malaise felt entrenched and pervasive, as though it had been building for a long time.

Greenberger and I were determined to build a top-quality team, but not everyone wanted to join us. In fact, it quickly became clear that we could only recruit people into government who wouldn't be forced to change their lifestyles fundamentally by taking the pay cut. Yes, the calling to serve the city was powerful but not as powerful as a mortgage or a child's tuition. Thus, we could persuade people who were already wealthy or worked in academics or for nonprofits where the compensation was comparable, or younger people who hadn't yet established a lifestyle. Anybody else, forget it.

So we had to get creative—and twist arms. Greenberger reached out to Rob Walsh, who had run the Union Square Partnership (the Business Improvement District around Union Square) for the Department of Business Services. A few years earlier, I had unsuccessfully tried to recruit him to a senior position at NYC2012 before he left to take a job in Charlotte, North Carolina. When I called him to sell him on it, he was running the organization dedicated to reviving the downtown there. He was reluctant to leave, but I persuaded him at least to come up for an interview. When I asked him what his proudest achievement there had been, he talked about a trolley that circulated within the district. I taunted him: "You mean a train to nowhere? You seriously would rather build a train to nowhere instead of helping to rebuild your city in its moment of need?" It took him just a few minutes to change his mind.

For our Commissioner of Consumer Affairs I picked Gretchen Dykstra, who had effectively built the Times Square BID into a powerful instrument to revive the physical and spiritual heart of the city. I had gotten to know Dykstra through the Olympic bid, and she had always struck me as one of the most energetic, passionate people I'd ever met. She signed on right away.

Greenberger and I also began to think about a staff in City Hall. We decided that we needed a team of people working for us directly who would be our eyes and ears regarding the agencies, local elected officials, community groups, and others. Unfortunately, there was hardly any money to pay for a staff. Altogether we could afford six. We had no idea whether that would be enough. As it turned out, no one was older than twenty-eight, but each would turn out to be a real star, and all would go on to great careers.

During my six years in government the team in City Hall would grow much larger, and I would have the opportunity to play a key role in hiring dozens more for the agencies that reported to me. We gradually gained a reputation for the quality of our team, which made it easier to recruit great people. Over the years I had refined a simple, standard interview of candidates that proved pretty infallible. Buried in a longer interview (as a courtesy) were four questions, the only ones I really cared about: (1) How would your coworkers describe you? (to understand the applicant's depth of self-awareness, which I consider the most valuable attribute someone can have, particularly as part of a team); (2) Describe in detail your most recent performance evaluation (I want diligent, hard workers; if someone doesn't get a great review, I assume they are not); (3) What is the best idea you have ever had? (to test creativity; you would be surprised how many people get stumped on this one, and I ask it because I only want people who can connect unobvious dots); and, finally, (4) Address a specific question on our agenda (to determine that the candidate had given real thought to what we were doing and actually was passionate about it). On each of the four dimensions—self-awareness, diligence, creativity, and passion—I rated them on a –1 to +1 scale. If a candidate didn't score 3.5 (half points were allowed) or higher, we didn't hire him or her.

The biggest personnel mistake I made during those early days was not bringing my long-term assistant, Marla Pardee, to City Hall with me. At Oak Hill, Pardee and I had developed an incredible working relationship and great personal chemistry. She got in at seven a.m., was a wizard at somehow never messing up on scheduling or rescheduling any of the hundreds of meetings each month, and knew pretty much everyone I had ever talked to. When I had signed on, I had understood that she made too much money at Oak Hill for government. She also didn't live in the city, which was a requirement for employment in City Hall.

So, I left her behind and settled for the administrative assistant of my predecessor. After about two days, I realized that she was never going to be able to keep the pace necessary in my new role. For two months, I felt like I had an anchor tied to my leg. Finally, I had had enough and just decided to put Pardee on the EDC payroll and get her a nonresident waiver. So, a couple of months into 2002 we had a pretty complete team. We had a real sense of being on a common mission. But that is not enough to get anything done. It requires a tremendous amount of interagency cooperation.

One of Greenberger's first innovations was the creation of the Economic Development Agency Council (EDAC), which brought together my staff, all the agency heads, and their top deputies biweekly. It started with twenty people and eventually grew to forty. The meeting usually occurred Tuesday afternoons around five p.m. The commissioners would sit at the table, and the staff would sit in chairs in a circle around us. A different agency hosted the meeting each time.

Every few weeks Greenberger organized the meeting around one specific problem we were trying to solve. What were the strategies we were employing? What were the holdups? What were the resources we needed? How should people work together? My job was to listen and demand action, knocking heads together when necessary.

The junior staff loved to complain about the meetings: they were time-consuming, they argued, and the Commissioners were all shamelessly trying to impress me. But, in fact, the staffers were pretty good at amusing themselves. While we were talking, they kept a constantly running, mocking commentary on the proceedings on their Blackberries. When one Commissioner known for going long settled into a drone one afternoon, for example, one staffer group-texted, "Andy has that 'Why did I ever leave Goldman Sachs' look again."

They played jokes. Once they told me before the meeting that I had won the Sexiest Public Servant Award to see how I would react. Suffice it to say no such award existed, but I certainly believed it! Such goings-on were not wasted time—they bonded the staffs across agencies. They began to have common goals, which facilitated our ability to work together. That was no small achievement—many of these agencies hadn't worked collaboratively for decades. I think the best testimonial to EDAC was that about six months after it started, we had a bunch of other agencies that didn't report to me asking if they could join because they wanted that sense of camaraderie and communication.

After a few months, I told the Commissioners I wanted them to prepare strategic plans that would describe their most important priorities for the next year, the resources they were going to require, what kind of "return" (financial or otherwise) they could hope to generate from the investment of time and money they proposed, what risks there were, what the process would be, and what other agencies would need to be involved. With the exception of Alper, I don't think a single one had ever done a strategic plan. Then I dropped the big bombshell: they were going to have to prepare PowerPoint presentations for their own teams and EDAC. You would have thought I was speaking Urdu when I mentioned the dreaded P (for PowerPoint) word. No one had ever done a PowerPoint presentation—in 2002!

In this way, we introduced some basic business concepts—business plans, risk and return, accountability and deadlines, disciplined cross-functional collaboration, and PowerPoint—into government. It was, to my knowledge, the first time that had ever been done in New York City.

A fair amount of grumbling ensued at first, but ultimately the agencies dove into the process with enthusiasm. The Commissioners were encouraged to involve longtime staffers, who actually had the deepest knowledge, in the development of the plans. One of the pleasant surprises was how many of them relished the opportunity to be heard within their agencies and to actually think systematically about what they were trying to accomplish. So, just a couple of months into our term, we had a set of priorities we had all agreed upon and a common sense of what we had to do to achieve them. It was a good thing because we were already behind.

CHAPTER FOUR

OPEN FOR BUSINESS

JUST BLOCKS FROM my new office, the collapse of the Twin Towers had not only blown a hole in the city's heart but also shredded the district that had been New York's historic birthplace and created a fiscal nightmare.

With our team in place, our top priority had to be to stabilize the population in Lower Manhattan. Fortunately, it appeared that we would have the resources to do the job. Within three weeks of 9/11, President George W. Bush promised a $20 billion package of financial assistance to the city. Some of that money consisted of a pool of funds designated for incentivizing businesses and residents to stay in, return to, or relocate to Lower Manhattan.

Before we arrived in City Hall, Mayor Rudy Giuliani and Governor George Pataki agreed that the vehicle for managing disbursement of these funds would be a new corporation, the Lower Manhattan Development Corporation (LMDC), controlled by the state and the city, although the state would be the dominant partner. It wasn't until Mike Bloomberg was elected that the city was given equal representation on the board, but, in what would turn out to be a fateful concession, the Governor had the right to select the Executive Director, who would manage the operations of the corporation on a day-to-day basis.

Pataki and Giuliani chose the Chair jointly. For that critical role, they selected John Whitehead, the universally well-respected, former Co-chair of Goldman Sachs. A decorated World War II veteran, Whitehead had risen from a relatively modest background to become the head of the most powerful investment bank in the world. He then "retired" and became Deputy Secretary of the State Department in the Reagan Administration and then Chair of AEA Investors, a large private equity firm that was really an investing club for former CEOs and wealthy families. With a long list of other corporate, civic, and nonprofit leadership positions to his credit, Whitehead's reputation for integrity was unimpeachable, which made him an ideal choice to lead LMDC. By the time he was tapped, however, he was seventy-nine years old. Nevertheless, his courtly manner hid reserves of energy and a fierce and very stubborn determination to get his own way.

My role in all of this was to lead the rebuilding from the city's perspective. Essentially, that meant interfacing with LMDC. Although the city's representatives on the board were supposed to be independent, in practice they would report to the Mayor and me and would act in accordance with city policy. Yet as we entered City Hall, LMDC had essentially no staff. To stanch the outflow of people and businesses from Lower Manhattan, we had no time to wait. So the staff members of EDC and its state counterpart, the Empire State Development Corporation (ESDC), worked intensely and with unprecedented cooperation to develop retention and attraction programs and then to sell them to the targeted constituencies.

By the end of February 2002, nearly $700 million was allocated and much of it disbursed. The success of the residential program astounded all of us. We offered significant incentives to encourage the repopulation of the area. Grants of up to $12,000 over two years totaling $227 million were awarded to more than thirty-nine thousand households. Within months of the announcement of the program, vacancy rates in Lower Manhattan, which had reached 45 percent, plummeted to about 5 percent.

The business retention and attraction program posed more difficult calculations. Should we reward companies that had already committed to return to Lower Manhattan? What about companies that could never leave the area because of a dedicated customer base or some other reason? Should the grants be awarded on a per-employee basis or that of economic contribution to the area? Should companies closer to Ground Zero get more than those farther away? What if a company's employment was low in the area, but its impact in other parts of the city was significant? We debated these questions intensely while staving off the relentless pleas from companies facing relocation decisions or threatening to leave the area.

Frustrated with the endless discussions, after a few weeks Sharon Greenberger and I retreated to a conference room in City Hall on a Sunday and developed a set of principles to guide the decisions. For example, we agreed that companies like American Express that had already committed to return to Lower Manhattan would not be penalized for making an early decision—a commitment that had sent a powerful signal to other companies about the area's future. We then created a mathematical formula based on these principles to allocate the money.

The formula made implementation a breeze. Because of the formula we could go to companies with specific amounts of incentive payments quickly, and because of the principles we could easily explain the reasoning behind the amounts. Very few companies had any objections, and nearly all of the businesses that had stayed in Lower Manhattan remained. Moreover, a large percentage of those forced to flee returned when space was available. The experience convinced me that in developing policy, it is wise whenever possible to start with a set of articulated principles. Randomness makes people uncomfortable and suspicious.

Clear rules also make turning away the undeserving—even if they are politically powerful—easier as well. Lehman Brothers, forced to evacuate its building after 9/11, quickly announced that it had acquired a new home in Times Square and would never return to Downtown. Yet at the behest of Chair and CEO Dick Fuld, representatives of Lehman came down to City Hall to demand that the company be allowed to participate in the business retention program. It was the only company that had the nerve to ask for money *not* to return to Lower Manhattan. It was a pleasure to be able to say no.

But it wasn't enough for the program to focus on Lower Manhattan. The entire economic structure of the city was dangerously flawed. At best, the boom-and-bust cycle that had characterized New York's history subjected the city to intermittent bouts of intense pain and poverty. In the bleakest scenario, it put the entire city at risk. Bloomberg and I realized that we had to take a more active role in smoothing the cycle not only to help us recover from the current downturn but also to insulate us from future ones. Part of the answer was to invest in the city when everyone else was pulling out. Bloomberg, the ultimate counterintuitive thinker and doer, had already embraced this strategy to achieve his multibillion-dollar personal fortune. He had founded Bloomberg LP during the depths of the early 1980s recession and then grew the company most aggressively during subsequent downturns. When we came into City Hall, we both believed that the condition of the city would eventually reverse and improve—it always had. We could use the recovery years to plan so that when the upturn came, we would be ready.

When we came into office, there were very few major development projects under way because the waning Giuliani Administration had lost steam. But largely as a result of NYC2012 we had a whole blizzard of ideas. A month after entering City Hall, on February 5, 2002, Bloomberg gave a major speech in the ballroom of the Regent Wall Street, just a few blocks from Ground Zero, outlining our economic development agenda at a special meeting of the Association for a Better New York, a civic organization. It was the first articulation of our "five borough economic development strategy."

After first describing many of the steps we were taking to get Lower Manhattan moving again, he then launched into our agenda. "We will change our orientation toward business. . . . The city will think of its job-creating, tax-paying employers, big and small, as valued clients." Although it seemed totally intuitive to him, it was a pretty radical notion to think of companies doing business in the city as clients of government.

For small businesses, he announced that we would transform the Department of Business Services into the Department of Small Business Services and then back that up with real action by creating small-business service centers and supporting the creation of many more business improvement districts that gave local businesses much more autonomy in their neighborhoods over trash collection, security, marketing, and other services.

Of course, a first priority had to be rebuilding Ground Zero—and all of Lower Manhattan. For the first time in the wake of 9/11, someone acknowledged that Lower Manhattan had been troubled before the attacks and needed to be "more vibrant, more exciting, and easier to get to" than ever before. But our vision had to go beyond Lower Manhattan. Bloomberg proposed creating new opportunities all over the city for companies looking for lower-priced space. We were going to focus on Downtown Brooklyn, Long Island City, Flushing and Jamaica in Queens, the Hub in the Bronx, and St. George in Staten Island. He added,

Perhaps the biggest long-term opportunity to expand our economic base is in Hudson Yards, the area surrounding the Javits Center on Manhattan's Far West Side. Block after block after block, the surrounding area is dominated by aging warehouses, open parking lots, and auto body shops. The nearest subway is a half a mile away. . . .

We need to bring mass transit to the area, including the No. 7 line, the Long Island Railroad, Metro North service on Amtrak's old Empire Line, and enhanced ferry service. We need parkland and better access to the Hudson River Park. And we need to rezone the area to accommodate commercial and residential growth.

By doing these things, we will unlock the potential of the surrounding area, turning Manhattan's last frontier into one of the world's great spaces. To accomplish this we must start right now.

Then came the key to it all: "We face many tough years of rebuilding ahead. We must sustain the spirit and unity that we enjoy today. Hosting the Olympic Games in the year 2012, with their fixed deadline and the worldwide attention they can generate, will be the spark that keeps us going through the difficult periods. Ultimately, they can also celebrate our rebuilding efforts too."

Finally, he concluded with a nod to perhaps New York's greatest Mayor, who in another time of great economic and emotional difficulty managed to find the resources and inspire a city to rethink its future and then get it done:

Fiorello La Guardia, who was as much a dreamer as he was a mayor, once said, "Sometimes I see the City of Tomorrow, with marvelous parks and buildings, finer hospitals, safer and more beautiful streets, better schools, more playgrounds, more swimming pools. It will be a reality someday." . . . Together we must direct the tremendous intellect, talent, and dedication of all New Yorkers to make that City of Tomorrow our New York today.

This work will be our legacy. Let's get started.

So we did. Facing remarkable obstacles, Bloomberg laid out the most ambitious economic development plan any Mayor of New York had proposed since La Guardia. Now we just had to do it. And we had to do it at the same time we had the million everyday balls in the air that are the ordinary stuff of running a city of eight million people.

One of my favorite examples of the day-to-day actions I had to take during those first months was to oversee the sale of a property of which the city had come into possession on Columbus Circle, at the southwest corner of Central Park.

Edward Durrell Stone, a reasonably prominent mid-twentieth-century architect, designed the building as a museum for the art collection of an heir to the A&P supermarket chain fortune, Huntington Hartford. At the time of its opening, architecture critic Ada Louise Huxtable called it a "die-cut Venetian palazzo on lollipops." Eventually, Hartford closed the museum and gave the building away. Eventually it was deeded back to the city. It had been sitting empty for several years. After a bidding process, the Giuliani Administration was all set to award the building to Donald Trump when Bloomberg came into office.

We put the sale on hold and rebid it. Because preservationists had their eyes on the building and because of its rather odd structure and state of disrepair, there were only a few bidders. We narrowed it to two. One was a small, but promising, museum, then the American Craft Museum, now known as the Museum of Arts and Design, which wanted to expand into a more prominent location. The other was "The Donald," as he was known in New York, who planned to turn it into a luxury boutique hotel that, if my memory serves correctly, would have been clad in gold (that could be an exaggeration!).

It was an easy choice. We wanted the museum, which we thought could be a magnet for Columbus Circle. The only problem was that Trump offered more money, all in cash, whereas the museum had no money and would have to pay us over many years. And this was 2002, when New York had no money. In June 2002, we chose the museum. The call to Trump was a lifetime highlight for the staffer who let him know our decision. He said that across the phone lines, he could feel Trump's face getting redder and redder and could picture his arms waving wildly as he absorbed the verdict. Trump then unleashed a series of threats, invectives, pleas, and finally, whimpers.

The story does not end there. I don't think I heard from Trump for eighteen months until *The Apprentice* debuted on NBC. The next day, out of the blue, he called me just to tell me the ratings of the show. And then for the next three weeks thereafter, like clockwork, he called to report the ratings. I never understood why. (I will confess, however, that I generally enjoyed a good relationship with Trump. We didn't always agree, and sometimes he could be a bit of a bully, but he was helpful on the Olympic bid and a handful of other issues.)

So, while we were doing the day-to-day work, we started thinking about New York's competitive position compared with that of other leading cities around the world. Coming from careers in the private sector, Bloomberg, Andy Alper, and I tended to think about the city as we might about a business. Like a business, a city offers a portfolio of products and services and has a cost structure that our customers—employers, residents, and visitors—constantly evaluate against others. As with any business, there are going to be situations in which a city can't compete well for a variety of reasons, such as space or cost, and there are going to be others in which it can. Our job was to figure out which was which.

One of the first things I did upon getting into office was to ask the management consulting firm McKinsey & Company to help us evaluate, pro bono, New York's competitive position on an industry-by-industry basis. We asked whether subsegments within certain industries were well suited to New York. One obvious example of that was in the financial services industry. We not only asked whether the front office (the traders, salespeople, investment bankers, and investment managers) needed to be in New York but also we separately evaluated the cost structures of the banks to understand if we could compete for the back office (the accountants and clerks and the information technology personnel, for example) too. Whether this sounds like an obvious enough step or not, it was novel to New York City government.

Several surprising conclusions emerged. First was the firm belief that we should not pay companies to stay in New York. As we studied the economic incentives previous administrations had offered companies, we began to understand that almost always, the companies and their legions of paid consultants played the city. Inevitably, the city would get in a bidding war with other cities that resulted in New York's providing tax benefits and other incentives to companies to induce them to do something they were going to do anyway.

This policy was immediately tested. In the waning days of the Giuliani Administration, the city had entered into sweetheart deals with the Yankees and Mets in the forms of nonbinding letters of intent for the city to subsidize new stadiums for each to the tune of about $400 million apiece. In addition, it entered into a $1.1 billion package of incentives for the New York Stock Exchange (NYSE) to move into a new facility across the street from its existing home on Broad Street in Lower Manhattan. Just over a month after being inaugurated, Bloomberg killed the stadium deals, saying the city just didn't have the money. He felt that there was no way the teams would leave anyway, especially after 9/11. That was that.

The NYSE posed a far knottier challenge. Despite the devastation just a few blocks from its headquarters, the staff of the NYSE had acted heroically in the days after 9/11 to get the stock exchange up and running less than a week after the tragedy, providing a morale boost to the city and the nation. Moreover, the deal with the NYSE wasn't just concocted in the final days of the prior administration. It had been in the works for years. The NYSE was also one of the most powerful symbols of Lower Manhattan; it had been there for two hundred years, having been founded under a buttonwood tree in 1792 not far from its current location. So the periodic threats from Richard Grasso, its CEO, that it would leave Lower Manhattan if it didn't get a package of incentives made many advocates for Lower Manhattan shudder— particularly after 9/11.

One of the best things about joining the Bloomberg Administration was that Bloomberg spent his own money on the campaign and had accepted no outside contributions, so he came into office owing fewer favors than any Mayor before him. He couldn't be bought. He would always say, "My Plan B is better than most people's Plan A. Just do the right thing."

Bloomberg, from his perch at his company with its near-omniscient information, saw the ebb and flow of the securities markets more clearly than anyone and believed that physical exchanges were likely to be a relic of the past. Personally, I wasn't convinced that the NYSE needed a new building with an expansive new trading floor either. I had been in to see Grasso about six months earlier in a completely different context. At Oak Hill I had been weighing investing in two different deals that embodied two very different possible futures for the NYSE: one involved the acquisition of a specialist firm of market makers—the guys who stand on the floor of the NYSE balancing buy-and-sell orders—and the other an investment in a company called Datek, a leading electronic brokerage firm. One was a bet on the physical future of the NYSE, the other on an electronic future that would need much less space. I wanted advice from Grasso on which way the market was heading. He said he honestly didn't know.

In our new roles, Alper and I began digging into the details of the NYSE building. With Grasso's ambivalence echoing in my mind, I just couldn't shake the notion that this was a really dumb deal. At one point, I actually went to Grasso and reminded him of our conversation about the future of physical trading. Now he backtracked and was a lot more certain about the need for physical trading (hence, space). The mere hint that we wouldn't adhere to Giuliani's nonbinding commitment made him sputter vague threats.

Getting out of the nonbinding agreement was still harder than it looked because the city was already paying $3 million a month to hold on to the new land for the project and had agreed to pay $160 million to demolish an apartment building on the proposed site—it had even sent out eviction notices to tenants. The city also had made a $22 million down payment on the $220 million purchase of an office building at 23 Wall Street owned by JPMorgan Chase.

Yet finally, a few months into our term, we told Bloomberg we shouldn't support the deal. He agreed. We just couldn't convince ourselves that investing in a new building made any sense. The fact that the city had already invested a lot of money was irrelevant to us. If there's one thing you learn in business early in your career, it is to avoid throwing good money after bad. We concluded the money already spent was bad, and we were likely to waste a lot more subsidizing a building that likely wasn't necessary. Besides, we didn't believe the NYSE would leave—and change the name to the NJSE, especially after 9/11.

Alper and I walked down to the NYSE to let Grasso know. He had an old-fashioned, massive office, filled with toys and knick knacks representing the thousands of companies that the NYSE had taken public during his term as CEO. To get to the office, you had to pass through metal detectors and layers of guards (which would have been understandable in the post-9/11 era except that it had been that way for years). He also kept it uncomfortably hot. I am not sure if he did it on purpose for psychological brinksmanship or if that was just how he liked it. In either case, it caused his guests to sweat profusely.

Despite the hints at our skepticism, I don't think Grasso ever really believed we would walk away. The message we delivered was brief but unmistakable: the city couldn't justify a $1 billion investment in a new fifty-story building for an entity that wasn't sure it would need the space. As we delivered the verdict, Grasso's face turned beet red, but the room suddenly felt frigid. There was nothing else to say. We got up and left.

A few days later, Bloomberg went on WABC Radio and publicly delivered the final blow: "In this day and age, if they were ever thinking of moving away, 9/11 must have ended that. Nobody's going to desert New York City at this point in time." Despite all of the calls of doom that predictably followed, the NYSE didn't move, a few years later Grasso was forced out of his position, and trading is now overwhelmingly electronic. The project would have been a colossal waste of money.

A second consequence of our strategic analysis of the city's competitive position was that we realized the city had to work harder to develop alternative commercial districts outside of Midtown that would be appealing to different kinds of tenants. This was, in effect, the mission of Chuck Schumer's Group of 35 efforts, and we took the analysis further and decided to implement it. With McKinsey's help, we interviewed CEOs of companies large and small to understand what was driving locational decision making. Not too surprisingly, a big factor was the cost of space.

The cost of space was something we could clearly address, however. The city's office space had traditionally targeted large companies seeking luxury office space, almost exclusively in Midtown. But that meant a range of companies, even entire industries, were being priced out and snapped up by other cities, including across the river in New Jersey. For a couple of decades, anyone who drove along the West Side Highway could look across the Hudson River and watch as the skyline of Jersey City seemingly exploded out of the ground while New York City added very little new office space. Losing these businesses reinforced our dependence on a narrow slice of industries, which made our entire economy vulnerable.

We decided that we had to invest in creating a variety of new or enhanced office districts that would allow companies options at several different price points. We saw Midtown as the premium product, Lower Manhattan as the midlevel product, and Downtown Brooklyn and Long Island City in Queens as the value-oriented products. If our commercial districts were retailers, Midtown would have been Saks or Barneys, Lower Manhattan would have been Macy's, and Downtown Brooklyn and Long Island City would have been Target. In addition, we decided to focus on a few niche areas—Harlem, with its proximity to Midtown at much lower cost; Jamaica, Queens, close to JFK Airport; and Flushing, Queens, near LaGuardia, with a heavy Asian American concentration.

The Giuliani Administration's strategy for attracting or retaining businesses was relatively straightforward: lower crime, and they will come. And, in reality, it worked well. The decline in crime was dramatic, and it gave employers confidence that New York City was a place where they could invest and build the future of their companies. Total employment in the city during his term increased from 3.37 million to 3.67 million.

But we felt we needed to add more value. We decided these districts would be the most attractive to businesses if they were mixed use and filled with residents, retail stores, and, ideally, visitors. As we looked around the city, we were aware that perhaps the most successful "emerging" office district was Park Avenue South from Grand Central Terminal to Union Square. During the Giuliani era, commercial rents there had grown substantially in tandem with an expanding and more affluent residential population attracted by a bustling restaurant scene and vibrant retail district, all of which created twenty-four-hour activity on the streets and sidewalks. Although the analogy to the other commercial districts was not perfect, it became an article of faith for the entire team that we would focus on creating multiple mixed-use districts.

Thus, within a few months of the beginning of the administration, we started planning for major redevelopments in all of these districts that placed an emphasis on quality of life, broadly defined. In time, we invested in transportation, parks, housing, cultural activities, and other necessary amenities, such as new schools and health-care sites, to make neighborhoods more attractive for residents and workers and therefore employers.

But we knew that none of these development initiatives would matter if people simply refused to come to New York City. Giuliani had begun to restore New York's battered image from that of a dirty, drug-shattered city overrun with violent crime. After the attacks, all those gains in the public imagination were lost. From 2000 to 2002, international tourism plummeted by 25 percent as the world, fed by the media, imagined a city of cratered holes, lurking terrorists, and burning buildings.

As we identified our new business districts, implemented programs to revive Lower Manhattan, and pushed for the Olympic bid, we launched the effort that would make success in all those areas possible: rebuilding New York's image. Over time, that strategy became far more sophisticated, evolving from a defensive reaction to a full-out offensive. In 2002, though, we had just one objective: send the message that New York was open for business.

However, we had virtually no money, a skeptical public, and limited time. The longer it took to turn the city's image around, the more the budget would continue to bleed, businesses would close from lack of patrons, and negative attitudes would become more deeply entrenched in the public mind. It was a self-defeating cycle, and the longer things spiraled the harder it would be to pull out. We were looking for any chance to tell our story we could find.

That meant taking some risks. The city was already committed to hosting the World Economic Forum (WEF), the annual January gathering of business, nonprofit, and governmental leaders normally held in the Swiss mountain town of Davos. To demonstrate WEF solidarity with New York and in a show of defiance of terrorism, in November 2001 its founder, Klaus Schwab, offered to move its 2002 meeting to New York, which Mayor Giuliani and Governor Pataki readily accepted. It was a gift. The sight of thousands of opinion leaders from around the world, trailed by hundreds of journalists, was an invaluable way to begin communicating to the world that New York was still a safe and fun meeting place.

The transition to the new administration was flawless. The NYPD, the many agencies that manage large events for the city, the City Hall staff, the New York business community, and the WEF scrambled to pull together the event, of which the results would be pivotal—either proof that New York was not yet ready to return to the world stage or that we could be trusted again.

Everyone worked together seamlessly to make New York a magnificent host. (And, as my driver, Richie Corley, and I hurriedly shuttled from one event to the other along the transportation cordons the NYPD had set up, it would be the only other time I would get to use the lights and sirens in my city car. A couple of years later, after one of my fellow Deputy Mayors was tracked by a WCBS-TV helicopter using lights and sirens to speed her daily commute to City Hall, Bloomberg ordered them all removed!) A second opportunity was presented in March 2002 by Robert De Niro and Jane Rosenthal, the founders of TriBeCa Productions, who proposed a film festival in just a few months to "celebrate Lower Manhattan." They asked for the city's blessing and support and the Mayor immediately said yes.

Finally, the National Football League (NFL) had an idea. As with all of the major professional sports leagues, New York City is the NFL's hometown. Its commissioner at the time, Paul Tagliabue, had grown up across the river in New Jersey and attended New York University Law School. Even though he had spent most of his professional career at a Washington, DC, firm where he had been counsel to the NFL, he remained a passionate New Yorker. In May 2002 Tagliabue led a contingent from the NFL office down to City Hall to broach an idea. The season was scheduled to start on September 5 across the river in New Jersey, when the New York Giants hosted the San Francisco '49ers in the league's first-ever Thursday night game. The NFL proposed a massive rock concert in Times Square immediately preceding the kickoff to be broadcast across the country. Tagliabue was not shy about acknowledging the publicity benefits to the NFL, but he and his team also believed strongly that images of hundreds of thousands of people singing and dancing in Times Square just five days before the first anniversary of 9/11 would demonstrate to the world that New York's recovery was well under way and reemphasize the indomitable spirit of New Yorkers.

A few days after the meeting with the NFL, I convened a meeting in the Committee of the Whole room of the key players involved in planning big events. The room was packed. Ray Kelly brought a team, as did Commissioner of the Department of Transportation Iris Weinshall. Cristyne Nicholas, who ran NYC and Company, the city's convention and tourism agency, was there to add her perspective on what impact such an event would have on New York's image. The risks were obvious. Would people perceive a big concert just before the anniversary as in poor taste? A City Hall team, led by then-First Deputy Mayor Patti Harris, was already planning the 9/11 commemoration, and it was clear that it would be a massive and emotionally draining undertaking, with leaders in from all over the world because the annual UN General Assembly would convene right after the anniversary. Would the combination of the equivalent of New Year's Eve in September, the 9/11 anniversary, and the UN General Assembly back-to-back-to-back be just too much to handle? There was also the unavoidable, ongoing threat of terrorism. How easy would it be for a lone terrorist to walk into the crowd or into a subway station and blow himself up? After all, we were only eight months after the attacks.

The upside was also obvious. Our economy was in tatters. We all understood that in the days leading up to and including 9/11, news coverage would be dominated by images of the planes hitting the Twin Towers; the thunderous collapse of the buildings; the debris at the site, still being removed; the impromptu memorials still springing up; and, most heartbreaking, the memories shared by the friends, colleagues, and loved ones of the 2,753 victims of the attacks on the World Trade Center.

It would have been so easy to say no to a concert. But I can't recall a single person inside our administration objecting, demonstrating the can-do spirit that would increasingly characterize the Bloomberg Administration. The Mayor was totally supportive, so the planning began. Over the next four months Joe Chan, a Senior Policy Advisor on my staff, brilliantly coordinated a dozen city agencies with hundreds of city officials and managed the relationship and negotiations with the NFL to anticipate every possible issue and to work out the overwhelming logistical challenges.

Light rain threatened on the evening of September 5 but held off. The NFL lined up an all-star cast of performers, including Alicia Keys, Enrique Iglesias, and Bon Jovi (at one point during the planning process, the NFL said it was trying to get Pink and Nelly to perform. "Pink Nelly?" I asked. "Who's that?" I have never been allowed to forget it). The *New York Times* reported that the crowd, which stretched all the way to 57th Street, reached a half million.

Later that evening, I raced with Tagliabue in his police-escorted car out to the Meadowlands for the start of the Giants-'49ers game. We agreed that the night had been a tremendous success. As it turned out, ratings for the concert and the first-ever Thursday night game were extraordinary. Indeed, ratings and attendance for the entire NFL season set records. The NFL had successfully wrapped itself in patriotism and New York's recovery. We couldn't have been happier to let them do it. The images of a celebrating city went a long way toward changing our image around the country and around the world. From that point forward, tourism to the city began to climb, and it hasn't stopped rising since.

CHAPTER FIVE

THE US CANDIDATE CITY

THE SINGLE BIGGEST opportunity to tell the New York story was, in my mind, still to come: the Olympics. When we started the year, four cities—New York; Washington, DC; Houston; and San Francisco—remained in the competition to decide which city would be selected by the United States Olympic Committee in November 2002. The final decision would be made by the International Olympic Committee in July 2005. Winning the nod from the USOC was central to my entire agenda. With so many of our initiatives tied to our strategy of planning around Olympic venues—especially the plans for the Far West Side, the Brooklyn-Queens waterfront, Coney Island, and Flushing—we definitely needed the benefit of at least three more years of deadlines, which the international Olympic bidding process would impose.

The Olympic bid itself still wasn't too onerous during the first half of 2002, yet I was already swamped. In fact, from the time I took office until I left six years later, I never saw the street in front of my home during daylight on Monday through Thursday except when I had a parent-teacher conference or some other event at the kids' school (right across the street from our house). I never had time to exercise, so I quickly started the practice of commuting to City Hall by bike. My early morning excursions led me to initiate the effort to complete a bike path around Manhattan.

On most Sundays, I was out meeting elected officials in their neighborhoods or visiting the sites of potential projects. One Sunday I might be going to church with the Councilmember from Far Rockaway, Queens, and the next I would be touring potential sites for affordable housing in East New York, Brooklyn. When the weather was warmer, often I would have the Department of City Planning give me a map marked with targeted areas, and I would set out on my bike with a colleague early on Sunday and do a forty- to forty-five-mile tour from home to and through one borough and back. There is no better way to get to know the fabric of a city than on a bike. Friday nights and Saturdays were almost inviolate to me—that was time spent with my family.

My dad's health continued to deteriorate, and during the first half of 2002, Alisa, the kids, and I flew out to Michigan every three weeks or so. He didn't step down from the bench until late spring, but by the time we visited him over the Fourth of July weekend, he couldn't feed himself and was struggling to breathe. Still, we had a wonderful weekend as we did some of the things he loved. We went to the zoo, had a cookout with his friends, and took him to see fireworks. As we said good-bye on Sunday morning, he seemed in great spirits.

So it was a complete shock when two mornings later Marla Pardee and Sharon Greenberger appeared with ashen faces and tears in their eyes at the door of a breakfast event I was attending. My brother Andy had called to say that Dad had died early that morning. At home less than a half hour later, I stared at the photograph on my dresser of Mom and Dad, looking so healthy and happy at Andy's wedding just six years before. They were just sixty-one and sixty-three, respectively, both with jobs they loved that gave them plenty of time to visit grandchildren, travel, and spend time with their many friends. They had so much to look forward to. There were no warning signs that just a few years later it would all be gone.

Two days later, on my forty-fourth birthday, we once again assembled at the Kaufman Funeral Home. As my brothers and I and our families stood in the first row of the large, packed chapel, a phalanx of judges—county, state, and federal—swooped down the center aisle, their black robes seemingly flowing in silent tribute to Dad, who had built a sterling reputation in the Michigan legal community. As we jointly delivered his eulogy and looked down on the huge crowd, we couldn't believe that we were in the exact same spot—just three years later.

I was back in City Hall five days later. There was just too much to do. Before I entered City Hall, we had already submitted our six-hundred-page bid book to the USOC. In 2001, we had hosted the Evaluation Committee from the USOC, which spent a few days in New York touring the proposed sites for the Games and quizzing us on the various aspects of our bid, such as our transportation and security plans, the availability of hotels, and a variety of other topics.

It had gone quite well. I caught a lucky break when the USOC appointed Charlie Moore, a gold medal–winning Olympian in the four-hundred-meter hurdles in 1952, as head of the committee. After his Olympic triumph, Moore had a successful career as a businessperson. When I had joined Lehman Brothers in 1984, one of the first projects I worked on was the sale of two small divisions of a New York–based industrial company called Clevepak Corporation, headed by none other than Moore. He was a very demanding client, but the sales had gone well, and we had maintained a relationship. The one big question he and the Evaluation Committee raised was, given the fractious politics of New York and the tortured history of attempting to build on the Far West Side, how confident were we that we would get the approvals for the proposed Olympic Stadium? Jay Kriegel and I assured its members we could get it done.

Under USOC rules, we were not allowed to lobby members of the 123-person USOC Board for our bid. In fact, we had no idea how they were going to make the decision. That kind of confusion was typical of the USOC. In the six years since I had first proposed bidding for the Olympics, there had been eight Executive Directors/CEOs or Presidents of the organization. One resigned because she had falsified her résumé; one had failed to report conflicts of interest. They tried bringing in two corporate executives to run the place. Both failed. In a sign of things to come, after the USOC decided to move ahead with the competition to select a US candidate city, USOC Marketing Director John Krimsky immediately imposed a 15 percent tax on all of the funds each city raised to support its bid. It was hard enough to raise the money without the millstone of a 15 percent penalty. (Several years later, Krimsky was arrested and then convicted on child pornography charges.)

The USOC decided that in order to simplify the final decision in November, it would cut the number of candidate cities from four to two, to be announced on August 27 at the Chicago O'Hare Hilton. That morning I was with my family in San Francisco on our first vacation since I arrived at City Hall. I left them early in the morning for the two p.m. announcement and met Kriegel at the hotel. We were not particularly nervous. Who would want to go to Houston or Washington, DC, in the summer?

Moore made the announcement that New York and San Francisco would advance to the final round. "Washington and Houston did not fall down," he said. "It was a question of riches from all four cities. It wasn't a unanimous vote, but it was a clear consensus." In reporting our advancement to the finals, the *New York Times* couldn't resist echoing a faint but growing chorus that my role in the Olympic bid was in conflict with my responsibilities as Deputy Mayor.

So, it all would come down to New York versus San Francisco on November 3 in Colorado Springs, home of the USOC. The early chatter was that it was too close to call. New York had the emotional appeal; San Francisco had the sex appeal. Given the size of our city, New York had more of the infrastructure in place (Mike Bloomberg was quoted as saying "San Francisco is a very nice, small town"), but there were concerns about our Olympic Village and stadium plans. The leadership of our bid was deemed stronger, but we had fewer links to the board members, and an Olympian led the San Francisco bid. In reality, nobody really had a clue. The USOC Board was a fractious, leaderless group, and we couldn't talk to its members.

At the end of the day, the vote would probably be determined by the one-hour presentation each city would make to the board in a big ballroom at the Broadmoor Hotel just a little more than two months away. That became the bid team's entire focus. We were determined to dazzle the board.

On the day before the Saturday presentation, we flew out to Colorado Springs on Bloomberg's personal plane and checked into the historic Broadmoor, one of the grand hotels of the West, with its own lake and a view of the Rockies—a very American setting. Our Chief Marketing Officer Amy Stanton and Doug Bernstein, a consultant, marshaled an army of producers, editors, graphic designers, and writers to develop a spectacular presentation. It told an emotional and compelling story with a lot of substance. We were going to take some big risks and have some fun, but we were only guessing whether it would pay off with our target audience.

The San Francisco leaders, presumably, thought the same thing. But they planned to add a special element to their presentation. The day before, they began telling USOC Board members, especially the athlete representatives, how they were going to divide the financial surplus a Bay Area Games would supposedly generate, with a special emphasis on giving money for athlete training. Kriegel saw this as a blatant attempt to "bribe" the voters, and we frantically lobbied the USOC and Moore specifically to instruct the board members that they should not take any mention of monetary surpluses into account in their decisions. Moore seemed sympathetic.

Our star-studded lineup was led by Bloomberg, of course, and included my Olympic hero Bob Beamon (originally from Queens), gold medal–winning swimmers Dara Torres and Donna De Varona, and former Executive Director of the USOC Harvey Schiller, a new New Yorker who was there to speak to the sports administrators on the board. Billy Crystal made a special guest appearance to make New York funny and approachable. The pièce de résistance was Rudy Giuliani, who just a year after 9/11 was still a hero. We had produced five films, all donated by the television production community, each designed to say something specific about New York, directed by leading commercial and music video directors. As the leader of the bid team, I led off and closed the presentation.

We gathered in the large ballroom of the Broadmoor in the morning for the rehearsal. I had butterflies (how could I not given the fact that much of my Olympic-driven city agenda and the Olympic dream I had been pursuing for eight years were riding on the outcome?), but I also felt oddly confident. I had seen each of the videos several times and knew they were amazing. I felt that the rest of our presentation was really compelling. The only thing I was worried about was whether Giuliani was going to make it because it was starting to snow heavily in Colorado Springs, and he wasn't flying in until later that morning. I hadn't seen what Billy Crystal was going to do, and that made me a little nervous too. We had only given him some guidelines about what to say, but the material was all his.

We started the rehearsal and basically glided through it. Everyone was on. Crystal was hilarious. The few people in the ballroom—the technicians and a few USOC staff members—responded just as we hoped the USOC Board would later that afternoon. The entire team, seeing the whole presentation for the first time, was almost giddy.

The only change I suggested to anyone was to Billy Crystal. I opined that he should eliminate a New Jersey joke the two board members from the Garden State might find offensive. He politely but firmly told me to mind my own business.

We left the ballroom and went to have lunch and then get dressed. Finally, we reentered the ballroom, wearing matching Brooks Brothers blazers, gray pants, and NYC2012 ties. Shortly after we entered, Moore addressed the board and admonished its members "to reject surpluses and legacies as they are for the most part hypothetical." The San Francisco team was furious.

We won the coin toss and elected to go second, opting to leave the last impression. We watched with growing excitement as San Francisco gave its presentation. It was fine, but not great. Its leaders didn't look professional, and they talked from notes. They didn't go into a lot of detail about their bid, erroneously assuming that the audience would have read the voluminous bid book. They had a video of Robin Williams (he and Crystal shared an agent who knew the New Yorker was playing a part in our presentation, so he volunteered to help his hometown—there are no secrets in Hollywood), but the production level was shoddy.

I led off our presentation, speaking personally about my Olympic quest, starting with my first Olympic memory, of watching Beamon. It was thrilling for me to figuratively pass the baton to Beamon, Torres, and De Varona. We described the venues in detail, outlining the Olympic X and emphasizing how nearly all of the events would be within the five boroughs, not spread throughout the region (as San Francisco's bid was). We addressed the concerns about the complexity of getting the stadium site approved by noting, almost subliminally, that we could always move it to Flushing Meadows, Queens, in the highly unlikely event we had to. Bloomberg got up and assured the board that New York would get everything done—a commitment he could keep because almost everything was under his control. "One government, one stop, one solution," he emphasized.

Interspersed in our presentation were the videos. One highlighted the diversity of New York, making the case that New York really is an Olympic Village every day and, therefore, would appeal to the IOC. Another included testimonials from famous New Yorkers such as Robert De Niro, Woody Allen, Jerry Seinfeld, Bette Midler, and Cardinal Timothy Egan about how welcoming and fun New York would be. Another was a funny video with other New Yorkers, such as the head of the trade unions, explaining how we get things done in New York. It started off with Donald Trump in his office in Trump Tower, surrounded by models of his construction projects, saying, "Well, there's no other city with the energy of New York. New York has energy like you've never seen. And, above all else, we can get it done, under budget. Everybody's head is going to spin!" People don't change.

Then came Billy Crystal. Rather than appearing by video, he arrived in person and performed a brilliant routine riffing off the opening of the Woody

Allen film *Manhattan*. He had the crowd roaring from the first line, and it didn't stop for the next three minutes and forty-seven seconds. He reminded the USOC that it would take some work to educate New Yorkers that "fencing is an event, not a felony." He told them New York was perfect for the Games. "All the foreigners are already there," he said. He asked the audience "to picture the Opening Ceremonies at the New Trump Stadium . . . I know he does!"

The jokes just kept coming. He quipped that New Yorkers would get involved in the Olympic movement in their own ways: "The Mets are helping out with drug testing. Martha Stewart is going to make Olympic license plates for the next three to five, unless she plea bargains. And Winona Ryder is getting us all of the Olympic uniforms for free." He concluded, "It's New York, Baby! It's always been an Olympic town and always will be. And best of all, it's not New Jersey!"

Although everyone loved Crystal, the show stealer was Giuliani. It had taken incredibly complex negotiations to get the former Mayor to Colorado, and up until game time we still weren't sure he would make it. He flew in from a speaking engagement in Kansas essentially to deliver two lines. But what lines. "New York will never let you down. Never has. Never will." You could hear the audience gasp. Without ever mentioning 9/11, his mere presence and the allusions to that terrible day and New Yorkers' determination to overcome any obstacle sent a powerful message to the fiercely patriotic group that this spirit was even bigger than the Olympics. Giuliani left right after delivering his lines, not even waiting to see whether we won.

The coup de grace was the final video, which closed our presentation. Directed by Sam Bayer, one of the leading directors of commercials and music videos at the time (and the future director of the remake of *A Nightmare on Elm Street*), it was set to John Lennon's classic song "Imagine" (Yoko Ono had personally given us permission to use it). It started with one runner holding a torch who began to run through the streets of New York. As the wordless film went on, the lone runner was joined by more and more people of every describable race and ethnicity. They ran with growing strength past famous landmarks such as the Brooklyn Bridge and the United Nations. The group, now a mass of humanity bound by a common purpose, ran past firefighters waving American flags in front of firehouses. As Lennon sang sweetly of peace and dreams, the runners, now a community of every color, age, and religion, ran through the confetti-filled streets with flag-waving crowds protected by police escorts until they eventually reached an imaginary Olympic

Stadium, where a young girl lit the Olympic flame, setting off laser beams that lit up the Empire State Building and the Statue of Liberty, ending in a spectacular fireworks display. Now you could hear the audience sniffling. We strode off the stage confident that we had won.

It didn't take long for the ballots to be counted. While we waited, we settled back into our assigned places in the ballroom as people came up to us and prematurely congratulated us. Even Charles Bagli, the skeptical reporter from the *New York Times* who would eventually become a fervent antagonist of our stadium plan, dropped his mask of objectivity and gave me a huge high-five, exclaiming, "That was incredible!"

Finally, USOC President Marty Mankameyer strode to the microphone on the stage. She announced, "With 59.2 percent of the vote, New York is the United States' candidate city!" The crowd rose to cheer. Jay Kriegel, Alisa, and I hugged each other. Mike Bloomberg and Billy Crystal high-fived. The rest of our team went crazy. I was ecstatic. Except for the births of my children and my wedding day, it was the happiest moment of my life.

Up to that moment, I hadn't really given much thought to what would come next. I just knew that if we didn't win, so much of the momentum we had constructed around the Olympic deadlines would be lost. I never would have imagined just how difficult winning could be.

CHAPTER SIX

THE VIRTUOUS CYCLE OF GROWTH

A LISA AND I flew home from Colorado Springs with Mike Bloomberg on Sunday morning still floating on the incredible emotional high from our victory, but I couldn't even take twenty-four hours to savor it. As soon as I landed in New York, I went home, hugged and spent some time with the kids, glanced longingly at the Giants football game on television, and then hopped on the subway for City Hall, where I had more than a dozen staffers assembled to finalize the housing plan our team had been working on for the past five months and the Mayor was going to unveil in just over a week. In the teeth of a recession, with the city's finances still a mess, we were set to announce a historic $3 billion–plus commitment toward building sixty-five thousand units of affordable housing.

New York is such a desirable place to live now. It has ridiculously high apartment prices—one-bedroom apartments in Manhattan and Brooklyn regularly sell for more than $1 million. So it is easy to look back and assume that building more housing would have been an obvious priority or investment. But that is twenty-twenty hindsight. When we came into office, the world was upside down: 9/11 had shattered Lower Manhattan and ripped a deep hole in the city's budget and its soul. When we embarked on our housing plan, pretty much everyone thought the city would face population flight and excessive vacancies.

Housing was so far off the radar that it barely came up in the 2001 mayoral campaign. Ever a stickler for accountability, Bloomberg issued a report a few years after he was elected detailing every promise he had made during his campaign and then reporting on how his administration had performed on each, ranging from merit-based pay for high-performing teachers to more composting. Affordable housing was mentioned only three times, with no commitment to actually build any.

The next logical question might be: Why at this juncture would we make a historically unprecedented commitment to affordable housing in 2002, when the general consensus was that people might leave the city, when we were facing huge budget deficits, and when no one was really focused on the issue? The fact is Bloomberg and I held a fiercely optimistic conviction that the city would eventually rebound.

I came into City Hall with only a vague sense that housing should be a priority. I had no real knowledge of the history of affordable housing in New York City. I didn't know that by 2002, one-third of New Yorkers lived in one of 1.1 million apartments or homes that were subsidized or regulated in some form by the city, state, and/or federal government. And I had no knowledge of the many specific programs, with their bewildering names and acronyms, cobbled together over the years to create and preserve the affordable-housing stock. But I did know one thing: New York had to grow, and when it did, we would have to find places for people at all income levels to live.

For a city, growth is good. That applies to the number of jobs and the number of visitors. But the most important metric of a city's health is population growth. In my mind, a city was like any other product. It had customers. It had competitors. It had to be marketed. How would you know if you were doing your job successfully? The answer: more people would choose New York over other places to live, and the population would grow.

Growth is not just a validation of worth; it is also what enables a city to make the kind of investments that improve the quality of life, attracting even more people. The opposite is also true. When the population declines, a city is forced to cut back on services, which makes it a less attractive place to live compared with other places, hastening its decline.

I first started thinking about the relationship between population growth and the health of a city when I started pitching the Olympic bid. After I made the presentation to the New York City Partnership, one of the business leaders who attended the presentation said I had to go see Lew Rudin. I had never heard of Rudin; I should have because he was known as "Mr. New York."

A leading real-estate developer, like most of his peers Rudin understood that the vitality of the city was great for his business, but unlike most of them he acted on that knowledge with creativity and passion. He had played an instrumental role in 1975 in bringing corporate executives and real-estate owners together to prepay real-estate taxes to support the bailout of the city at the depth of its fiscal crisis; he and his brother, Jack Rudin, had helped to boost the New York Marathon from a small event held only in Central Park for a few hundred runners into the five-borough global extravaganza it has become. He also helped to move the US Open to its new home in Flushing, Queens.

Rudin regaled me with stories of the fiscal troubles of New York in the 1970s and how the city's bailout unfolded. He explained to me the vicious cycle of decline that comes when cities lose population. First the tax base suffers. Then the city can't afford to pay for even basic services such as crime prevention and sanitation, leading to more population and business losses, which lead to more financial troubles and more fleeing people. In fact, during the 1970s alone, the population of New York City fell by almost eight hundred thousand people (more than the population of Boston). In 1971 alone, thirteen Fortune 500 companies left the city. Entire sections of Brooklyn and the Bronx were vacated. From 1970 to 1980, crime spiked by 33 percent because a depleted police force couldn't keep pace with the empowered criminals. By 1996, twenty years after the city's bailout, despite the painstaking efforts of three Mayors and their administrations, although the population of the city had started to grow again, it still hadn't recovered to where it had been in 1970.

If the failure of a city was linked to population loss, I began to reason, the success of a city relied on population growth. A core concept in economics is profit maximization, the process by which a firm determines the price and output level that generates the greatest profit. This principle dictates that businesses should produce goods and services to the point where marginal revenues equal marginal costs. That is, the business should stop producing at the point where it can't make any money because the cost of producing one additional unit is greater than the price at which it can sell it.

Critical to determining that level is understanding the difference between fixed and variable costs. Fixed costs are incurred by the business at any level of output, and variable costs change with the level of output, increasing with higher production. The same essentially applies to a city. For a city, each new resident is attractive as long as the marginal tax revenues from that one additional person are greater than the marginal costs of supporting him or her.

Because cities have already invested so much money in infrastructure (at least those in the developed world), adding the average new person will typically allow a city to make a "net profit" on him or her. The subways, the roads, the parks, the schools, the sewers, and the power plants have been built, and as long as they have capacity, additional people can be added without adding new costs. Running the subway costs roughly the same if 1 million people or 1.4 million people use it. Eventually, new investments might have to be made, but where there is excess capacity, this logic generally holds.

The increased net revenue can be invested back (we hope wisely) into improving quality of life—making the city safer, healthier, more convenient, more environmentally friendly, more fun and interesting, with greater educational and employment opportunities and improved housing stock—which, in turn, attracts more people, which generates more revenue, which helps to perpetuate this cycle. The same logic applies to attracting not only residents but also businesses and tourism. This is the virtuous cycle of the successful city. Its reverse, the vicious cycle of the unsuccessful city, is what afflicted New York in the 1970s and has devastated my hometown, Detroit, since I was a child.

A big part of the Olympic vision was to take parts of the city used for purposes perhaps well suited to the nineteenth- and even most of the twentieth-century New York economy and transform them into vital parts of a growing twenty-first-century New York by making them into new communities. But making them affordable to a wide range of New Yorkers was something I knew nothing about.

For that, my teacher became Jerilyn Perine, whom I had inherited as the Commissioner of the Department of Housing Preservation and Development (HPD). Perine was a gem of a public servant. She had been at HPD for seventeen years and had slowly risen up through the ranks until finally she was named Commissioner in the last year of the Rudy Giuliani Administration. She threw her hat into the ring to keep the job under Bloomberg, but ever self-deprecating, she did not expect to get it. Her appointment was announced before I became Deputy Mayor. Bloomberg loved people working for him who had spunk. Perine had spunk.

Normally Deputy Mayors prefer some say in who works for them, and I was generally very picky on this front. A short, blunt, fast-talking, wickedly funny woman, Perine had been in city government too long to want to work for someone who didn't want her. After the pleasantries, her first sentence was to the point: "Look, if you want, I can just go away," she blurted out.

I was so surprised that I didn't say anything. I just stared at her. "It is not good for either of us to be in a situation where we are not a good fit," she persisted. I paused before I answered, but then I grinned. "No. No. I've heard only good things. You and I will do this together." With Perine as my tutor, I threw myself into learning everything I could about housing, a subject I had no expectation of having to know anything about when I took the job. It was a slog.

I learned how eighty/twenty housing (which enables developers to use low-cost, tax-exempt bonds in exchange for reserving 20 percent of the units for people who make less than 50 percent of area median income) could be combined with the 421(a) program (which provides developers a partial tax exemption to use vacant or partially vacant lots) to provide enough of a subsidy to enable apartment buildings to be built. Perine and her staff piled briefing papers on my desk about historical subsidy programs in which the restrictions on many of the more than fifty thousand units were starting to expire.

She taught me about former Mayor Edward Koch's historic commitment to housing, which had helped to rebuild some of the neighborhoods that had suffered the greatest devastation in the 1970s. During the 1970s, the city faced the double-barreled problems of white flight and inflation. The ensuing fiscal crisis and population depletion devastated the housing stock. Property owners who had been facing the squeeze for years as richer tenants moved out and poor residents moved in were letting their properties crumble. The normal economics of property ownership—if you invest you get more money—had totally broken down. There was no advantage in fixing a broken window or a leaking roof.

The economics became so bad, in fact, that it made more sense for apartment owners in the worst parts of town, such as the South Bronx and Harlem, to abandon their properties and their tenants or to torch their buildings for insurance payouts. That's what led to the fires seen burning in the broadcast of the 1977 World Series and to Howard Cosell's famous (except he never actually said it) exclamation, "There it is, Ladies and Gentlemen. The Bronx is burning." An iconic photo just a few days before showed President Jimmy Carter, who had come to tour the South Bronx, standing forlornly in an empty lot.

Koch's greatest legacy was his housing program and the impact it had on rebuilding decimated neighborhoods. Before Koch, the city had taken over properties abandoned by property owners but only after they were delinquent in paying taxes for three years. The city would then try to manage them, restore them, or resell them to a better owner.

But three years was too long; by then, in many cases, the buildings had crumbled beyond repair. Koch lobbied hard to pass legislation that allowed the city to take properties after only one year of delinquency. As a result, the system was flooded with more than one hundred thousand of these *in rem* (in the city's possession) units. Koch and his staff then broke with traditional practice and used the city's capital budget—money reserved for long-term projects, such as parks and bridges—to partner with nonprofits and for-profit developers to rehabilitate housing stock and rebuild or refurbish the seized lots and buildings. New city, state, and federal programs were created to offer incentives, in the form of tax breaks or subsidies, to partners to encourage them to invest in building or restoring housing, most of which was mandated to be affordable to New Yorkers who otherwise wouldn't be able to live in the city. Koch spent an astonishing $5.1 billion on his housing plan. That's because the economics of housing in New York, even when land is available, can be brutal. Here's why.

The US Department of Housing and Urban Development (HUD) estimates that affordable rent is about a third of a family's gross income. That means a family making two-thirds of New York's median income in 2001 of $63,000—that is, $42,000 a year—could "afford" only $1,200 a month in rent. No developer, even if the land is free, could build an apartment building where the rent is $1,200 a month. Costs of construction and real-estate taxes in New York are just too expensive. He or she would have to charge much more than that to earn a reasonable profit. The only way to make up the difference is for government in some form to subsidize the difference. That's affordable housing—any housing subsidized in some form by the government.

Perine explained that for our administration to provide affordable housing, the challenge would be even harder than the one Koch faced. The city had almost no *in rem* stock remaining in its portfolio. When Giuliani came into office in the 1990s, he wasn't interested in the city's being an apartment owner or taking over what he considered private developer responsibilities. His basic marching orders to the housing agencies were to find ways to divest the remaining *in rem* stock as quickly as possible. Thus our team had next to nothing to build upon.

The problem was actually a lot bigger than the city's running out of vacated lots and vacant buildings. All over New York, developers were finding less land to build upon. Because of the city's outdated zoning code, which restricted the use of land to manufacturing rather than housing, it seemed that much of the developable space zoned for housing had been spoken for—a fact that was also putting upward pressure on existing rents, making the problem even more acute.

Perine was a passionate advocate of the city's responsibility to find decent housing for people who legitimately couldn't afford it and, up to a point, for not making neighborhoods the exclusive enclaves of the wealthy. She had grown up the daughter of a waitress and a shipyard worker in Prospect Lefferts Garden and Bensonhurst and was a fervent believer in the power of mixed-income communities.

For lower-income New Yorkers the situation was grim: the city had a perpetual housing shortage for its lower-income and middle-class residents alike. In 1999, 356,000 households were doubled up living with another household, the average New York family paid 29.2 percent of its income for housing, and 27.2 percent of all renter households in New York paid 50 percent or more of their income in rent. By 2001, the number of families in our homeless shelters was beginning to increase again too.

But Perine shared our optimism about New York's future, which anticipated more people would arrive (and worsen the housing problem). New York was attracting about 150,000 immigrants a year. The average age of the arriving immigrants, often our city's poorest residents, was twenty-eight, about seven years lower than the average age of city residents. They would be starting families.

So, after the first three months in my job, I had learned four things about affordable housing (in addition to a lot of acronyms): (1) New York had an acute housing problem only likely to get worse; (2) the city didn't have land or property upon which to create affordable housing; (3) building affordable housing is expensive; and (4) the city didn't have any money. So, to produce affordable housing, we were going to need money and sites, neither of which we had.

The answer to the site question, we agreed, was rezoning. Zoning is very technical, but its basic purpose and function is to divide a municipality into districts or subdistricts that are, for the most part, distinct from each other, with the use of property (industrial, residential, commercial) within each district's being reasonably uniform. For example, you wouldn't want someone building a smoke-belching factory next to, say, an elementary school.

The last major overhaul of the zoning code in New York had been in 1961. In 1961, there were 847,000 manufacturing jobs in New York City. By 2002, manufacturing employees had fallen to about 140,000. Despite the decline, many areas of New York were still zoned exclusively for manufacturing and industry. High density, mixed-use zoning was largely limited to parts of Manhattan. It was clear that an update was desperately needed.

The challenge was that in New York rezoning was a particularly cumbersome process, demanding intense input from the local communities and lengthy environmental review. In 1975, the city established the Uniform Land Use Review Procedure (ULURP), which mandates the process that applicants (the city or private developers) must follow when they want to change the official land-use designation of an area. After an application with the Department of City Planning is filed, the first key step is a detailed environmental impact statement (EIS), a very long document that discloses all the possible effects of changing land use. It is very rigorous and demands findings on everything from traffic counts to sewage drain-off. It can take hundreds of pages, and it might take a year to complete.

If the EIS is certified by the Department of City Planning as properly completed, the petitioner can enter the ULURP, which provides an orderly process for community input into local land-use changes. The main vehicle for this review is local community boards, whose representatives are selected by the borough presidents. Inevitably, there are savvy advocates opposing the action. Although the vote of the community board is only advisory, its opinion is given deference as the process proceeds, so it must be carefully considered.

The relevant borough President (there are five, one for each borough) then reviews the petition. Although a city charter revision in 1989 largely neutered the Borough Presidents' powers to create policy, they are still given an important advisory role regarding land use. After review by the relevant borough President, the plan goes to the City Planning Commission, controlled by the Mayor and chaired by the Commissioner of the Department of City Planning, for approval. Then the plans have to be approved by the Land-Use Committee of the City Council, and then the City Council as a whole. Great deference is given to the views of the local Councilmember.

Because rezonings require so many steps and so much effort, recent administrations have tackled just a couple at a time and have completed at most a handful during a four-year term. Almost from the very beginning of our era, in large part because of our Olympic bid, we started out with a whole set of them we wanted to complete before the IOC decision in 2005. Three and a half years to plan, get the EIS done, and get the plans approved was a split second in New York time. As we began thinking about housing more, the need to get more rezonings done became more of an imperative.

Over twelve years, the Bloomberg Administration would propose 140 separate rezoning actions. To put it another way, we would rezone 40 percent of the entire city! Only two of the Bloomberg Administration's proposals would be defeated.

Critical to every single one of them was Amanda Burden. She was a master of walking the streets of a neighborhood, understanding the local conditions, and listening to the needs of the community. No one was better at marshaling our arguments and allies at the community board meetings and then listening to their concerns and bringing them back so we could craft responses that would either win them over or at least demonstrate responsiveness, which would soften the local Councilmember. In time, we got better at the entire process and could anticipate the issues, often taking a more aggressive position than we knew the community would find tolerable so we would have something to give away at the last minute. Burden called it "leaving a little juice in the lemon."

There was no issue on which this game played out with more predictability than the percentage of affordable housing to which we would commit in our larger rezonings, such as along the Brooklyn waterfront, on the West Side of Manhattan, and in Harlem. We even developed a simple formula. We would start negotiations with the community and the City Council by offering to make 25 percent to 28 percent of all housing units in the proposed rezoning area affordable, with the percentage dependent upon the cost of property in the neighborhood, which would determine the cost of the subsidy necessary. We knew the community would ask for a percentage in the low to mid-30s. Inevitably we would compromise somewhere in the middle.

In time, I became a huge fan of the ULURP. Its rigid deadlines created a rhythm to the process that was predictable and, in an odd way, comforting. More importantly, although the process was time-consuming, every one of the rezonings ended up better because of the community involvement dictated by the process. We never fundamentally compromised our plans, but they were always more sensitive and thoughtful than we ever would have figured out on our own.

I will confess that some of the biggest rezoning battles in my tenure happened not in the neighborhoods but behind closed doors between Burden and me. She viewed herself as the steward of neighborhood context; I was much less sensitive to that given my focus on creating much more housing; perhaps being more attuned to the economics of building, I tended to push for us to "build up." Sometimes, our different philosophical orientations led to real tension—even one or two screaming fights—but ultimately, I think, the beauty of our relationship was that we pushed each other and came to compromises that brought us aspirational, sensitive, and feasible rezonings.

In the 140 neighborhoods the Bloomberg Administration rezoned, there were commitments to about seventy thousand units of affordable housing, leaving a large inventory of sites in areas rezoned and available for building after Bloomberg left office (something upon which his successor has capitalized as he seeks to achieve his own ambitious housing goals). Over time, we would add new tools to facilitate the acquisition and development of land, including reform of brownfield remediation laws; creation of a revolving credit facility to help small developers acquire properties for affordable housing; and even expansion of the use of new approaches such as inclusionary zoning, which essentially creates affordable housing out of air (more on this in Chapter 10). In all of this we were guided by the conviction that if you don't have the land, you won't have an ambitious affordable-housing program.

The second thing you need for affordable housing is money. Where we were going to get this in 2002 wasn't obvious. However, as I struggled to learn about the intricacies of loans and tax incentives as ways to promote housing growth, I was increasingly drawn to a sleepy agency, the Housing Development Corporation (HDC). I had not heard of HDC until Perine told me it was in my portfolio. Created by the New York State Legislature in 1971 to supplement the city's budget, HDC is a 501(c)(3) nonprofit organization whose primary purpose is to finance the preservation and development of multifamily housing in New York City. It is controlled by the city, and its Chair is the Commissioner of HPD. Basically, it is a city-controlled bank that finances affordable housing.

Prior to the Bloomberg Administration, HDC was a backwater. Under Mayor Giuliani, it was even worse. He used it as a dumping ground for political patronage, most notably of Russell Harding, whom he named its President. Harding did not have a college degree or any housing experience, but he was the son of Raymond Harding, the longtime head of the Liberal Party in New York, one of Giuliani's earliest and most ardent political allies. As Mayor, Giuliani kept the senior Harding close as an advisor. In addition to Russell, Giuliani hired another one of Harding's sons, Bob, who would eventually become a Deputy Mayor in the Giuliani Administration. (I dealt with him frequently, both while he was in City Hall and afterward, and thought he was very competent.)

On our tour of the agencies right after Bloomberg's inauguration, Sharon Greenberger and I made a stop at HDC. Bloomberg hadn't picked a President of HDC yet, so it was up to us to recommend one. Harding made a presentation about HDC. We could see instantly that he was largely ignorant about housing finance. Even to a housing neophyte like me, he clearly knew nothing. He was asked to move on. In a rush to get someone into the job, I gave the top post to the bearded, soft-spoken, and sober Chuck Brass, an HDC veteran who actually was able to answer our simplistic questions during the presentation and seemed to know the most about the agency.

After Harding left, an investigation revealed that he was worse than incompetent. He was corrupt. He had used agency dollars to pay for fancy electronics, spa treatments, and trips to Hong Kong, Vancouver, and Las Vegas. While in Vegas, he had even used city money to arrange for a helicopter tour of the Grand Canyon and tickets to see Siegfried and Roy. Eventually, he pled guilty to embezzlement and possessing child pornography. He served jail time and later, tragically, committed suicide.

After Brass started, he gave me a more comprehensive explanation of HDC. He handed me a stack of HDC financial statements. Fortunately, if there's one thing I'm very good at, it's reading financial statements of financial institutions. In fact, at Oak Hill Capital, my private equity firm, the single biggest success we had was the acquisition of the largest failed savings and loan (S & L) in the wake of the S & L crisis of the late 1980s. I was a member of the small team that rescued the bank, which a year after our acquisition had become the most profitable S & L in the United States. As a result, I was quite comfortable with the way banks made their money, especially with how much equity they required to support the loans they made.

Despite Russell Harding, HDC was making a lot of money. It had made long-term loans in the 1970s and 1980s, when interest rates were high, and had financed those loans at rates not nearly as high. By the 1990s, with interest rates lower, HDC was able to refund its own debt at dramatically lower rates, whereas many of its borrowers either couldn't or didn't refinance their loans. As a result, it was earning a large spread on its book of business.

Because HDC also had tough underwriting standards, the default rate on the loans it had made was very low. It also had a very low leverage ratio—the ratio of loans outstanding to equity. I could see almost instantly that HDC could do a lot more. By mid-year 2002, I knew enough to ask Perine and Brass whether we could begin to think as ambitiously as Mayor Koch had, using a more aggressive HDC as the financial bulwark and the rezonings to provide a big proportion of the sites we would need. Perine was immediately game. Brass was much less so, at first. In the turmoil of the Harding era, Brass had to be the guardian of the institution. He couldn't change speeds quite as quickly.

Over the next five months the teams at HPD and HDC, with some help from a few of the other agencies, worked on the plan. Over those months, with my encouragement, it grew more ambitious, and the team became more enthusiastic. After twelve years of the David Dinkins and Giuliani Administrations, in which selling off *in rem* stock was pretty much the entire housing strategy, longtime bureaucrats and new recruits to city government grew excited about having a big impact. It was what many of them had come into government to do. During the run-up to the announcement of the plan, Perine was diagnosed with breast cancer, had surgery and then chemotherapy treatments, and didn't even seem to miss a beat. That was the depth of her dedication.

As we drew closer to the mid-December date we had targeted for the release of the housing plan, its contours were gradually coming into focus. A central focus would be on the rezonings, but we also debated how we would streamline the processes to make underused city-owned property, including the remaining *in rem* inventory, more readily available for disposition. We decided to make funds available to accelerate the process of cleaning up brownfield sites, making them available for housing. In a time of significant austerity, we found ways to make HPD's funds go further by subsidizing some less costly, moderate-income housing, but we also sharpened our pencils and figured out how to avoid spending excessively on HPD maintenance and then redirected the savings to building new units. A significant focus, we decided, would be on preserving existing subsidized housing that would be lost unless we intervened. We even gave the plan a name: New Housing Marketplace Plan.

The focus on a marketplace illustrated a key Bloomberg-era principle: government has a critical role to play in creating markets where they don't otherwise function, but the role of government should be limited to the minimum amount necessary to enable the markets to function effectively. At the end of the day, there is no way that government can do it alone; the vast majority of money that we expected to be invested in our housing plan would be from the private sector.

Still, a key element not resolved was how much HDC would contribute to the plan. In the last two years of the Giuliani Administration, HDC provided just $25 million to $35 million a year from its reserves to support affordable housing. I was ready to triple that. Brass was nervous at first, but I persisted. Finally, he agreed to increase the amount to $70 million a year. I called him and Perine into the bullpen at City Hall and pushed for more. "Why can't we leverage this even more?" I demanded. Brass looked uncomfortable. "We can, but we could risk lowering our bond rating," he'd say. "Our cost of borrowing capital could go up."

I was nonplussed. I knew that going from an AA rating to something a notch or two lower was really about optics, not economics. "That couldn't cost us more than ten to twenty basis points (.1 to .2 of a percent). I'm not concerned about that. Any other reasons?" Silence. Eventually, I just forced the issue. Just a short time before the plan was presented to the public, HDC increased its commitment to $100 million a year.

About two weeks before we were going to share our plan with the public, we needed to get the final sign-off from the Mayor. I wanted Perine to do it because, after all, no one knew it better. But she was terrified. Somehow she had it in her mind that after all her work she would be derailed. I helped her by working with her to hone the presentation for the boss. I kept making her pare down all the complicated information in the plan to a comprehensible story.

Finally, we were ready. We arrived at the meeting as a team, and Perine ran through the presentation. Bloomberg listened politely but didn't say much. At the end, he simply said, "Okay," and got ready to walk out. That was it, the green light. I could see that Perine was shocked and, what is more, she wanted to share more. I could see that she was going to start explaining more details. Bloomberg has an expression he uses a lot when someone has made the sale but is inclined to keep talking, running the risk of saying something that will cause him to change his mind: "Close the traveler." (I still have no idea where it comes from.) I hadn't heard that yet, so I just winked at her, as if to say, "Okay is good."

She got the message, and so on December 10, in front of a packed audience at the New York Housing Conference luncheon at the Sheraton in Midtown, the Mayor unveiled the plan. Outlining how we would spend $3 billion to preserve or build sixty-five thousand units of affordable housing, he declared: "We're the world's second home, a magnet for people from around the world who want to build better lives for themselves and their families. That new generation of ambitious and hardworking New Yorkers deserves just what my parents struggled to achieve and what all parents want for their children: the security that only good living accommodations in safe and stable neighborhoods can provide. Without these homes and neighborhoods, New York will lose these people—and lose its future. That's why affordable housing is fundamental to our long-term economic prosperity, and this commitment demonstrates that in these difficult budget times, the city has found innovative new ways of funding affordable housing."

Among the housing advocates in attendance, many of whom had been consulted in the months leading up to the plan, he got an overwhelmingly appreciative reaction. Some were just pleased that the Mayor would make an effort in financially troubled times and that the city was committing itself to firm targets.

Although there was an article about the plan in the *New York Times,* it really didn't get much attention. I believe there are several reasons for that. First, housing wasn't really on anybody's radar screen, other than that of the band of housing advocates. Second, we had just announced a plan to spend a lot of money, but we really hadn't done anything yet. At that point, the press and the public didn't really appreciate that when Bloomberg says he is going to do something, he does. And, finally, in retrospect, there were so many pieces to the complex plan that it was hard to understand it. I don't think even I fully understood how transformative it would be.

In 2004, the side effects of her ongoing cancer treatments forced Perine to resign (she is still receiving treatment at the time of this writing but is otherwise reasonably healthy). It was a great personal loss for me, but I was fortunate to recruit a star as her replacement, Shaun Donovan. Donovan was a self-described "housing nerd" who, after receiving undergraduate and graduate degrees from Harvard, had spent nearly his entire career in affordable housing, including a stint in charge of multifamily housing at HUD under President Bill Clinton and then the Secretary of HUD Andrew Cuomo. When Bloomberg and I interviewed him, he was a Managing Director at Prudential Mortgage, where he led a group that made loans for affordable-housing projects. Bloomberg and I were attracted by his public-private experience and his encyclopedic knowledge of affordable housing.

By 2004, it was already clear that the economy was recovering. Justifying our optimism, the city's population exceeded its pre-1970s population levels, further intensifying the pressure on the housing market. By 2006, only three years into our plan, we decided we had to do more. Donovan and his deputy, Rafael Cestero, along with Emily Youssouf, who had replaced Chuck Brass as president of HDC, proposed a big increase—to 165,000 units costing $7.5 billion over a ten-year time frame from the start of the original plan. To reach this supersized goal, which would be 50 percent greater in dollar terms than the Koch program, Donovan took tools deployed by Perine, honed them, and added new ones to the arsenal.

The pace of rezonings, under Burden's driven leadership, accelerated. Our appetite for sites on which to build became even more voracious. I used my clout as Deputy Mayor to insist that all of the city's public agencies meet with me to discuss sites that might be available. I pushed hard to get these agencies to hand over sites they might otherwise have protected. The Department of Education dedicated a building that housed two failing schools slated to be closed anyway. I pressed the Department of Transportation to sink some of the city-owned parking lots underground so we could build above them. Occasionally, I went a bit overboard. My former staffers still like to tease me about the time I suggested we deck over the Brooklyn-Queens Expressway to create more land. After I left, HPD and HDC partnered with the New York City Housing Authority to build affordable housing on public housing sites.

The 2006 expansion relied even more heavily on partners beyond HPD and HDC, although the capital funds from the HPD budget were increased and HDC contributed even more. Donovan and Cestero created the New York City Acquisition Fund with a group of philanthropic foundations to generate the capital to support the construction and preservation of thirty thousand units; they partnered with the state government to provide funding for supportive housing for the formerly homeless; and they redirected funds owed to the city from Battery Park City to pay for more housing.

A hallmark of the plan from the very beginning was that it needed to be flexible. We realized that we weren't ever going to be smart enough to predict how the housing market was going to change over the course of what would be an eleven-year program. As Perine reflected back on the original concept: "The Plan was always intended to be a dynamic, renewing document that should be reviewed and adjusted at regular intervals." Through a booming market into 2008 to the depths of the financial crisis to the aftermath of Superstorm Sandy, the plan was modified by my successors as Deputy Mayor and the leadership of HPD after Donovan left to become the Secretary of HUD (and then later the Director of the Office of Management and Budget in the White House).

Nothing illustrated the complexity of the decision making we faced as a result of changing market conditions more than our decision not to preserve the rent-stabilization features at Stuyvesant Town and Peter Cooper Village on Manhattan's East Side. The massive complex of 110 red-brick apartment towers stretched from 14th Street to 23rd Street between 1st Avenue and the East River. It housed roughly twenty-five thousand residents. The project had been the brainchild of Robert Moses, who in the 1940s had wanted insurance companies and banks to get in the business of "slum clearing."

Through its right of eminent domain, the city gave Metropolitan Life (known as MetLife) the right to bulldoze eighty city acres to build the complex. It then gave the insurer twenty-five years of tax exemptions as long as it would keep the rents affordable to middle-income families. The first buildings opened in 1947. The deal was extended in 1974. By 2005, MetLife's obligation to retain a significant amount of the rent protection had expired, and the values of rental residential real estate were so high that MetLife decided to sell the complex in an auction process that began in 2006. To justify the price MetLife could command, it was inevitable that the new owner would seek to eliminate the rent protection.

This change was not going to be popular with the tenants, but we felt strongly that the role of government was not to interfere in the fairly negotiated bargain a private company had struck with city government. MetLife had fulfilled its end of the bargain for almost sixty years. It seemed that the only option we would have was to provide enough city subsidy for the tenants so that the winning bidder would not be economically disadvantaged by maintaining the lower rents. One of the bidders, it turned out, was the tenants themselves, who wanted to turn Stuyvesant Town and Peter Cooper Village into a co-op, offering units to tenants who wanted to buy at low prices and selling off the apartments of people who didn't after their apartments left the rent stabilization program. Cestero set up a "swat team" to begin analyzing the potential cost of subsidizing tenants using all of the usual tools: tax breaks, low-cost financing, and even outright cash subsidies.

To be clear, the rent protections at Stuyvesant Town and Peter Cooper Village were just that—controls on rent. Tenants of any income could rent the units at the complex, but the owners could only increase rents based on increases approved by the Rent Guidelines Board, a Mayor-controlled board charged with calculating increases in property owner costs and passing them on to tenants. Most of the rent-protected units were not occupied by tenants whose income would have qualified for the rents they were paying under our subsidy programs.

This was a critical distinction at the center of our analysis. Every unit created or preserved under the New Housing Marketplace Plan was subject to controls on rent increases, *and* every tenant had to be qualified by income. They were truly affordable-housing units. Why does this matter? Because if the city were to find a way to intervene and help preserve the low-cost units at Stuyvesant Town and Peter Cooper Village and shift hundreds of millions of dollars from other parts of our housing plan to this complex, we felt strongly that we needed to achieve true affordability there just as with the other 165,000 units in the plan.

The plan for Stuyvesant Town and Peter Cooper Village that Cestero and the team presented would have converted the roughly six thousand units subject to rent protection into truly affordable units with rents capped for low- and moderate-income tenants. Each unit, upon vacancy, would have to be rented to a tenant whose income qualified as low or moderate. This would have been a dramatic change to the affordability commitment at the complex but would mean that the city's subsidy would be targeted only to families in need.

As Cestero and his team were analyzing the cost of providing the subsidy, the auction process got hotter and hotter, eventually reaching $5.4 billion, which only increased the cost of the subsidy even more. We had no right to stop the sale. The only option we had was to step in and provide funds to pay the difference between market rents and the subsidized rates. At that price, he calculated that the city would have to spend almost $900 million, or more than his agency's entire capital budget for two years.

So we faced a difficult choice. We could spend $900 million to provide true affordability. We did not believe at the time that politically we could spend money to preserve rent stabilization for people who didn't qualify under our income tests. The alternative, we figured, was to spend less money on up to five thousand units on the site designated as the home for the Olympic Village, across the river from the United Nations in Queens, and have a lot of money left over to create a lot more affordable housing across the city. In the real world, where money is not infinite, what's the right, even moral, thing to do? We decided not to intervene. I still have qualms about the decision. Maybe we should have pushed back harder on MetLife. Maybe we could have found a way to partially subsidize tenants based on income. Honestly, I'm not sure.

Today, the site in Queens in which we decided to invest is on its way to becoming the largest moderate- and middle-income housing development built in New York since the 1970s. The site will contain almost five thousand units (almost all of which will be affordable to families earning $60,000 to $145,000 a year) and include schools, retail stores, and eleven acres of waterfront park (all designed to withstand the flooding and severe weather that might come with climate change).

In 2010, in the wake of the financial crisis, the buyer of Stuyvesant Town and Peter Cooper Village, Tishman Speyer and its partners, defaulted. At the time it was the largest commercial mortgage default in US history. In 2015, the property was sold for $5.3 billion. The Bill de Blasio Administration committed $144 million to preserve rent stabilization of five thousand units for twenty years, but at roughly $3,000 a month (which under standard rates of affordability, only families earning roughly $150,000 a year can afford). It was a different plan at a different time.

When Bloomberg left office at the end of 2013, it was clear that his administration would fulfill its commitment to building or preserving all 165,000 units, albeit one year late. The financial crisis in 2008–2009 would require budget cuts that forced the delay. The plan housed a half million people, or 6 percent of New Yorkers, in housing that they otherwise wouldn't have been able to afford. In the end, $8 billion of public investment was made. It was the largest city-driven affordable-housing program ever completed in the United States. Dozens of new approaches were tried, often in response to changing financial conditions and new needs. A focus on excellence in design and on community building became central to the city's approach.

HPD prepared a map of New York City as part of its retrospective on the New Housing Marketplace Plan with a dot placed on every site where we built or preserved a unit. It paints a remarkably beautiful picture. There are dots covering most of the map, indicating new or saved affordable housing in almost every neighborhood. But it looks more like the work of Georges Seurat, the nineteenth-century pointillist painter, than it does that of Jackson Pollock, the twentieth-century abstract expressionist best known for his drip paintings. The map seems much more deliberate, with the heaviest concentration of projects in three areas of the city—the South Bronx, Upper Manhattan, and Central Brooklyn. Each of these was among the areas of the city suffering from the highest incidence of poverty and social dysfunction.

In each of these areas we brought dramatic change. Whether in Harlem or Manhattan, Mott Haven in the Bronx or Bedford-Stuyvesant in Brooklyn, to name just a few, the first few thousand housing units that came online, accompanied by appealing new playgrounds and public spaces, investments in schools, traffic improvements, and other community-building features, all required government subsidies. Over time, the neighborhoods became more diverse, private investment was attracted, and a functioning market for non-subsidized housing emerged. Ultimately, that is the measure of success. Can government be the catalyst of a real market that enhances the quality of life for members of the community at all income levels?

Without question, we made mistakes. Although targets are powerful devices for focusing and building support for an ambitious objective, there is always the risk that the numbers become the end in themselves. There is a risk of getting deals done just to meet the targets, sometimes at the expense of addressing the underlying housing problems. Money can be poorly spent, and we were probably guilty of not doing enough retrospective evaluation to determine where our investments had an adequate return and then using that data as part of a feedback loop to better target our money or to analyze the impact of our efforts on, for example, how city-financed deals were affecting land prices.

The bigger, more important, and politically charged question is whether we did enough to stem the tide of rising rents in the city. That is closely related to the issue of gentrification, although they are not the same issue. It is worth considering deeply because this is perhaps the most important issue facing the city.

First some facts: There are 2.2 million rental units in the city (I focus on rental units versus owned units because those are the ones in which local government policy has historically played a role). They house nearly five million New Yorkers. Of that total, 13 percent are subsidized in some form, and 47 percent are rent stabilized or rent controlled. The vast majority of those are rent stabilized, that is, regulated by New York state law, which dictates a process that limits rent increases and imposes tenant restrictions (which itself is a form of subsidization, but a more indirect one because all other renters bear the burden of its restrictions). Importantly, rent stabilization laws do not dictate a particular level of tenant income. In all the affordable housing programs the city runs, tenants qualify by income. In rent stabilization, it doesn't matter what your income is. This means that the lowest-income tenants do not necessarily get the benefit of the cheapest apartments. The remaining 40 percent of the rental units are unregulated or, effectively, market rate.

There is no question that rents went up during the Bloomberg Administration. Over those twelve years, median rents in the city went up by about 15 percent, adjusted for inflation. At the same time, median incomes of renter households across the city, also adjusted for inflation, went up by only 2 percent. As a result, rents on average assumed a higher percentage of income. According to a report by the New York University (NYU) Furman Center, the rent burden for households in New York City (defined by HUD as the total number of households that paid more than 30 percent of their income for housing) increased from 43 percent to 54 percent between 2000 and 2013. The same period also brought a net decline of about one hundred thousand in the number of units subject to rent stabilization.

Could we have altered that dynamic? The first option would have been to try to change the rent stabilization laws by lobbying the state legislature in Albany. There are several ways an apartment can lose rent-stabilization protection; the most common occurs under state law—when an apartment is vacated, the property owner can increase the rent on that apartment by up to 20 percent per year. And the apartment can be decontrolled when the rent increases to more than $2,000 a month, which can be accelerated when the owner makes qualifying tenant improvements he or she can amortize into the rent. Because the owners have very powerful influence on the Republicans who control the state Senate in Albany, we never thought a material change in the law was possible. But that might have been too passive an approach, particularly after the financial crisis. I think there was an opportunity to advocate for and achieve real change—at least to raise the threshold for decontrol and to make it harder for tenant improvements to qualify for the rent increase. Granite countertops shouldn't count the same as a new boiler.

The rent guidelines process sounds very objective, but it is complicated and can be subjective. We tried to play it right down the middle and pass along only the legitimate costs. We could have sided with the tenants' organizations and skewed the results to lower the rent increases, but we chose not to, reasoning that the long-term result would be inadequate investment in buildings and, more ominously, the introduction of uncertainty into the system, which would have negative consequences for new investment in affordable housing. Obviously, we could have produced more affordable housing to try to keep pace with the unexpected demand the incredible population growth fostered. That would have required more money, and our commitment was already huge.

Perhaps the biggest cause of the problem was a national and even global one. Incomes simply did not rise fast enough to keep pace with housing inflation. This is largely a function of national and global economic forces, although, as I discuss in Chapter 8, we were very aggressive in our efforts to produce more, better-paying jobs.

I'm sure too that we could have been more sensitive in some cases to the combined effects of our zoning and affordable-housing policies, particularly where we expected dramatic neighborhood change. There isn't any evidence to support the conclusion that the growing problem of housing costs was greater in gentrified areas. The NYU Furman Center did a separate analysis that divided neighborhoods into three groups—low-income neighborhoods that experienced higher than median rent growth, low-income neighborhoods that experienced lower than median rent growth, and high-income neighborhoods. The first group was labeled as gentrifying neighborhoods, including Harlem, Greenpoint-Williamsburg, Bedford-Stuyvesant, and several neighborhoods in the South Bronx.

Certainly, rents increased in the gentrifying neighborhoods (30.1 percent, unadjusted for inflation) more than in the nongentrifying neighborhoods. But incomes also went up in the gentrifying neighborhoods (6.2 percent, unadjusted for inflation) whereas they declined (–7.5 percent) in nongentrifying neighborhoods. More significantly, the rent burden in gentrifying neighborhoods increased less (from 42.3 percent in 2000 to 52.9 percent in 2014) than in nongentrifying neighborhoods (from 45.7 percent to 58.5 percent). Rising rents affected everyone but more in the neighborhoods that didn't gentrify because the residents' incomes in those neighborhoods went down. The study couldn't determine if low-income households in gentrifying neighborhoods were forced out of their neighborhoods. It is clear that new housing was added to the housing stock.

Unquestionably, though, the character of neighborhoods changed. Many new buildings went up. And, as the Furman Center study demonstrated, the new residents were unquestionably different from the residents there before but in somewhat surprising ways. The biggest change was in the percentage of residents with a college degree. In the gentrifying neighborhoods, it went from 16 percent to 29 percent. In the nongentrifying neighborhoods it went up as well, but by a much smaller margin, from 14 percent to 18 percent.

Gentrifying neighborhoods also attracted more young people and families without children.

From a racial perspective, there wasn't much change. The white and Asian share of the populations of the gentrifying neighborhoods went from 25 percent to 29 percent, whereas in the nongentrifying neighborhoods it remained consistent. The African American population fell slightly across the city but only by two percentage points, more in gentrifying than in nongentrifying neighborhoods. All of this indicates that the single biggest change in the gentrifying neighborhoods is that better-educated people of the same races typically moved into these communities.

Was this a bad thing? I don't think so. When those new people moved in, they brought new investment with them. New stores followed. There was greater demand for city services (although crime came down in all neighborhoods pretty much evenly). That was a benefit to everybody. Property values went up, which helped many long-term owners of homes, most of whom had little wealth otherwise.

Bloomberg used to say that the best way to avoid gentrification (and to have rents go down) is to make the city worse. Then people won't want to come (or stay), property values will come down, and investment will dry up. We did that in the 1970s. I think what the gentrifying neighborhoods show is the virtuous cycle working the way it is supposed to. More people come, more revenue is raised for the city, and more services are provided. A consequence, though, is that when there is more demand for housing, supply needs to keep pace. We rezoned 40 percent of the city to help do that. We spent $8 billion to make more housing affordable, a program we started when we didn't have the money and no one was calling for it, and then we more than doubled down just three years later.

During his campaign to replace Bloomberg in 2014, Bill de Blasio criticized our administration for our record on affordable housing. He argued that we had not done enough. After he was in office, he even changed the name of my former job to Deputy Mayor for Housing and Economic Development. The plan he's announced calls for two hundred thousand units, just thirty-five thousand units more than we actually built or preserved, for the most part using the tools we pioneered or refined. He is benefiting from our rezonings, which created much more potential supply. Most importantly, he is able to pay for it because the virtuous cycle in the city has actually worked, and the city has record revenues flowing through its coffers.

CHAPTER SEVEN

REALITY AT GROUND ZERO

FINISHING AND ANNOUNCING the housing plan were not the only immi-
nent deadlines I faced as we flew back from Colorado Springs. Just two
days after Mike Bloomberg was set to unveil the housing plan, he was slated
to announce our vision for the future of Lower Manhattan.

In the very early days of our first year, the emotional fallout of 9/11 was
every bit as tangible as the bits of wreckage still being pulled from the site.
The city lost police officers and firefighters. The Port Authority, which owned
the site, lost eighty-four people. Then there were all of the victims' families—
ever present and grieving. All of that anger and loss quickly coalesced around
possessing the future of the World Trade Center site—restoring the skyline
and nursing Lower Manhattan back from the dead were everyone's deepest
desires. And that was the problem.

Anyone from any entity with any possible connection to that hallowed
land wanted a say in its future. Because I was Deputy Mayor of New York
and rebuilding was in my title, I was one of those vying for a place at the
table. It seemed a sacred responsibility. It also seemed common sense that
New York City, through the Mayor's staff, should have a say in reinventing its
iconic skyscrapers and the neighborhood they had come to define. I would—
but not at all in the way I first imagined.

My original vision of the city's role in the rebuilding of the Twin Towers
died from a thousand small cuts, as they say, but one seven a.m. meeting at
City Hall in early May 2002 perfectly encapsulates what went wrong.

I liked the early hours, when few people were around, other than the Mayor. So it was a great time to catch up with him, get organized for the day, and think through difficult problems that I didn't have time for in the constant crush of daily meetings. By the time I got home at night I was too tired to think clearly. Increasingly, though, my morning time was encroached upon.

I had asked the top staff from the Lower Manhattan Development Corporation—the entity charged with rebuilding Lower Manhattan—to come to City Hall to see if we could at least begin the process of putting together a financial outline for rebuilding the 9/11 site. Where did we envision spending money, and where was it going to come from? Then–Executive Vice President Kevin Rampe of LMDC led its delegation. (He would eventually become its President.) Rampe was an appointee of the Governor.

At my request, Roy Bahat, one of my Senior Policy Advisors at City Hall, had done a great deal of work to catalogue various funding streams, especially the $20 billion of funding the federal government had committed, that might be available to help rebuild Lower Manhattan and pay for the dozens of projects already being discussed, such as the new transit infrastructure the Port Authority and the Metropolitan Transportation Authority were urging. It was already clear that the "uses" of funds were going to be much greater than the "sources," and an approach to evaluating the trade-offs to be made was going to be needed.

At this point, I still somewhat credulously took for granted that all the parties would want to cooperate and that we ultimately shared the same goals. In fact, up to this point the city and the state had generally cooperated well.

Rampe slowly examined the detailed spreadsheets Bahat had prepared. Then he looked up and asked pointedly, "Roy, is this coming out of your end or ours?" Bahat, who was taken aback, responded: "I don't know what you mean. I thought the way this worked was we were all just going to work together to figure out the best plan and go from there." Rampe, in a condescending voice, said to my twenty-five-year-old staffer: "Roy, this isn't Harvard. This isn't Oxford [Bahat had been a Rhodes Scholar]. This isn't McKinsey. This is politics." Bahat was stung. But I had had enough. "This is ridiculous," I said. And I got up and walked out of the room.

There would still be years more of petty infighting and worse. But to me that meeting marked the moment when I began to reckon with my own naiveté about politics and government. My background was in business, and I have to admit that I came into office more than a little Pollyannaish.

I thought that if I did my best to cooperate, we could all work together to articulate the plan that best balanced all of the competing interests using the resources we could muster.

Up to that point a feeling of goodwill, driven by the sanctity of the mission, had characterized the city's relationship with the state. Yet I vastly underestimated the resistance and resentment my involvement on behalf of the city would cause. Over the next ten months, I would get a brutal education in the politics of personal ambition, the limits to the powers of the Mayor's office, and the dynamics of the relationship between the city and state and the Mayor and the Governor. As a result of learning the limits of my position, I began to get a better grasp of my areas of influence as well. Eventually the lessons learned would help me redirect my energies and reshape the southern tip of Manhattan Island.

The stage for the clash was set long before Bloomberg was elected. The power struggle between the state capital in Albany and the state's largest, attention-grabbing, money-generating city hasn't changed much since Albany became New York's permanent state capital in 1797. However, it hit a modern nadir when George Pataki was elected Governor. That's because even though both he and New York's new Mayor, Rudy Giuliani, were (nominally, in Giuliani's case back then) Republicans, when Pataki ran for office the first time, in 1994, Giuliani endorsed his Democratic rival, three-term Governor Mario Cuomo. It must have seemed like the smart thing to do at the time. There hadn't been a Republican Governor since 1974, and the city is highly dependent on the Governor's goodwill in many different ways. However, in the big midterm Republican sweep that fall, Pataki defeated Cuomo in what was perhaps the biggest upset in the election cycle.

There are many ways in which a Governor can punish a Mayor, and Pataki went straight for the jugular. He appointed Giuliani's political rival George Marlin the Executive Director of the Port Authority of New York and New Jersey. Marlin had run against Giuliani from the right as the Conservative Party candidate in 1993, and the two despised each other. The Port Authority, a joint venture of the state of New Jersey and the state of New York, had been established in the early 1920s through an interstate compact authorized by the US Congress to develop and administer much of the complex transportation infrastructure shared by the states within a twenty-five-mile radius of the Statue of Liberty, including bridges, tunnels, shipping terminals, and airports. It was a perfect spot to place a thorn in Giuliani's side.

Over the years, the goliath Port Authority had experienced mission creep; increasingly the Governors of both states used it to fund their pet projects. The biggest pet of them all was the building of the World Trade Center (WTC), which then-Governor Nelson Rockefeller, encouraged by his brother David Rockefeller, insisted the Port Authority build. In fact, the WTC was a source of great pride for the Port Authority. Not only did it dominate the skyline but also it generated tens of millions of dollars in rental income.

With his independent power base, Marlin immediately went to war with Giuliani. There were battles over how much rent the city should get from the Port Authority for La Guardia and JFK airports, which were on city land. The Port Authority was paying a minimal $3.5 million a year. Marlin wouldn't agree to pay more, so eventually Giuliani refused to renew the leases. Without the certainty that the leases would be renewed, the Port Authority had increasing trouble raising the capital to fund improvements to the airports. Marlin and Giuliani also fought over fares on the PATH, the train system that runs between New York and New Jersey. It got so bad that eventually Marlin was replaced. But the bad blood between the Port Authority and the city still ran deep.

In the wake of 9/11, Giuliani and Pataki had a detente. Partly because both were deeply affected by the tragedy and felt a sincere responsibility to ensure that the site was rebuilt, they cooperated extremely effectively in the months afterward. They worked with local representatives in Congress, especially with Senators Chuck Schumer and Hillary Clinton, to secure $20 billion in funding for the rebuilding. As they began to think about how the site was going to be cleared and rebuilt, they also found someone they both despised more than they did each other. In the two months after 9/11, right up until the day of the mayoral election, pretty much everyone thought that the next mayor was going to be Democratic candidate and city Public Advocate Mark Green. Both Pataki and Giuliani wanted to keep Green, whom they found smart, arrogant, often obnoxious, and philosophically very much out of step, as powerless in the rebuilding process as politically possible.

On November 2, 2001, four days before the mayoral election, the Governor and the Mayor agreed on the creation of LMDC and ultimately vested control of it in the Governor. To further cement his hold on power, on January 9 Pataki selected Louis R. Tomson to run the day-to-day operations at LMDC. Tomson was, to my mind, typical of many of Pataki's appointees—chosen not because he brought any special expertise to the job but because he would be completely loyal to the Governor. He had started out as a lawyer in private practice, had come into the Pataki Administration, and then the Governor promoted him to Chief Policy Maker for Energy and Communications. He was very smart and had a reputation as a deft operator.

Even though the odds were stacked against the city when Bloomberg first arrived in City Hall, he made a sincere effort to make peace. Just after he took office he invited Pataki, Governor Jim McGreevey of New Jersey, Pataki's appointed Executive Director of the Port Authority Joe Seymour, and their wives to dinner at his Upper East Side townhouse and toasted to a new era of cooperation.

At first it seemed as if cooperation might be the order of the day. In early February, at my suggestion, Alex Garvin, whose work on the Olympic plan was largely done, was appointed Vice President for Planning, Design, and Development for LMDC. This was especially comforting because in his interview for the post, Garvin discussed with Tomson many of the things he and I agreed needed to be done to make Lower Manhattan more appealing. He brought with him Andrew Winters and Chris Glaisek, members of our NYC2012 planning team.

In the aftermath of their destruction, the Twin Towers were immediately wrapped in a veil of nostalgia. But the truth was that their impact on Lower Manhattan had been severe. In the 1970s, as the WTC was built, 22 percent of all Manhattan jobs were Downtown. By 2000, the area only had 19 percent—it had lost about sixty-four thousand jobs. At night the area was a ghost town. The shops and restaurants were mostly run down. Having worked in Lower Manhattan twice, I knew it was unappealing.

Although there were many reasons for the decline of Downtown, the WTC was a major contributing factor. It had been a planning disaster. It was built on a "superblock" that cut off access to the rest of Lower Manhattan in every direction. In an area largely characterized by small, narrow, dark, and confusing streets that dated back to precolonial times, it truncated the one street—Fulton Street—that traversed Lower Manhattan from river to river. A building adjacent to the WTC, 2 Greenwich Street, cut off a major north–south thoroughfare. It was built on an elevated, concrete plaza that stifled the street life all around it. The wind off of the Hudson whipped around the site, making its central plaza difficult to cross, let alone enjoy. It was so unpleasant that it was often closed to the public. There was also a huge underground mall that, although popular with commuters, sapped retail activity from the local streets.

Garvin and I were not alone in thinking this way. The local business community and the universe of architects and planners who immediately got engaged in thinking about the site's future almost unanimously agreed that the tragedy offered an opportunity to rebuild better than before. More important, that view was shared by Larry Silverstein, who just a month and a half before 9/11 had agreed with the Port Authority to lease the Twin Towers and other portions of the site for ninety-nine years (effectively a purchase) in what was billed as the largest real-estate deal in the city's history and one of the largest privatizations ever.

After Garvin was in his job, one of our first collaborations was to develop a set of principles we hoped would help to guide rebuilding the site and the area immediately around it. Released in April after significant public input and minimal objections, they emphasized restoring the street grid and re-integrating the site with the neighborhood; enhancing mass transit service; building a permanent memorial for the nearly three thousand people killed at Ground Zero; promoting commercial, residential, retail, and cultural activity; and creating more park space—in short, a mixed-used neighborhood that appropriately recognized the need for a memorial right in the middle of it.

In March, Pataki, yielding to Bloomberg's complaints that he had too little influence at LMDC, agreed to expand the board to fourteen people from eleven, increasing the number of mayoral appointees to seven from four. Yet, despite those outward signs of progress, by late spring it was becoming clear to my staff and me that our attempts to build consensus around a clear blueprint of where we were going were stalling. In fact, it seemed we were intentionally being thwarted.

From my perspective, probably the biggest obstacle was turning out to be Pataki's amorphous but apparently grand ambitions. As Pataki's man on the ground, Tomson filtered many of LMDC's activities through a political lens—specifically the lens of what it would take to get Pataki reelected as Governor and then to raise his profile to the national level. I assumed that included an eventual run for President in 2008. (His desire to run for President was bizarrely confirmed when he competed for the Republican nomination in 2016, ten years after leaving office!) So much of what LMDC undertook—studying transportation, approving architecture plans, consulting victims' families—seemed to be contrived to gather maximum public attention.

In mid-March, for example, Tomson told the staff of LMDC that Pataki wanted to put together a design for Ground Zero so that he could have something to announce on July 4. It was so bad that the planning team for

LMDC used to joke that LMDC should be called the Lower Manhattan Committee to Reelect the Governor.

If it were just setting dates toward some political calendar, that might not have been so hard to swallow—in fact it might have helped move things forward. But the calculus for what Pataki and his inner circle—essentially Tomson and Seymour—thought would get him reelected was not shared with the rest of us and often seemed counterintuitive, blocking straightforward progress.

Part of the challenge was that Tomson could be very emotionally volatile. At some meetings, he'd be extremely humorous and productive and say things such as, "Let's agree we're going to get three things done." The next meeting you'd come in and he didn't speak or would lash out. He was also gone a lot. He lived upstate and would arrive on Tuesday morning and leave on Thursday.

Tomson generally resisted shared planning—he regarded it suspiciously as the city's attempt to take away power he might need to deploy on behalf of his boss. My early success placing Garvin, Winters, and Glaisek at LMDC probably turned out to be a negative because it fed Tomson's paranoia that the city, often personified by me, was trying to use LMDC to forward the city's agenda. During his first three months on the job, he referred to Garvin's small staff derisively as the "Planettes."

Getting Tomson to agree to the simplest analysis could be torture. For example, 10.5 million square feet of office space was destroyed on the World Trade Center site on 9/11. But just because the offices was destroyed did not mean it necessarily made sense to rebuild them all back: jobs had been migrating uptown for decades. Yet in considering rebuilding, Tomson blocked all attempts at a basic financial analysis of whether all that office space was still needed Downtown. Would the Port Authority be able to recoup in rent the costs of rebuilding the entire space? It sounds like a crass question, but the Port Authority is a public agency with a duty to use its resources responsibly. But Pataki and his staff did not want to hear that kind of talk. They just wanted to rebuild what had been there. It was what Silverstein demanded, and it became their mantra.

This was obviously nonsensical, not just to us, but to knowledgeable outsiders. At some point, Tomson orchestrated a very private meeting—maybe ten or fifteen people, including David Rockefeller, who was Chair and CEO of Chase Manhattan Bank in the late 1960s. I wasn't at that meeting, but it was described to me afterward. Rockefeller spoke in a quiet, bemused voice:

"Well, back in the '60s when we thought about the rebuilding of Lower Manhattan and sort of the reenergizing, we did studies," he said. "We thought about what would this community really need—how much office space, how much . . . I don't, you know . . ." He never finished the sentence; he was too much of a polite gentleman, but the question he was implicitly asking—how much office space do we need Downtown?—was clear.

If my staff and I faced suspicion from LMDC, we faced ten times more resistance from the Port Authority, which saw the city and LMDC as interlopers. One WTC, or the North Tower, was where the Port Authority had its office and was the first tower hit by the planes in the terrorist attack. Eighty-four employees, including Executive Director Neil Levin, died in the attacks. The Port Authority functions on two levels: the top leadership, made up of political appointees, and then the staff of engineers and technical people, many of whom were lifers. As tenured bureaucrats, the staffers were fairly immune to what those above them wanted. And the emotion of 9/11 made them fiercely tribal.

When it came to rebuilding, the Port Authority did not really want to share or consult with anyone. From its point of view, it owned the underlying land, and although it had leased the buildings to Larry Silverstein, it alone had the legacy and the technical know-how to rebuild. So the creation of LMDC was an insult to begin with. As the focus began turning to how to rebuild, and Garvin—always perceived as my agent—advocated for an open design competition that the Port Authority wouldn't control, this drove its professional staff almost mad.

Direct negotiations between the Port Authority and the city were even worse, exacerbated by the lingering anger over the airport battles of the past. The tension was manifested largely in ongoing lack of cooperation and openness. Although my relationship with Seymour, at the top of the Port Authority, was very cordial, my team in City Hall and the planning team at LMDC were fighting a ground war with the Port Authority's planning staff. Very quickly the feuding grew so intense that the Port Authority outright refused to meet with Glaisek, one of the members of Garvin's planning team, on basic questions of easements and street placement, leaving the more diplomatic Winters to do most of the negotiations.

Winters managed to maintain relationships with everyone in the rebuilding process, and as a result, he was able to sustain a degree of objectivity about the power dynamics between the city (as represented by me) and the Port Authority and LMDC. Here is his description:

On numerous occasions I would hear Joe [Seymour] or Lou [Tomson] make comments about the fact that Dan was working for $1. I think this all plays into the great divide between them. In addition to the historic/ structural divide between City and State; Dan was not only an urban/ urbane NYC guy vs. their upstate backgrounds. Dan was not only Jewish and from the business world, but also seen as an interloper in their world of politics, made doubly insulting by volunteering to do work that they got paid good money to do.

After all, a part of the power base of any Governor and his economic development cronies is the ability to give away make-work jobs at economic development agencies, and Dan was not only from a different world, he was playing by totally different rules. It came off as a sense that Dan thought he was better than everybody else—smarter, wealthier, etc.,—but they would show him that the exercise of political power was an area where they had the upper hand.

Rampe, the Pataki appointee who later became a friend, has a slightly different interpretation of the tension. As Rampe saw it, the men I was dealing with were highly evolved and skilled political beings, but years in government service had taught them to suspect that everyone had an angle—usually, like themselves, for self-glorification or glorification of their boss. So they hypothesized that my real goal in getting involved was to somehow promote myself or the Mayor over the Governor by advancing the Olympics, or even more darkly, by sabotaging the WTC because I had real-estate interests on the Far West Side. (I owned tiny interests in a few buildings on the Far West Side in which an affiliate of Oak Hill Capital had invested. The total value of my stakes was less than the salary I gave up every year.)

Pataki's guys frequently took swipes at me in the press, suggesting not so subtly that unnamed others questioned my motives. Charles Gargano, Chair of the Empire State Development Corporation, the state equivalent of the Economic Development Corporation, told the *New York Times*: "There was speculation that some didn't want the rebuilding of Ground Zero because they thought there was a better real estate market elsewhere." No facts. All innuendo.

The results were tragicomical. When I went to Tomson and said, "Wouldn't it be great if we could use some of the funds for rebuilding Lower Manhattan to build a park along the East River?" what he heard was, "Doctoroff is trying to take funds away from the office towers that are important to us so he can use them for his own ambitions to bring the Olympics to New York." In short, it was impossible for me to have a straight conversation with him.

If I am truthful, there was one other factor that limited my standing among the players for Ground Zero, and that was the Mayor. In so many little ways he telegraphed that he did not think that Lower Manhattan would ever return to being the financial capital of the world, let alone New York. Like many other former investment bankers, he had left Downtown for Midtown years before. He started and then built Bloomberg LP on Park Avenue—almost as far away from Downtown as he could get. "Dan," he would tell me in private meetings, "they are just not going to move Downtown. It is not that attractive."

Occasionally, he would blurt out thoughts in the press that would complicate matters. In June, for example, he told the victims' families that the memorial on the site shouldn't be too big because that would make the area too much like a "cemetery." It was classic Bloomberg, not wrong, but not exactly politically sensitive. It could have been worse, though. Giuliani, the heroic ex-Mayor, was urging that the entire site be preserved as a memorial.

Although I was slow to understand the causes of my blocked progress, the frustration was building to a head. Finally I boiled over. We were somewhere deep into negotiating preliminary issues necessary to begin the process of rebuilding the site, and every point had become combative. I went to a meeting to discuss efforts to accelerate rebuilding Seven WTC, just to the north of Ground Zero. Everyone had to make adjustments to make this possible. The city, for example, had to move an entire street. All the Port Authority had to do was take one easement and move it a foot.

Sure enough, that became the sticking point. It was as if its representatives were planning to fight and get nothing done. In what would become an unfortunate and all-too-frequent refrain for me when it came to the rebuilding efforts at Ground Zero, suddenly I slammed my hand down on the table and yelled, "This is bullshit, and I'm leaving."

There was no way LMDC and the Port Authority were going to make plans for something as important as the WTC without public input. New York City has a long history of public participation in design and architecture. The city's fifty-nine community boards and their committees hold public hearings on buildings and land use all the time. The City Planning Commission and the City Council and its committees also hold hearings. The entire city had been attacked, and virtually everyone who lived there felt he or she had a stake in the rebuilding.

Garvin pushed aggressively to ensure that even though legally there was no requirement for formal public input into the rebuilding process, the intense interest from the public and the media should be respected. At Garvin's urging, in April, Tomson contacted a Washington, DC–based, nonprofit organization, AmericaSpeaks, which had developed interactive technologies that facilitated discussions of public policy issues for thousands of participants. LMDC signed it up to conduct an event called Listening to the City, which would take place at the end of July at the Javits Center, after the preliminary plans had been developed. The idea was to give anyone a chance to come and express his or her opinions about the plans and aspirations for the site. One sign of the pent-up demand for input was that within a week more than 4,000 people signed up for the event.

With this big event now scheduled, it was clear that the small architecture firm Garvin had initially hired for the early design process, Peterson and Littenberg, might not be up to the task. So Tomson asked fifteen other firms to respond to a request for proposals (RFP) to provide design advisory services for the site. On May 22, LMDC awarded the commission to develop a site plan to the firm of Beyer Blinder Belle. Only LMDC and the Port Authority cast votes—three each—and the city had no say.

With that apparently settled, Tomson went on vacation for a month to Scandinavia. In his absence, Garvin and I made some progress. For example, we got the city, LMDC, and Silverstein to agree that Greenwich Street (running north–south) and Fulton Street (running east–west) would be re-inserted through the site and would assume their pre-WTC roles as thoroughfares through Lower Manhattan, essentially cutting the site into four (unequal) quadrants, which assured that it would be reconnected to the rest of the street grid.

However, that grid, combined with the Port Authority's insistence that architects include three big requirements—ten million square feet of office space, six hundred thousand square feet of retail, and an eight-hundred-room hotel—meant that, in reality, there was relatively little flexibility left for Beyer Blinder Belle to develop a site plan.

Even given the constraints, the work the firm generated was very disappointing. Garvin and I and several LMDC Board members worried that if the plan were presented to the public, it would be an embarrassment. My good friend Roland Betts, who sat on the LMDC Board, and I then put together a working group of representatives from the Port Authority, LMDC, city, and state to quickly consider other alternatives.

To improve the field of options on short notice, the working group turned to architects who had already prepared plans for the entire site for other parties. David Childs, who would eventually be the architect of One World Trade (the so-called Freedom Tower), had just finished a plan for the site for Silverstein. Cooper, Robertson had developed one for Brookfield Properties, the large real-estate company that owned the World Financial Center, across the street from Ground Zero. We also included two of the more promising schemes Peterson and Littenberg had done for Garvin before Beyer Blinder Belle was chosen.

While Tomson was still on vacation, the working group agreed to present those four plans along with two from Beyer Blinder Belle at the Pataki-mandated exhibition at Federal Hall on July 16, 2002, and then allow them to be discussed as part of the Listening to the City event four days later. Given the limited time frames involved, the plans necessarily weren't complete designs, but they reflected a diversity of imagination and design. At least they would give the public a sense of the possibilities, we reasoned. It seemed like a pretty inoffensive, commonsense solution, but when Tomson returned from his long vacation he was furious.

If that wasn't complicated enough, on June 29 Pataki met with the victims' families and out of the blue, without consulting the city or the Port Authority (as far as I know), made a promise that there would be no rebuilding on the footprints of the Twin Towers. The Governor's spur-of-the-moment promise had profound ramifications.

It was shocking that he would make such a significant decision without consulting anyone. I heard about it the next day when it was reported in the papers. As Bloomberg would later say, declaring the footprints inviolable drove the building process from that point forward. "Once you say that, you've set the scale of the memorial, you've set where the other buildings on the site will be, and you've set the cost," he told the *New York Times* in 2006.

In the short run, Pataki's declaration certainly meant that the plans being prepared for public review had to be overhauled. Tomson ordered Beyer Blinder Belle to make plans "similar to the other four plans, but avoid building on the footprints" and add two of their own. As a result, Beyer Blinder Belle created six plans and, given the limitations, turned them into six variations on a bland theme. Basically, they were just simplistic bulk diagrams that avoided any consideration of the site's importance or its relationship to the rest of Lower Manhattan. The changes they made were so significant that the architects for Brookfield Properties later told the press they didn't even recognize their designs when they were posted.

I saw none of this. While the redesigning was taking place, my father died, and I went back to Detroit for the funeral. I was out of the loop for nearly a week. Garvin was apoplectic. He could see that the designs were going to be a public embarrassment—he imagined he would be blamed. He reached out to Sharon Greenberger to warn the Mayor what he would see when he previewed the plans three days before the planned event at Federal Hall.

Bloomberg was deeply disappointed. He wanted to know why there was not more housing, why the buildings were so large and blocky, and why there was no design for the park space. Garvin, who was there, overheard Bloomberg asking incredulously if I had approved the plans. A representative from the Port Authority told him that I had. Of course, I had not. Bloomberg then announced that he would not attend the press conference at Federal Hall three days hence, where the plans were presented to universal derision.

Redemption came at Listening to the City the following Saturday. It was truly an inspirational moment. If the terrorists had meant to deal a blow to democracy, instead they had created the most democratic design event in the world. In addition to the 4,300 people who showed up at Javits Center on Day One, 200 more people attended an overflow event two days later. Moreover, an additional 800 people participated in online dialogues held from July 29 to August 12.

It didn't take long into the process to realize that the crowd hated what they were seeing. The attendees were asked if they approved of the plans. Only two of them were approved of by an even majority. They were not sparing in their comments. The biggest insult: the plans "look like Albany."

The rejection was so widespread and conclusive that the Port Authority and LMDC were backpedaling almost immediately. Even before the event, LMDC Communications Director Matt Higgins was explaining that this was just a beginning. I must admit I was thrilled—thrilled that the public had spoken and thrilled that the people had told the public sector to start listening. I got up to speak and told the crowd, "If I had to sum up what I heard today in one phrase, it would clearly be: Don't settle. Do something great."

After the second Listening to the City event, the Governor and LMDC did a complete turnaround. Acknowledging the anger, they announced a new competition for the WTC and surrounding area. Unlike the first tightly held, controlled design, this one was to be an open, global competition.

As everything got more and more complicated, I became convinced that the rebuilding process would be better served if just one governmental entity were in control—and, needless to say, to me it seemed clear that should be the city. But with the cards we had been dealt, that just wasn't going to happen. Other than the bully pulpit, we really didn't have control of anything—not LMDC (and all of the federal money that flowed through it), the Port Authority, the MTA, Battery Park City, or the New York State Department of Transportation, which managed the highway that ran down the West Side of Manhattan adjacent to the site. The only asset we possessed was the leverage Giuliani had left us by refusing to renegotiate the airport leases.

The Port Authority was finding it harder to finance airport improvements because it couldn't tell potential debt holders with certainty that it was going to be managing the airports in the future. One warm evening in late July, Bahat, my point person both on the Port Authority renegotiation and on Ground Zero, was studying spreadsheets he had prepared for both projects. He had a flash of insight: the city was looking to collect from the Port Authority about $100 million in lease payments annually for the airports (plus back rent), and in the Port Authority's deal with Silverstein it had negotiated to collect about $100 million in annual rent on the WTC site. So why not swap? The city would give the Port Authority the land under the airports, and it would give the city the land under Ground Zero. Because of the back rent, to make it even, the city would also get some upfront cash. If the city owned the land underlying the WTC, we reasoned, the Port Authority would go away, and LMDC could too. The city would then be left alone to decide what was best for what was arguably the most important site within its borders and then to work out a deal with Silverstein. We brought the swap idea to the Mayor, who loved it instantly and suggested that we see if the state had any interest.

We broached the idea with Seymour, who said it was interesting, and he would raise it with the Governor. A few weeks later, word leaked to the press (not from us) that the city and state were discussing the land swap. The press and public reactions were very positive. On August 6, the *New York Times* editorialized that it was "the most creative idea to arise from the Lower Manhattan redevelopment process so far. It deserves prompt and serious consideration."

But despite his public assertions at the time to the contrary, the Governor never took us seriously. At the end of August, Governor McGreevey told the *New York Times* that a deal was "unlikely." Tomson, Gargano, and I would discuss the idea periodically over the ensuing weeks, but they never really engaged. By early September, it was pretty clear that it wasn't going to happen. Some years later, Seymour was asked in an interview why the Governor had let us go through the motions for so long. His response: "Sometimes the Governor likes to watch the turkeys dance."

Well, I was tired of dancing. By late August, I knew we had to change our focus. We were never going to exert any real, direct control over the site. At critical moments in the rebuilding process, we might be able to use the mayoral bully pulpit and the leverage the unresolved airport leases gave us. (In October 2003, I would finally break the stalemate and negotiate a massive increase in annual rents to $93.5 million a year and then, increasing from there, a $700 million upfront payment, a share of the lease payments the Port Authority was to receive from the WTC site, and $50 million for projects in Queens to use at the city's discretion, which helped us with local Councilmembers.)

Bloomberg and the rest of our administration were also aware that we had to use our influence carefully because of how dependent we were on the Governor for so many other things, including education reform, our precarious budget, and the Olympic bid, including our plans for the Far West Side.

If we couldn't control Ground Zero, why not spend more of our energy on things we could control—such as the rest of Lower Manhattan? We controlled the streets, the parks, and the security; we collected taxes in the rest of Lower Manhattan; and we were responsible for land use. With the exception of Ground Zero, Battery Park City, and some highways, Lower Manhattan was our canvas. We could paint something bold and creative on it. And no one denied that it needed help. So, beginning right after Labor Day 2002, our strategy shifted. At Ground Zero, with LMDC and the Port Authority, the city would begin playing zone defense to ensure that nothing stupid happened in the rebuilding process, but for the rest of Lower Manhattan we would be aggressively on offense.

A part of that strategy would be to try to get the use of a portion of the $20 billion in federal funds committed to the rebuilding. Eight billion dollars of the funds were in the form of Liberty Bonds, tax-exempt bonds that could be authorized by the city or state to help private businesses lower their costs of borrowing, and various tax credits that could be used to retain or compensate businesses in Lower Manhattan. The rest of the federal money, more than $12 billion, was appropriated for two broad purposes—for disaster relief and assistance, including security and antiterrorism, and for economic recovery and rebuilding. Much of the first category was given to the Federal Emergency Management Agency, but it also included grants for rebuilding the West Side Highway, for emergency ferry service, for damaged federal offices, and for local antiterrorism efforts. The biggest chunk of the remainder was the most flexible. These funds—$2.7 billion—were for loans and grants to retain and attract residents and businesses to Lower Manhattan. They were to be funneled through HUD's Community Block Development Grant program and would be administered by LMDC. Of these funds, $700 million had already been allocated for the very successful business and residential attraction programs the city and the state put in place in early 2002. The rest was up for grabs. We felt we could use those funds to remake Lower Manhattan.

The opportunity to reimagine the place where New York had been born was irresistible to everyone at the many city agencies I brought together to consider the future of the area. We tried to ask ourselves what Lower Manhattan meant to New York, the United States, and the world. Everybody was struck by the fact that the tallest building in the world had been built in Lower Manhattan five times. So Lower Manhattan's DNA was aspirational.

We brought in outsiders to help. Garvin surreptitiously joined our working group and contributed many of the ideas eventually included in the plan. We reached out to a wide variety of constituents. We asked them what Lower Manhattan meant to them. Paul Goldberger, the celebrated architectural critic at the *New Yorker,* came in and described it as New York's lodestar.

We identified so much that made Lower Manhattan unique. It was surrounded on three sides by water, but the water was inaccessible because of the highways that ringed it. It had cobblestone streets with historic buildings. It had canyons of historic (and not so notable) office buildings. We asked what it didn't have. Good infrastructure. Residents (there were only twenty thousand or so in Lower Manhattan). Retail. With the exception of Battery Park at Manhattan's southern tip, it didn't have parks.

We analyzed transportation access. Twelve subway lines converged there, but when we compared Lower Manhattan and Midtown in terms of accessibility from the metropolitan region, Lower Manhattan was at a distinct competitive disadvantage. We commissioned a study that showed that many more millions of people within the metropolitan area could get to Midtown within forty-five minutes than to Lower Manhattan. So from a transportation point of view, unless that dynamic could be shifted, it was always going to be priced lower for office space, but from a residential perspective, it had incredible access.

Over the course of those three months a remarkable team of dedicated public servants created a bold vision for a new Lower Manhattan completely different than any place on earth because it would rest on a foundation of modern infrastructure and Lower Manhattan's historic assets. It would be uniquely of the eighteenth, nineteenth, twentieth, and twenty-first centuries.

As we prepared to unveil the plan, I pushed the team hard. It wasn't going to be enough to talk in generalities. Unlike the Port Authority and LMDC, we would detail what we were going to do and where the money would come from. And we would develop a world-class presentation. The plan itself needed to be rich in visual images because we understood people would need help imagining the grubby area's brilliant future.

Only two days after we unveiled the New Housing Marketplace Plan, we assembled again to present the Mayor's Vision for Lower Manhattan. This time the venue was Regent Wall Street, one of the city's great spaces. The large event space is housed in a columned, Greek revival–style building that has over the centuries served as the New York Merchants' Exchange, the New York Stock Exchange, and the US Customs House. Our presentation was in the main atrium, with seventy-foot-high ceilings—a perfect match for our towering aspirations.

First, Bloomberg dispelled the commonly held view that our work would be done when the WTC site was rebuilt. In fact, only twenty seconds of the thirty-one-minute speech were spent discussing the rebuilding of Ground Zero. We had to wipe away the gauzy nostalgia for Lower Manhattan and recognize that we had to reinvent the whole thing. Taking a sacrilegious swipe at the Twin Towers, Bloomberg asserted, "We cannot assume that a grand design for the site will solve the problems of Lower Manhattan. . . . We've done that before. . . . The Twin Towers' voracious appetite for tenants weakened the entire downtown real estate market."

We were going to reimagine, reassess, and reinvent. "Lower Manhattan must become an even more vibrant global hub of culture and commerce, a live-and-work-and-visit community for the world." We proposed more than a dozen new parks, including a network ringing the waterfront. We called for ten thousand new apartments over ten years and the services, such as schools, retail, and other amenities, to support them. The West Side Highway should be shrouded in seven hundred trees, making it the "Champs-Elysees or Commonwealth Avenue for Lower Manhattan." Ferry service to take Lower Manhattan residents and workers to and from the area would be vastly increased. To address the fact that New York is the only global city that does not have a one-seat ride from its airport to its center city, we proposed direct train lines from the WTC site to JFK and Newark Airports and proposed specific ways to pay for them.

The response was tremendous. "Mayor Michael Bloomberg's long-awaited plan for Lower Manhattan is a bracing tonic for anyone dispirited about the future of downtown New York City," raved the *New York Times* editorial page.

While our administration was racing to complete our Vision for Lower Manhattan, the LMDC (with extensive city input) was finalizing the first round of its design competition. Exactly a week after our presentation, LMDC put on its own big show. It held the unveiling of the six finalists at the Winter Garden, a ten-story, glass-covered atrium with thirty-foot palm trees in the middle of the World Financial Center. It had been damaged on 9/11 and had been reopened in time for the event. On the morning of the announcement, it was packed. With Garvin as master of ceremonies, it was an engrossing display of the possibilities for the site.

All the designs were sophisticated and worthy of consideration, but very quickly two sets of plans emerged as the favorites, that of Uruguayan-born architect Rafael Viñoly and that of Polish-born, Berlin-based Daniel Libeskind. By February 3 the two would be named official finalists.

Libeskind sketched an ensemble of angular, crystal-like buildings that rose in height as they traveled north and then west around the site, culminating in what would be the tallest building in the United States. It was to be 1,776 feet tall, which is why Pataki called it the Freedom Tower. The buildings were positioned—like Stonehenge—so that on the morning of every September 11 the angles of the sun would mystically create a "wedge of light" (I never really understood what he meant, but Libeskind was a mesmerizing storyteller). The center of the site, in Pataki's sacred memorial quadrant, was basically left to be decided. The centerpiece of Viñoly's plan was the memorial, for which he proposed two cylindrical, one-hundred-story-high scaffolds of steel designed to evoke (especially when dramatically lit at night) the destroyed Twin Towers. The towers would not be office space—they would be arrayed around the intricately crafted, light-filled ghosts.

The Viñoly plan was particularly daring, and the LMDC Board was falling in love. Betts, who ran the board's Architecture and Design Committee, was particularly smitten. He worked closely with Viñoly and engineers to make sure that the design could actually be built.

By February 2003 the LMDC Board members were ready to choose their architect. They needed to show it to the politicians first. The meeting to preview the two finalist designs never made it onto Bloomberg's calendar. LMDC leaders insisted it was not their fault, but I doubted that. So Pataki alone got the viewing.

On February 25, the committee met to finalize its decision. The votes were clearly for Viñoly. The only voices who spoke up clearly for Libeskind were Seymour and Garvin. It seemed so clearly in the bag that it was rumored Libeskind had packed his bags and headed to the airport.

The next day, the meeting between the Governor and the Mayor took place. I attended the meeting with Bloomberg. Neither of us had particularly strong views about the designs. He leaned toward Libeskind (he thought the Viñoly plan "looked a little like two beer cans"), and I slightly favored Viñoly. Both of us were fine with honoring the outcome of the design process. The Governor arrived late, however, and was in an unbelievably foul mood. During the presentation, Pataki blurted out that he hated the Viñoly plan. "It looks like a skeleton," he spat. Then he began to pick apart the details. There was a museum placed above the ground between the Twin Towers. "I would never walk under there. It could collapse."

Betts, who was there with other representatives of LMDC, the Port Authority, and the Governor's and Mayor's offices, was ready to debate, but the Governor was not in the mood. He was hostile. After fifteen minutes, he said he had a phone call and disappeared from the room. A few minutes later Bloomberg was called out to follow him. Pataki told Bloomberg that he couldn't vote for the Viñoly plan. Leaning toward Libeskind himself, the Mayor wasn't going to put up a fight. When they returned, they announced to a stunned silence that Libeskind had won the competition. There was no vote.

Betts was floored. He couldn't believe that the Governor alone would decide the fate of such an enormously important public undertaking. He was completely alienated from the entire process. I honestly didn't feel strongly enough about the choice to protest. Bloomberg and I both knew that we needed the cooperation of the Governor on so many things, including getting money for our plans for Lower Manhattan. And we were already watching with great satisfaction as our ambitious plans were getting under way.

CHAPTER EIGHT

FIVE-BOROUGH ECONOMIC DEVELOPMENT STRATEGY

AS 2002 CAME to an end, the recurring dream I had about swimming to the surface and being plunged down by an invisible hand disappeared. It had been a brutal and exhausting year, but with the end-of-the-year Olympic bid victory and the nearly unanimously enthusiastic responses to the housing and Lower Manhattan plans, I felt a sense of relief and, more importantly, accomplishment.

Although Mike Bloomberg had completed his first year in office and clearly had the city pointed in the right direction, it was far from fixed. Ground Zero remained an ugly, open gash across Lower Manhattan, and psyches across the city were still fragile. Budget deficits loomed. The outpouring of love for New York from around the world hadn't disappeared, but over time it had lost some of its potency (as a headline in the satirical newspaper, the *Onion,* put it in the immediate aftermath of the attacks: "Rest of U.S. Temporarily Feels Great Affection for New York"). People were still scared to visit the city, hampering efforts to rebuild our tourism industry. Our tentative gains in residents, jobs, and reestablishing normal life still felt like they could all be reversed. Collectively as a city, we still held our breath, as the city still felt vulnerable.

But New York had made it through that first, traumatic year and emerged intact. The city had shown a stubborn, determined resolve that gained strength with every day of distance from the attacks. The spirit that emerged was a particular New York blend of compassionate connection bonding the city, combined with an equally powerful and widely shared FU attitude directed at the terrorists. That refusal to be cowed had enabled us to begin the pursuit of our ambitious agenda at what was certainly one of New York's lowest moments. On my end-of-year vacation, I slept more soundly than I could remember.

It would be months before our international competitors were anointed for the Olympic bid, providing a temporary reprieve that allowed me to direct my full attention to the next round of New York projects. The previous year had been a frequently brutal crash course in city politics, and I had made some rookie mistakes. But I felt like I had started to grasp how to navigate the bureaucracy, the various egos, and the range of constituencies.

As 2002 came to a close, we had an immediate emergency. Since the reforms precipitated by the 1975 fiscal crisis, New York City had been required to balance its budget every year. The restriction stemmed back to a time when the city couldn't meet its debt obligations and nearly went under. Intense negotiations with the state yielded a series of conditions that enabled the city to restructure its debts and avoid bankruptcy, at a cost. The Financial Control Board had been created by the state to oversee the city's finances and ensure that the annual operating budget was balanced (debt for capital projects could be incurred).

During our first year, the state had been in a forgiving mood. So Bloomberg, with the assistance of Deputy Mayor Marc Shaw—who had run the Metropolitan Transportation Authority, served as Budget Director for the city, and been a legislative staffer in Albany—negotiated a onetime exemption. The agreement allowed the city to borrow $1.5 billion to close the budget gap for fiscal year 2003 (which ended in June 2003).

It was essential relief. But the prospects for the next year looked even bleaker. Some estimates of the 2004 fiscal year budget deficit were as high as $8 billion, and it was pretty clear that the state wasn't going to make another exception.

With his back against the wall, Bloomberg did the responsible thing. He got the City Council to agree in December 2002 to a whopping 18.5 percent increase in the city's property tax rate, which had been frozen for ten years. In addition, he and the City Council agreed on two new and temporary personal income tax rates for higher-income households (4.25 percent for people earning more than $100,000 annually and 4.45 percent for those with incomes over $500,000 per year) and a temporary two-year sales tax rate increase of .125 percent. The city was not going to be getting any cheaper.

All of this was on top of some other unpopular policies Bloomberg pushed through. At the very end of 2002, he and relentless Health Commissioner Tom Frieden (who would go on to become the Director of the federal Centers for Disease Control and Prevention), convinced the City Council to enact the Smoke-Free Air Act, a pioneering ban on smoking in restaurants and bars. On its tenth anniversary, the law would boast overwhelming support (and be credited with reducing the proportion of adult smokers from 21.5 percent to 15 percent and the percentage of smokers under the age of eighteen by half to 8.5 percent). It would be widely copied around the world. As it went into effect in March 2003, however, the Mayor was denounced by many as a "Stalinist" attacking personal liberty. Seers came out of the woodwork with dire predictions that it would crush nightlife and usher in a new puritanical age in the city. "The attitude at every place I know is that this is the most asinine law they've ever heard of," Michael M. Thomas, a chronicler of New York society, told the *New York Times*. "I know of no more detested law than this."

Bloomberg now gets the credit he deserves for taking principled but unpopular stances. But at the time, predictably, he was hated. In November 2003, Quinnipiac University released a poll showing that 61 percent of New Yorkers would refuse to have Thanksgiving with the Mayor. The *New York Post* gave the poll the memorable headline "Thanksgiving with Hizzoner? Stuff It, NYers Say!" Only 23 percent of New Yorkers said they wanted to see Bloomberg reelected—the lowest such rating in the history of the poll. Any goodwill established in his first year was quickly gone.

Taxes were only a temporary fix. We needed a structural solution to improve the city's financial outlook. But here were more obstacles. New York wasn't just considered an expensive place to do business (and getting worse)— it was deemed next to impossible, with a dense thicket of regulations, impassive bureaucrats, outdated technology, and fees designed to ding.

Getting permits to open a business often involved dozens of applications across multiple agencies. Because many agencies lacked computers or an online presence, that meant multiple in-person visits to offices scattered across the city to pick up and drop off forms. It wasn't clear where to get help, and businesses often expressed the view that the city was working against them, not with them. Leaders of big businesses felt that the city viewed them primarily as ATM machines.

We had our work cut out for us, which makes the results especially impressive. When Bloomberg took office on January 1, 2002, there were 3,671,700 people employed in New York City. When he left office twelve years later, there were 4,120,800, an increase of 11 percent to an all-time record. The numbers continued to grow substantially in the years since, building off the momentum generated during the Bloomberg Administration. New York City's job growth was more than double the national growth rate and occurred even though its largest industry, financial services, declined. More importantly, for the first time in recorded history, employment in New York recovered from a major recession (the financial crisis of 2008–2009) faster than the nation as a whole. All of this suggests that the growth of the city's economy was not an accident. It was the result of a strategic approach premised on this key insight: you could attract business to the city by thinking of the city like a business.

The development of our strategy began with an honest assessment of New York City's strengths and weaknesses relative to other cities around the nation and around the world. In 2002 we had hired McKinsey & Company to evaluate the city's job situation industry by industry. McKinsey interviewed dozens of CEOs—some headquartered in New York, some based elsewhere—to understand why they had (or hadn't) chosen to locate their companies in the city. McKinsey talked to their employees to understand their perceptions of New York.

The company analyzed the cost of doing business in New York versus other places and then applied that knowledge to the cost structures of businesses on an industry-by-industry basis. Together we tried to understand what companies perceived as the obstacles the city placed in the way of their success. We looked at employment trends by industry. Although there were certainly some differences of opinion, for the most part there was a striking consensus on New York's positive and negative attributes as a place to do business.

On the positive side, the first thing nearly all mentioned was the energy level of the city. That was closely related to the second most common thing we heard—New York was the most open city in the world. The President of a major Japanese bank, who had managed his bank's outposts in London, Sydney, Paris, and New York, articulated it most poignantly. When I asked him what his favorite city was, he responded by blushing. "You'll laugh at me," he said. Assured that wouldn't be the case, he continued in his strongly Japanese-accented English. "New York is my favorite city in the world because it is the only place in the world where when I walk down the street, people ask me for directions."

My first reaction was to stifle a chuckle. But I quickly realized that the bank president had actually said something remarkably profound about New York. What he meant was that no matter who you are, no matter where you come from, no matter how hard your accent is to understand, New Yorkers naturally assume that you are from New York. That creates a sense that anyone can feel at home there.

This has been true from the city's earliest days. Founded as a trading center in the New World by the Dutch West India Company in 1624, nineteen years later New York's five hundred inhabitants were native speakers of eighteen languages. Today, it is still a city of immigrants—from around the nation and around the world.

In my mind, that forges a link between openness and energy. The act of immigration is fundamentally an act of optimism. The immigrant believes, almost by definition, that the place he or she is going to is better than the place he or she is leaving behind. A city of immigrants, then, is a city of optimists who infuse their new home with a unique sense of purpose. Writer E. B. White, in his small but legendary work *Here Is New York,* described it best: "The Settlers give it passion. Each embraces New York with the intense excitement of first love, each absorbs New York with the fresh eyes of an adventurer, each generates heat and light to dwarf the Consolidated Edison Company."

That's why studies show that New Yorkers walk and talk faster than people in almost any other place in the world. The capacity to attract highly ambitious achievers from everywhere was cited by many respondents to McKinsey's surveys as a key competitive advantage for New York. It is also why New York has such a powerful brand. Just as we were starting in City Hall in 2002, the media and advertising firm Young and Rubicam published its annual evaluation of the strength of global brands and found that New York City ranked thirteenth out of more than 2,400 brands measured. We were the first city by far and in very good company—several Disney brands and Oprah Winfrey were among the twelve that ranked ahead of us. By contrast the United States ranked only forty-third. Although the sympathy for New York after 9/11 certainly played a role in our position, studies before and after have demonstrated the hold New York has on the global imagination.

The negatives from the survey were equally clear. Some knocks on New York were unfair—but one was undeniable. It was an incredibly expensive place to do business. In fact, McKinsey evaluated twenty-five different factors on which the city could be compared to other cities when companies made location decisions. The four on which the city performed the worst all related to cost: cost of living, cost of real estate, taxes, and cost of doing business. Over the past half century, a trend had emerged: jobs that needed to be in the city for some reason stayed. But many of those that could move to cheaper locations were in the process of doing so—or had already.

That meant the industries that generated the bulk of our business-related tax revenues relied heavily on intellectual capital. Financial "activities" were clearly the most important. In 2002, they represented only about 13 percent of the jobs but generated about 24 percent of the city's economic output. We also relied on industries such as media and advertising, higher education, and professional and business services (law, accounting, architecture, and engineering). Taken together, those industries represented 24 percent of employment and a disproportionate share of the economic output of the city. Just before we took office, the growth industries included health care, which relied on the local market for customers and therefore expanded with the population.

This trend was offset by a decline in wholesale trade, construction, and most significantly manufacturing, which since World War II fell from over 25 percent of the total job base to about 4 percent by the time the Bloomberg Administration came into City Hall.

We had also begun to see the "disaggregation" of companies, in which businesses were moving some functions away from New York because they could be done more cheaply elsewhere or required fewer employees because of technology. The classic case of this was financial services. Total employment in financial services had actually declined in New York from 1990 to 2000 from about 530,000 to 480,000 people just before 9/11. Within financial services, back-office employment (administrative and data processing personnel, for example) was dropping faster than the rise of the more highly paid front-office personnel (traders, salespeople, and investment managers). That was fine for New York's budget but not for the tens of thousands of middle-class workers displaced.

It was pretty clear from the outset that there wasn't going to be much we could do about costs, certainly not in the short term. We had hundreds of years of history to demonstrate that real-estate costs go down only when times are bad. There isn't a lot a local government can do about personnel costs. We had already raised taxes, not lowered them, and our financial situation remained dire. There would be no relief from that direction.

One solution Bloomberg, Andy Alper, and I discussed was to diversify our tax base so that we weren't so dependent on the financial services industry, which made us vulnerable to the painful effects of market contractions. If we wanted to be able to provide a consistent level of good services through good times and bad, we needed a broader foundation. There was also a physical component. We needed to spread the job base more evenly across the five boroughs instead of relying so intensely on Manhattan. That would give companies more choices in terms of cost and quality, enabling us to appeal to a broader range of businesses.

So, armed with the work McKinsey did for us, plus the benefit of Bloomberg's, Alper's, and my combined seventy-two years of working and building businesses in the city, we began formulating a strategy. In time, we would call it the Mayor's Five-Borough Economic Development Plan, but back then we just based it around a handful of key principles:

1. **No incentives to stay:** We would not incentivize companies (or parts of companies) to stay in the city. Offering to pay companies to stay might be politically popular in the short run, but ultimately it was a fool's errand in which every single company would threaten to leave in order to get in the queue for handouts.

2. **Improve customer service:** The city would treat its job-creating, tax-paying businesses like customers. Bloomberg was particularly fanatical on this point. His company, Bloomberg LP, was generally regarded as one of the most responsive companies to its customers anywhere, engendering remarkable loyalty among its users, and as Mayor he didn't understand why a city should be any different.

3. **Create or enhance alternative business districts:** We needed to recognize that businesses are not all the same and require different options at multiple price points. We decided to develop alternative commercial districts outside of Midtown appealing to different kinds of tenants.

4. **Diversify our employment base by focusing on our competitive strengths:** Our detailed analysis of our strengths and weaknesses had given us a strong belief of where we should be

competing and where we would be wasting our time. Although our strategy would evolve over time, it was best articulated by dynamic President of New York University John Sexton at a retreat for our economic development team. New York, he reminded us, is already strong in the "FIRE" (financial services, insurance, and real-estate) industries. It was time, he asserted, for us to focus just as much on "ICE" (intellectual, cultural, and educational) endeavors. FIRE and ICE. Everybody loved that.

Bloomberg had sent a clear, immediate message on incentives when he killed the baseball stadium and stock exchange deals. But just as quickly, we began communicating that the administration would offer a new level of responsiveness toward the businesses that stayed. Alper began making "client" visits, meeting one on one and in groups with leadership of the city's largest businesses. He quickly built a client coverage team, recruiting people with experience in key industries to be our well-informed emissaries. They would play an important role in addressing issues for companies already based in the city and in easing the way for businesses considering relocation to New York.

We also developed a plan for small businesses, transforming the Department of Business Services into the Department of Small Business Services. Commissioner Rob Walsh overhauled the agency during his twelve-year tenure, increasing by 50 percent the number of business improvement districts; creating NYC Business Solutions Centers, which provided support and financing to small businesses; streamlining the licensing and permitting process; linking businesses and potential workers through the creation of Workforce One career centers; and strengthening the city's Minority and Women-Owned Business Enterprise programs.

We also began to aggressively pursue office space development in new areas of the city, to provide businesses a greater range of cost and quality options. Rezonings were coupled with plans for infrastructure enhancements to create dynamic, mixed-use communities. In each case, we developed detailed plans that highlighted extensive investment in transportation, parks, streetscape improvements, housing, schools, and other amenities to make the districts more attractive for workers and their employers.

Finally, we identified specific industries in which our analysis had shown that New York could compete more aggressively—some obvious, others surprising—and developed targeted interventions. Not every strategy worked, but overall a new range of industries flourished, so that when the financial crisis struck the nation in 2008 and deepened into 2009, despite our dependency on the securities industry, New York's economy was more resilient than that of the nation as a whole. Some examples of our industry-based interventions included the following stories.

FILM AND TELEVISION PRODUCTION

ALTHOUGH NEW YORK City is one of the most iconic, photogenic backdrops in the world, the list of films set in New York but shot elsewhere goes on and on. When we came into City Hall, insiders joked about *American Psycho*, a movie starring a young Christian Bale as a murderous investment banker in Manhattan. What could be more New York than a psychotic investment banker? Nothing. But where was the movie filmed? Toronto. And with it went hundreds of jobs that could have gone to New York carpenters, electricians, caterers, stagehands, and production assistants, not to mention actors and actresses.

As we made our rounds of companies doing business (or not) in the city in the early weeks of the administration, leaders in the film and television industry, such as Harvey Weinstein, then of Miramax, told us why they filmed their movies and TV shows outside of the city whenever they could. We heard three main reasons: costs, facilities, and service. What did they mean by service, we asked? "Try getting a permit to shoot on a street of New York," we were told. "It is torture."

In the 1960s, producers were often required to obtain fifty or more permits from many different agencies to shoot their projects on the streets of New York. Faced with a decline in the number of movies shot in the city, Mayor John Lindsay created the nation's first-ever one-stop shop for issuing permits, appointed an aide to liaise with the industry, and established a police unit to control crowds during filming. Eventually, this grew into the Mayor's Office of Film, Theatre, and Broadcasting (MOFTB).

By 2002, the office had atrophied. Employees were still working on electric typewriters, permits required quadruplicate forms, and applicants had to go in person to the office of the MOFTB to fill out the forms, then return in person to pick up the permits after waiting for a few days. No wonder that in 2001, only nine TV shows were shot in New York.

When I described this mess to Bloomberg, he said I had to reach out to one of his key employees at Bloomberg LP. Katherine Oliver had been the general manager of Bloomberg Television and Radio. "She's the one,"

Bloomberg said. I interviewed her and was so impressed with her energy and preparation for our interview that I immediately offered her the job. "KO," as she was known, started in August 2002, and within a few weeks the office was starting to hum, not clack. Computers replaced typewriters, and the permit process was streamlined.

KO was relentless in promoting the industry, and she understood that if we wanted more projects shot and more people employed in the city, then it wasn't enough to give them the right to shoot on the streets. We needed sound stages and support space, including makeup and dressing rooms, green rooms, storage rooms, and offices. The limited facilities in Long Island City and Astoria, Queens, or at Chelsea Piers on Manhattan's West Side, wouldn't be enough.

Fortunately, the Giuliani Administration had embarked on an effort to develop production facilities that we inherited. Its staff had imagined the old Brooklyn Navy Yard as the new home for a film and television studio complex.

One of five original navy yards founded by President John Adams in 1801, the Yard, a three-hundred-acre parcel nestled on an inlet between the Williamsburg and Manhattan Bridges, was once the most storied US shipbuilding facility. Ships forged in its workshops would go on to lay the first transatlantic cable, hunt down slave-trade pirate ships off of Africa, and fight in some of the most famous and infamous US naval battles. Its most notable ships included the USS *Maine*, which sparked the Spanish-American War when it sank; the USS *Arizona*, which was sunk at Pearl Harbor; and the USS *Missouri*, which hosted the peace treaty signing that ended World War II. By 1945, it had become the world's busiest shipyard, employing seventy thousand workers.

But peacetime, the steady decline of urban manufacturing, the cost of labor in New York City, and the rise of the South's political power (which led to the growth of military shipyards there) were not kind to the Brooklyn Navy Yard. In 1966, Secretary of Defense Robert McNamara shuttered it along with more than ninety other military installations across the country. The Nixon Administration eventually sold it to the city, which spent the next two decades trying to salvage the shipbuilding and ship repair industry without success. Finally, Mayor Edward Koch created the Brooklyn Navy Yard Development Corporation, opening the site up to manufacturing and commercial activity. By 2001, there were fewer than three thousand workers employed in a motley mix of dilapidated buildings amid the almost unused dry docks. The Yard became a money-losing drain on the annual city budget, with hundreds of millions of dollars in deferred maintenance piling up.

The Giuliani Administration saw its potential, however. Its staff dreamed up the idea that this largely inaccessible place (there isn't a subway station within a fifteen-minute walk) would be an ideal spot for a movie studio. And, when staff members put out a request for proposals for a tenant, it seemed they were right. A fierce battle for the right to build the studio ensued. Ultimately, Robert De Niro and Harvey and Bob Weinstein lost out to a father-son team of New Jersey real-estate developers, David and Doug Steiner.

The minute we got into office, with the city reeling from 9/11, the Steiners tried to renegotiate the deal. I stood firm and they backed down, but it was not an auspicious start. Even when the Steiners were set to open the studio in October 2004, we still didn't believe that they would make their rent payments. Chair of the Brooklyn Navy Yard Alan Fishman, a successful banker who was also the leader of several major Brooklyn-based nonprofit and civic groups, called me to warn that Doug Steiner might bankrupt the place in six months.

Boy, were we wrong. Steiner Studios became a huge success. Within a year, the Steiners came to us and said they wanted to rehabilitate an additional building they could rent out to tenants related to TV and movie production, such as set and costume designers. They maintained that they couldn't take the risk both of paying rent and doing the extensive renovations the building required. So we gave them a 225,000-square-foot building and made it rent free as long as renovations were under way. Turns out it was a smart deal. Sooner than we ever imagined, the entire space was rented. Before the end of the Bloomberg Administration, they began a third major expansion bringing that total footprint to over one million square feet. The Steiners now own the largest production complex outside of Los Angeles.

It also attracted unusual tenants. Brooklyn College founded a film school there—the first film school ever embedded in a working studio. The students get hands-on experience, and the largely white industry gets a pipeline of young minority talent. Carnegie Mellon, the prestigious Pittsburgh-based research university, created a graduate school for interactive technological arts (i.e., gaming and film special effects) there as a result of the competition Bloomberg created to lure an applied sciences campus to New York.

In total, the city contributed $35 million to Steiner Studios for environmental remediation and utilities. Meanwhile, the Steiners invested $350 million and have more than paid the city's investment back in rent. And that doesn't include the jobs and the tax revenue they generate.

They also weren't alone. Across the city, new film and TV production spaces popped up over the next decade. By 2013, the square footage of sound stages and film and TV production space in New York City had doubled. As much as I would like to credit KO's customer service approach to the industry with generating the increased demand, the success also reflected a strategy we avoided in almost every other circumstance—tax credits.

As KO settled into her role, we embarked on a more detailed assessment of our competitive position for attracting film and TV production. We hired Boston Consulting Group to do the analysis, which pinpointed the final and most significant obstacle: money. Although producers and actors generally preferred to take advantage of our incredible backdrop whenever appropriate, ever sensitive to their volatile bottom lines, they just couldn't afford it. The states and provinces with which we were competing offered generous incentives, typically in the form of tax credits that could be deducted against the costs of production there.

We decided that to compete we had to do the same. So in August 2004, KO and industry leaders convinced the state legislature to enact a law providing state tax credits under the Empire State Film Production Credit program and authorizing the city to provide a film production tax credit, which the city did a few months later. The city's program, the first and only municipal-based tax credit for film and TV production in the country, created a pool of $25 million in tax incentives over the next four years, matched by $50 million from the state to anyone filming 75 percent of a feature film or TV series in the Big Apple. (Producers got a 5 percent city tax credit and 10 percent state tax credit for so-called below-the-line costs such as catering, scene scouting, and set building.)

KO enhanced the tax incentives with a marketing program, Made in NY, that offered, among other things, free advertising on bus shelters that we received as part of a deal with the Spanish company Cemusa, which had won the bus shelter and newsstand advertising concession from the city. The program was announced at a joint press conference with the Mayor and Governor and comedian Mel Brooks, the first to take advantage of the incentives. Brooks said the initiative had convinced him to film the cinema version of his Broadway smash *The Producers* in Brooklyn—that and the food. "The bagels, just the bagels alone," he cracked. "You go to Toronto, they're mushy." (During a hug, Brooks, in fine form, taped a piece of paper to Pataki's back that said "Gov.") *The Producers* would be the first film shot at the new Steiner Studios, demonstrating the combined power of our strategy of service, space, and incentives.

The incentives were such an inducement that all of the allocated funds, supposed to last four years, were used up in eighteen months. The city and the state extended and expanded the credit in 2006, and then when that money ran out in 2007, we decided to let the state go it alone. I was afraid we were creating a monster because the producers were getting more and more demanding, playing us off against other states in a ruthless competition for their business. Their lobbying efforts paid off with the state, though, which has continued to expand its tax credit program. As of 2017, the state was paying out $420 million annually. New York City, of course, is the major beneficiary of that expenditure.

According to a report by Boston Consulting Group in 2012, despite a nationwide industry decline in employment in the filmed entertainment industry over the previous decade, New York City employment grew by forty-four thousand to one hundred thousand over that period. Spending on movies increased by 70 percent, and TV productions grew by 82 percent. In 2015, 52 television shows and 336 movies were filmed in the city, all for an investment on our part of $60 million, some ads on bus stop shelters, and great customer service.

MANUFACTURING

I CAME INTO office thinking manufacturing was essentially a lost cause, as did the Mayor. Much of our rezoning strategy was built around former industrial areas that were never going to come back. The evidence seemed incontrovertible. After World War II there were a million manufacturing jobs in the city. By 2002, there were only 140,000 left; by 2003, it was down to 125,000, and then about 5,000 more were lost every year. When we came into office, the only manufacturer in the city with more than 400 jobs was Cumberland Packing Corporation in Brooklyn (which made Sweet 'N Low and other sweeteners at the Yard but eventually closed the manufacturing plant and moved it out of state).

As we negotiated our deal with the Steiners, however, I began to study the Brooklyn Navy Yard more closely. The three thousand workers at the Yard were employed in an interesting array of businesses. There were ethnic food manufacturers, stage set builders, and the manufacturer of Kevlar bulletproof vests. It seemed many of the businesses that thrived there had something in common: they had all found their competitive advantage in their relationship with the city. That could have been because the city was a customer, the local population was a natural market or a good place to test their products, or they were primarily dependent upon another industry in the city.

There must be other similar businesses that could be attracted to the Yard, with its cheap rents, I reasoned. It didn't take more than a little due diligence to understand what held this back: the Yard was crumbling. Some of its basic infrastructure dated back to the Civil War. In July 2004, we committed to invest $71 million in capital funds to stabilize the place with the hopes of creating an initial eight hundred jobs and building the foundation for more.

At the same time we were focusing on the Yard, my staff was hearing from existing manufacturers and their advocates that our own policies were making it harder for manufacturers to continue to operate in the city. There were complaints about excessive ticketing of industrial truck fleets and lack of respect for industrial businesses, some of which was attributable to my own rhetoric, especially as I pushed some of the bigger rezonings of industrial areas. Those rezonings were the source of some of the biggest concerns. It seemed that no area of the city would be safe from our rezoning machine, which began to increase speculation in property. In some cases that pushed up rents, but more often it just created enough uncertainty about the future of the property that business owners began to question whether they could stay in the city. In some cases, that concern alone prompted them to move out.

As a result of this feedback, Bloomberg and I convened a task force staffed by the Economic Development Corporation to study the issue. The task force members interviewed leaders of five hundred manufacturing and industrial businesses and held roundtable sessions in each borough. They studied the concentration of industry in each neighborhood of the city and cross-checked that with a longer-term view from the City Planning Department about where it expected the greatest residential growth to occur.

The result of this six-month effort was a comprehensive policy to support New York's industrial sector that the Mayor announced in January 2005 with the creation of the Mayor's Office of Industrial and Manufacturing Businesses, which would oversee a network of neighborhood ombudspeople who would liaise with their "clients" and act as their advocates with city agencies and City Hall. This office would administer a set of grants, enhanced sanitation services, and employee training programs. Most importantly, we created sixteen industrial business zones (IBZs) where there was a still heavy concentration of industrial and manufacturing businesses and where the city made an unprecedented commitment not to rezone these areas for residential use. To encourage businesses in nondesignated areas to move into IBZs, we offered a tax credit for relocation expenses.

Still, the Yard was the place where I saw the future of manufacturing in New York. In 2005, I offered Andrew Kimball, who had been the Chief Operating Officer of NYC2012, the job of shepherding the Yard's expansion. Kimball had never run a business before and knew nothing about real estate or even manufacturing, but I completely trusted him and assured him that he would be well tutored by Fishman. I gave him a dual mandate: maximize return on investment and maximize job creation.

Kimball and Fishman developed a strategy to position the Yard as a sustainable industrial park using cutting-edge green technology, which would enable it to become a magnet for forward-looking industrial businesses. The city agreed to fund $210 million for such capital improvements as the development of additional industrial buildings and the renovation of a historic entryway to make it happen.

The city mandated that new buildings and full-building renovations be certified according to Leadership in Energy and Environmental Design (LEED) standards—a rating system to evaluate the environmental performance of a building. They constructed the first multitenant, multistory, industrial, LEED Silver buildings in the United States, which included the city's first roof-mounted wind turbines. When repaving the roads, they used permeable asphalt. When they undertook major sewer projects, they added storm-water management systems such as water-absorbing plants. They collected rainwater for reuse. They even went as far as to use solar-powered trash compactors, solar- and wind-powered street lamps, and eco-friendly cleaning products.

To be sure, none of this happened overnight. A lot of space was being used to house city agencies and long-term tenants that weren't going to be moved or converted quickly. The Department of Citywide Administrative Services, for example, had a parking lot there that it used to repurpose old city vehicles. It took four years of effort for me to force it out of there.

But in the meantime, Kimball and Fishman's repositioning of the Yard was working magic. The rest of the campus began to attract the kind of socially responsible and tech-driven companies we desired. Niche manufacturing using laser cutters and 3D printers arrived and settled in. The Yard began to have a brand that stood for sustainable industrial design.

Not only did this make the Yard a magnet for visitors from around the world looking to build their own sustainable industrial parks, but this brand, so true to the new Brooklyn's values, began attracting people and businesses to the surrounding neighborhood. By 2017, the Yard was home to more than 330 businesses employing more than seven thousand people and generated an estimated $2 billion per year in economic impact for the city. And the model is being copied in other parts of the city, such as Industry City in South Brooklyn, a privately owned complex of industrial buildings Kimball left the Brooklyn Navy Yard to run.

Admittedly, we were slow to focus on the manufacturing sector. Had we moved faster, perhaps we could have stanched the job losses. By 2010, there were only seventy-six thousand manufacturing jobs in the city. Since then, the number has stabilized for first time since the end of World War II. "This is the most encouraging news for New York City manufacturing in decades," said Executive Director Jonathan Bowles of the Center for an Urban Future, one of the leading critics of our early inaction.

LIFE SCIENCES

THE MCKINSEY ANALYSIS indicated that the life sciences industry should be a focus. It was a natural. Drive up 1st Avenue in Manhattan, and there is one prestigious academic medical center after another. New York University Langone. New York Presbyterian. Rockefeller University. The Hospital for Special Surgery. Memorial Sloan Kettering. And that's just one avenue. Back in 2002, New York ranked in the top three states in terms of life sciences–related patents and federal funding for research.

Indeed, the medical and health-care industries were already very large employers in the city (491,600 employees in 2001), but relatively little of that employment was driven by pharmaceutical, biotech, or other life science businesses. We had two large pharmaceutical companies headquartered in the city, Pfizer and Bristol-Myers, but that was about it—and Bristol-Myers had been moving employees out of the city for decades. There was very little translation of all of the research into new businesses. Although New York captured about 6 percent of the research grants funded by the National Institutes of Health, its startups received almost none of the venture capital funding invested in life sciences. Typically when companies were formed based on ideas developed in New York institutions, their founders quickly decamped to Boston, San Diego, or the Bay Area to begin their corporate lives.

We were not the first to identify this as an opportunity. Back in 1984, the Port Authority sponsored a study that identified the gap between all of the academic work done in the city and new company formation. In the late 1990s, the New York City Partnership, under dynamic and aggressive longtime executive Kathy Wylde (by 2000 she would become CEO) went on a crusade to rally the academic institutions to work together to address the issue. Her heroic efforts resulted in the creation and joint funding of a common research facility, the New York Structural Biology Center, formed by nine leading research institutions to provide advanced instrumentation in structural biology, something none of the institutions could afford on its own. Its formation was heralded as a sign of recognition that for New York to be competitive nationally, its institutions needed to cooperate.

Emboldened by that success, in 2001 the Partnership issued a report detailing why New York had failed to develop a life sciences cluster despite the obvious advantages. The missing ingredients were identified as the shortage of wet lab space (laboratories where chemicals, drugs, and other material or biological matter are handled in liquid solutions requiring special ventilation or piping), the absence of an entrepreneurial culture within New York's academic centers, and the lack of early stage venture capital.

We were persuaded by the Partnership's logic. Our goal was to create a real life sciences cluster. Harvard Business School Professor Michael Porter first popularized the importance of industry-based clusters in his 1990 book *The Competitive Advantage of Nations*. He defined a successful cluster as a geographical area containing a critical mass of resources and skills related to an industry. That concentration leads to greater innovation, productivity, and new business creation—which in turn attracts more companies in the field. In New York, we were familiar with the concept—our economy was built on our financial services, media, and professional services clusters. But they had grown organically, not by governmental initiative.

Of the three factors identified by the Partnership, we concluded that as a government we couldn't do much about the entrepreneurial culture in academic medical centers, and we weren't going to create a venture capital industry. Instead, we focused on two things. The first was attracting business. We could identify and court pharmaceutical and biotech companies that might benefit from being in New York. Alper formed a team focused on life sciences at EDC, and its members began a domestic and international road show to convince companies to relocate at least some of their operations to the city to take advantage of our incredible academic research capabilities.

At the same time, we decided to focus on developing affordable wet lab space where new companies could take root. The statistics were stark. In 2003, Boston had twelve million square feet of commercial wet lab space, and New York had a fraction of that. To close the gap, we identified a parcel of city-owned land between Bellevue Hospital and NYU Langone Medical Center along the 1st Avenue corridor.

But we hit some snags. An intake center for homeless people had to be moved. The Coroner's Office had placed a temporary 9/11-related morgue on the site that took years to move (nearly proving Doctoroff's First Rule of Government: everything temporary is permanent). It took six years for the winning bidder, Alexandria Real Estate Equities, to finally open a beautiful three-hundred-thousand-square-foot building in 2010.

In the meantime, our efforts to attract existing pharmaceutical or biotech companies to the city were frustrating. Our team met with hundreds of them and got no takers. Companies didn't see New York as a home for the life sciences. We were too expensive. We didn't have the space. Even after Alexandria's new building opened (the fact that Alexandria was willing to invest in New York was a result of our outreach efforts), its first tenants were large companies such as Pfizer. Because of the cost of development in Manhattan, the space was more expensive than most startups could afford.

When an affiliate of the Partnership issued a new report on the state of the life sciences industry in 2016, its evaluation was pretty much a repeat of the 2001 report: "Historically, New York has been a leader in life science discoveries and patents, but has lagged thriving commercial hubs like those in Massachusetts and California when it comes to capturing life science jobs and attracting capital investment to build companies."

I've reflected a lot on why our efforts failed to produce as much as we'd hoped, at least in the short-term. First, we were just naïve in thinking that biotech and pharmaceutical companies were going to locate operations in the city because we were New York, especially after 9/11. We just didn't have enough to offer them. Second, I think building clusters is hard, especially when there is little culture of entrepreneurship in the target industry. The fact that so much of the intellectual capital existed within university structures where there were immature processes to achieve commercialization was a huge liability. We certainly could have worked harder to bring the academic institutions into working more with the private sector and government, the way the Partnership succeeded with the Structural Biology Center. Finally, a place-based strategy almost by definition takes a long time and is difficult when getting anything developed has a long lead time. We always believed that for the industry to succeed we would have to offer lower-cost real estate, which could be accomplished by developing the alternative business districts that were always part of our plan for the city, but as we will see in subsequent chapters, that means playing the long game.

Still, there are signs of hope that some of the seeds planted for life sciences during the Bloomberg Administration are actually bearing fruit. Alexandria opened a second building in 2013, and its anchor tenant is the US headquarters of Roche, the huge Swiss pharmaceuticals company, which moved from its home across the Hudson River in New Jersey. A Seattle-based venture capital firm took space there to support small, scientist-run companies. So did a biotech company spun off from Rockefeller University. Encouraged by the success of Alexandria, developers are creating space suited for the life sciences industry in lower-cost neighborhoods such as Harlem and South Brooklyn. The venture capital industry, increasingly drawn to the city by New York's growing technology sector, is starting to look at life sciences startups, which are increasingly requiring information technology expertise, a historical strength in the city. Maybe it just takes time to grow a cluster from a small base of little commercial activity, even when the intellectual capital is there.

HIGHER EDUCATION

EVERY YEAR, THE New York metropolitan area swells with an estimated seven hundred thousand college and graduate students who bring their vitality and wallets (not to mention friends and parents) with them. But higher education has had an impact on the city far beyond its raw numbers. The universities enrich the city's research, intellectual, and cultural scenes; the students and their families generate increased demand for the housing market; and after leaving school students become a critical source of employees for local businesses. Increasingly, they even play a role in building a startup ecosystem in the city.

Growth in higher education occurs when three things happen: the city is a place where students want to go, the institutions can accommodate a growing number of students, and the schools expand their programs, drawing new students. The prerequisite to everything is improving quality of life. For example, applications to NYU and Columbia University skyrocketed in inverse proportion to crime levels almost from the time it became apparent that New York was becoming safer in the mid-1990s.

More direct intervention came when we helped guide institutions through the city's complicated land-use process as they pursued plans for more space. That was the case with Fordham (which went through a dramatic expansion at its Lincoln Center campus in Manhattan), NYU, Baruch, Pace, Juilliard, the New School for Social Research, and the publicly owned schools of the City University of New York.

The mother of all expansions appeared on our radar screen when President of Columbia Lee Bollinger made a visit to City Hall from his Morningside Heights campus in May 2003. With him was Robert Kasdin, a longtime friend of mine who oversaw everything at Columbia outside the university's academic departments. Kasdin had given me a heads-up that Bollinger and he wanted to show a "big idea" to just the Mayor and me. We eagerly awaited the meeting.

Bollinger's desire to expand Columbia's thirty-six-acre campus was no secret. Ever since being installed as Columbia's president the year before, he had often been quoted as saying he was going to stake his presidency on ensuring that Columbia had adequate space to meet its future needs (Columbia had only about half as much space per student as Harvard). How he planned to do that wasn't at all clear, especially given the historically white, elite university's fraught relationship with its largely low-income, African American neighborhood—tension that exploded in protests when the university proposed building a gym in Morningside Heights in the 1960s. The gym would have had a separate entrance and facility for the community on a lower level—a design that many took as racially discriminatory. Columbia was scarred by the "Gym Crow" episode and for thirty-five years never attempted to build anything bold.

When Bloomberg and I came into the Committee of the Whole room for our meeting, Bollinger and Kasdin had placed a huge wooden model of West Harlem on the large, ornate wooden table in the center of the room. As we stood over the model, Bollinger explained his plan. Columbia wanted to expand its campus into a gritty area to its north and west known as Manhattanville, filled with auto repair shops, tenements, and small manufacturers. He described it as an "industrial slum."

As Bollinger pointed at the model, he explained that the university had been working with Renzo Piano, the Italian, Pritzker Prize–winning architect, on a master plan for the seventeen-acre, almost seven-million-square-foot expansion. It would extend from Broadway to the Hudson River from 125th to 133rd Streets. Their intent was to have the campus be far less closed to the surrounding community than the existing campus was. The first phases of this twenty-five-year project would be heavily focused on the sciences.

Then came the shock: Columbia had quietly bought up almost 40 percent of the land in the area and was in negotiations to buy more, Bollinger confided. Bloomberg and I glanced at each other, knowing what the other was thinking: "These guys aren't fooling around!" Bollinger's intention was to acquire all of the property in the area. They needed it all because they planned to build a "bathtub," or a big basement for the whole site, just as at the World Trade Center site. The bathtub would house all the infrastructure—the parking, freight delivery, energy, and so forth. Now it was clear why they had come to us: such a project would almost certainly require using eminent domain to buy out any property owners who refused to sell.

As the meeting neared its end, Bollinger turned to us and asked point-blank whether we would be supportive. Without pausing for even a second, Bloomberg, the longtime Chair and largest donor to his alma mater, Johns Hopkins University (or any university, for that matter), said, "Absolutely."

Over the next four years, our economic development team worked with Bollinger and Kasdin and their team to get the plans approved. Columbia had hired Piano because they wanted the campus to take an open, more European approach in contrast to typical walled-off US campuses. Although Piano had the right sense of urbanity, Columbia didn't have the experience to guide him to get the job done. Amanda Burden and Manhattan Director of City Planning Vishaan Chakrabarti took Columbia in hand. They insisted that Columbia develop design principles leading to a more coherent vision for the entire site.

Getting plans approved was never easy. But other than the two rezoning projects rejected by the City Council during the twelve years of the Bloomberg Administration, this one was the hardest. There was strong opposition from the surrounding community (although much less from within the affected area because there were so few people living there), which feared gentrification. Community meetings that Columbia held to discuss its plans were almost always long and contentious. The attitude of many in the local area was expressed by Chair of the Coalition to Preserve Community Tom DeMott, who told the *New York Times*, "We'll stand in front of the bulldozers." In fact, the local community board even proposed its own plan for Manhattanville.

Through it all, my staff, especially Mat Wambua, a Senior Policy Advisor on my staff in City Hall, stood with Columbia. We guided its community engagement strategy; helped the school position its physical plan so it would have "a little juice to squeeze out of the lemon," as Burden put it, when it came time to negotiate with the local elected officials; pushed the state, in charge of the eminent domain process, to move at the speed Columbia needed; and then helped Columbia negotiate with US Representative Charles Rangel, the dean of Harlem politicians, to hammer out a "community benefits agreement." The university committed $150 million to fund community priorities such as supporting local nonprofits and investing in affordable housing. It also promised additional benefits such as providing access to its facilities and hiring locals to work on the project.

Sometimes these city building efforts can lead in unpredictable directions. In 2006, while I was working closely with Columbia and frustrated with our efforts in the life sciences, I thought perhaps we should try to create our own health-focused academic campus to help accelerate the life sciences cluster. Working with Dean of the Bloomberg School of Public Health Al Sommer at Johns Hopkins and a team of experts, we developed an idea for a global health commons on Governors Island, the unused 172-acre island eight hundred yards off the southern tip of Manhattan. Our thought was that we could leverage the ecosystem of academic medicine, financing, global nongovernmental organizations, and philanthropy based in New York to create a hub for global health on the island, which the city and state had acquired in 2003. We hired consultants to develop a business plan that centered on convening leaders in the field, including academic researchers on the island. Bloomberg was even interested in funding it.

That plan died slowly after I left City Hall, but it was reborn in a different form when Seth Pinsky, a young star who had ascended from a low-level position at EDC to become its president in just five years, initiated an effort to accelerate the growth of the technology economy in the city. With the explosive growth of the Internet, many of New York's traditional industries, including media and advertising, information services, retail, and finance, were migrating online. Pinsky, under the leadership of one of my successors, Deputy Mayor Bob Steel, developed a multipronged strategy to make New York more competitive in attracting digital companies, especially startups. That included expanding Internet connectivity; fostering a network of incubator and coworking spaces to provide less expensive, easy-to-access space; and communicating New York's appeal to technology companies and entrepreneurs.

The centerpiece of the strategy, though, was the development of a competition to bring a top-tier applied sciences and engineering campus to New York. Pinsky acknowledges that the idea of the campus had its roots in the global health commons. In fact, one of the four sites the city offered to bidders for a proposed campus was Governors Island.

At the end of 2011, Bloomberg named Cornell University and Technion-Israel Institute of Technology the winners of the competition for their proposal to build Cornell Tech on Roosevelt Island, a sliver of an island in the middle of the East River between Manhattan and Queens. When fully built, the two-million-square-foot, state-of-the-art campus will be home to more than two thousand graduate students and 280 faculty and staff dedicated to "new approaches to commercializing university technology, new levels of strategic collaboration between companies and universities, and new curricula for graduate education."

Even without counting Cornell Tech, employment in higher education grew by 44 percent during the Bloomberg Administration—and continues to grow. By contrast, the number of people employed nationally in higher education during that time grew by 28 percent.

TOURISM

AS WE TACKLED New York's job market, our goal was not only to stabilize the economy but also to rebuild the foundations, broader and deeper, for a more stable future. As we entered 2003, one key industry remained in shambles.

Tourism had long been a big part of New York's economy. In 2003, it brought in more than $1.35 billion in taxes from income, sales, property, hotel, and other sources, and it directly employed 220,000 people, many of whom were immigrants on the first rung of the economic ladder. But in the wake of 9/11, the number of visitors and hotel occupancy plunged, taking away the livelihoods of tens of thousands of employees. Just over 12,000 were laid off in the first month after the attack.

I knew the industry well. Because of NYC2012, I had been on the board of the tourism bureau, a not-for-profit company that received a significant percentage of its funding from the city, before becoming Deputy Mayor. In fact, I had even come up with its new name—NYC & Company (an improvement over the clunky New York City Convention and Visitors Bureau). So when I became Deputy Mayor and assumed responsibility for overseeing the city's tourism strategy, I understood that three things common to every business that had ever underperformed its potential were going to have to be addressed if we were going to bring our tourism business back. Reputation. Money. People.

Our reputation had effects beyond the economy because tourism wasn't just a simple financial metric. It reflected something deeper about perceptions of New York around the world. Had our message about the city's safety resonated, or were people still resistant and afraid? Were we attracting mostly gawkers and mourners to Ground Zero, or were traditional tourist hubs thriving? Did people remain intimidated after they arrived, or were they pleasantly surprised, even delighted, as evidenced by repeat visits? We were regarded as one of the most open cities in the world—or at least congratulated ourselves on being so. But did everyone actually agree? Or was New York viewed by some (many?) as an aggressively diverse, liberal, dirty, dangerous bastion where they would never be welcome? Tourism was a way to take the temperature of the world, and in 2003 the warning signs were there.

These questions had taken on particular resonance for me since the start of the Olympic bid, when I began seeing the city through others' eyes. I knew we had our work cut out for us. Our public spaces *were* dirty, with dingy bus stops and derelict newsstands clogging the streetscape. Not everyone *was* always welcome—Republicans, for instance.

Before the international phase of the Olympic bid commenced—the other competing cities wouldn't all be announced until later in the spring of 2003—there was little to do on that front. But like a host preparing for one massive party, we could take a hard look at our home and start getting it in shape for guests.

The Bloomberg Administration had already begun tackling New York's dented image in our first year with the World Economic Forum and the National Football League kickoff in Times Square. But those opportunities had come to us. Buoyed by those early successes, I wanted to be far more proactive in attracting events—and not the ones you'd expect.

As we started to identify possible opportunities, we collided with one of the city's long-standing problems. Most major events require you to bid for the privilege, which means assembling a comprehensive proposal that dives into every detail, from budget and funding sources on the front end to plans for policing and traffic control on the back end. Yet New York City had no permanent organization that did this. NYC & Company had a paltry budget of $14 million a year (half contributed by the city) that made it hard to attract top people to its staff and limited what it could accomplish. Its main job had evolved into luring conventions and trade shows and then helping them book hotel rooms. So every time the city wanted to bid for a big event—such as an award show or an athletic championship—we had to start from scratch, creating a temporary host committee to pull everything together.

In order to compete effectively for major events, we needed a permanent host committee in the form of an independent agency devoted solely to luring big events. I committed to doing it in City Hall but imposed some limits. Although the city would pay for staff, none of the money used to bid for the events could come from taxpayer dollars. Even though the goal was to raise revenues for the city, politically it would look unseemly if we laid out money for so-called fun and games while still cutting things such as firehouses to balance the budget.

Maureen Reidy, a former accountant and then the president of Donald Trump's Miss Universe Organization, would run the new agency, which we dubbed NYC Big Events. In a response that would surprise no one today, when I called "The Donald" for a reference, his main feedback was that she was the "most beautiful accountant in the world." Reidy, the daughter of a New York City firefighter, certainly had the drive, smarts, and charm required for the job.

She needed it all after I insisted that the city should bid for counterintuitive events. I told her that the events should say something surprising about New York or reach out to an audience that might otherwise be hesitant to come to the city. When we hired her in July 2003, we were already pitching for the 2004 Republican and Democratic National Conventions, but Reidy had the idea that we should pitch for the Country Music Awards (CMAs). It was genius.

Few might have guessed it, but New Yorkers were the second largest buyers of country music in 2003 after residents of Los Angeles, according to Nielsen SoundScan. Still, it wasn't going to be an easy sell. At that point in their thirty-seven-year history, the CMAs had never been held outside of Nashville. When Reidy cold-called longtime CMA Executive Director Ed Benson to suggest the idea, there was a very long pause, after which all he said was, "Now that's an idea."

The combination of New York's post-9/11 appeal, the creative approach we proposed to exposing the huge New York market to country music in a way it hadn't been before, plus hosting in the world's biggest media market ultimately convinced Benson to move his event for the one and only time from its traditional home of Nashville.

The pitch Reidy honed conveniently gelled with our notion that events were not just for the few who attended but should have a surrounding value proposition that could be shared by the entire city across all boroughs. So as the awards approached in November 2005, Reidy had weeks of events planned under the motto Country Takes New York. Country stars taught in the public schools; others gave free concerts in subway stops across the city.

Within a couple of years after we hosted the CMAs, New York surpassed Los Angeles to become the biggest market for country music in the nation. Just as an entire NFL season had been given a turbo boost by the kickoff in Times Square, so too did the country music industry see a positive shift in consumption of its products by having an event in New York.

We had other victories. We got the Latin Grammys to leave Miami. But perhaps the biggest coup was the 2004 Republican National Convention. Although we bid for both parties' conventions, the one I really wanted in New York was the GOP's. New York is traditionally a Democratic stronghold—out of a city of more than 8 million people, only a few more than half a million are registered Republicans. And for us, what could be better than 4,800 delegates, most of whom were influential in their local communities and had never been to New York, trailed by 15,000 members of the international media?

When Bloomberg went to Washington, DC, to hand deliver our bid proposal to Chair of the Republican National Committee Marc Racicot, he was greeted with deep skepticism that Republicans would ever be welcomed in New York. After all, George W. Bush had lost in the five boroughs to Al Gore by 78 percent to 18 percent.

We played to their sense of patriotism, but we also made the case that given the Bush Administration's commitment to the city after 9/11, which few New Yorkers could deny had been exemplary, the Republicans would be warmly welcomed. We pointed out that given our position as the media capital of the world, events that took place in New York got more attention than if they happened anywhere else. We made the point that the last two times Democrats defeated Republican incumbents to win the presidency, they had done so in upsets after very successful conventions in New York City—Jimmy Carter in 1976 and Bill Clinton in 1992.

Bloomberg put his personal credibility on the line by committing that he would raise any funds necessary to put on a spectacular convention. That overcame one of the most significant logistical concerns, because putting on an event in New York typically costs at least 50 percent more than in other cities. The CMAs were a clear example: the awards required a ten-day rehearsal in the broadcast arena. To rent Madison Square Garden for that long, organizers would need to work with dozens of unions for a total cost of about $3 million. In Nashville, the cost was $100,000.

So at the end of August 2004, with the third anniversary of 9/11 just days away, the entire Republican circus came to town. There were parties all over the city: from private dinners at "21" Club to an over-the-top dance party at the Copacabana. Although our contract with the GOP required us to fulfill needs large and small, from the red carpet for the delegates to the twenty-two thousand gift baskets serving as farewell treats, Reidy and Kevin Sheekey, Bloomberg's trusted political guru and communications wizard, who co-led the effort, were determined to go way beyond what was expected. It was Sheekey's idea to house the media in the old, largely unused Farley Post Office across 8th Avenue from Madison Square Garden, where the convention took place. To help reporters avoid standing in long security lines every time they exited or entered the arena to file a story, he insisted we build a $750,000 pedestrian bridge over 8th Avenue to connect the two. They didn't stop there. Reidy hired Barneys, one of the city's toniest retailers, to set up a spa to keep our media guests well massaged. A happy media is smart business.

Bloomberg raised $81 million, including his personal donation of $7 million. We estimated that the four-day session generated $255 million in economic activity and brought in more than forty-seven thousand visitors. Even today, whenever I run into people from the Republican National Committee who worked with us to organize the convention, inevitably they gush that it was the best convention the Republicans ever had.

If there was one large, negative mark on the convention, it was the arrest and detention of 1,821 protesters, bystanders, legal observers, and even some journalists. Every political convention is an ideal forum for protests, and we certainly had more than our share, particularly given the intense opposition to the Iraq War. Hundreds of groups organized protests, culminating on Sunday, August 29, 2004, in a huge march including a procession of one thousand flag-draped coffins commemorating fallen soldiers. For the most part, the protests were peaceful and didn't disrupt the proceedings at Madison Square Garden.

With the anniversary of 9/11 so close it would have been an ideal time for a terrorist strike, and the entire city was on edge. The New York Police

Department, with ten thousand officers and hundreds of bomb-sniffing dogs on duty, rounded up protesters, sometimes in bright orange nets, and hauled them off to a grimy, temporary detention facility in an unused pier on the Hudson River. Ten years after the convention, the city agreed to pay $18 million to settle the civil rights claims of people arrested. For New York City, with its long history of skillful and patient policing that carefully preserved First Amendment rights, it was a regrettable shift.

Because the significance of the protesters' arrest wasn't broadly apparent, the Republican National Convention had exactly the impact we had hoped. New York was now being viewed as a much more welcoming place, especially by people who wouldn't have ordinarily been drawn to it. Still, I was skeptical that our counterintuitive event strategy would be enough to enable us to compete for visitors and their dollars with other cities spending a lot more to promote their attractions. Like any good consumer products company that has to compete for customers, we needed to spend money on advertising and promoting ourselves. Our top competitors, Las Vegas and Orlando, spent $153 million and $35 million annually, respectively, on their equivalents of NYC & Company compared with our paltry $14 million. Competition internationally was also fierce. Even Toronto spent more on promoting itself, and both Hong Kong and Singapore spent significantly more. Many of these cities donated hotel taxes to their convention and visitor bureaus. Not New York. New York had no money. In fact, with a projected deficit of $8 billion and vast tax increases enraging large swaths of the city, we'd have to get creative about funding.

We settled on two main strategies to generate revenue. First we would have to exploit the untapped value of the city's brand and assets through licensing and sponsorship deals. To do this, we created the world's first municipal marketing agency. The idea came from the city's chief legal officer, Corporation Counsel Mike Cardozo. Prior to joining the Bloomberg Administration, Cardozo had been outside counsel to several of the professional sports leagues, including the National Basketball Association. The leagues and teams generate a lot of revenue by licensing their logos and other trademarked property and by selling sponsorships to companies who want to be associated with them.

The city, despite having one of the most powerful brands in the world, did neither. In fact, Cardozo noted, it did the reverse. It failed to enforce the rights it had. He watched as merchandise using the logos of the New York

Fire Department and New York City Police Department flew off the shelves, but nearly all of it was unauthorized so the city didn't capture any of the benefits.

In April 2003 we created NYC Marketing and hired Chief Marketing Officer Joe Perello. Perello came from the sports marketing world. He might have been the most enthusiastic guy in the city, especially when it came to branding an entire municipality. For him, it was a dream job, and he leapt at the opportunity. "I've always idolized New York," he gushed at our interview.

Perello immediately started the search for sponsors. Because the idea of municipal marketing was still very much in its infancy, we got a lot of publicity for our efforts—not all of it positive. We had to explain what the plan was not. It was not to force every street seller of schlocky New York T-shirts to pay us a royalty. It was not about renaming bridges or tunnels for sponsors either. We were aware we were selling a city, not a sports league.

Still, we were somewhat taken aback by the level of controversy our first big deal created. In September 2003, Bloomberg announced a five-year, $166 million deal with the Snapple Beverage Corporation. The deal gave Snapple the exclusive right to sell pure fruit juices and water in vending machines in our public schools and a larger selection of beverages, including ice teas and chocolate drinks—it owned Yoo-Hoo!—in the six thousand vending machines in public buildings.

To us, the deal seemed like an obvious win. It got the highly sweetened, caffeinated, expensive sodas such as Coke and Pepsi out of the schools, replaced largely by juice and water at no more than one dollar apiece. The money we made from the program went to finance after-school sports programs for middle schoolers. We had the complete support of Schools Chancellor Joel Klein. In addition, Snapple agreed to spend $12 million a year on promotional campaigns featuring New York City.

What we hadn't anticipated was the anger of Pepsi, a company based in suburban New York. There are a million kids in the city's public schools and more than a thousand vending machines. Pepsi didn't like losing that business, especially because of the suggestion that it lost it based on considerations of health. Pepsi's lawyer actually told Perello: "I am not going to sue you. I am going to get [Bill] Thompson [the city's Comptroller, who was planning to run against the Mayor in the next election] to do it."

Thompson did indeed come after us. He accused us of noncompetitive bidding, saying that Octagon, a marketing company that helped broker the deal, also represented Cadbury Schweppes, which owns Snapple. We ended up in front of the City Council defending the deal. Perello was terrified, but by the end of the hearing he was charming the City Council and swatting away its members' objections. (At the end of the day, we would get only about a third of the money Snapple had committed because the deal was dependent in part on sales in the vending machines, which were disappointing.)

The biggest source of revenue for promoting the city, I hoped, would also solve a different problem. Most people take the newsstands, bus stops, and other so-called street furniture for granted. But the Olympic bidding process had made me acutely aware of how our city looked to visitors. Every time I passed a rotting, rusted bus stop shelter or newsstand, I cringed. As I traveled around the world, I became painfully aware of how beautiful such street furniture could be—especially in Paris, then thought to be our top competitor for the 2012 Games. Paris's public toilets were like elegant little houses. Why couldn't New York aspire to the same?

But we quickly learned that replacing the bus stop shelters and kiosks wasn't going to be easy. Bruce Ratner, a major real-estate developer who had been the Commissioner of the Department of Consumer Affairs during the Koch Administration, told me he had tried to replace them . . . in 1979. Mayor Giuliani had gone through a years-long procurement process and then didn't end up awarding the contract to anyone, reputedly because the bidder favored by one of his major supporters wasn't going to win.

It was so hard because the stakes were so large. There's a lot of money to be made on ads placed on the sides of those structures, especially in New York. With our dense population and relatively high average income levels, New York was viewed as a prime market by outdoor advertisers. In fact, the city was, in Perello's words, "the Super Bowl of outdoor marketing."

Yet we were being wildly underpaid for this asset. Under a long-expired contract with Viacom Outdoor, the city was receiving only about $12 million annually, plus we were allotted 2 percent of the advertising space for public service announcements. We knew it was worth much, much more. The city had an estimated 3,500 bus shelters and 350 newsstands. Given the then-current advertising rates, Viacom was generating maybe $75 million a year from the ads.

At our instigation, in 2003 the City Council passed a bill that led to the issuance of an RFP for the design, installation, and maintenance of bus shelters, newsstands, and pay toilets (for some reason, the *New York Times* editorial page was obsessed with pay toilets, so we threw in the option to build some of the money-losing structures into the RFP), with bids due in August 2004. Because nothing in a big city ever goes without controversy, it took longer than we expected. In this case, part of the reason was the negotiations among different interests on our side. Perello wanted to generate as much money as possible, and the Department of Transportation (DOT) cared more about safety. The flashpoint came over Perello's proposal to have the advertisements on the bus shelters on rollers so they could flip every thirty seconds. DOT worried that it would be too distracting for drivers. I didn't buy it, but to buy peace I reluctantly sided with DOT.

Alper, Commissioner of DOT Iris Weinshall, and Perello did a masterful job of managing the proposal process, and after several rounds of back and forth with several bidders in July 2005, we awarded the franchise to Cemusa, a Spanish company. We loved its modernist, clean design and, of course, the money. Cemusa agreed to pay the city four times what we had been receiving (a minimum of just over $1 billion over twenty years). But it got better: we reserved 22.5 percent of the ad space for ourselves, allowing us to promote whatever city initiatives we saw fit. And, better still, Cemusa agreed to give us a similar amount of out-of-home inventory in the European and Latin American cities where it had contracts. That gave us a perfect platform to promote the city globally. It was a grand slam.

The number of domestic visitors reached a record high the following year. But it was clear that we needed to do more. Despite the efforts to beef up our tourism infrastructure, by 2004 the number of international visitors was still 6 percent below 2001 levels and 22 percent below 2000 levels. This was a bigger problem than it might have seemed: international visitors might have been just 15 percent of visitors to our city, but they accounted for 40 percent of visitor spending. We needed more of them.

A study of other cities, led by Marc Ricks, one of the Senior Policy Advisors on my City Hall staff, compared New York with other cities and discovered a series of actions we could take to promote ourselves better. Some cost money, but others were just common sense, such as a best-in-class website, better signage, or even a simple calendar of events that could help travel agents convince their clients who had already seen the city's iconic postcard attractions such as the Statue of Liberty and the Empire State Building to come back. It was clear that the team at NYC & Company didn't have the capacity to take our efforts to a higher level.

In all, a targeted total investment of $35 million from the city (five times the amount the city had been funding) would be enough to turbocharge growth in tourism. In his State of the City Address in January 2006, Bloomberg announced an audacious goal: "50 by 15"; that is, to attract 50 million visitors to New York City by 2015 (compared with 42.6 million in 2005).

Before handing over the money, I wanted to combine the new constellation of agencies, including NYC & Company (to which the city contributed half of the money and with which it had significant influence but still maintained an independent board), NYC Big Events, and NYC Marketing (which reported directly to me) under unified leadership.

With a $35 million prize dangling, it wasn't hard to convince the board of NYC & Company to replace its leadership. For the new CEO, Chair of NYC & Company Jon Tisch and I approached George Fertitta, who had recently sold his successful advertising firm. He was close friends with Tisch, and one of his satisfied clients had been Bloomberg LP.

As soon as we met him, we knew Fertitta was perfect. An ebullient, native New Yorker who looked a dozen years younger than his actual age of sixty, with the energy of a thirty-year-old, he came in completely prepared, offering dozens of suggestions about how we should rethink the selling of our city, such as opening low-cost sales offices in international cities, promoting all five boroughs to expand the city's tourism offerings, and using targeting to encourage repeat visitation. It was love at first meet. Shortly thereafter, we announced his appointment and created the first fully integrated tourism and marketing office (it has now been copied across the country) with a budget of $41 million, keeping the name NYC & Company.

Fertitta knew what we needed and was utterly confident we could get there. He told an audience of executives at the "21" Club that fifty million visitors by 2015 would be a "layup." He set about remaking the agency. Nearly 90 people left, and about 140 new people came onto a staff that numbered only about 175. Fertitta deemphasized advertising and employed a more cost-effective communications strategy but still built the capacity to do in-house ad campaigns with a fast turnaround. He also opened NYC & Company offices in eighteen different countries, which allowed us to run promotions specially tailored by region, speaking to visitors in their language in a more genuine way, but the offices also acted as press conduits, quickly reacting to both good and bad news.

By leveraging the inventory with Cemusa, we were able to come up with ads and get them up nearly overnight from our backyard to dozens of places across the globe. Fertitta ran 150 separate campaigns in five years. Two days after the Marriage Equality Act went into effect in New York, allowing for same-sex marriage, Fertitta placed "NYC I Do" ads across the country, encouraging gay people to come to the city to get married. When Brazil's currency strengthened, he ran ads encouraging its citizens to come to New York to shop because it was so cheap.

Needless to say NYC & Company met its goals and then some. In 2002, we drew thirty-five million tourists; by 2011 we had hit fifty million—four years early. The Mayor then demanded fifty-five million. By the end of the administration, I was long gone, but the engine Fertitta and I had put in place was still chugging along and had brought us nearly to the Mayor's target. In the six-plus years Fertitta led NYC & Company, domestic visitation increased by 12 percent, international visitation increased by 52 percent, and New York's share of the lucrative market for overseas visitors to the United States increased from 28 percent to 33 percent. All of those tourists created huge demand for new hotels and the construction and services jobs that came with them.

Over the twelve years of the Bloomberg Administration, the number of hotel rooms nearly doubled, from fifty-five thousand to ninety-five thousand. The number of jobs in tourism and related industries increased by 136,300. In 2014, the *New York Times* declared tourism and its associated revenues "one of the biggest successes of the administration."

<hr/>

The final numbers tell a clear story about how we fundamentally reshaped the city's economy. While Bloomberg was in office, total private employment in the city grew by 449,000 jobs, or 12 percent. By contrast, national job growth over the same period was only 5 percent. While he was Mayor, the economy became more diverse, and our reliance on financial services diminished. In 2008, for the first time in recent memory, the city went into a recession more slowly than the rest of the nation and emerged from it more rapidly.

In addition, and as important, the city's economy diversified geographically, just as we hoped it would. A 2017 report by the New York City Comptroller found that between 2000 and 2015, the number of businesses in New York grew by 16 percent. What was more remarkable was the fact that overwhelmingly, the business growth occurred outside of Manhattan. Brooklyn increased by 48 percent, Queens by 33 percent, the Bronx by 26 percent, and Staten Island by 22 percent. Manhattan was down by 2 percent.

In the areas identified by NYU's Furman Center as gentrifying (see Chapter 6), business growth was even more stunning. Central Harlem grew by 99 percent, Greenpoint/Williamsburg by 70 percent, Bedford-Stuyvesant by 63 percent, and East Harlem by 58 percent, for example. But even in non-gentrifying areas, the growth in businesses was an impressive 36 percent. This growth occurred in a wide range of industries and the number of minority-owned businesses increased in every borough (from 2007 to 2012).

Were we just lucky? I don't think so. The best proof of that is the fact that for the most part, the industries and neighborhoods that we focused on were among the ones that grew the fastest—and much faster than they did nationally. For each industry we targeted, the city developed a multilayered strategy and pursued it aggressively. Of course, not everything worked out exactly as we had planned. But we applied common principles across every field: uncommon public-sector customer service, carefully targeted investment, and thoughtful attention to finding the right space in a tightly constrained city. Only rarely did we use financial incentives. Although it is certainly too early to declare victory over the city's boom-and-bust cycle, New York's economy is more diversified geographically and industry-wise, and more resilient.

CHAPTER NINE

OLYMPIC TRUTHS

ONE NIGHT IN June 2003 I found myself at the Prague Hilton bar. I had finished a bottle of Italian red wine with new friend Alex Gilady, the International Olympic Committee member from Israel and an executive with NBC, who was about twenty years my senior. He was kindly but firmly delivering some unpleasant news that made me wonder for the first time why I had volunteered to become both Deputy Mayor and de facto leader of an international Olympic bid.

I was in Prague to attend the 115th Session of the IOC. The following month the IOC would officially name the nine competitor cities bidding for the 2012 Games: New York, Paris, London, Madrid, Moscow, Istanbul, Rio de Janeiro, Leipzig, and Havana. By the time of this meeting it was pretty clear who would be competing, so the Prague session marked the kickoff of the international phase of the bid. It was one of the first of what would turn out to be dozens of international Olympic events I would attend over the next two years as I tried with increasing desperation to juggle my full-time job at City Hall with the growing demands of the bid.

Really, the entire strategy in winning the Olympic bid was to woo the 116 members of the IOC, who would vote on the host city in just a little more than two years in Singapore. My job was to get to know them, to learn their special needs and concerns, and to get them to trust me. This arduous task was made more complicated by anticorruption rules. You were not supposed to visit with these delegates unless you were at an official Olympic event. Thus, I was not really in Prague to sit in the hall in the Hilton but to lie in wait outside the hall or in the lobby or bar of the official hotel after the formal session ended so I might introduce myself or be introduced by a friendly intermediary to as many individual IOC members as possible to begin the process of developing a relationship. That was what leaders of other cities' bids were doing too. They seemed to know lots of people there, but I knew no one.

The IOC members had gained their elite status through a byzantine, often mysterious process. In some cases, it was the result of a personal relationship with the very powerful President of the IOC. From 1980 to 2001, that had been Juan Antonio Samaranch, a Catalan who had been the Minister of Sport late in the Franco regime. Most IOC members had been appointed under his watch. Samaranch, a masterful political strategist, had rightly been credited with the enormous growth in the popularity and revenue-generating capacity of the Olympic Games that had occurred since the 1980 US boycott of the Moscow Games, culminating in the spectacularly successful Olympics twenty years later in Sydney.

Samaranch was succeeded by Jacque Rogge. A successful orthopedic surgeon, Rogge was both a noted rugby player and sailing champion who had ascended to his role of IOC President by leading the Belgian Olympic Committee and then the European Olympic Committee.

Perhaps in reaction to Samaranch's dominating personality and tenure, Rogge was a more formal, reserved head who did not seek to exercise political influence and power and, depending on your perspective, either created a vacuum of leadership or allowed others to play a more impactful role.

Although no one became an IOC member without the President's blessing, there were several routes to membership. The first was to be involved in the Olympic movement through an international sports federation (IF), which exists for every Olympic sport. The IFs promote the interests of those sports around the world. A perfect example was the President of the Federation Internationale de Volleyball (FIVB), Ruben Acosta of Mexico. An IOC member since 2000, Acosta had led the FIVB since 1984, popularizing his sport with more revealing player uniforms and TV-friendlier rules, leading to explosive growth in sponsorship revenues. He had even built a gleaming new FIVB headquarters in Lausanne, Switzerland, where the IOC happened to be headquartered. Other IOC members who had gained that status through their involvement in powerful IFs included Lamine Diack of Senegal, President of the International Association of Athletics Federations (IAAF; the athletics, or track-and-field, federation), and Sepp Blatter of Switzerland, President of the Fédération Internationale de Football Association (FIFA; the world football—soccer—federation). Some members came from winter sports federations, such as ice hockey, figure skating, and bobsledding—each had an equal vote on the decision about where to host the summer Games even though his or her sport wouldn't be involved.

A second route was to be involved through National Olympic Committees (NOCs), which have authority for the Olympic movement within each country and oversee that country's teams and bids. The USOC was one of 202 of these organizations. The USOC receives no support from our national government despite being chartered by an act of Congress and, as a result, needs to raise all of its funds privately. It does this largely by selling sponsorships to corporations and through a deal negotiated with the IOC in the early 1980s that gives it a cut of the IOC's global sponsorship rights (VISA and Coca-Cola are longtime "TOP" sponsors, for example) and US television rights. This arrangement would play an unexpected role in our bid. In most other countries, there is a very close relationship between a National Sports Minister, often a cabinet-level position, and the NOC, which receives significant governmental funding.

Other members were granted membership into this elite club through their service to a sport or to the Olympic movement, because they had played a key role in hosting prior Olympic Games (two of the three US members of the IOC, Jim Easton and Anita DeFrantz, had both been involved in the successful organization of the Games in Los Angeles in 1984), or perhaps because their fathers had been members. A small subset of members were specially elected by Olympic athletes, who voted after every Summer and Winter Olympic Games for their peers, but their terms were limited to eight years (unlike those of many of the other members, who were given lifetime appointments or termed out at an advanced age).

And then there were the royals. Princess Nora of Liechtenstein, Prince Albert of Monaco, Sheikh Ahmad Al-Fahad Al-Sabah of Kuwait, Princess Anne of Great Britain, the Grand Duke of Luxembourg, the son of the Emir of Qatar, and the sister of the King of Spain were all members. Although they might have had a connection to a sport or an NOC, everyone really understood why they were there—to lend prestige and an elevated aura to the IOC.

In total, the 116 members of the IOC hailed from every continent but Antarctica, making it like a mini United Nations, but one that contained the head of the weightlifting IF from Hungary and the future King of The

Netherlands. My first impression of the group, watching the proceedings from the back row in the Hilton, was that Europeans seemed to dominate. They tended to be the leaders of the IFs. Indeed, as I scanned the IOC membership roster for maybe the fiftieth time trying to memorize names, faces, and backgrounds in case I had a chance to meet any of them, I was reminded just how many Europeans were in the IOC. There were four from little Switzerland, four from Italy, three from Russia, three from Great Britain, and so on. Meanwhile, the United States, which supplied more than 50 percent of the money to the IOC through television rights and sponsorships, only had three.

The IOC Session was one of the few gatherings at which nearly all of the members were in attendance. This meeting was especially important because the IOC would select the winner of the 2010 Winter Olympic Games (they selected Vancouver), so the proceedings were infused with a special buzz from the bidding cities; thousands of their frenzied supporters, staffs, and consultants; and the media. The ever-present and very influential IOC staff corralled them all.

My main guide to this boisterous bazaar was Charlie Battle, an Atlanta-based lawyer who had helped lead his home city to win its successful bid for the 1996 Games. Naturally warm with an easy, Southern charm, Battle had done many members favors when he was bidding and then hosting the Games and, by all accounts, remained adored by many of them. He was at my side in Prague, as he would be for the next two years at most of the other events I attended, helping me to learn the strange customs of the Olympic movement and trying to help introduce me to whatever Prince or Olympic-gold-medalist-turned-delegate happened to wander by. In addition to Charlie, I also had a team of young international relations staffers who specialized in knowing everything about members and then helping to develop strategies to win them over; they were organized by continent and would sometimes accompany me on trips. One of my European wranglers was Tania Paessler of Spain, who joined me in Prague.

What made this meeting in Prague particularly memorable was the introduction to Gilady. Gilady is someone who used to be known as a "Man of the World." Although Israeli, he lived mostly in London and had a house on the Costa Brava in Spain. He was always dressed impeccably in tailored suits and moved fluidly between four or five different languages. Battle had introduced me to him during that day, and later that evening, when I saw him in the lobby, he asked me to join him for a drink in the bar. He ordered a very expensive bottle of red wine, and just the two of us sat there for a couple of hours. As he smoked his Cuban cigar, he probed my background, how I came to lead New York's bid.

Almost instantly, probably because of our shared Jewish background—Jews were a rarity in Olympic circles—he took an almost paternal interest in me. (There was one other Jewish IOC member, Carlos Nuzman, the head of the Brazilian Olympic Committee. He led Rio's short-lived bid for 2012 and then its successful 2016 bid. We too became very friendly.) At one point, Gilady put his hand on my knee and told me that he wanted to tell me how the game was really played. In his deep voice and Israeli-accented English, he laid out a very complete set of obstacles that I had not fully considered. Over the two-plus years until the decision was made, I'd say no one was as honest as he was about what I would really face.

"You will never get more than eight votes," he said. I was stunned. Eight votes meant New York would be the first city eliminated, a humiliating defeat. "How can you know that for sure?" I stammered. "No one knows for sure," he conceded, "but how the votes will split in the first round is the most difficult. America is not positioned well."

As a US bidder, I was learning, I was battling perceptions, payback, and anger for slights and irregularities of which I was only barely conscious when I started the process. The first issue was the scandal that had erupted five years before involving Salt Lake City's winning bid to host the 2002 Winter Olympics.

After Salt Lake City won, local reporters began sniffing around, demanding to know the real costs of winning the bid. They were blocked at every turn. Then, in November 1998, a reporter turned up the fact that the Salt Lake Organizing Committee was paying the private school tuition for an IOC member's child. Suddenly, multiple investigations were under way, including one by the US Department of Justice.

The search turned up plenty of grubby trading. IOC members had let themselves be bought with lavish travel, cars, private tuition, and trips to brothels. Much of this was not technically illegal; it was the way business had always been done. Yet in the end, the IOC was embarrassed into setting up a fairly stringent set of rules on how bidders could interact with delegates. More painfully, it expelled ten delegates and suspended another ten on corruption charges.

Needless to say, not everyone enjoyed the American sense of righteousness. For many IOC members, this was just part of the process. Worse, the ramifications were widespread and, according to Gilady, would affect our bid. This was especially true because the US Congress pressured Samaranch into making a pilgrimage to Washington to testify regarding the IOC's misdeeds. After much resisting, he finally acquiesced and, in December 1999, trailed by an entourage of two dozen staffers, lawyers, and advisors, answered questions from the House Subcommittee on Oversight and Investigations for a grueling, humiliating three hours.

The deep bitterness was still fresh in 2003. One member, the former Mayor of Lima, Peru, had been accused of taking gifts—which he insisted unequivocally was not true. As he told Paessler, "Unfortunately, unless the US lets Bush make a public apology I can't vote for you." Well, that wasn't going to happen.

My visit to Prague was just a few months after the United States invaded Iraq. According to Gilady, that was certainly going to hurt us with a number of the members from the Middle East. They could accept the invasion of Afghanistan, he explained, but "President Bush's invasion of Iraq seemed more personal." Whereas Britain had supported the US invasion, France had clearly not, which would inevitably help Paris, thought to be the leading contender.

The goodwill that had built up after 9/11 had been utterly squandered. The world began narrowing its eyes at the United States, seeing only its arrogance, its warmongering, its disrespect for other traditions and cultures. And that arrogance was seen as having a personal component too. In the Olympic world, so many people could relate a tale—either involving themselves or someone they knew—who had trouble getting into the United States. Many wondered out loud how we could hold an Olympics in a country now so unfriendly to visitors.

Our other big problem was that the last Summer Olympic Games held in the United States, in Atlanta in 1996, was perceived, fairly or unfairly, as a logistical disaster. At the Opening Ceremony, a man dressed as a security guard and carrying a loaded handgun managed to slip through security checkpoints without a credential or a ticket and was only arrested ninety minutes before the start of the proceedings, attended by President Bill Clinton and numerous other heads of state. Later on at the Games, there was a bombing in Centennial Park in the heart of Downtown Atlanta that killed two people. Long waits and frighteningly crowded conditions plagued rapid transit trains. Inexperienced drivers staffed the bus system for Olympic athletes and spectators, causing people to miss events. A much-vaunted IBM computer network that was supposed to supply fast results to reporters failed. Meanwhile, sellers of schlocky merchandise were permitted to operate in Downtown Atlanta, creating a bazaar-like atmosphere. International newspapers began to call the Atlanta Games the "Glitch Games"; these Games were regarded in the international press and among many IOC members as the worst in two decades.

The privately funded Atlanta Games also ran into financial difficulties in the closing weeks before the Opening Ceremony. In the end, the Games made a small profit, but financially the process of getting to the finish line was painful. After the Atlanta Games, the IOC tightened up the requirements for bidding cities, requiring them to have financial guarantees from their host governments. This too would have repercussions for our bid.

All of this, Gilady piled on, paled in comparison to our biggest issue: the fraught relations between the USOC and the IOC. The roots went back to the 1984 Olympic Games in Los Angeles. In 1979, Peter Ueberroth, the owner of a highly successful travel company, became the CEO of the Los Angeles Organizing Committee, charged with hosting the 1984 Games. Los Angeles had had virtually no competition to become the host city. The two prior Games had been beset with problems—the murder of Israeli athletes by the Palestinian Liberation Organization had marred the 1972 Games in Munich, and the 1976 Games had been a financial debacle for their host, Montreal. To make matters worse, Ueberroth assumed his post with the Los Angeles Organizing Committee just months before President Jimmy Carter mandated a boycott of the 1980 Moscow Games because of the USSR's invasion of Afghanistan. The Olympic movement was in deep trouble.

Ueberroth came to the rescue by reinventing the model. He negotiated a huge television contract with ABC and sold very lucrative sponsorships both nationally and internationally. Whereas Montreal had generated $9 million from sponsorship rights, Los Angeles produced $123 million. Whereas US television rights in Montreal generated $25 million from ABC, in Los Angeles that figure was nine times greater. The well-organized Games were a huge success, drawing enormous crowds in person and on television, despite the fact that the Eastern Bloc boycotted the Games in retaliation for Carter's 1980 boycott. The Games also were financially lucrative. The Los Angeles Organizing Committee earned an unprecedented profit of $232 million that later was used to support youth sports activities throughout Los Angeles and to create an endowment for the USOC. For his efforts, Ueberroth was named *TIME* magazine's "Man of the Year" in 1984 and received from the IOC the honor of the Olympic Order in gold. The US television rights and global sponsorship deals Ueberroth negotiated created a huge windfall for the IOC, which he shrewdly convinced the IOC to share with the USOC (the USOC got 20 percent of the TOP sponsorship revenues and 12.75 percent of the US television revenues).

That relationship, Gilady explained, was going to be a problem for New York nearly twenty years later. "No other country gets a share of their local television rights or the TOP sponsorship revenues. And they resent the fact that America does."

"Why?" I asked. "Hadn't Ueberroth saved the Olympics? Didn't the United States still contribute a disproportionate share of the worldwide revenues from TV rights and sponsorships?"

"Ah," he intoned in his Israeli-accented, deep voice. "Things aren't always so rational when it comes to money." He went on to explain that I had to look at it from their perspective. The rest of the world had developed and grown less dependent on the United States over the previous twenty years, and the other countries wanted the United States—and the USOC, specifically—to show them some respect by acknowledging that fact.

It was after midnight by the time we parted and I headed back to my room, thoroughly depressed. Gilady had no reason to bullshit me. I trust my instincts when it comes to judging people, and, to me, he was only trying to be honest. Besides, he worked for NBC, which already had the rights to broadcast the 2012 Games. If the Games were held in New York, it would be a boon to them.

When I got to the room, Alisa, who was with me on the trip, was asleep. I just lay there dwelling on Gilady's words. As depressed as they had made me, I just couldn't let myself believe them. How could I? So much—especially the value of the Olympics as a catalyst to getting things done in New York—was riding on NYC2012.

CHAPTER TEN

MANHATTAN'S LAST FRONTIER

WHATEVER I WAS hearing, I still believed that our exceptional bid and a campaign that powerfully promoted New York's assets could overcome these obstacles. So we pushed ahead with projects linked to the bid hurtling forward across the city, from Downtown Brooklyn to Harlem to the waterfront in Queens. But no plan was more crucial than our vision to remake the Far West Side of Manhattan.

Alex Garvin and I had targeted the vast, largely abandoned swath of land in the middle of Manhattan for redevelopment years before I entered City Hall. We were drawn to its extraordinary potential immediately as we began assembling potential Olympic sites in the late 1990s. At first, it was part of the impressionistic set of plans that we flung together for our initial Olympic presentations, meant to spark listeners' imaginations. We chose locations we thought would be memorable, emotional, and motivational without necessarily doing the due diligence to determine if they were actually feasible. In those early pitches, I asked people to envision an Olympic Village rising along the Hudson River on new landfill just north of Battery Park City. Traveling up the Manhattan waterfront to Midtown would lead to the city's most ambitious new neighborhood in a century, anchored by a soaring Olympic Stadium. The entire stretch could be linked by a restored elevated rail line that snaked along the edge of the river. Repurposed as an original, magnificent, public space, the rail line could provide a whimsical Olympic connector.

After Garvin and I got serious about drilling down to venues and details, we realized the Battery Park City plan would never survive an environmental review. As a result, we moved the Village across the river to the Queens waterfront, facing the United Nations. That meant we no longer needed the rail line. But the West Side Olympic Stadium—and with it plans to revitalize the Far West Side—stayed intact through all the changes.

The more we'd studied it, the more sense it made. As the marquee Olympic site, the stadium was subject to particular scrutiny by the International Olympic Committee. It had to be eighty thousand seats at least to accommodate fans for the Opening and Closing Ceremonies as well as the popular track-and-field events. The athletic federation rules also required that the field be seventy-four yards wide—far bigger than a US football stadium, at fifty-three yards wide. That meant no existing stadium in the region could handle the requirements—and we would never have enough money to build a new one on our own.

As a result, we realized we'd need to partner with a team to build a temporary stadium that could be converted into a smaller, permanent venue. But here, too, we were limited. We heard through unofficial channels that the IOC didn't want a baseball stadium conversion, which would require massive temporary structures; that's what Atlanta had done, and members felt it looked cheap, with bad sight lines. That ruled out Queens because we thought the only team willing to play there was the Mets.

Remarkably, the Far West Side plan fulfilled the IOC's and sporting federation's complex technical requirements, avoided pitfalls we had been warned against, and advanced New York's own development needs, passing the most important test for every venue plan.

The area—roughly from 30th to 42nd Streets between 9th Avenue and the Hudson River—was Manhattan's last frontier. It had never been developed despite its proximity to two of the most active transportation hubs in the world—Pennsylvania Station, which receives all commuter trains from New Jersey and Long Island, and the Port Authority Bus Station, which runs commuter buses throughout the region and beyond.

Still, transportation was a major problem. There was no subway west of 8th Avenue, meaning that to get all the way to the river from the last stop was a fifteen- to twenty-minute walk. In fact, the one big fixture of the area, the Javits Center, had to have its own shuttle bus because it was so far from hotels in Midtown. Even if that constraint could be solved, most of the area was still zoned exclusively for industrial uses, meaning no apartments or office buildings were allowed. As a result, on the twenty-four square blocks west of 10th Avenue—prime land in the middle of Midtown Manhattan—there were only eleven small residential buildings.

Instead, the area was dominated by parking lots, vacant lots, largely underused warehouses, and the frequently traffic-snarled entrances to the Lincoln Tunnel. Despite overall employment growth for the city for the previous ten years, on the Far West Side in the same period it had actually gone down.

At the heart of this wasteland was a six-block active railyard owned by the Metropolitan Transportation Agency and used by the Long Island Railroad to store its commuter trains. We weren't the first to recognize the site's potential. In the early 1920s, the Yankees considered moving there when they were seeking their own stadium, frustrated at being tenants of the New York (baseball) Giants at the Polo Grounds in Northern Manhattan (fatefully, they relocated to the Bronx instead). In the 1980s, prescient MTA Chair Richard Ravitch arranged the train tracks so that columns might be inserted between them to support a deck that could hold future buildings, imagining that the rights to build above the tracks might someday be worth a fortune. Without that foresight, it wouldn't have been possible to do construction without stopping train traffic, a nonstarter.

In 1993, the Yankees surfaced again after team owner George Steinbrenner made one of his perennial threats to move the team out of New York City. Governor Mario Cuomo suggested a new stadium on the MTA yards. Rudy Giuliani seconded that suggestion when he pushed it as a new home for the Yankees in 1996.

As our venue search intensified, I was convinced that the West Side was the only location for our Olympic Stadium too. It was also very clear that the Yankees' effort was never going to happen. The local community fiercely objected, fearing that the eighty-one home games a year would pose insurmountable congestion problems. Governor George Pataki, who took office in 1995 after defeating Cuomo, was less excited about moving the Yankees from their historic home in the Bronx. His objections were dispositive because he controlled the MTA, the owner of the site.

I knew from the start we were going to face a vicious political battle if we proposed any kind of stadium, but I thought we might be able to improve the odds if the after-Olympic use was a football stadium. After all, concerns about traffic might be mitigated by the fact that a football team plays only ten home games a year (including two exhibition games). The obvious tenant for the new football stadium was the New York Jets, who played in Giants

Stadium in the Meadowlands (evoking the New York Yankees playing in the home of the other New York Giants before 1923) and whose lease there was going to expire in 2008.

But we knew we couldn't sell a football stadium alone—and the inevitable critics might be right to reject us if we tried. Garvin and I decided to make the stadium part of a broader plan to transform the forlorn area. If a primary purpose of the Olympic bid was to overhaul New York's outdated land use on a deadline, then a plan built around a stadium in the heart of the Far West Side was the ultimate expression of that strategy. So Garvin and his little team of two recent architecture school graduates and I began audaciously planning an entirely new neighborhood despite not having any government positions or authority to implement it.

We quickly identified some key components. Even before 9/11, it had become clear there were very few sites for new office buildings in Manhattan and even fewer with the zoning that would have made such construction possible. As a result, the 1990s saw a spate of companies, such as the securities firm UBS, flee New York City for easily buildable sites outside the city that could accommodate then-fashionable uses such as large trading floors. (Of course, it didn't help the city's case that our neighbors, New Jersey and Connecticut, offered massive tax and other incentives.) At the same time, the average age of large commercial office space in Midtown Manhattan was almost fifty years, which meant that the buildings frequently couldn't provide the amenities or generous open floor plans large office tenants now desired.

New York also faced another major problem. The Javits Center, one block north of the West Side railyards, was inadequate and had been from the day it opened in 1986. At 840,000 square feet of exhibition space, it was less than half the size of competitor centers in Chicago and Orlando. By 1998, it was only the fourteenth largest convention center in the United States—an embarrassment. Moreover, it lacked the meeting room spaces and conference facilities offered by other centers. As a result, it couldn't compete for large, lucrative conventions, such as that of the American Medical Association, that would have brought in thousands of visitors to flood New York's hotels and restaurants. Instead the Javits Center had to settle for trade shows such as the annual boat and auto shows, which drew a predominantly local crowd, with low spending during brief visits to the city.

So when our little band started our bootstrapped planning exercise in 1998, we had a vague notion that the area west of 9th Avenue was the key to solving a host of Olympics- and city-related problems. Not only would the Olympic Stadium provide a stunning Olympic showcase on the Hudson River and a new home for the Jets but also it would enable an expanded convention center and spur construction of desperately needed expansion space for the Midtown office market.

We realized immediately that our plan would require a new mass transit connection. We hired Parsons Brinckerhoff (PB), a leading engineering consulting firm, to help us evaluate possible options. PB, which had a close relationship with the MTA, quickly concluded that the cheapest and most effective solution would be to extend the No. 7 subway line from its current terminus at Times Square west under 41st Street and then have it turn south at 11th Avenue and end between the site of the proposed stadium and the Javits Center at 34th Street and 11th Avenue.

The beauty of the No. 7 line extension was that it was one of the only lines in New York's subway system that traveled east–west. As a result, it intersected with almost every other line, meaning that virtually anyone could reach the site with no more than a single train change. In addition, the No. 7 made a stop at Grand Central Station, which would make it easier for commuters from Westchester (and eventually Long Island commuters after the long-delayed East Side Access project, which will bring commuters from Long Island to Grand Central, is completed). For commuters from New Jersey, a major ferry terminal was nearby, and New Jersey Transit and the Long Island Railroad passengers came into Penn Station only three blocks away. We assumed that a shuttle system could be developed to take passengers from Penn Station to the area. The No. 7 extension was equal parts common sense and absurdly ambitious—there had not been any major subway construction in New York for more than a generation.

Garvin refused to rest there. A particular interest of his was in the "public realm"—the parks, squares, marketplaces, streets, and even highways that can be created or transformed to add dynamism to even the most sterile-seeming place. He tutored me on the value parks and open space can create for the areas that surround them.

He told me the story of Grand Central Station. Around a century earlier, the area had been an ugly tangle of dangerous open rail tracks, with trains belching thick, black smoke into the air as they streamed in and out. In 1902 a fatal train crash occurred just north of the old Grand Central Depot. A southbound train had overrun several signals and collided with another southbound train, killing fifteen people and injuring forty more. The outcry that followed prompted the New York Central Railroad and city officials to consider alternatives to running a large railyard in the middle of a rapidly growing city.

The plan that emerged required sinking tunnels under and putting decking over the railyards, relying on technology recently pioneered by Thomas Edison to electrify the trains and vent the smoke. Planners designed a new, broad boulevard with a spine of elegant landscaping down the center to run over the deck, culminating in a majestic new train station.

The combination of the new Park Avenue and Grand Central Station terminal formed the core of what was to become the greatest business district in the world, Midtown Manhattan. To capitalize on this newly desirable real estate and to create better-scaled development sites, the city extended Madison Avenue in the middle of the huge blocks between the new Park Avenue and 5th Avenue to the west, which would become one of the world's most desirable shopping streets.

Garvin and I decided to steal the Park Avenue playbook and apply it to the Far West Side. We would create a platform over railyards and then build a new boulevard running down the middle of the superblock between 10th and 11th Avenues, creating attractive development sites for residential and commercial buildings on either side. We too would include lush landscaping down the center—only our park and boulevard would be much wider than Park Avenue to accommodate playgrounds and other amenities for a mixed-use neighborhood. Just past the new subway stop at 34th Street, the boulevard would widen farther and then curve to the west, forming a new six-acre park on a platform built over one-half of the railyards. This new park, which would be bigger than Trafalgar Square in London, would be surrounded by new office, retail, and residential development and, we said, maybe even a new Madison Square Garden. And directly to the west, across 11th Avenue over the other half of the railyards, would be our new stadium, which could be connected to the adjacent Javits Center.

As we developed this vision, we shared it with our Facilities Advisory Board, which included the heads of several city agencies. The board loved the historical reference to Park Avenue; the fact that we had incorporated mass transit, open space, and mixed-use development; and that our target tenant for the stadium was a team that would play only ten home games a year.

The presence of city agencies on the advisory board made them feel included in the development of the plans. As a result, the territorial jockeying that can occur when public officials believe an outsider is attempting to do their jobs for them was minimized. Instead, they became advocates for the plan and our emissaries to Mayor Giuliani, successfully persuading him to include the idea in his State of the City Address in January 1999.

As I sat in the audience, Giuliani laid out our plan as a vision he shared for the city's future. He showed a map to the audience with a new stadium connected to an expanded Javits Center and an extension of the No. 7 line. It included a new home for Madison Square Garden, just as we had suggested. But the aspect that caught the most public attention was that instead of touting the Yankees for the stadium, the fanatical Yankees fan now wanted to woo the Jets.

By this time, we had also managed to secure the nonpublic support of Governor Pataki. That was a little harder. Jay Kriegel tried to mine every relationship he had, pretty much everyone in the state of New York, and yet we couldn't get a meeting. Finally, I was having lunch with Roland Betts, the codeveloper of Chelsea Piers, the huge sports and entertainment complex opened on the waterfront just a few blocks to the south of our proposed site for the stadium. Chelsea Piers had been pretty much the only thing built on the Hudson River waterfront in decades. Betts and his partner, Tom Bernstein, understood better than anyone did how hard it was to get anything done in that area, so I consulted him often. (He was also a member of the United States Olympic Committee Board and a huge believer in our effort.) As I was describing how difficult it was to get the attention of the Governor, he said, "No problem. I can get you a meeting with him. He was at Yale the same time I was." Sure enough, he called the Governor while I was sitting there, and we met at Chelsea Piers a few weeks later. Kriegel and I made the pitch, and the Governor gave his endorsement as long as the plan was to lure the Jets back to New York.

That May, Leon Hess, the owner of the Jets, died. His will stipulated that the team be sold. Goldman Sachs was retained to sell the team, and a battle ensued between Woody Johnson, an heir to the Johnson & Johnson fortune, and Charles Dolan, Chair of Cablevision, which owns Madison Square Garden. Johnson offered $635 million, the third-highest price ever for a professional sports team and the most ever paid for one in New York. It was a staggering price for a team that had barely eked out a profit over the years. The deal closed in January 2000.

The Jets' limited profits and the high price Johnson paid meant that his need for a new stadium would be acute. At Giants Stadium, the Jets were struggling. In addition to the demoralizing visuals signaling their status as second-class citizens, they didn't get a share of sponsorships, corporate boxes, or concessions, and they also had to pay 15 percent of revenue in rent—all in all, a bad deal. Johnson was serious enough about a new stadium that by June he hired Jay Cross as the Jets' president. Cross's appeal was that he had come from the National Basketball Association's Miami Heat, where he had led the development of the American Airlines Arena. He had also planned the new Air Canada Centre Arena in Toronto.

I asked Johnson's investment bankers at Goldman Sachs to reach out to him and Cross to set up a meeting. Kriegel and I hosted them in the offices of my private equity firm to lay out the Olympic pitch. After we described our plan, Cross looked at me and asked, "Where do you plan to host sailing events?" "Breezy Point [Queens]," I responded. "Why do you ask?" "Because I was on three [Canadian] Olympic sailing teams." "Good," I said. "Now you can plan two venues!"

Over the next nine months, Johnson and Cross invested a massive sum in developing their new stadium. Whereas we had sketched out only a vague sense of how the stadium and its various configurations would fit on the western railyards, Cross built a team of architects, structural engineers, cost estimators, and dozens of other consultants to figure out how and when it could actually be done, what it might look like, and how much it would cost.

In January 2001, the Jets released the results. They had taken our idea of a simple, outdoor stadium to a completely different level. The biggest additions to the plan were that the stadium would have a retractable roof and that it would be connected to the Javits Center via a tunnel under 34th Street, allowing the stadium to be converted into an immense, 220,000-square-foot exhibition and convention hall, which would give the Javits Center a space unlike any competing convention center in the world. There would be meeting rooms interspersed throughout the building to make the Javits Center more attractive to conventions. They coined it the New York Sports and Convention Center to emphasize that this facility was more than just a stadium. Instead, it would be a valuable addition to the city's woefully inadequate convention space. I thought it was a remarkably artful addition. It also solved the thorny political problem of co-opting Bob Boyle, the Chair of the Javits Center, a close Pataki confidante and an early critic of our plan.

By that time, we had been working on our own bold move: the subway extension. The fate of the No. 7 train—and our plan to deck over the railyards at all—rested in the hands of the MTA, a state-controlled agency. So as the Jets embarked on the design phase of the stadium, we began our outreach to officials in the state capital.

Albany's corruption was legendary. (At one point in 2015, both the leaders of the Assembly and the Senate had been convicted of graft, and in the previous decade "more than 30 state lawmakers had been convicted, sanctioned or accused of wrongdoing," according to the *New York Times*.) But back then, I was very naive. I thought if we honestly explained our good intentions and demonstrated the obvious boost it would give the city, we would get the help we needed. I soon realized my error and developed an aversion to Albany, viewing it as a place to avoid. The capitol felt like a hall of mirrors where nothing was ever as it seemed and everything was always at least a little distorted. This was an equally dangerous attitude.

Yes, the self-dealing was rampant, and mutual back scratching was the norm. Many of us straightforward business types in the Bloomberg orbit never really understood Albany's language of allusions and half-truths and hints. Not my style. Yet, if I had to do it over again, I would spend more time learning how to master Albany and less time trying to avoid it. That way I might have caught the signals I was getting.

We began by approaching Assembly Speaker Sheldon Silver in 2000. Sadly, Shelly, as he was universally known, was the ultimate creature of Albany. A large bloc of his fellow Orthodox Jews formed the core of his support in his Lower East Side district, which had elected him reliably since 1976, often by 80 or 90 percent of the vote. The few times I met with him, always at his office on Broadway in Lower Manhattan, he struck me as being Don Corleone–like. Uncharismatic, heavyset, with a wide, pale face, he sat behind an oversized desk. I always had the impression that the room was dark even if it wasn't. He made you wait before you could approach, leaving you half expecting that you had to kiss his hand. Even as you sat across from him, he mumbled almost indecipherably so that you went away unsure of where you stood. He exercised power through obfuscation.

Like a Mafia don, he could be particularly vindictive. In 1999, the Republicans in the State Senate, backed by Governor Pataki, had proposed the repeal of the commuter tax, just under half of 1 percent tax on the paychecks of the hundreds of thousands of people who commuted into the city every day from the suburbs. The tax, which had existed since 1967 and had until then stirred virtually no resistance, generated up to $360 million annually. It was a crucial revenue stream for New York City, which plowed the money into streets and other infrastructure costs. When the commuter tax repeal came up for a vote, Silver, the self-described defender of New York City's interests in Albany, let it pass. It turned out he had struck a deal in an attempt to win one extra seat for the Democrats in the State Senate (which he didn't get). But many speculated that the real reason he sold out the city was to exact retribution on Mayor Giuliani, with whom he was not on speaking terms. Whether that's true, based on his character it was perfectly plausible.

Silver had become Speaker in 1994 and was the most cynical of politicians. Even other Assembly members admitted that he was motivated by only a few things. His top priority was getting reelected, and therefore he tended very carefully to the needs of his district, which included Lower Manhattan. Of course, he also cared passionately about preserving his position as Speaker. As we know now, Silver was also personally corrupt. It would take until 2015 to come out, when he was arrested and convicted on seven counts of corruption that involved failure to disclose payments from law firms seeking favors from the state on everything from real-estate tax reductions to asbestos abatement. He was expelled from the Assembly, disbarred, ordered to pay millions of dollars in fines, and sentenced to twelve years in prison. Due to a subsequent Supreme Court decision that changed the standard of corruption by public officials, an appeals court concluded that the lower court judge's instructions to the jury were incorrect and overturned his conviction.

But back in 2000, we knew there was no way around the man, so Kriegel shared our vision of the Olympics with him personally. His visit came at a touchy time. Some Assembly members, fed up with Silver's tight-lipped management style and complete control of power, had attempted a coup. One supporter of the coup called Silver's leadership a "virtual dictatorship." But by an 85–63 vote, the coup failed. The leader of the rebellion, a representative from upstate, lost his job in Silver's brutal backlash. When Kriegel went to meet with him, Silver appeared more sensitive to the feelings of his fellow Assembly members, especially those from the city who had backed him in the coup attempt. Kriegel speculated that under the circumstances he would naturally defer to the handful of his members from the West Side, who opposed any development in their districts.

Silver gave no hint of this, however. Instead, Kriegel came back with a good news/bad news/no news report. Silver seemed positive about the idea of the Olympics. One win. On the stadium, he said, "I don't care about your stadium." On the No. 7 subway line extension, Kriegel translated the response in his own inimitable way: "Shelly says, 'No fucking way.'" The state controls the MTA, which runs the vast transportation network critical to New York City, so its budget is controlled in Albany. Silver said there wouldn't be one nickel of state or federal funds for a No. 7 line until his 2nd Avenue subway was completed down to the Lower East Side.

New York is a subway-driven city. That's how our citizens get around—about 5.5 million of them a day. But whereas the West Side has four lines that run under 8th Avenue, 7th Avenue, 6th Avenue, and Broadway, respectively, the East Side is served largely by one subway line, under Lexington Avenue. Unsurprisingly, this line had become the city's most overcrowded by far, with an estimated 1.3 million daily riders.

For nearly a century, people had been complaining about the lack of subway access on the East Side. As far back as 1919 a new line had been proposed for 2nd Avenue, but the idea died under the weight of the Great Depression. Since then, the idea had been resurrected and abandoned multiple times, including a brief construction phase that started in 1972 and stopped three years later because of more budget woes. If Silver wouldn't fund one or two stops on the No. 7 line until the entire 2nd Avenue line was revived and completed down to his district, we couldn't count on its being done until the 2060 Olympics.

Kriegel called me as soon as he got out of the meeting. "This is a disaster," he said with his typical understatement. I asked him to repeat what Silver had said precisely. "Shelly said there would be no MTA funds available." I pushed a little harder. "So, Shelly didn't say that we couldn't build a subway, just that we couldn't use state funds, right?"

The truth is that getting any money from the MTA had always scared me. The MTA had spent about $64 billion in the previous twenty years rebuilding a system that had deteriorated badly throughout the financially calamitous 1960s and 1970s and had a huge backlog of projects on its priority list necessary just to bring the system up to the elusive standard of acceptability it called a "state of good repair." The MTA's focus was on improving the rider experience and system performance, not on economic development. That's why no new subway line had opened in New York since 1989. And even that one was just a small extension at 63rd Street. An extension of the No. 7 was never on anyone's list.

So, Silver's statement was confirmation that we were going to have to find the money—it was clear that the cost of the No. 7 extension would be close to $2 billion, and with the infrastructure and the boulevard between 10th and 11th Avenues, we were looking at $2.5 billion or more—ourselves.

This is where my background in finance came in handy. Although I was no expert in municipal finance, I had read a little about Chicago's extensive use of something called tax increment financing (TIF). Although there are a lot of variations on the idea, a TIF basically works like this: a governmental or quasigovernmental entity raises bond debt from private investors on the condition that the proceeds are invested to make improvements in a specific district. The debt holders agree to be paid back only out of the incremental tax, fee, or other revenue generated out of the district during the life of the debt. The underlying assumption is that the improvements will enhance the district, encouraging other private investment in the area, which will generate new tax and other revenues.

Let's say a city needs to raise $100 million for a new park its leaders are convinced will encourage private investors to develop new residential buildings nearby. But the city doesn't want to or can't raise new debt on its own balance sheet. A TIF would allow the city to create a new entity, controlled by the administration, that would issue $100 million in thirty-year bonds. The city promises that it will use the funds only to build the park and pledges the incremental amount of tax and other revenue (mostly property taxes, but it could be other things such as sales taxes on construction) in a designated area around the park to the new entity for the thirty-year life of the bonds. The risk the bondholders take is that development doesn't happen and there aren't enough new taxes to pay them back. If that occurs, the bonds default and the investors lose their money, but the city isn't on the hook. The idea here is that the project essentially pays for itself.

Beyond that, I knew pretty much nothing. Kriegel asked around to find the MTA's most respected financial advisor, and the name he kept hearing was Bob Foran, an investment banker at Bear Stearns. So I reached out to Foran, and the next day he walked up Park Avenue from his office to mine. He proceeded to give Kriegel and me a crash course on financing big transportation projects and on TIFs specifically. Foran had recently helped the MTA with a large restructuring. He knew the people there and their stresses. He also had managed dozens of large-scale municipal financings around the country. He pointed out that TIFs had been used across the United States since 1952, but they were controversial because of some high-profile defaults. Plus, the TIFs were typically smaller—much smaller—than we would need. Oh, and there was one other issue: it wasn't completely clear that TIFs were legal under New York State law.

Still, Foran was inspired by our Olympic vision and the ambition behind the plan for the Far West Side, and he agreed to volunteer his help based solely on our promise that we would retain him and Bear Stearns to help us raise the money if we ever got that far (given that we were a little nonprofit with no authority to do anything at this point, our promise didn't mean a whole lot). Foran did his work—for free. He talked to real-estate developers, looked at current tax rolls, analyzed the historical office and residential development patterns in the city, delved into the age of existing office buildings in Manhattan, and then produced a variety of development scenarios for the Far West Side assuming the No. 7 line extension and related infrastructure projects were completed. He then looked at different options for taxing new real estate in the area and different financing options, ultimately producing a detailed model to determine whether we would be able to pay back the debt. In essence, the question his models tried to answer was, "If you build it, will they come?" (Foran became the Chief Financial Officer of the MTA in 2010.)

Foran ultimately concluded to his own satisfaction that our plan for the Far West Side was financeable. We prepared a presentation that we could shop around to the MTA, to city officials, to business leaders, and to the trade unions. The specificity and originality of the idea impressed everyone. The MTA leaders loved it. Who wouldn't? We were proposing that they could build the first subway extension in twenty-five years, and they wouldn't have to pay for it!

By the time the Jets announced their ambitious, detailed design, we had a realistic plan for extending the subway that didn't rely on state funding. As we shopped the idea around, it gained currency in more official circles, especially within the Department of City Planning. In December 2001, the very last month of the Giuliani Administration, it announced the completion of a study titled *Far West Midtown: A Framework for Development*. The report presented a comprehensive plan for the revitalization, calling for zoning changes, investments in infrastructure, open-space and urban design guidelines, and a financing strategy that was, well, almost exactly like ours. "The Far West Midtown plan is designed to pay for itself," a press release accompanying the report said. "It anticipates that infrastructure improvements will be financed and built as redevelopment proceeds."

This followed on the heels of a report by Charles Schumer's Group of 35 that called the need for more high-rise office buildings critical to the city's future. The study identified three areas for rezoning to accommodate growth: Long Island City (Queens), Downtown Brooklyn, and the Far West Side of Manhattan. It called for sixty million square feet of office space across the city and endorsed our conclusion that extension of the No. 7 line was essential.

As a candidate, Bloomberg had strongly supported the extension of the No. 7 line and the rezoning of Hudson Yards. These had been things we had talked about getting done when he interviewed me. So by the end of 2001, right before I became Deputy Mayor, we couldn't have been in better shape.

As Amanda Burden, our City Planning Commissioner, describes it, "We had a perfect layup."

We had to move fast when we came into office to continue the momentum. Right away, we set a challenging deadline. Although NYC2012 hadn't even been selected yet as the US candidate city, we announced that the entire West Side plan needed to be approved by the final IOC vote in July 2005. That would give us around a year to turn our rough concept into an actual plan, another to get the environmental impact statement done and figure out the financing, and a third year to actually get the plan approved, which would require reviews from the local community board and borough President and approvals from the City Planning Department and the City Council. All along the way, we would have to have extensive consultations with thousands of stakeholders, including community groups, opinion leaders, members of the City Council and state legislature, the trade unions we expected to be our biggest supporters, and the media.

Quickly we mobilized. Within weeks of our arrival in City Hall, we formed a multiagency task force—we needed to go step by step, block by block in what would be the biggest rezoning in the city's history. Burden and Director of the Manhattan Office for City Planning Vishaan Chakrabarti took the lead, and by June 2002 they had hired a team of outside architects, urban designers, landscape architects, sustainability consultants, traffic consultants, and structural engineers. During that first year, the plan got more detailed and specific, but the contours of it didn't change much, so that by November 2002 the City Planning Department and the consultants were able to hold the first official public hearing, which outlined the assets and challenges in the area and a vision and road map for change. A more detailed plan was presented publicly in early 2003.

Perhaps my major contribution during this period was to find a replacement for the awkward names we had been using for our new neighborhood—Far West Side or Midtown West. Having come up with the monikers "The World's Second Home" and "An Olympic Village Every Day" to describe the city as part of NYC2012, I fancied myself an amateur branding wizard. One Saturday afternoon at home, I sat down with a piece of paper and drew a crude map of the area, labeling each major element on the map including Penn Station, the Hudson River, the Caemmerer West Side Storage Yard (the official name of the MTA yards), the Javits Center, and so forth. In playing with different combinations of the names, I thought the best one was Hudson

Yards. Kriegel argued for Penn Yards, but I pulled rank. Thus was born the name of a new New York neighborhood.

The fully fleshed out plan had four components:

- **A rezoning plan** to reshape Hudson Yards as a mixed-use community with new residential, commercial, and public open space, including approximately 28 million square feet of office space; 12.6 million square feet (12,600 units) of residential space; 1.5 million square feet of hotel space; and 700,000 square feet of retail space;
- **The extension of the No. 7 subway line** to serve Hudson Yards, with two new stops;
- **A new multiuse sports, exhibition, and entertainment facility** with approximately 30,000 square feet of permanent meeting room space. The stadium configuration would have seating capacity for 75,000, whereas the exposition configuration would offer 180,000 square feet of exposition space. The facility could also be converted into a plenary hall that provided maximum seating capacity of approximately 40,000;
- **The expansion, renovation, and modernization of the Javits Center**, including the construction of 1 million square feet of new exhibition space plus additional space for meeting rooms, banquet halls, and other facilities, along with the development of a new convention hotel, all in addition to the extra space the stadium would provide;

In short, we were asking to build the equivalent of Downtown Seattle or Downtown Minneapolis on a small, square patch of Manhattan, a city within a city.

Critical to all of this was the financing. Although I had taken our financing plan using the TIFs as a dog-and-pony show to a variety of people before joining the Bloomberg Administration, I had never actually presented the idea to New York City's Office of Management and Budget (OMB), the city government's chief financial agency. It oversees both the expenses and capital budgets and is charged with evaluating the efficiency and cost-effectiveness of city services and proposals. It also helps implement the city's borrowing and bond programs and conducts legal reviews of capital projects for financing with bond proceeds.

For Director of OMB Bloomberg had selected Mark Page. A Harvard graduate with a law degree from New York University, Page came to work for the city right out of law school during the depths of the city's financial crisis in 1974 and had been at OMB since 1978. Page was proud of the smart financial stewardship of his office, which had led to the steady upgrade of New York City's bonds ever since. In some ways, Page could not have been more different from Bloomberg and me. A profile of him in the *New York Observer* noting the fact that he was the great-grandson of financier J. P. Morgan described him as a "budget aristocrat" both "dour" and "erudite." I wouldn't describe him as dour as much as shrewdly skeptical. Whereas Bloomberg and I, both self-made businessmen, tended to be can-do and optimistic, Page had seen lots of Mayors and their staffs come and go and knew where the pitfalls lay. His job was to protect the city against people like me with no experience and crazy new ideas.

When I first pitched the financing plan for Hudson Yards, despite Bloomberg's vocal support for it, Page balked. His concerns were many and not unreasonable. Property taxes were guaranteed first by law to secure the city's general obligation debt. If we created a special levy that skimmed those property taxes for alternative bondholders, it might be illegal, he argued. He was also concerned that because the city typically gave new office development tax exemptions for ten to fifteen years, the debt wouldn't be self-supporting for a very long time. Although he agreed that $2.5 billion was probably too much debt to put on the city's balance sheet at a precarious financial time, he pointed out that doing it on the balance sheet would be cheaper.

I pushed back, but very respectfully. Although he could be sarcastic, there was never anything political about Page. I respected his role as a guardian of the city's financial position. Over the course of more than a year, I worked very hard to get him onboard. We met every couple of weeks. He and his staff had good questions about our financial model. They asked us to run alternative scenarios assuming different tax structures and slower paces of development. At the OMB's request, we explored what a different mix of residential and commercial development would mean for the financial sustainability of the structure.

I showed Page and his team historical development patterns—and the ages of the existing commercial building stock—to help them gauge whether our assumptions were unreasonable. We examined every single possible commercial development site in the city to demonstrate that other than the World Trade Center site, there were no alternatives for large-scale commercial development. We shared our interviews with the largest employers in the city, who were demanding larger, more open floor plans that couldn't be accommodated in existing buildings. Page put me through a yearlong course in the financial management of New York, and his final exam was the financial model that would underpin our financing structure. Although today Page jokingly calls me the "Marketer in Chief" and reports that he drank "my Kool-Aid," in reality I got an A on his test. He believed the numbers. By early 2003, we had his approval to move forward.

This was a critical milestone. Page was the voice of credibility for New York with the credit rating agencies. So they listened when he argued that if the city were to grow, Hudson Yards would be successful, making it as good a bet as any general obligation bond. Page also worked intensively with the city's lawyers to find a way to issue the bonds legally. Page's credibility with the City Council gave its members the confidence, when we were getting ready to issue the bonds in 2006, to insist that the city guarantee the interest on the bonds, which reduced the risk to investors and in turn reduced the amount of interest the city had to pay bondholders.

Unfortunately, even using our financial strategy, we couldn't raise enough money to cover everything we hoped to do. By 2004, the total tab had reached close to $3 billion. We didn't believe we could raise any more money than that. As a result, we had to choose between building the extra station at 41st Street and 10th Avenue and building the parks around the remaining station. We chose the parks because I thought they were critical to developing the sense of place that would attract developers and tenants to the heart of Hudson Yards. Besides, the Hudson Yards area had fewer trees, shrubs, and bushes than any other neighborhood in the city.

This led to some MTA disappointment. Its leaders couldn't complain too much; they weren't paying for it. However, the decision led eventually to a shouting match with Senator Charles Schumer. Chuck is a close friend. There is never any doubt where his heart lies. There is no greater advocate for the city. He stood with us on almost everything we tried to achieve. In many ways, it was his Group of 35 effort that gave Hudson Yards its legitimacy. Other than regarding the stadium—which he privately doubted but refrained from publicly criticizing out of friendship—we never disagreed. Except when he learned that I had killed the second station, he called me, screaming. I screamed back. He called me arrogant, claiming I was going to kill the development potential of the area he had worked so hard to promote. I called him a bully. I said that the focus had to be on and around the railyards; they were the center of the plan. I complained that he was ignorant of the financial pressures I was dealing with. He hung up.

We joke about it now, but at the time it left me shaking. I had alienated our biggest supporter in Congress and had been arrogant in doing it. I called him back the next day and apologized and offered a compromise: although we were not able to build a second full subway stop, we agreed to carve out a cavern and preserve a right of way to the street level so that someday there might be a second stop.

Even as we pursued the financing agreement, we were also undertaking an EIS. Mandated by federal, state, and city law to cover all jurisdictions, the EIS is essentially a disclosure document. It analyzes the effects of the proposal on land use, zoning and public policy, socioeconomic conditions, community facilities, open space and recreational facilities, shadows, transit and pedestrians, urban design and visual resources, air quality, noise and vibrations, public health, and so on. In short, the impact on pretty much everything has to be analyzed, requiring an astounding level of detail so that plans can be evaluated on every criterion.

In US history the longest EIS document ever submitted was for the Yucca Mountain Nuclear Waste Repository in Nevada. Yucca Mountain took fifteen years to get approved and was never built. The second longest, at six thousand pages, was for the rezoning of Hudson Yards. By June 2004, we had a fully baked financial plan and a draft EIS, so the Department of City Planning could formally "certify" that we could enter the seven-month formal land review process with the city. Given that we were seeking changes that would completely alter the feel and population of the Far West Side, the approval went shockingly smoothly. We weren't just asking for permission to build a few tall buildings in an area where there were none, but blocks and blocks of them.

Selling such density to the City Council and local residents is usually nearly impossible. So the effort we had spent to develop a comprehensive, mixed-use plan and then sell it to the many stakeholders before we entered the review process paid enormous dividends. The boulevard and plaza on the railyards added significant green space. We set aside a prime site on the eastern railyard for a new cultural institution that would also be accessible from the High Line directly to its south. We had no idea what that cultural institution would be, but the commitment of one of the best sites at the very heart of this new district sent an important signal that this wasn't just about making money for developers.

In addition to creating a mixed-use neighborhood, we believed that it should also be a mixed-income community. That was consistent with the goals of our New Housing Marketplace Plan, which held that every new development we spurred should have a significant percentage of affordable housing. After the plan was in place, we set an initial target of 25 percent of the units to be subsidized for low-, moderate-, and middle-income residents in every rezoning undertaken by the administration.

During the planning process the team at the City Planning Department and my senior staffer on Hudson Yards, Ann Weisbrod, were constantly out in the affected community with its elected officials to gain a nuanced understanding of their concerns and desires. The plan that emerged reflected the hundreds of hours of outreach they did. For example, although there were only 150 housing units west of 10th Avenue, there was (and is) a vibrant community to the east toward 9th Avenue. The plan required the tallest buildings to be closest to the river and then tapered their height as they moved toward 9th Avenue and the relatively low-slung neighborhood known as Hell's Kitchen. We carefully calculated spacing and setbacks for those buildings to make sure there would be adequate light between the new skyscrapers.

Toward the end of the seven-month approval process, the City Council typically asks for extensive modifications, even in a modest rezoning. We braced ourselves for draconian demands given the unprecedented scope of the Hudson Yards plan. It never happened. In the case of Hudson Yards, the City Council members asked for only very minor changes, the largest of which was to reduce the amount of commercial space by four million square feet to twenty-four million square feet. Given that our projections didn't anticipate the last four million square feet being built until about 2030, that didn't seem like a big deal. A second concession we made was to increase the percentage of affordable housing from 25 percent to 28 percent. We had assumed the ask for more affordable housing was coming, so we were prepared to offer specific suggestions about how to get there. That added to the seriousness of our response, which built greater trust with the City Council members.

By then, there was one member of the City Council I would never trust again: Speaker Gifford Miller. One night late in 2004, just as we were heading into the land review process, I got a call at home from him. It was the first time he had ever called me at home, so I suspected it wasn't just to chat. He prefaced the conversation with an expression of his support for the Hudson Yards rezoning. Then his tone became softer and a bit less confident. He began talking about the mayoral election that would take place the next year, indicating that he planned to run against Bloomberg. "Why do you want to do that? You're only 35—you have plenty of time," I said. He explained that he would be term limited out of office the next year, and by the end of Bloomberg's second term, he would be out of office for four years and effectively invisible. Besides, he thought Bloomberg was vulnerable.

By this point, I had a sense of where this was going. Finally, he got to the point. "Dan, I knew we had a deal, and I agreed to stay neutral on the stadium [if I would support the saving of the High Line—see Chapter 11], but I just can't do it. My core constituency is strongly against it, and if I'm going to have a chance, I have to come out against it. I'm sorry." I lost it. For the next ten minutes, I yelled at the Speaker of the City Council, the leader of the body that would have to approve all of our plans. I called him dishonest, a scum, completely untrustworthy. I screamed that I had upheld my end of the bargain completely and that he was placing his personal self-interest above the interests of the city. He was immovable.

Although I'd like to give all the credit for our smooth sailing to our careful planning, another reason was that our potential critics were distracted by the stadium (see Chapter 16). I used to joke frequently that if you want to pass a big rezoning, be sure to throw in a stadium as a distraction. Sadly, it was all too true.

On January 14, 2005, our Hudson Yards rezoning officially passed the City Council by a vote of forty-six to one.

CHAPTER ELEVEN

AN ABANDONED FREIGHT LINE

A S OUR HUDSON Yards plan progressed, another project on the West Side was clamoring for attention. Alex Garvin had noticed the rusting, elevated rail tracks early in our search for Olympic sites, but after we eliminated the High Line from our plan, I had paid it little mind.

In fact, it was a little too far ahead of its time, even for us. I had a vague notion from our very first Olympic presentation that the High Line could be repurposed. Others in Chelsea who had been living near it or owned property around it for decades had very specific ideas. Some wanted it destroyed; others wanted a park.

In 2001, the High Line was a massive, two-track, steel-girded, sunlight-blocking anachronism. It had been constructed in 1934 as an elevated freight line by the New York Central Railroad to replace the street-level tracks that carried goods to the factories and warehouses that dominated the Far West Side of Manhattan from 34th Street all the way down to Soho. Before the High Line was built, the street along which most of the tracks ran, 10th Avenue, was known as "Death Avenue" because of the high volume of fatal accidents caused by pedestrians' unsuccessfully testing their luck darting across the tracks. The elevated line was conceived to go through the centers of blocks, enabling trains to directly deliver milk, meat, produce, and raw goods to the factories along the route, and then to pick up the finished products to start their journeys to market.

Within two decades, however, interstate trucking reduced the need for rail traffic while simultaneously hastening the decline of manufacturing in New York. The High Line carried its last train in 1980—three carloads of frozen turkeys to plants in the Meatpacking District. Around the High Line, the district lost its vitality. It became the home to mini storage businesses, parking lots, and gas stations. Drug addicts and prostitutes, who found the shadows of the High Line a great place to do business, prowled its streets.

But because New Yorkers are always reinventing their city, others found uses for the empty warehouse spaces. First clubs colonized the vast floor spaces. Then in the 1990s, art galleries priced out of Soho began moving into the neighborhood, giving it an artistic, edgy vibe. As the neighborhood became hipper, landowners suddenly saw possibilities. Those who owned property under and adjacent to the High Line, including a mix of local businesses and outside speculators, began lobbying the city to remove the High Line so that they could build on their parcels. Soon enough they had the ear of Mayor Rudy Giuliani, and the city began to process a demolition order.

But two young Chelsea residents, Joshua David and Robert Hammond, had met at a community board meeting at which representatives of CSX, the company that owned the High Line, disclosed plans to tear it down. They discovered a shared love of the High Line and decided to fight to preserve it. In 1999, at almost the last minute, they formed an advocacy group called Friends of the High Line (FHL). They have since acknowledged that at that time they did not know exactly what the elevated structure should become, but they followed their instincts that demolition would be detrimental to the neighborhood. They started organizing to save it.

The resistance enraged Mayor Giuliani, who began attacking FHL. But in New York's topsy-turvy, nonconformist social world, the Republican Mayor's ire served only to attract the attention of celebrities such as actor Edward Norton and fashion designer Diane von Furstenberg. She and her husband, media billionaire Barry Diller, committed to join the resistance and fund a large part of the effort to save it.

FHL won over some members of the political establishment too. Gifford Miller, a young City Council member representing the Upper East Side, had gone to Princeton with Hammond. Miller's mother, a distinguished designer of public gardens, saw the potential of the project. Miller's support was important because he was not yet subject to a recent term-limits law, meaning he would likely become a senior member of the City Council after the next election in November 2001. Another huge proponent of saving the High Line was none other than Amanda Burden.

In May 2001, the *New Yorker* published Adam Gopnik's essay about the High Line, with Joel Sternfeld's hauntingly beautiful photo essay "A Walk on the High Line" alongside the text. All of a sudden, the creative and design community was energized. In June, Design Trust for Public Space, a not-for-profit advocacy group, organized a forum with city, state, and federal government officials to explore the feasibility of adaptive reuse of the structure. With its higher profile, FHL began doing real fundraising and intensified the legal action to prevent the High Line from being torn down. The group kept losing but still managed to slow the demolition. This only made Giuliani and the landowners press forward with greater determination.

By the time we came into office, the High Line was just one court decision away from its doom. The question was: Would the Bloomberg Administration stop the demolition order?

Within days of my arrival in City Hall, Randy Mastro, a Deputy Mayor under Mayor Giuliani, called to ask for a meeting. Mastro was representing the thirty-eight landowners who owned property under or abutting the High Line. Mastro was so familiar with City Hall he strutted into the Committee of the Whole room trailed by a large contingent of his clients. One of them was pulling a red wagon containing a jagged block of concrete. Before we even had finished the introductions, Mastro blurted out that the piece of concrete had fallen from the High Line. "It nearly killed a passerby!" he shrieked. "The High Line is a threat to the safety of New Yorkers. It has to be torn down immediately!" I ordered an immediate inspection of the High Line that revealed some risks, so we spent the money to put netting on the underside to be extra safe.

But the High Line's allies were also organized and newly powerful. After the election, Miller had become Speaker of the City Council, its most powerful member, and Burden was the new Chair of the City Planning Commission. They both made the case for saving the High Line. New to government, I immediately felt pulled in two directions. Sharon Greenberger made the wise but obvious suggestion that maybe the right thing to do was to actually visit the High Line. She got permission from CSX to allow us to take a walk on the tracks to see what all the fuss was about.

The day of our walk could not have been less hospitable, a bitter, cold day in early February. We had to climb through a chain-link fence on a property next to the High Line to get up top. Everything seemed gray: the sky, the river, the buildings, and the steel of the tracks. Even the weeds that colonized the tracks seemed bleak and brittle. The wind was howling, and we were shivering. It couldn't have been less appealing. As I walked the length of it with Greenberger, we admitted to each other that we just didn't get it. We couldn't envision a park out of that sea of gray.

Yet we didn't issue the demolition order. Why? I guess it was a couple of things. Mostly, Bloomberg had supported the High Line during his campaign. Burden was incredibly passionate about it. She could wax rhapsodically about the potential of the park. She helped me to imagine the beauty of the flowers in springtime and the unique vantage point from which to see the city. She brought in pictures of the Promenade Plantée in Paris, a popular, elevated linear park built less than a decade before on an obsolete railway line.

As Burden was making her case, a greater vision was beginning to form in my head. Everyone else was thinking about the High Line as a separate thing, but I started to connect a few dots. The new boulevard Garvin and I had envisioned between 10th and 11th Avenues would terminate in the park on the platform over the eastern railyard. At the southern end, the platform would be thirty feet above ground, exactly the same elevation as the High Line. Might it be possible to walk through a park all the way from Times Square down to the Meatpacking District?

Money was an obstacle. While the city was in the middle of a financial free fall, it would be well-nigh impossible to find the tens of millions (much more, as it turned out) to restore the High Line. I called FHL back to City Hall and said it was time to get real. If they were serious, they had to act seriously.

In their own book on the High Line, Hammond and David recall this meeting and describe me as "intimidating." They quote me as saying, "Don't show me pretty pictures. We have so many parks now we can't afford." I think what I really said was that I needed to see an economic feasibility assessment: How much would this thing cost to save and restore, and how could we justify the expense in financial terms? FHL hired a consultant who produced a report showing that it would cost $65 million to save the High Line, which would produce $140 million in incremental tax revenue over twenty years. The incremental tax revenues would be generated by developers who would build new buildings around this new amenity through the heart of the neighborhood.

HR&A, the consulting firm, and FHL played me brilliantly. They suspected I would be a sucker for their arguments. In effect, they were turning my Hudson Yards tax increment financing district approach on its head. For the Hudson Yards, I argued that if we *build* a railroad, they will come. FHL made the case that if you *save* a railroad, they will come. They'd presumably also seen my Olympic pitch (by then, pretty much everyone had), in which I used historical data on the impact on property values in the wards surrounding Central Park after its opening to justify the Olympic effort.

After that meeting, I had more or less decided to support the preservation of the High Line, but I didn't say anything to anyone outside of my immediate team, not even Burden. Shortly after, in the early spring, Miller asked to see Jay Kriegel and me, and we arranged a meeting. Kriegel and I strolled under the rotunda to the other side of City Hall, where the City Council was located, and plopped down on chairs in his very generous office. After a few pleasantries, he got down to business. "Dan," he said, "there's only one thing in your world that I care about."

"What's that?" I innocently inquired, suspecting what was coming.

"I don't care what else you do, just save the High Line. I will do anything else you want."

At that moment I felt like I had found the bottle with the genie inside granting me one wish. It took me about five seconds to ask for my wish. "I want you to support the stadium," I said. He turned white. Miller was a skilled politician. You don't get to be Speaker at the age of thirty-two otherwise. He had a bright future ahead of him, including an expected run for Mayor someday, and he knew the stadium would be controversial among his natural constituency of Manhattanites.

After thinking about it for a minute, he responded, "What if I agree not to come out against it?" I hit his bid. "That works for me." And so we made a very clear deal that afternoon. I promised to support the High Line, and he promised not to oppose the West Side Stadium. Only one of us would keep his word.

Indeed, the High Line was saved, and it has turned into one of the most successful new parks to be created anywhere in the country in the past few decades. The renaissance of the High Line has created a new urban legend. The heroes are two young men who suddenly emerged with a vast following of locals, and their inspired and almost magical advocacy demanded the preservation of this abandoned trestle as something uniquely pure, pristine, and natural.

As they stood against the formidable forces of the city and its powerful real-estate interests, they evoked the biblical image of two Davids taking down Goliath, and as the Davids emerged victorious, the aged, decrepit structure was suddenly transformed into a sparkling, brilliant urban treasure. In a sense it is true that the High Line would not exist today but for the vision and determined efforts of our heroes, David and Hammond.

But there is more to the story. Had there been just these two Davids and their loyal band of followers, they might have stopped the destruction of the High Line. But it isn't clear that they could have added anything in its place. That required the second chapter of the High Line story and some quiet heroes at City Hall.

The story of the High Line is really about what can happen when an inspired private sector teams up with a determined and creative public sector. That's when the real magic happens. That collaboration not only saved the structure but cleared the thicket of obstacles that stood in the way of the project, designed a unique urban oasis, got it built, and then devised a public-private partnership to pay for its construction and management. There was no precedent or road map, so we made it up as we went along.

After we made the decision to stay the High Line's execution, it fell to the team in the Bloomberg Administration—led first by Laurel Blatchford and then by Marc Ricks and including Burden and the City Planning Department, the Economic Development Corporation, the Parks Department, the Law Department, and others—to convert the High Line to a park through the federal government's Rails-to-Trails program. CSX was game but feared litigation and therefore would cooperate only if we somehow convinced all thirty-eight property owners to completely change their position and sign a document saying they supported keeping the High Line intact.

Then we had to get the Surface Transportation Board, the federal agency in Washington, DC, that oversees Rails-to-Trails, to approve our plan, which it would do only if we could meet its stringent requirements. Then we had to find the financing at a time when we didn't have any money. And last, but certainly not least, we had to design and then develop an approach to the long-term management of an elevated park, which has all sorts of unique challenges and triggers arcane regulations such as the Frozen Turkey Rule. That rule held that all elevated structures must have eight-foot fences because some teenagers had once actually thrown a frozen turkey from a bridge onto a highway below.

In short, we needed to pull a miracle out of thin air. Seemingly, the most insurmountable obstacle was going to be the landholders. Although some of them were relatively unsophisticated, their leader was the wily Jerry Gottesman, head of Edison Properties, a parking and mini storage empire. Nearly seventy years old, he had never sold a property and was generally known to be irascible, painfully patient, and a skillful negotiator.

Gottesman was our lowest common denominator. We understood that if we could appease him, we could get the rest of the landholders onboard. But that was going to be brutal. We couldn't buy their property. We couldn't afford that, even if we had wanted to. We did have one weapon, though: we could rezone the area, West Chelsea. Like Hudson Yards, the core area surrounding the High Line—from 10th Avenue to the Hudson River, from 30th Street to 14th Street—was still zoned for manufacturing and industrial use. That hadn't stopped gallery owners from taking advantage of the cheap rents and establishing a thriving district, but it meant that there could be no residential, retail, or office space. Agreeing with HR&A's approach, we quickly concluded we had to upzone the area. "If you *save* it, they will come," became our approach.

Although upzoning can create enormous value in an area for which there is expected to be demand for the newly possible uses, it is never easy. The surrounding community is always going to be wary of a flood of newcomers into the area straining services and infrastructure. The affordable housing advocates are going to demand that a significant portion of any new housing built is subsidized. In the case of West Chelsea specifically, we had a thriving gallery district we didn't want to price out of the market. Many of the galleries had relocated there after being forced out of Soho as it was taken over by upscale retailers and luxury loft apartments.

Christine Quinn, the City Council member from West Chelsea and Hudson Yards to its north, was a passionate advocate for affordable housing. Very quickly, Blatchford on my team developed a great working relationship with her, knowing she would play a key role in our plans for her district. Although Quinn made it very clear she was likely to oppose the stadium, she was not opposed to change in her district otherwise (and she was a very strong proponent of saving the High Line) as long as it was equitable, largely meaning our plans had to include a fair component of affordable housing. The Department of Housing Preservation and Development and the Housing Development Corporation began to think about what that would mean.

But the upzoning wasn't necessarily going to help the people we really needed to win over—the owners of property under the High Line. If the High Line remained in place, they couldn't build anything, or at least couldn't build on the part of the property over which the High Line passed. So we realized that to appease the property owners we would have to give them something of equal or greater value than they would have received if the High Line had been torn down, and we had to do it without using any money in the city budget.

How do you provide value without having any money to pay for it? It was a question we wrestled with for months. Then our resident illusionist, Vishaan Chakrabarti, suggested that we create value out of thin air by permitting a transfer of air rights throughout the district.

Here's how it works. In New York, zoning prescribes a maximum density for each parcel of land. To the extent that the building on that site is less dense than the maximum permitted, the owner has the right to sell the difference to an owner of an *adjoining* property. So, if I own a five-story building but could build up to ten stories, and my next door neighbor wants to build a fifteen-story building even though he is also only permitted to build up to ten stories, he can purchase my rights and build up to fifteen stories. In effect, zoning looks at the average of the two. This can produce some very funky results, and there are exceptions, but this mechanism of transferring "air rights" is pretty well established in New York.

There are only a couple of examples in New York in which the zoning law permitted a transfer to *nonadjoining* properties. The most recent attempt had been in the 1990s, when the city wanted to save the historic playhouses of the Theater District. It gave the theater owners the right to transfer their unused air rights to nonadjoining properties in the Times Square area, but because the permitted density was already so great there, other property owners saw little need to purchase them, so no real market was created.

By preserving the High Line we were going to disadvantage the owners of property under the High Line in two ways. They couldn't build to maximum capacity because the High Line was in the way. And we made it harder for them to transfer air rights to immediate neighbors because we intended to place restrictions on building in the middle of blocks to preserve space for galleries. To solve this, Chakrabarti learned from the Theater District example. He proposed a maximum density for the buildings along the avenues and permitted an increase in that density (up to a maximum) only if the owner of the receiving site purchased air rights from the owners of property under or next to the High Line. They could transfer their air rights to any permitted site in the district. Chakrabarti argued this would create a vibrant market for the air rights.

It took a full year or so of negotiating over every block and property until everyone found enough to like. Gottesman held out to the very end. Ricks, one of my Senior Policy Advisors, who was brilliantly coordinating both the Hudson Yards and West Chelsea initiatives, had to call a meeting with all of the landowners without Gottesman to communicate directly to them how favorable the deal was (New York Police Department officers were under strict instructions not to let him or his team into the building). Many landowners worried they wouldn't be able to sell their air rights. One asked, "How do we know anybody will buy these air rights?" Sitting front and center in the room was Jeff Blau of Related Companies, one of the most aggressive developers in the city. Without hesitation Blau raised his hand and said, "We're buying." At that moment, the anxiety and uncertainty in the room dissipated. After that meeting the negotiating dynamic changed quickly, the landowners agreed, and Gottesman, who got the most favorable deal of all, grudgingly went along. (In 2015, Gottesman sold his property, for which he paid almost nothing, for $870 million!) For the community, the fact that the High Line was going to be preserved was the price they were willing to pay for the taller buildings.

By the end of 2003, in the midst of our attempts to move forward with our Hudson Yards plan, the city also made its official application to the Surface Transportation Board. The Rails-to-Trails program, which allows creative uses for abandoned rail lines, is not only about green uses but also mandates conserving a national rail network in case of emergency. This meant that we had to not only keep a rail line on the High Line but also demonstrate how we would hook it back into the national rail system and allow for rail service along it to be restored, if necessary, through a process called "rail banking."

This didn't present a big problem up to 30th Street, but then we hit trouble. At that point, the High Line suddenly veers to the west toward the Hudson River and then curves around the western railyard until 33rd Street, where it dives to its terminus in the middle of a site owned by the Javits Center. How that would ever come into play in a national emergency we couldn't imagine, but we weren't going to change federal law. The Jets had to figure out how to incorporate the High Line into their plans. I made the presentation myself to the Surface Transportation Board at the Federal Building in Lower Manhattan, and it signed on.

As the High Line project moved ahead, we encountered resistance from some unanticipated places—our own Parks Department, for example. The preliminary estimates of the costs of saving the High Line were coming in much higher than FHL had estimated. It was clear that it was going to cost hundreds of millions of dollars, not the $65 million the group had thought. And like all of our agencies in the post-9/11 period, the Parks Department was already strapped for operating funds. Adrian Benepe, the Parks Commissioner, legitimately asked how it could afford to manage a new park at thirty feet in the air no less. The Parks Department also raised the question of how it would look to have the billionaire Mayor fund a park in Manhattan likely to be enjoyed mostly by tourists and relatively well-off people in the neighborhood.

I felt this was rebuttable because of our Olympic agenda, which assumed new venues and refurbished parks in all five boroughs. But the question of how to find both the capital to build the High Line and then pay for its ongoing operations was a challenge. Our saving grace was that as the plans for the rezoning proceeded, it became clear that the scope of potential development in the surrounding area was going to be greater than we had thought too, giving us some greater justification for spending more.

After we had settled with the landowners, the West Chelsea rezoning steamed ahead, so to speak. It passed on June 23, 2005—five months after the Hudson Yards rezoning—by a vote of 50-0. The High Line was saved. Twenty-seven percent of the four thousand new housing units expected to be created there would be affordable.

But there were many other Olympic-inspired projects under way.

CHAPTER TWELVE

BROOKLYN DREAMS

THE DAY I started as Deputy Mayor, I changed my commute, of course. Instead of heading inland to Midtown Manhattan's towering office district, I started riding my bike down to the office at around five-thirty a.m. from our brownstone on the Upper West Side along the waterfront bike path in the new Hudson River Park before crossing to City Hall near the bottom of Manhattan Island.

The six-and-a-half-mile ride in the dark, with no one else around, took about twenty minutes. As I rode along the river early in the morning, the lights would twinkle onto the river from the forest of new towers sprouting on the other bank in Hoboken and Jersey City. Suddenly, I was shadowed by a truth about the regional economy that I had only sensed earlier: New York City was getting its lunch eaten by its neighbor to the west.

During the 1990s, as New York put its resources into battling crime, New Jersey greedily lured our businesses with tax breaks and new, affordable, glass and stainless steel towers. It was enticing our young families with spacious new three-room condos with spectacular views of Downtown. Census data show that Hoboken increased its total number of housing units by nearly 14 percent and its total number of households by 29 percent from 1990 to 2000. During the same period, Jersey City built twelve million square feet of office space on the Hudson waterfront—or about as much as Lower Manhattan lost on 9/11. Thirty-two firms moved from Manhattan to Jersey City in 2000 alone.

New Jersey's relentless bid for our business and families highlights another aspect of New York's competitive dilemma. As an international capital of finance, our competitors were London and Hong Kong. In theory, it might have made sense to work with New Jersey to strengthen the entire region as a destination compared with these other world capitals, or other regional business centers, and we both might have benefited. After all, we shared such tourist attractions as the Statue of Liberty and sports teams such as the Giants and Jets. The Port Authority was established to enable just such cooperation. But the fact is that it is just too hard to get things done well across state lines. It is challenging enough to get things done in any one city or state alone. Each has its own agenda, each its own time frame, each its own allocation of capital, and they rarely sync up.

Before I entered City Hall, I had tried to work with officials from New Jersey on the Olympic bid and realized one thing: it was hard to get them to respond. That wasn't necessarily because they disagreed with what we wanted to do—although they might have—but because they didn't see what a New York Olympics would do for them.

In fact, while in office, I came up with only a semi-jokey formula that I immodestly called Doctoroff's Theorem, to calculate the degree of difficulty of getting anything done: degree of difficulty = $x + 3y + 10z + \infty$, where x is the number of city agencies involved, y is the number of state agencies, and z is the number of federal agencies. You add infinity if the Port Authority is needed in any way at all. So you can see why I usually tried to do things that could get done completely within the five boroughs and, therefore, within our power.

As I began to ponder our competitive situation compared with New Jersey more deeply, I began to think more and more about Brooklyn.

Why shouldn't Brooklyn be our competitive response? Compared with the sterile environment along the Hudson River in Hoboken and Jersey City, Brooklyn could offer so much more. It too had miles of underused waterfront. It was tightly linked to Midtown and Lower Manhattan by a far more developed subway system and three road bridges. As a bonus, it also had its own supply of gas, meaning it could have an independent source of fuel for electricity and generators in case of another debilitating attack on Manhattan, which had real appeal after 9/11. It had superior housing stock in the form of acres upon acres of brownstones, elegant multistoried family homes with backyards that often retained turn-of-the-century details such as wood-carved staircases and inlaid floors. It had the region's most successful and innovative cultural institution outside of Manhattan in the Brooklyn Academy of Music, and it had the Brooklyn Museum, many smaller arts organizations, and a dozen local colleges.

Moreover, the key issue holding back the borough—a high crime rate—was in retreat. That was part of the complicated legacy left by Rudy Giuliani. After 9/11, Giuliani had won nearly everyone's admiration for his strength in rallying the city. So when I got deep into the economic development areas for which I was responsible, his record was disappointing. The city planning, housing, and economic development agencies under his watch had atrophied. In some cases, his Commissioners were subpar or even worse.

Still, Giuliani's intense focus on reducing crime throughout the city was the foundation that made all else possible. Crime and the perception of crime had been driving businesses and middle-class homebuyers away from Brooklyn for decades by the time he arrived in office in 1994. In 1950, Brooklyn had a population of 2,738,000, and by 2000 it was down to 2,465,000. The virtuous cycle in Brooklyn had painfully ground into reverse.

The statistics from the Eighty-Fourth Police Precinct, which covers much of Downtown Brooklyn, tell the powerful story of the Giuliani effect. From 1994, when he was sworn in, to 2002, when Mike Bloomberg came into office, the murder rate had declined 72 percent, rape 77 percent, robbery 79 percent, felony assault 54 percent, auto theft 80 percent, and so on. It was an astounding sea change. When crime had been tamed enough, residents of the borough could dream again. Suddenly things that seemed impossible before—such as clean streets and going out alone at night—seemed not only possible but just within reach. That was Giuliani's other great gift to the city: new hope.

By 2000 Brooklyn had a new sense of possibility. As an example, a local developer, David Walentas, had long before purchased property under and around the Brooklyn Bridge largely ignored for decades and was turning it into a cool neighborhood known as DUMBO. Young people into the arts and music scene began squatting in abandoned lofts in Williamsburg. A private foundation founded in the 1980s, the Prospect Park Alliance, led the transformation of the dilapidated Olmstead-designed park in the center of the borough into a gleaming oasis of green attracting more and more families to brownstones in adjacent Park Slope.

From the Olympic bid process, I actually knew quite a lot about the Brooklyn waterfront in both Williamsburg, where Alex Garvin and I had planned a new park, and in Brooklyn Heights, where we had wanted to place a stunning swimming and diving venue that the community quickly rejected. But the rest of Brooklyn was still unfolding for me.

What became clear right away was that there was no coherent thinking about Brooklyn as an alternative to New Jersey. In my first month or so in City Hall, I had six almost back-to-back meetings with governmental, community, cultural, and business leaders in Brooklyn, all pitching individual projects. Not one organization put its idea in the context of the whole borough, let alone described its place in a broader strategy for the city.

The first meeting was with our own City Planning Department, which pushed for a plan developed at the end of the Giuliani Administration for a rezoning along the Greenpoint-Williamsburg waterfront that had gone nowhere. Meanwhile, the staff of the Brooklyn Navy Yard wanted to use the dilapidated industrial park much more ambitiously. The community group advocating for a park on the unused piers below Brooklyn Heights was frustrated that for more than fifteen years its efforts were mired in government bureaucracy and inattention. Jim Whelan, then Executive Director of the Downtown Brooklyn Council, and his leadership group, including Bob Catell, the CEO of Brooklyn Union Gas, and Don Elliott, a lawyer and former Chair of the City Planning Commission, wanted the new administration to focus on what was becoming a back-office enclave in Downtown Brooklyn. Marty Markowitz, Brooklyn's borough President and biggest booster, was dedicated to bringing a professional sports team to Brooklyn. Finally, I met with impresario Harvey Lichtenstein, who had just completed a thirty-two-year tenure as President and Executive Director of the Brooklyn Academy of Music (BAM). After he retired in 1999, he devoted all of his efforts to the BAM Local Development Corporation, whose aim was to turn the vacant land around BAM's main theater into a multibuilding, multicultural district.

Based on these six meetings, a pattern emerged. Some of these civic leaders came with two different groups. Bruce Ratner, arguably the most ambitious real-estate developer in Brooklyn, attended as a board member of two organizations. Similarly, Alan Fishman, the chief executive of the Independence Community Bank, attended two meetings. I asked Joe Chan, my Senior Policy Advisor for Brooklyn, why there seemed to be so little coordination. Chan, who would lead many of our efforts in Brooklyn over the next five years, simply shrugged.

Presented separately, each of the projects seemed to make sense, but I quickly began to believe that they were far more powerful when seen together. That meant we should start to think of Brooklyn as a separate city, with a mixed-use downtown filled with arts, recreation, and parks at or near the core, surrounded by incomparable housing and other amenities radiating into the already strong neighborhoods surrounding Downtown Brooklyn and new ones along the nearby waterfront. All of which would be just a short subway ride from the more dense and expensive Manhattan. How could New Jersey ever compete with that?

No one shared such ambitions for Brooklyn more than Markowitz. A larger-than-life character, the political version of Ralph Kramden in *The Honeymooners*, Markowitz had been elected at the same time as Bloomberg. A longtime Brooklyn pol, Markowitz had over-the-top love for his borough. However, he didn't have much power, so he manifested his enthusiasm by posting wacky signs on the several bridges connecting Brooklyn to the rest of the city. For traffic entering Brooklyn they would say things like "How Sweet It Is" and "Believe the Hype." On the upper and lower levels of the outbound Verrazano-Narrows Bridge, he posted: "Leaving Brooklyn/Fuhgeddaboudit!" And for the Manhattan-bound side of the Williamsburg Bridge, finally overcoming the city's Department of Transportation worries that it would be too distracting, he got a sign saying "Oy Vey."

Markowitz wistfully longed for the Brooklyn of his youth, when it was the borough of strivers and its heart was the baseball team, the Brooklyn Dodgers. In Markowitz's mind (and in the minds of many other longtime Brooklynites), the Dodgers' move out of Brooklyn after the 1957 season was the event that led to the borough's long slide. The Dodgers' owner, Walter O'Malley, had wanted to build a domed stadium in a largely inactive train yard on Atlantic Avenue near the heart of Downtown Brooklyn, where there was a confluence of five subway lines and a Long Island Railroad stop. Robert Moses had other ideas. So O'Malley took the team west. In 2002, the site was still mostly vacant. Markowitz often told a joke that illustrated his feelings about O'Malley: Question: "If you had a gun with two bullets and you had to choose between Stalin, Hitler, and O'Malley, who would you shoot?" Answer: "O'Malley two times."

He was obsessed with bringing in a new professional team. Markowitz's passion helped me see Brooklyn as it wanted to be seen. The professional sports team he imagined would symbolize Brooklyn's reemergence with rising pride and ambition. Brooklyn wanted to be a big-league city in its own right, rather than an appendage of Manhattan; a team would signal that Brooklyn had come back into its own fifty years after the loss of the Dodgers.

Almost right away we would start the planning for several projects, which could then be combined into a consistent narrative. We would turn Downtown Brooklyn into a vibrant mixed-use district, we would focus on the waterfront in Greenpoint-Williamsburg, and we would finally launch Brooklyn Bridge Park, which would enhance both the waterfront and Downtown Brooklyn. And we would kick New Jersey's ass!

Because Lower Manhattan had lost 13.4 million square feet of office space on 9/11, a top priority was to remake Downtown Brooklyn, which was so central geographically but so underdeveloped. As Whelan nicely put it, Downtown Brooklyn was the hole in the doughnut. Downtown Brooklyn's commercial district was surrounded on all sides by residential neighborhoods. By our calculations, some seventy thousand people worked there, including support staffers for bankers at Bear Stearns and JPMorgan Chase. Yet despite this, it had become an indistinct, unappealing area. In order to survive the economic downturns of the 1970s, local merchants on the central Fulton Street Mall had turned to selling shoddy clothing and beepers out of low-rent storefronts. The area was deserted and scary at night. Over the years, it had essentially acted as a no-man's land and thus a barrier between upscale Brooklyn Heights and more crime-ridden areas such as Vinegar Hill and Fort Greene. Flatbush Avenue, a vital corridor through the center of Downtown Brooklyn that could have connected all the neighborhoods, was bereft of any commercial development except car washes, bail-bond dealers, and vacant car dealerships. Traffic passed through, but people rarely stopped.

The last mayor to focus on Downtown Brooklyn was Edward Koch. Koch pushed the development of MetroTech Center, an office park that accounted for most of Downtown Brooklyn's eleven million square feet of office space. To my mind, MetroTech's greatest contribution was that it brought the Cleveland-based real-estate company Forest City Ratner to Brooklyn. Bruce Ratner, who ran the New York arm of the firm, was one of the rare developers in New York who saw potential in some of the more run-down areas in Brooklyn and was willing to invest. But after Koch left office, efforts to make MetroTech attractive to private business floundered. Heavily gated for security reasons, it never seemed welcoming; it was more like a fortified detention center. Although it had a very high occupancy rate, the banks kept back offices there largely because of rich tax incentives. The city began putting its own back offices there to take up space not being used by the private sector.

Then, after 9/11, given the loss of space in Lower Manhattan, there was a citywide office space crunch. We needed to jump-start the Downtown

Brooklyn revival, and quickly. We brought together the Economic Development Corporation and the City Planning Commission to do an in-depth study of the area. They concluded that we should develop a plan to accommodate a large increase in office space, but just as important, to encourage a large mix of retail and high-rise residential uses that would make the area much more dynamic and integrated with the neighborhoods all the way down and into a future Brooklyn Bridge Park.

Of course, not everyone liked these ideas at first. Affluent Brooklyn Heights preferred being an island unto itself. The merchants on the Fulton Street Mall feared rezoning would bring in large chain stores that would put them out of business. The poorer neighbors on the east side of Flatbush worried that they would be cheated out of their fair share of development dollars as had happened in the past. Moreover, many of the residents of Brooklyn were suspicious of high rises. They liked that their borough was not Manhattan. The unofficial ceiling for height in the area was forty-two stories, or 512 feet, as set by the Williamsburg Savings Bank building on the edge of Fort Greene. Most of the residential areas surrounding Downtown Brooklyn never rose above four-story row houses.

Amanda Burden and her team, Joe Chan and leaders of the community such as Bob Catell, and Jim Whelan led the outreach efforts to local residents, attending countless meetings with them—some of which I attended. Our intent was to reassure everyone that growth could be good for all. Just fifteen months after taking office, on April 14, 2003, we were ready for the announcement of our plan. We held a press conference at City Hall and then made presentations in Downtown Brooklyn to local community organizations announcing that the city was proposing to rezone the area and would commit $100 million toward its revitalization over the next decade.

Up until this point, the biggest problem with the local zoning code was that it did not allow for density or for enough mixing of residential and retail uses. Our proposed rezoning allowed for much higher density in the more blighted areas just beyond the traditional residential neighborhoods. We zoned for towers that would allow 4.5 million square feet of additional office space, enough for 8,500 workers, plus 700,000 square feet of space for shopping. The zoning would also permit a thousand new apartments in high rises along Flatbush and Livingston Avenues, a street that connected Flatbush Avenue to Brooklyn Heights. Not knowing how much demand there would be for office space, and acknowledging the growing residential demand in Brooklyn for young professionals, we gave developers the flexibility to develop residential or commercial buildings.

By allowing greater density, we basically freed private developers to make investments. The $100 million the city promised to pony up was for spaces that would bring the neighborhoods together—including new parks; a new performance venue; new medians and plantings along Flatbush Avenue, the Fulton Mall, and Boerum Place; and improvements to infrastructure throughout the area. As part of the rezoning, we also insisted shop owners meet requirements for the attractiveness of their storefronts. In part because the office space losses of 9/11 were still motivating people to act, the plan got a great reception.

As I had learned through the housing initiative, winning the favor of the local City Council representative could be the key to a rezoning. One of my favorites, James E. Davis, was elected to the City Council from Brooklyn's Thirty-Fifth District during the same election in which Bloomberg was elected Mayor. Because the Thirty-Fifth was an elongated district that ran along Flatbush Avenue from almost the Manhattan Bridge to Prospect Park and encompassed BAM, he was essential. We wanted to bring him onto our side from the start.

A naturally gregarious man who had been a police and corrections officer, he was more than willing to work with us, but he wanted to make sure his side of Flatbush Avenue, the poorer side, was not forgotten and that it too received private investment. The first time he met me I saw him whispering with my staff. He then announced, "I am going to ask him." He turned playfully to me and said he noticed my slightly darker skin coloring and curly hair and wondered if I "had a little 'brother' in me." This got a big laugh out of the entire room.

Davis was a ferocious advocate for his district. For our part, listening to him and taking in his concerns about Flatbush Avenue helped and improved our plan. As our relationship bloomed, he had me to his house for Sunday lunch after he took me to five churches in his district in Fort Greene and Clinton Hill. He taught me to duck in and out of an active church service without offending anyone. He would bow his head toward the pastor and make a little hand gesture of apology, and then we were out the door.

His support of our Downtown Brooklyn proposal and the commitment we made to facilitate development on the east side of Flatbush were reasons I think it had relatively easy sailing. In fact, I realized just how crucial he was after a tragedy that occurred a few months after our first meeting. In July, Davis had invited a political rival to a City Council meeting at City Hall. The rival had a history of violence and in a stunning moment unsheathed a gun and shot Davis on the floor of the City Council. He died later at the hospital. It was heartbreaking. He was replaced by a City Council member far more hostile to development.

Although I grew to be a fan of extensive community input, the many stages of the rezoning process made it vulnerable to hijacking by individuals or small groups who could cleverly and disproportionately affect it. In the case of Downtown Brooklyn, as one example, we had to deal with a lone homeowner, Lewis Greenstein of 233 Duffield Street.

Unlike Robert Moses, with rare exceptions we avoided using eminent domain. In the case of the Downtown Brooklyn master plan, however, we moved to condemn 130 residential units to get the parks we needed. One was 233 Duffield Street. Greenstein, who had lived in the mid-nineteenth-century home for twenty-six years, put up a spectacular fight. With almost no evidence at all, he claimed that recesses in his basement had been used to hide slaves on the Underground Railroad.

It was a canny move because it immediately touched off the issue of racial insensitivity. The city ran its own yearlong investigation, which could find no concrete evidence slaves had ever come close to Duffield Street. But the community rejected the findings. So we hired an independent historian who, with no real evidence, from our perspective, decided there might be a link. After a two-year process, large investigative costs, and accusations of racism joyously trumpeted by the tabloids, the city caved. We changed the name Duffield Street to Abolitionist Place. The house was saved. So too was the rezoning, approved by the City Council in June 2004, in a vote of 47–0, with one abstention. One down, two to go in Brooklyn.

The next rezoning on the docket was for Greenpoint and Williamsburg. Together, these two neighborhoods, which run from the Newtown Creek (a canal that forms the border with Queens) to the Brooklyn Navy Yard, have roughly two and a half miles of East River waterfront. Greenpoint, not served by a direct subway line to Manhattan, had remained a largely untouched, middle-class neighborhood with a concentration of residents of Polish origin for decades. But next door, Williamsburg, on the L line, was experiencing one of the more interesting transformations in the city. After World War II, it was a bustling neighborhood filled with Hasidic Jews who were Holocaust refugees from Romania and Hungary, along with Puerto Ricans drawn to the neighborhood's industrial jobs, including those at the Domino Sugar Refinery, whose factory and sign on the East River were clearly visible from both bridges.

In a familiar story, as industry declined, unemployment and gang violence grew. The crusading NYPD Detective Frank Serpico was shot on a drug stakeout on Driggs Avenue in 1971. But in the 1990s, as crime retreated, young artists and musicians checked out the area because of its low rents. Illegal conversion of industrial lofts into apartments soared.

Williamsburg's energy caught the attention of the City Planning Department during the Giuliani Administration. The first time I met with the department, early in 2002, a team led by Brooklyn Director for City Planning Regina Myer and a young colleague of hers, Howard Slatkin, gave an in-depth presentation about rezoning the neighborhood. The plan proposed changing two miles of industrial waterfront into a riverside esplanade with parks and made it easier for developers to build high-density residential towers to accommodate as many as seven thousand new apartments over a 170-block area behind the park.

It was a huge project that might normally have required months of consideration. But the Olympic bid planning done by Garvin had focused on this vast unused waterfront as an ideal site for various sports, which dovetailed nicely with the department's ideas. So a prompt rezoning was consistent with the needs of both the Olympic bid and the City Planning Department's concept of future development. As the team members from the City Planning Department finished their presentation, they seemed to brace themselves for my reaction. I said yes without hesitation. There was a moment of stunned silence. Then celebration. We were going to move forward rapidly.

We made the plan public in June 2003, just two months after the Downtown Brooklyn plan was announced. However, unlike Downtown Brooklyn, Greenpoint-Williamsburg did not go smoothly. There was much more local opposition to our proposed height increases. The affordable housing advocates argued passionately that the plan didn't include enough affordable housing. We readily accepted that and made clear that our intent was that longtime residents not get priced out of a gentrifying market. Our New Housing Marketplace Plan had substantially increased the funds and tools available for affordable housing, but given the scope of the Greenpoint-Williamsburg plan, it wouldn't be enough. We needed new approaches.

There was a little-used option in the city's arsenal called inclusionary zoning: in return for being able to build a taller building than the zoning would typically allow, the owner of a property agreed to add affordable housing to the project. The affordable housing can be done on- or off-site. In order to make it worthwhile for the owner, the value of the additional density has to be greater than the cost of the affordable housing, which is generally going to come at a loss. In effect, the city agrees to allow a developer to build taller or denser than ordinarily allowed for the site.

The problem was that neighborhood advocates usually wanted both height limits and lots of affordable housing. Could we convince them that the trade of height for affordable housing was worth it? Before we could use this tool, I had to convince my own team, especially Amanda Burden. She had an almost religious zeal about "context." That meant that the height and density of buildings had to be "appropriate" for their surroundings. For example, you shouldn't put high rises in the middle of a brownstone neighborhood. Although context seemed a very vague concept, I generally agreed with her, although she could take things to extremes.

Once we had an argument about a proposed eighty-eight-story building about two blocks from Ground Zero. I was eager to get pretty much anything built in Lower Manhattan, but Burden called it "out of context." "Out of context, out of context," I fumed. "What does that even mean in Lower Manhattan? The tallest building in the world was built in Lower Manhattan five times. Lower Manhattan has always been about aspiration, and that's even more important now!" On that one she agreed, but she was much more dug in on Greenpoint-Williamsburg. The original plan the City Planning Department proposed had maximum height limits on the waterfront towers of thirty-two stories. Burden was convinced that inclusionary zoning, which would have increased that maximum height, would push the buildings into the dreaded zone of "out of context," so she dragged her heels.

As we were gearing up to release the Greenpoint-Williamsburg plan, I called a meeting in City Hall among the various agencies to discuss the analysis. After a stormy exchange, Shaun Donovan and new Deputy Commissioner of HPD Rafael Cestero came up with a 33 percent density bonus in return for 20 percent affordable housing. This eventually became our formula. After we resolved the issue among ourselves, we then had to sell the new proposition to the community. Myer and Chan led the outreach with community groups and elected officials. Despite their efforts, it was a struggle. Community opposition to the rezoning was growing, and local politicians who had seemed so supportive were wavering.

The third major Brooklyn project we embarked on right away was Brooklyn Bridge Park. Standing on the famous promenade in Brooklyn Heights back in 2002, not only would you get a fabulous view of the skyscrapers of Lower Manhattan but also you would look down to see the always congested

Brooklyn-Queens Expressway, and beyond it, miles of piers and cargo bays on the Brooklyn side of the East River. Owned by the Port Authority, by then these cargo operations lay largely unused and decaying. In the early 1980s the Port Authority closed them because it had built a new shipping operation in New Jersey that could handle the much larger, modern containers. The Port Authority announced plans to sell the waterfront property, from the piers to Old Fulton Street, to developers.

The community was outraged. Its members wanted a waterfront park, so there was deadlock for a decade. The residents were persistent. In 1998, a citizen group formed the Downtown Brooklyn Waterfront Local Development Corporation to undertake a public planning process for a new park that they cleverly called Brooklyn Bridge Park. By September 2000, they had authored the illustrative master plan, which presented a conceptual framework for turning the entire area from the Manhattan Bridge to Atlantic Avenue into a glorious park. Our Olympic swimming pier proposal barreled into that plan. As much as we argued that the Olympic bid could be the catalyst to finally turning the piers into a park, we made no progress and abandoned the idea. But they made no progress either. They got little traction from the Port Authority or from Governor George Pataki, who controlled the Port Authority's New York interests.

As we began considering our Downtown Brooklyn and Greenpoint-Williamsburg plans, Brooklyn Bridge Park was a no brainer. It was an attraction that would draw people from all over the city (and hopefully, the world); it was also a vital link between the waterfront neighborhoods we hoped to create to the north and in Downtown Brooklyn, only half a mile away.

This was only four months into our administration. We decided to join with the state to buy the piers from the Port Authority and launch the park together. On May 2, 2002, Governor Pataki and Mayor Bloomberg signed a Memorandum of Understanding dedicating state and city funding to the park and providing for the creation of the Brooklyn Bridge Park Development Corporation (BBPDC) to oversee its design and construction. But the state outfoxed us. Because we agreed to split the substantial costs of building the park with the state at 60 percent from the state (partly funded by the Port Authority) and 40 percent from the city, we allowed the state to name the BBPDC Chair and the Executive Director. It also had one more appointee to the board.

Before we knew it, the state not only insisted on being in charge of overall design of the park but also was impossibly secretive about its plans. In what would be a comical, almost textbook, example of Doctoroff's Theorum, the state-designated members of the staff in charge of the designs would attend joint meetings on the park but then, on the order of their boss, refuse to show us plans or answer any of our questions. It was insanity. Over the course of the next four years, progress was slow. The BBPDC went through two executive directors. It seemed as if we would never get the park built.

The lesson here was that whenever joining with another agency of government, especially at a different level, always try to control the appointment of the person leading the day-to-day work. Management control equals actual control. It doesn't matter that you have the same number of board seats or any other levers of control. The leader is almost always going to be loyal to the entity that appointed him or her. The acquisition of the Brooklyn Bridge Park piers had happened too soon after we started in City Hall for us to understand that.

Pretty much the same thing happened with Governors Island. Sitting in the middle of the inner New York Harbor, just four hundred yards across the Buttermilk Channel from the Brooklyn Bridge Park piers and eight hundred yards off of the tip of Lower Manhattan, Governors Island is a 172-acre oasis that had served as a major headquarters for the US Army and then the Coast Guard since just after the Revolutionary War. In 1995, the Coast Guard announced that it would vacate the island.

Garvin and I had toured the site as we began our search for Olympic venues shortly afterward, and we became enamored of it as a potential Olympic Village home. Ultimately, we decided to forego it—we didn't believe the International Olympic Committee would sanction a site where the only way to get there was by boat. Still, its beauty, with its 360-degree views of the harbor, was undeniable.

When Bloomberg entered City Hall, the island was vacant and deteriorating but still owned by the federal government. In the post-9/11 period, when the federal government was willing to do whatever would help New York, President George W. Bush indicated that he would be willing to offer it to the city and the state for a nominal sum. In order to justify that price, the federal government required that there could be limited commercial and no permanent residential development on the island and that the National Park Service would retain the twenty-two acres of the island that contained historic forts. Although the maintenance costs would be very high given the infrastructure needs and the large number of historic buildings on the island, we jumped at the chance to acquire it.

Over time, we came to realize how fortuitous this was and that, as a general rule, whenever the city has a chance to acquire a valuable piece of property, especially one that can be used for permanent infrastructure, just grab it, almost no matter the cost. We assumed that at a minimum it could be a great park, another amenity in our evolving waterfront strategy. It would add another jewel in the emerging crown of great parks we envisioned ringing the harbor, including Brooklyn Bridge Park and the parks we wanted to build around Lower Manhattan and on the rest of the Brooklyn waterfront in Greenpoint-Williamsburg.

So, on January 31, 2003, after months of negotiations, the US government sold the remaining 150 acres of Governors Island to the people of the city and state of New York for one dollar. Mayor Bloomberg and Governor Pataki handed the money over to President Bush in the Oval Office.

In the months we were negotiating with the federal government, the city and state worked out a governance arrangement. This time we got a better deal: we got to pick the Executive Director, and we agreed to rotate the Chair position every two years. Even still, just as in Brooklyn Bridge Park, things moved slowly because a state agency managed the administration of the new entity.

WORLD TRADE CENTER

BEFORE

Ground Zero days after 9/11. Credit: US National Archives' Local Identifier: P7375-20, 2001

AFTER

The World Trade Center site, anchored by the 9/11 Memorial & Museum, surrounded by towering office buildings and an iconic transit hub, 2017. Credit: Joe Woolhead

ATLANTIC YARDS

BEFORE

The proposed site of the new stadium for the Brooklyn Dodgers (in 1955!) at the corner of Atlantic and Flatbush Avenues was still vacant fifty years later. Credit: Forest City New York, 2012

AFTER

The Barclays Center, home of the Brooklyn Nets and the New York Islanders, at the same corner in 2012. Credit: Brooklyn Events Center, LLC

THE HIGH LINE

BEFORE

An abandoned, overgrown High Line in the 1980s. Credit: James Corner Field Operations

AFTER

The High Line (shown in 2014) is now the third-most visited site in New York City, after Central Park and Times Square. Credit: Mark Wickens

HUDSON YARDS

BEFORE

Manhattan's last frontier, the Far West Side, 2009. Credit Joe Woolhead

AFTER

Rendering of the Far West Side, as it will look when it is completed in the mid-2020s. Credit: Related Companies

BEFORE

Looking east on 30th Street on a Monday morning in May, 2000. Credit: © Joel Sternfeld; courtesy of the artist and Luhring Augustine, New York

AFTER

The High Line looking east at Hudson Yards, America's largest-ever development, 2017. Credit: Joe Woolhead, 2017

LONG ISLAND CITY, THE QUEENS WATERFRONT

BEFORE

The waterfront in Long Island City, Queens, 2006. Credit: Wikimedia Commons, user_ matanya, 2006

AFTER

The waterfront in Long Island City, Queens, 2017. Credit: Joe Woolhead, 2017

WILLIAMSBURG

BEFORE

Kent and 6th Streets in Williamsburg, Brooklyn, 2002. Credit: Alex Garvin, 2002

AFTER

Kent and 6th Streets in Williamsburg, Brooklyn, with perhaps America's highest concentration of hipsters, 2017. Credit: Joe Woolhead, 2017

CHAPTER THIRTEEN

WALTER O'MALLEY BE DAMNED

TO BE A big-league city, you need a major league sports team. If it had been a separate city in 2002, Brooklyn would have been the fourth most populous city in the country, and yet Brooklyn hadn't had its own major league team in nearly half a century. Hence one of the most ambitious and controversial of all our large-scale plans: Atlantic Yards and its beating heart, the Barclays Center and the Brooklyn Nets.

So how do you bring a professional sports team to a city? It starts with a rich guy (or gal) buying a franchise. Marty Markowitz, Brooklyn's ultimate booster, was dead set on bringing a team to Brooklyn. He even called the Dodgers in Los Angeles to see if they'd sell. He quickly enough settled on Bruce Ratner.

Ratner, one of the largest real-estate developers in Brooklyn, could sense that Brooklyn was potentially on the edge of blossoming. Owning a team, as he readily admitted, was not really his passion, but building an arena and a surrounding development made him excited. Ratner had spent his career in development, much of it in Brooklyn, but many of his projects—such as MetroTech—were, quite frankly, unmemorable and becoming outdated. He aspired to leave a greater legacy.

With some arm-twisting from Markowitz, he became persuaded that he could be a kind of hero if he brought sports back to Brooklyn. Although the team would be a huge risk financially, he believed he could make a lot of money by doing massive-scale housing and office development around it.

In early 2003, Ratner came to City Hall with an audacious plan that borrowed from our plans for Hudson Yards. He would build a huge development on the railyard at the convergence of the two major thoroughfares in Brooklyn—Atlantic and Flatbush Avenues—right next to the Brooklyn Academy of Music, Brooklyn's premier cultural institution. Our administration had just renewed the city's commitment to the creation of a broader cultural district around BAM that Rudy Giuliani's Administration had made to BAM's legendary impresario, Harvey Lichtenstein.

Ratner's plan, designed by world-renowned architect Frank Gehry, called for a new arena surrounded by no less than seventeen towers that would encompass 2.1 million square feet of commercial space and 4,500 residential units. It was the largest private development plan the city had seen since Battery Park City rose near the tip of Manhattan in the 1980s—other than the other railyard plan we were then developing on Manhattan's Far West Side. Back then Brooklyn's potential wasn't obvious. As Ratner was giving his presentation, Michael Kalt, a Senior Policy Advisor on my staff, leaned over to me and whispered, "The guy has balls."

Ratner was only really guessing at the size, cost, and architecture of the project as well as the benefits to the community. At that nascent stage, that's all that was possible. He also didn't have a team nailed down. Initially, he proposed buying the New Jersey Devils.

The symbolism inherent in the site was particularly rich in this case because the site where he was proposing to develop the arena was atop the Long Island Railroad's Vanderbilt Railyard, at nearly the same spot where Walter O'Malley had wanted to build a stadium for the Dodgers almost fifty years earlier. The site had awesome potential for the obvious reason of the centrality of its location and its incredible access to transportation: the nine subway lines, two lines for the Long Island Railroad, and several bus lines all converged there.

For more than half a century, projects had been proposed for this clearly underused site. Yet development had been piecemeal. One of those projects was by Forest City Ratner itself, which had built a mall adjacent to the site in the 1990s. But it was widely despised by architecture critics for being lightless and ugly with no common areas such as food courts.

Ratner, a canny and intuitive operator, understood his likely critics and worked quickly to appease them. After his first presentation, he swiftly adjusted his proposal in response to criticisms to make it more appealing to Amanda Burden, who was generally skeptical of the quality of his work. At the urging of Markowitz and me, Ratner turned his attention to the New

Jersey Nets, also for sale. Although the most losing team in basketball, the Nets seemed a better fit with the energy and interests of Brooklyn residents than did a hockey team.

A major league team, even a losing one, is expensive. Ratner won the team with a bid of $300 million, the second-highest price ever paid for a basketball team at the time, beating a rival bid from an investor group in New Jersey.

That cost was only part of the risk. As he contemplated buying the team, Ratner didn't have any of the approvals for the Brooklyn arena, much less the housing and office towers that would make the deal financially possible. He didn't have an agreement from the Metropolitan Transportation Authority to move the eleven tracks that crisscrossed the Vanderbilt Yards or the clearance to condemn twenty-one acres and raze them. The team was already losing tens of millions of dollars a year, and while he would be waiting to move the team the losses would only mount because its New Jersey fan base, knowing the team was likely going to be deserting it, would flee. I thought it was a crazy risk, but, hey, it was his money.

My role in this was to be as supportive and reassuring as possible. The Mayor and I promised Ratner that the city was behind him. I went as far as to talk to the investment bankers selling the team, telling them how great the Nets would be for Brooklyn and how supportive the city was. I helped to get the state on board, a necessary step because the MTA owned most of the land Ratner needed. Ratner had carefully studied our deal with the Jets to build the West Side Stadium, where we agreed to pay for "infrastructure" (in that case the roof and the platform) if they would pay for the stadium, and he wanted a similar deal. So, the state and city each pledged about $50 million.

The first public reaction to Ratner's plan could not have been more positive. In August 2003, the *New York Times* broke the story of efforts to move the Nets as part of a larger development and was effusive in its enthusiasm (the purchase of the Nets would not close until January 2004). Soon afterward, when Forest City Ratner presented the Gehry model of the entire project to the public, the applause was thundering. Herbert Muschamp, the architecture critic for the *New York Times*, raved: "A Garden of Eden grows in Brooklyn. This one will have its own basketball team. Also, an arena surrounded by office towers; apartment buildings and shops; excellent public transportation; and, above all, a terrific skyline, with six acres of new parkland at its feet. Almost everything the well-equipped urban paradise must have, in fact."

It helped that Ratner, who had worked in the Koch Administration, had a savvy understanding of the political system. He got the unions behind him by promising more than ten thousand construction-related jobs. He co-opted local advocacy groups. For example, he met with the Association of Community Organizations for Reform Now, which had often been a major thorn in developers' sides, and promised that nearly half of the 4,500 housing units would be affordable. In return, the organization promised it would support him at all of the public hearings and in the media. He got political support, in part, by spreading donations widely to local politicians and lobbying aggressively in Albany. (In 2006, he was ranked the third-largest lobbyist in the state.) He generated a lot of star power by giving rapper and entrepreneur Jay-Z a piece (less than 1 percent) of the Nets ownership.

Also, although Ratner is reluctant to admit this, I think he reaped a lot of benefit from our simultaneous efforts on the Far West Side of Manhattan. For starters, his concept of a development built over railyards, with a stadium or arena at its center, was very similar. Even the name he initially gave the project, Atlantic Yards (which later became Pacific Park), echoed Hudson Yards. Then, there was the fact that the Dolans, who owned Madison Square Garden and the Knicks and who arguably had the most to lose from competition in Brooklyn, were already busy fighting the West Side Stadium. They couldn't really fight both sports facility projects without looking too self-interested.

Ratner also learned from our Far West Side mistakes. For example, Andrew Zimbalist, an economics professor who made a specialty of analyzing the economics of sports stadiums, tore apart the Far West Side project, saying we were bilking the taxpayers. Ratner got out in front by hiring Zimbalist to do an analysis of his proposed arena. This time, Zimbalist came to the opposite conclusion: this arena could generate $818 million for the city and state in tax revenue.

Yet for all his sophistication, Ratner utterly underestimated one set of potential opponents: a new core of well-off, white families who had purchased brownstones and now did not want to see their neighborhood crowded by others. They were not the majority, but they were sophisticated in their use of media and influence. They organized almost immediately after the announcement in 2004, forming groups such as Develop Don't Destroy Brooklyn. They argued that the new arena would clog the local area with traffic and otherwise ruin the special nature of the neighborhood. These folks helped persuade City Council member Letitia James, who had taken James Davis's seat after he was killed, to come out against the project. (Another local councilmember, Bill de Blasio, who represented nearby Park Slope, came out in favor of it.)

Although we would eventually become masters of the Uniform Land Use Review Procedure, at this point not a single rezoning had been approved, and internally we had doubts about pulling off all we were trying to accomplish. Because the state owned much of the land, we decided that for expediency we would skirt ULURP and take advantage of the state's seemingly speedier process. With twenty-twenty hindsight, I am positive we could have placated our opponents in negotiations and gotten the process through ULURP. Instead, Ratner and the state faced years of lawsuits challenging everything from the environmental impact statement to the state's right to condemn properties for the public good.

As Ratner morphed the development in response to real-world economics—adding luxury units, reducing the total percentage of affordable housing closer to the 30 percent range toward which we normally guided most large-scale development, and dramatically increasing the total cost of development to more than $4.5 billion—his adversaries read evil into his every move. His critics and the tabloid press painted him as a greedy, manipulative developer. Ratner, like me, was a native midwesterner (from Cleveland) who came east to go to Harvard and then to New York for law school. He is also a dyed-in-the-wool liberal. He was an ardent Vietnam War protester and crusading Commissioner of the Department of Consumer Affairs in the Koch Administration. He honestly believed he was trying to do a good thing for New York and Brooklyn.

He had my sympathies, frankly. One of the hallmarks of the Bloomberg Administration, for better or worse, was that we were loyal to people who stuck with us. Ratner had sunk $300 million into a losing team based on our commitment that we would help him get his plan approved, and we felt honor bound to stick with him. So when Extell, a rival development group, made a bid for the right to build out MTA land that tripled Ratner's offer, we blocked it.

When the financials of the deal deteriorated, the city and the state upped our contributions to the project to $100 million apiece. We still thought it made sense, especially in light of our dreams for Brooklyn. Yet, as we entered 2005, Ratner owned a money-sucking team in New Jersey without a clear path to getting the approvals he needed to make his investment pay off. And right next door, despite our support, by 2005, the expansion of the BAM Cultural District was mired in planning and fundraising delays.

There was one other Brooklyn project we had started early that was also stalled. When we came into office, legendary Coney Island was rotting. It was another of the communities on which we believed we could shine an Olympic spotlight by placing a venue there and then building a comprehensive plan for the surrounding area. In this case, it would have been the place from which to watch Olympic sailing. But that was really just a pretext for focusing on the dilapidated area.

One of the world's most iconic urban amusement areas since the mid-nineteenth century, Coney Island drew millions of visitors to the wide beach; the boardwalk with famous sites and amusements such as Steeplechase Park, Dreamland, the Wonderwheel, and the Cyclone roller coaster; the Brooklyn Aquarium; the freak shows; the annual Mermaid Parade; and the celebrated Nathan's Famous Hot Dogs, with its annual Hot Dog Eating Contest.

Yet Coney Island had been in decline for more than seventy years, the victim first of the Great Depression, then the migration out of Brooklyn to the suburbs after World War II, and then poor city housing policy placing a disproportionate share of public housing in the area, which merely accelerated the concentration of poverty and the area's deterioration. By 2001, the sense of hopelessness was pervasive. Coney Island was the virtuous cycle turned vicious in its most dramatic form. The great amusements were a shadow of their former selves.

We came into office determined to restore Coney Island. We didn't delude ourselves into thinking that it would be quick or easy. But by September 2003, we had created a local development corporation to work with community leaders and local elected officials to develop a plan that would once again make Coney Island a major local and tourist destination while being sensitive to local concerns and navigating the complex racial issues in the area. But there was a looming problem. A developer had speculated on property home to many of the amusements at the core of our plan, claiming that he wanted to enhance the amusement district and develop housing around it. We didn't believe him. Coney Island was dead in the water.

So, by early 2005 our ambitious Brooklyn plans were stalled. Although we had been successful at getting the Downtown Brooklyn plan approved, the Greenpoint-Williamsburg rezoning was facing increasing pressure from the local community and politicians. We were locked in a battle for control over Brooklyn Bridge Park with our state partners. Ratner was fighting financial, planning, legal, and public relations battles at Atlantic Yards. And Coney Island seemed to be going nowhere.

CHAPTER FOURTEEN

THE INTERNATIONAL OLYMPIC CAMPAIGN

THE CHALLENGES ON the Far West Side and in Brooklyn paled in complexity next to the massive Olympic operation now humming along. By 2004, our Olympic staff had grown to more than one hundred members and consultants charged with two main, daunting tasks. Half the team was making sure we met the International Olympic Committee's formidable bid requirements regarding every aspect of how a candidate city would host the Games.

It's only when things go terribly wrong—such as the recent Olympics in Rio—that the public realizes the complexity of mounting a safe, successful Games. Bidding cities must demonstrate full mastery of every detail more than seven years in advance.

The three-volume tome containing all the required information is known as the bid book, a 562-page bible in French and English covering seventeen required topics, including customs and immigration, medical services, accommodations, security, transport, technology, media operations, culture (every Olympic Games is accompanied by a Cultural Olympiad!), venues, the Olympic Village, and so forth. When finally mailed out, each beautifully designed, white leather–covered book weighed more than three pounds.

But it wasn't enough to just say what you were planning to do; you had to prove it. This was reflected in the guarantees we had to provide. If we said, for example, that the Waldorf-Astoria was going to be the official IOC hotel, we needed a contract with it that detailed the availability of rooms and facilities and the rate it would charge. If we wanted to use Madison Square Garden for the duration of the Games (and Paralympic Games to follow), we needed a signed agreement. Early on, Andrew Kimball, our Chief Operating Officer, put together a list of all of the guarantees we would need, as well as the officials who would help us fill those requirements, in a single-spaced document. It ran to nearly fifty pages.

We needed approvals or guarantees signed by nearly every level of government, from the President of the United States to the Governor of New Jersey to the County Executive of Nassau County (the county bordering Queens). We needed the US Secretary of State, for example, to guarantee entrance into the United States by anyone with an Olympic identity and accreditation card. We needed the US Secretary of Labor and the Secretary of Homeland Security to guarantee the temporary entry of Games-related personnel prior to the Olympics. We needed the Administrator of the US Environmental Protection Agency, the Commissioner of the New York Department of Environmental Conservation, and the Commissioner of the New York City Department of Environmental Protection to guarantee that all construction for the Olympics complied with environmental regulations. And so on.

We had to guarantee that we would control all ad space outdoors, in airports, and on subways before and during the Olympics to prevent ambush marketing, and we concluded that we would also need special legislation to enforce the protections. We obtained agreements with 191 separate hotels and with five colleges for dormitory space. Guarantees of adequate security and medical care were especially complicated. Although the Olympic Games received a special designation as a national security event from the federal government, thereby involving the Secret Service, we were required to ensure that one law enforcement agency would be empowered to coordinate all security activities. Getting the Secret Service to accept the New York Police Department in that role was complicated, delicate, and unprecedented. But Jay Kriegel and Kimball succeeded.

Then we had to come up with a budget that would convince ourselves, elected officials, the media, our business leaders, our supporters, and, most importantly, the IOC that we could pay for everything necessary to host the Games—including providing the twenty-seven different venues for the competitions—without relying on government funds. From my very first presentation in May 1996, I had promised that this could all be done without governmental funding, and I wasn't about to back away from that now. Besides, if Los Angeles and Atlanta (barely) could do it, New York, the media capital of the world, certainly could too. The biggest chunk of spending was going to be on the venues. The good news was that we really didn't have to change much from the proposal we had submitted to the United States Olympic Committee before it picked New York as the US candidate city in 2002.

The bad news was that constructing, renovating, and creating venues cost a lot. The New York area had great facilities for its ten professional sports teams but not many that could accommodate Olympic sports. We had always assumed that wherever possible we would rent existing facilities—such as Madison Square Garden, the National Tennis Center (which hosts the US Open every September), and Yankee Stadium—or temporarily retrofit existing ones such as the Javits Center, which would host six sports. In some cases, we would undertake expensive upgrades to existing facilities that would leave a legacy, such as the historic 369th Regiment Armory in Harlem, slated to become the home for boxing during the Games, or the dilapidated NYPD shooting range in the Bronx, which would be replaced with a state-of-the-art shooting facility. In some cases, we would have to build expensive temporary venues, such as an aquatics center in a new park on the Williamsburg waterfront (it was still a lot cheaper than building a permanent one). The rest—nine venues, including the Olympic Stadium on Manhattan's West Side, the arena that developer Bruce Ratner was planning to build in downtown Brooklyn, and a new rowing center in Flushing Meadows–Corona Park in Queens—would be completely new and permanent additions to New York's constellation of sporting venues to be enjoyed for generations.

In addition, our budget had to include expenditures for other necessary Olympic facilities, such as an enormous broadcast center for live coverage to every country in the world; a massive media center for the rest of the world's press; and the Olympic Village. In those cases, we assumed private developers would build them, and we would just pay to make them usable for the Games. In each case, we had to develop real designs and cost them out to ensure that our estimates were credible. To get it all done I asked Alex Garvin and Andrew Winters to come back to NYC2012. Fortunately, they did.

Most notably, Garvin held a worldwide design competition for the Olympic Village, with more than seventy submissions from architects around the world. Thom Mayne, who later won the Pritzker Prize, won this contest. The elegant, yet modernistic design for the Village, surrounded by water on three sides and situated right across the East River from the United Nations, contained a variety of "ribbon" apartment buildings that traced the shoreline and curved around a central green. In total, we planned to spend $795 million of our $3.1 billion budget to pay for facilities.

The $795 million did not include the contributions from other parties, such as the New York Jets or Forest City Ratner, the owners and primary users afterward of the two largest facilities. In only two cases did we assume the city would contribute anything—$60 million for a new indoor pool in Flushing Meadows–Corona Park planned for years that would have been used for water polo and $80 million to purchase the land to build the park on the Williamsburg waterfront, part of the much larger rezoning there, which would serve as the venue for aquatics.

In almost every case in which our Olympic plan placed a permanent venue, the city developed a comprehensive plan for the surrounding neighborhood, including housing, infrastructure investments, transportation upgrades, streetscape improvements, new schools, and parks in addition to the sports facilities. Because we would have to demonstrate to the IOC that our plans were feasible, getting those plans approved before its decision gave our efforts urgency not common in government.

Normally, such rezonings can take years, even decades, to happen because every neighborhood group weighs in with its own agenda. But the Olympic bid really did work its magic. In part, it was because our venue plan seemed to spread the benefits around the city fairly. It was also because New Yorkers saw in the Olympic Games a reflection of their own city, especially after 9/11 ("New York is an Olympic Village every day!" I persisted in reminding virtually everyone I met). People from all walks of life, from every community, and of every race were truly excited to be part of it—polls showed all along that around 70 percent of New Yorkers supported hosting the Games, and we benefited from that enthusiasm in all sorts of ways. Key city unions signed a "no strike" pledge if we won the Games. That 70 percent support also stimulated other government agencies to act promptly to aid the bid. Our rezonings wouldn't have sailed through the City Council as easily without evidence of broad public support. Nor was it likely the state legislature would have agreed to provide a guarantee to the IOC that it would fund $250 million to cover cost overruns if we failed to generate enough Olympic revenues had public support not been so strong.

Locking down the logistics was almost nothing compared with the emotional challenge of the second major task we had before us: winning the hearts and trust of IOC members. There really is nothing like bidding for an Olympics. It is a kind of international political campaign, given the thrust and parry that takes place between the competitors in the glare of great media attention. There's a secret ballot at the end too. However, there is no polling, so you have no way of knowing how you are actually doing. All of this produces a profound sense of insecurity that rises and falls based on the last good or bad conversation you've had, the last positive or negative article you've read, or the last rumor you've heard.

Although we had dozens of people dedicated to parsing every piece of information about every IOC member we could, ultimately it would largely come down to whether they trusted me. As the founder and face of the bid, my biggest job was to get out to see as many IOC members as possible. This meant finding frequent opportunities for very brief trips out of the country whenever I had a chance to meet available IOC members and to build the personal relationships that could make the difference. In the two years between my trip to Prague and the decision in Singapore in July 2005 I was out of the country for a total of 136 days.

This sense of insecurity was compounded by the limited ability we had to meet or even contact IOC members. As I noted earlier, as a result of the Salt Lake scandal, the IOC changed the rules so that the only contact bidding cities were supposed to have was at officially sanctioned, Olympic-related events. The vast majority of these took place in Europe, which only made my job more difficult relative to that of our competitors, all of whom were European (in May 2004, the IOC eliminated as candidate cities Havana, Leipzig, Istanbul, and Rio de Janeiro). Each of our remaining competitors (London, Paris, Madrid, and Moscow) seemed to have influential IOC members on its team stumping regularly, made that much easier by their proximity, especially to Lausanne, Switzerland, where the IOC was based and where many ongoing activities involving members occurred. Our three US IOC members, on the contrary, all lived in California and were less influential and less available.

In time, as I began to get to know many of the IOC members better, they would drop hints that some of our competitors were playing a little fast and loose with the rules. Several members let it be known that other bidders had visited them in their hometowns, a clear violation of the rules. Apparently, the IOC staff had heard some rumors of this but had let it slide. So I began to do it too.

I never saw any evidence of corruption. Perhaps the most bizarre situation happened when I made a private visit to the IOC delegate in Beirut, who had invited me to come visit him in his hometown. After he picked me up at the airport, he showed me his elegant home and then drove me around his beautifully rebuilt city. At one point, we pulled into a parking lot and sat there for a moment until a black Mercedes-Benz pulled up. Both my host and the other driver opened their windows, and the other driver handed my host an envelope. He took it, handed it to me, and motioned for me to open it. In it must have been $10,000 in cash. Confused, I handed it back. There was no mention of a bribe, and I am still not sure what the entire sequence signified.

It was also pretty clear that our competitors' national governments were playing a far greater role in their bids than our federal government did. Despite concerns that our President was a liability on the world stage, the George W. Bush Administration was very helpful. But it was undeniable that it was not a matter of national importance for the United States whether New York won an Olympic bid in the same way the governments of Tony Blair or Jacques Chirac declared that it was for Britain and France. Although the federal government had done some important things, such as easing the ability of IOC members and their families and international sports officials to get visas (we even sent each IOC member a gold-plated "get into the country free" card that gave him or her a special hotline number to call when coming to the United States—the number was staffed by NYC2012 personnel with a direct link to the State Department), we were never able to mobilize our ambassadors in the way other countries did to establish relationships and openly advocate with IOC members on their home turf.

Occasionally, the influence of our competitors' political leaders extended a bit further. Mike Bloomberg asked Colin Powell, a native New Yorker who was then US Secretary of State, if he would be willing to help out his hometown. To our delight, he was very enthusiastic about our bid. Some months later, he happened to be meeting with the Prime Minister of Senegal, whose Sports Minister was an IOC member. Powell reported back to Bloomberg that he had passionately made a case for New York and urged the Prime Minister to encourage his Sports Minister to vote for us. But the push was to no avail. It turned out that Tony Blair had been there first. "With all due respect, Mr. Secretary," Powell reported the Prime Minister as saying, "Tony Blair promised to double British foreign aid to us." The fact that the United States gave four times as much aid to Senegal as Britain did—even after the increase—was beside the point. The United States couldn't and wouldn't play that game.

On the individual level there were a few unsavory characters. In June 2004, I went to Zurich to visit Sepp Blatter, an IOC member and the President of the Fédération Internationale de Football Association, the all-powerful international soccer governing body, and some of his staff to press our case. I brought one of my Europe specialists, Iva Benson, who was Croatian and spoke German and French. The meeting was ostensibly to talk about soccer and the Olympics, and Blatter's associates asked me lots of questions about the stadium and whether I thought having the Games in New York could be a catalyst to building interest in soccer in the United States. But Blatter spent the meeting looking almost exclusively at Benson. Afterward, as we were walking to the elevators, he said to her in an aside in German: "You have beautiful dimples. You should be in my family." In 2015, Blatter would be forced to step down from FIFA and banned from participating in the sport for the next six years because of bribery charges associated with his bidding for the World Cup.

Then there was Mario Vasquez Raña, a Mexican billionaire and media magnate. As the President of the Pan American Sports Organization, the organization of the national governing bodies of the Americas, he was reportedly the gateway to several votes of Latin American IOC members. He invited Bloomberg and me to visit him in Mexico City. When we landed, we walked across the tarmac to Vasquez Raña's helicopter, took off, and a few minutes later landed on the rooftop of his complex. Downstairs, he greeted Bloomberg, staffer Tania Paessler, and me. His office was filled with pictures of him with famous people who had come to visit him. As he showed us the pictures, he said several times what an honor it would be to take a picture with Bloomberg and to interview him for his publications. He offered us some of his homemade tequila.

Vasquez Raña got what he wanted: he interviewed Bloomberg and published the interview in all his newspapers and magazines, and, of course, he added another picture to his wall. We got what we wanted too. He committed his vote to us and firmly declared, "We Americans must support each other," implying that he would encourage other Latin American members to vote for us. Eventually, he would betray us.

Bloomberg was an incredible trooper throughout the bid process. He traveled around the world, ignoring the inevitable shrieks of local opponents and the media that he was pursuing frivolous trips when he should be in town dealing with important city issues, let alone the risk that he would be out of town when a crisis happened. He never wavered. He came with me to Athens for the 2004 Games; to Dubrovnik, Berlin, and Accra, Ghana for the meeting of the African Olympic Committee. He was always charming with the IOC members, who were honored that he had made the effort to come. And over time, he evolved both his own eloquent pitch for a New York Olympics and a demonstrable passion for the bid. He inspired our bidding team, raising their spirits, their game, and their hopes.

His commitment was really tested in Accra. Each of the five bidding cities was given fifteen minutes to make its pitch. I was going to lead off, and Bloomberg was going to conclude. Out of respect for the delegates in attendance, many of whom spoke French and not English, I decided to give some of my remarks in French, a language I had last spoken in high school, and then not very well. I went a couple of minutes too long, and then Bloomberg took over. Just as he was getting ready to deliver his closing pitch, the Chair of the African Olympic Committee, a Major General from Togo, interrupted him and commanded him to stop. He was over the limit. Bloomberg had traveled more than five thousand miles to Ghana only to be cut short. He just laughed it off.

While we were out wrangling votes, we had other setbacks. At the Athens Olympic Games, on a beautiful evening on the rooftop terrace of the IOC hotel overlooking the Parthenon, I was approached by one of the South Korean IOC members with whom I had developed a warm relationship, who told me that he wanted to speak with me in confidence. We stepped inside, where I could hear him better, and almost in a whisper, he said, "I thought you should know that some people involved with the Paris bid have been telling members of the IOC that New York's bid is the 'Jewish bid.'" Sigh.

As the bidding process intensified, we got better and better at understanding the members and their interests. I brought on my former City Hall staffer Roy Bahat to coordinate all our international relations, activities, and contacts or, really, member management. He created spreadsheets to keep track of the IOC members. Benson, Paessler, and the rest of our international relations staff catalogued potential connections we had to them, no matter how obscure. (Who are their wives or third cousins?) They recorded any specific concerns the members had noted about New York, or pretty much anything they said about the bidding cities. They noted their interests and hobbies. (Is his daughter an equestrian? Does her nephew want to come to college in the United States?) We kept it all on file.

Because we were permitted to speak with them by phone (e-mail was almost never used by the IOC back then), Bahat made sure I called certain members at least once every three weeks to maintain a minimum of steady contact. We were also allowed to send them materials supporting our bid.

Our marketing team, led by our creative and indefatigable Chief Marketing Officer, Amy Stanton, concocted a steady stream of interesting and visually compelling communications, including a big box filled with little mementos of New York and letters from individual New Yorkers, including people they knew personally, making the case for New York. We even sent each one of them a key to the city.

Some members were immovable no matter how hard we tried or how naturally supportive we thought they should be. If ever there were a natural voter for New York, it should have been Richard Carrion, the Chair and Chief Executive of the Banco Popular, the large San Juan, Puerto Rico–based bank. Carrion thought of himself as an American. He was even on the board of Verizon. During the course of the bid process, the two of us actually developed a friendship that went much deeper than most. To help cement our position, I suggested that he be the Grand Marshal of the Puerto Rican Day Parade in New York in 2004. The parade, which takes place every June, gathers huge crowds, and he was ecstatic to be waving at the cheering throngs. We even held a reception for him at Gracie Mansion.

I considered him a vote in the bank until I actually asked him. We were at dinner with his wife, Conxita Martorell, and Juan Antonio Samaranch Jr., who was promoting the bid for Madrid, and his wife. During dinner, I heard for the first time the heartrending story of how after he and his first wife had divorced he was depressed until he was introduced to Conxita—who had made him deliriously happy—by Juan Antonio Samaranch Sr. He was eternally grateful. My heart sank as Carrion told me that even though his head was with New York, his loyalty was with Madrid, and he would vote for the Spanish city. He was one of the few members willing to tell me to my face that he wouldn't vote for us. (Tragically, Conxita passed away in 2016.)

I was away so much courting votes that the *New York Daily News* finally caught on, christened me "Travlin' Dan," and actually published my away schedule. I didn't really care. I felt entirely confident that despite my being gone so long my City Hall office was productive. But the travel was taking its toll.

Every time I needed to take a trip, I dreaded it. Even though most people, even those who know me well, think of me as outgoing, I'm actually more of an introvert. I have never been able to walk into a room filled with people and just go up to someone and introduce myself. In structured or prearranged meetings, I'm fine. But waiting around in a lobby until I spied someone to grab, often a person with whom I had nothing in common and who didn't speak English well, brought out my biggest anxieties.

At first, these forced conversations felt painfully unnatural. Worse than that, I was bad at them. The members, comfortable with the process, were looking for leisurely conversations about family and politics; they did not want to be hard sold. Frequently, they wanted to drink a lot more than I did. My staff had to rein in my hard-charging, New York, can-do business attitude. I was told to drink more, make light banter, grill people less in conversation, and hold off on pitching New York. "They feel like they were interrogated there," they would complain. "You just have to let the conversation slow a little."

The trips were brutal. I would often do round-trips to Europe or even to Asia in seventy-two hours or less. The routine was always the same, especially when I would attend an international sports meeting. I would land in the early morning; take a taxi to the hotel, where I quickly showered and changed; and then head down to the lobby or into the meeting, where I hoped to snag an IOC member. Usually, I was accompanied by Charlie Battle and one of the members of our international relations team, who arranged lunch and dinner, which would inevitably be followed by a late night at the bar. After most everyone had departed the bar, I would go back to my room to answer e-mails and make calls on city business. I would sleep for four or five hours and then groggily get up and do it all over again. By the time I got on the plane to go home, I couldn't think straight and would fall into a deep sleep before the plane took off. On several flights back from Asia, I slept the entire way back. When I got back to New York, I was never able to completely recover. After a long day in City Hall, I would trudge up the stairs in our townhouse crying out to Alisa and the kids only somewhat facetiously, "I'm so tired, I think I'm going to die." They thought it was mildly cute for a while, but soon enough they just rolled their eyes.

But it was no joke. My exhaustion only magnified one of my least appealing traits: my temper. My temper had always been a part of my management style, for better and worse. Sometimes my anger could be strategic, a tool to move petty bureaucrats forward. Once, Josh Sirefman and I had a meeting with the Port Authority, which had been dragging its feet again on some ridiculous aspect of rebuilding the World Trade Center. "Want to see me get angry?" I said to him with a wink. Then, during the meeting, at the predictable moment of impasse, I yelled and pounded my fist on the table. And, in fact, I was able to move the needle and get the results I wanted.

But in this period, my temper wasn't strategic—it was out of control. I was exhausted from international travel. I was under pressure to get an enormous amount done. And then I would go on diets, sometimes going weeks eating only a thousand calories a day (usually as part of a crazy bet—part of my competitive nature), and this would, I can now see, make me as irritable as a hungry child.

When in town, I dropped in on the NYC2012 office, just a few blocks from City Hall, as much as possible. Kriegel—who was driving the day-to-day NYC2012 effort forward with his special Kriegel obsessiveness, energy, and creativity—and I developed a routine of talking by phone every morning at six a.m., usually after I got to City Hall, and running down a full agenda of open bid issues, planned strategy, and objectives for the bid staff that day. Kriegel was a harder worker than I was. He was so relentless that I eventually banned him from sending messages to me between midnight and five a.m.

When I staggered off a plane returning from an Olympic-related visit to Seoul one Sunday night in May 2005, the last thing I wanted was a call from Joe Chan saying I needed to get to City Hall—immediately.

It was the night before a City Council vote on the Greenpoint-Williamsburg project. This rezoning had been far more difficult than the others. Now, on the verge of the vote we expected to win, the local City Council member, Diana Reyna, onboard up until this point, had suddenly left the room to take a phone call. When she came back, she was ashen and said she was going to pull her support—unless we came up with $1 million to support the extension of hours for a local day-care center.

It wasn't hard to read the tea leaves. The call had been from Vito Lopez, a New York Assembly member from Brooklyn and Chair of the Brooklyn Democratic Party, which still ran an old-fashioned, political machine operation. His girlfriend ran the nonprofit that operated the day-care center. Reyna had once been his chief of staff, and he was her patron. She owed her City Council seat to him. Lopez was also a thug. He would go on to be a subject of a federal corruption investigation and was censured and fined $330,000 by his own colleagues in the New York Assembly for sexually harassing young women on his staff.

As distasteful as the last-minute stickup was, we knew we had to comply. By now it was past midnight, and I was totally exhausted. But where could we get $1 million at that hour? Chan suggested I call John Mattingly, the relatively new Commissioner of the Administration for Children's Services. It was obvious that I had woken Mattingly from a deep sleep when I called.

"We've never met, and you don't work for me," I said by way of an introduction, "but I need a favor. The city needs a favor." To Mattingly's credit, he understood what was at stake and committed the money. In the end, we would never have done something corrupt, but more hours for a day-care center isn't a bad thing. And so Greenpoint-Williamsburg was approved.

Two pieces of the Brooklyn puzzle were in place.

CHAPTER FIFTEEN

PERMANENT JET LAG

LIKE A GENERAL deploying for a major military operation, I realized I was operating in numerous theaters, and they all needed to intersect to make the final drive triumphant. Whereas Jay Kriegel drove the NYC2012 efforts, my City Hall staff shouldered the day-to-day responsibility of coordinating the work of the agencies to move forward the huge volume of projects we had under way.

As a boss, I had two responsibilities—laying out the big vision and then enabling my staff to get it done. Enabling fell into two categories. The first was not being an obstacle. That meant if a decision had to be made or if an arm needed to be twisted, I had to do it quickly to avoid causing logjams. This was the era of the BlackBerry, and my staff and I made the most of it. I was on my BlackBerry as soon as I touched down overseas. When we were traveling and would get out of reach of the signal, I would get cranky and nervous. I was so addicted to the technology that I based my definition of a developed country—as opposed to a developing country—on whether I could get a signal. I remember the first time I visited Athens as a Deputy Mayor, in 2002, and it had no service. I couldn't believe a European country was this far behind. When I returned in 2004 for the Olympics, I was greatly relieved that Greece (briefly) had achieved first-world status. With Black-Berry, my staff claims, I was actually more responsive out of the country than in the country, when I was often in back-to-back meetings.

The other way we kept momentum was that my formidable, talented City Hall staff was trained to think like me. After Sharon Greenberger left in 2005 and Josh Sirefman took over as my Chief of Staff, he would tell new staffers, "Dan will want to know the following detailed set of information before we make a decision." As a result, many smaller meetings and decisions that might have slowed me down were taken care of routinely by others.

Delegating isn't always easy. You have to understand that not every decision will go exactly as you'd like. And if it doesn't, then you have to get over it. One time, Sirefman made a decision I didn't like, and I yelled at him for making the call without me. He stood up to me. "You can yell at me for a lot," he said. "You can say I made a stupid decision, but you can't yell at me for making a decision for you. I do that all the time. I make a hundred decisions for you a day." I had to agree and apologized (which I almost always did shortly after acting like a jerk).

My staff weathered the occasional tirades gamely and, in fact, bonded over the shared adversity of having to deal with me. Years later, at one of the get-togethers I periodically host for our City Hall team, someone came up with the idea of having everyone complete the following sentence: "I thought Dan was going to kill me when . . . " There were plenty of stories, most of them funny, thank goodness, like the one below:

> Dan is supposed to deliver remarks to something like the Spanish-American Chamber of Commerce. Or the US Chamber of Commerce in Spain. Or the Spanish Chamber of Commerce in the United States. I don't know. But someone at EDC decided it was essential that Dan speak to them. Did that person have any idea what he should say? No. No clue. "He'll know." Yeah, he'll know. FU. Anyway, my prep meeting to go over the remarks was cancelled, so he's now reading them for the first time, an hour before he's supposed to deliver them. Marla calls me to tell me Dan wants to see me in the bullpen. I go up. Now, it's not interesting that he's screaming questions like: "Why would anyone care about any of this?" What's interesting is that he's screaming so loud that the Mayor can't help but look over to see what the hell is going on, interrupting his conversation with Mark Page, who also feels compelled to watch. I can't help but look back at the two of them, but I quickly turn my attention back to Dan lest he actually kill me. When I sneak a look back at the Mayor, not only is he still watching, but now he's eating popcorn.

My staff members had various coping mechanisms. My assistant, Marla Pardee, who arrived by seven a.m. and was usually the first to interact with me, would take a mood reading every morning and pass it on to Sharon Greenberger. They jokingly called it the mood-o-meter. It basically came in two settings: (1) he is in a good mood, and (2) try again some other time. Pardee subsequently told me there were several occasions on which staff came to her to weigh whether they should pitch me on an idea and then walked away with the warning that now was not a good moment. Eventually, she placed a statue on her desk, and if it was facing forward it meant I was in a good mood, but if it was turned the other way, people knew to wait.

Greenberger had identified a four-part response cycle that I had to others' new ideas: (1) rejection, (2) reassessment, (3) acceptance, and (4) ownership. She joked that they could all occur within minutes. By her calling out the cycle, though, everyone was aware of it, could laugh about it, and just knew to wait me out.

My many trips and the relationships I was developing with the International Olympic Committee members left me feeling more optimistic about our chances as 2004 rolled on. Even Alex Gilady thought we were doing better. "Maybe now, you'll get fifteen votes," he suggested. That was progress. My optimism increased when in June 2004 the stadium's financial plan and initial environmental impact statement were done—and it looked like the United States Olympic Committee, one of our biggest millstones, might finally get its act together. Peter Ueberroth, the savior of the Olympic movement, was named the new USOC Chair.

Certainly, I thought, the IOC members and staff would appreciate his service to the movement. A highly respected businessperson who had gone on to become the Commissioner of Major League Baseball, he was on the board of Coca-Cola and then ran a profitable investment firm. Could there be any doubt he would help to bring order to the chaos that had been the USOC? What could be better than having him as our representative with the members, especially because it was clear by now that the three American IOC members weren't really in the inner circle and weren't prepared to really push our bid aggressively with their colleagues? As Kriegel said, "You can't win the bid without someone on the inside to lobby for you and give you inside information." Even though Ueberroth hadn't been part of the Olympic scene for a decade, I hoped he could help fill the void we felt so acutely.

Kriegel and I had flown out to Newport Beach, California, after New York had become the US candidate city in early 2003 to seek Ueberroth's advice and blessing for our bid. He received us graciously at his lovely home on a cliff overlooking the beach and the Pacific Ocean. It even turned out that I went to high school with his son-in-law. Ueberroth seemed truly supportive of our bid. He pledged to do everything he could to help. He did give us one major piece of advice. The IOC, he said, would keep making demands on us if we won the bid. "The only way to deal with them was to stand up to them from the beginning." It was sobering, but our concern at that point was winning the bid, and Ueberroth had not run the Los Angeles bid; he had been hired to run the Games after Los Angeles was selected. Sadly, our visit in early 2003 was the high point. Almost nothing turned out the way I had expected. None of the things we hoped to get from Ueberroth panned out. He was not an asset with IOC members. Rather than being grateful, they saw Ueberroth as the symbol of USOC greed because he had been the one to negotiate the deal that still gave (and would in perpetuity) the USOC a share of the US television rights deals and TOP sponsorship dollars. In turn, I suspected he was bitter that the IOC members didn't appreciate how much he had done to save the Games.

I had spent enough time with members of the IOC to appreciate that even a modest concession by the USOC on the deal Ueberroth had cut twenty years before would be a huge plus for us by demonstrating the respect from the United States that members craved. Several months after he was appointed USOC chair, he was in New York for an Olympics-related dinner I attended as well. I asked if we could talk privately after dinner. We went upstairs to his grand suite at the Waldorf. I pleaded with him to make at least face-saving concessions to the IOC, arguing that even a modest change would make a huge difference. He was polite and promised he would help. But he never did. I can't explain why. Maybe he considered the IOC members' desire for even modest changes a personal affront. Maybe he just thought a deal was a deal. In fact, for the entire six years he was USOC Chair, there was no progress on a deal with the IOC. Two years after he stepped down, his successor, Larry Probst, and the CEO of the USOC, Scott Blackmun, cut just the kind of deal I had been advocating. They made very minor concessions, and it completely changed for the better the relationship between the USOC and the IOC.

Our own relationship with the USOC went from not good to worse. A few months after we became the US candidate city, as the USOC kept asking for information and seemed distrustful, Kriegel proposed that the USOC place a staffer full time in our offices to act as liaison. It was a difficult challenge. Chris Sullivan did it with ease and skill, having full access to all of our activities, and quickly became a valuable, fully integrated member of our team. After Ueberroth became Chair, the demands for information and the attempts to exercise control increased.

We pushed back. We weren't getting enough value from the half-baked USOC efforts on our behalf (let alone from the 15 percent surcharge on all our fundraising the USOC was still charging us) to cede more control. The USOC had virtually no international relations staff, little presence or stature in Lausanne or at IOC events, and virtually no knowledge of or intelligence about IOC members. Frankly, this was startling and put us at a huge disadvantage compared with our competition.

Ueberroth, the savior of the Olympic movement, must have felt affronted. Kriegel learned later, when Chicago was bidding for the 2016 Games, that Ueberroth specifically complained about NYC2012, saying, "We're never going to let happen what happened with New York. Guys that went off on their own. We want to know everything; we want to control the bid." (Chicago was the first city eliminated in the IOC vote in 2009, which was won by Rio de Janeiro.)

Meanwhile, serious questions had suddenly arisen about the centerpiece of our plan—the stadium.

CHAPTER SIXTEEN

WEST SIDE STORY

JUST A FEW months earlier, everything had seemed on track. With klieg lights swirling outside to give the event the dramatic flair of a cinematic debut, Mayor Mike Bloomberg joined Governor George Pataki, Woody Johnson, and a cast of public officials and civic leaders at the Javits Center on March 26, 2004, to make a formal presentation to the public of the New York Sports and Convention Center and the expansion of the Javits Center.

We had conquered a series of obstacles to reach this point, and this was to be a triumphant moment. The hotels and labor unions had been persuaded to support the full project, including the West Side Stadium, in part by including a long-sought expansion of what everyone knew was an inadequate convention facility. We had used an innovative financing plan to generate the money to build the subway extension and convinced the skeptical and conservative budget watchdogs that the strategy was sound. We had made progress on rezoning the entire forty-five-block area around the stadium, galvanizing astonishingly consistent support for such a massive reimagining. And so far we had survived growing "local" opposition, even though it was being fanned and apparently financed by CEO of Madison Square Garden (MSG) James "Jimmy" Dolan.

On this last front, there was cause for concern. Dolan was so opposed to the stadium that the night before the announcement, he actually had called the Governor and made an explicit threat: "If you go forward on this, we are going to go nuclear. We are going to become enemies."

Charles Bagli, the longtime real-estate reporter at the *New York Times*, described the unveiling as follows: "The event was a result of the single-mindedness and perhaps the naïveté of the deputy mayor for economic development, Daniel L. Doctoroff. The stadium and convention center expansion are the crucial components of the city's bid for the 2012 Olympics, which Mr. Doctoroff cobbled together before he entered city government. He has sought to ram them through the usual political and economic barriers like a fast-moving train, but he still has a long way to go. The announcement yesterday was his way of saying the train was leaving the station." On the last point, at least, Bagli was dead on. Although I should have been proud to reach this day after nearly ten years against all odds, I was deeply anxious. We had less than a year before a team of IOC evaluators would make its site visit to New York to inspect all of our venue sites and assess our plans, and I was determined to have an approved and financed stadium agreement to show it.

The Jets addressed the assembled media and laid out their plan for the stadium. It seemed like a design that could inspire pride in every New Yorker. Jay Cross and his team of architects and engineers, led by Kohn Pedersen Fox Associates, had designed a brilliantly luminous box, rising against the Hudson River, that would become one of the most flexible and technologically advanced stadiums in the world. Its signature visual feature was a glass-veil facade—the first of its kind—that had chameleon-like properties because it could be adjusted to let light filter through in varying intensities, creating effects that ran the gamut from opaque to transparent.

Beyond its glistening exterior, it was also a magical testament to adaptability: the roof could retract or close, and all the seating and flooring could be completely moved out or rearranged within a twenty-four-hour period, allowing it to accommodate a football game on Sunday, a floor show for a plastics convention on Tuesday, and then plenary seating for all eighteen thousand attendees of the Scientific Sessions of the American Heart Association the next week. The building could even be configured to host the Final Four, which had long since moved out of traditional basketball arenas. As the design evolved, the integration into an expanded Javits Center became even more complete. The NYSCC would have even more meeting rooms, and the connection to the Javits Center under 34th Street would be even more seamless. The Javits Center itself would double in size, expanding to the north by two blocks and to the south by one block.

The new stadium elegantly solved the problem of meeting the Olympic requirement for a wider field to accommodate track-and-field dimensions by constructing a temporary section of the stadium on its west end on top of a temporary platform over the West Side Highway. When the Games were finished, the temporary part of the stadium would be torn down, and the permanent glass facade would enable beautiful vistas of the river. It was incredibly creative and iconic.

The cost of the stadium was estimated at $1.4 billion. Under the city and state agreement with the Jets, which we detailed that day, the team would pay $800 million to build the stadium and fund convention improvements. The city and state would each contribute $300 million, which would fund what we called infrastructure. This included $375 million for the platform over the railyards and $200 million for the roof, which we reasoned made it possible for the NYSCC to be used as a convention facility (after all, the Jets didn't need a roof to play). The way we saw it, the Jets were going to pay $800 million toward the cost of an expanded convention center and would get the right to use the building for football ten days a year (or more in the unlikely event they made the playoffs!). All in all, it seemed to me as if the city had cleverly gotten the maximum leverage from its public investment dollars to encourage the private sector to finance a major part of an expanded convention center. Significantly, the Jets agreed to fund any cost overruns, which would become meaningful over the course of the next year, when the costs would balloon to $2 billion.

Yet by the time we made the announcement in 2004, we were already running a rearguard action. Our opponents had started organizing years earlier, and we had been to some extent lulled into complacency. The opposition was being led by Dolan. Charles "Chuck" Dolan, Jimmy's father, was a tough but respected businessperson who built a cable empire worth billions. He had been a cable pioneer, wiring buildings in New York, helping to found HBO, and negotiating to show sports and live music events to subscribers long before anyone else did. Gradually, he built a cable monopoly business in part of the city, Long Island, and eventually nineteen states. He used his fortune to purchase Madison Square Garden and the New York Knicks and Rangers.

In 1995, Charles Dolan handed the leadership of the company to one of his sons, James. Unlike his steady, midwestern-bred father, Jimmy was erratic and explosive. A guy who seemed to get more pleasure from playing rock music than running his company, Jimmy was widely disliked. He picked fights with content providers, such as Fox and Disney, that left city residents under constant threat of being blacked out of major events such as the Super Bowl and the Academy Awards. He was despised for meddling with the Knicks, who never won a championship under his leadership. But most concerning were the legendary tales of his screaming at employees, alienating talent, and generally having tantrums.

From the start, everyone knew that the Dolans might be trouble because of the perceived competition the NYSCC might pose to Madison Square Garden and other MSG-owned properties such as Radio City Music Hall. So there were efforts to co-opt them. And for two years we thought they were working. When the Giuliani Administration first put together its framework for the development of the Far West Side, a new MSG was included.

The Dolans had been talking about the need to update MSG for a long time, but whether they really wanted to move was unclear. When Cross first released sketches for the West Side Stadium, he got a call from one of the Dolans' underlings who said he had seen the plans and noticed that the Jets were on the Hudson and MSG was inland. "You know Jimmy is a water guy," he told Cross, referring to the younger Dolan's penchant for racing sailboats. Cross said, "No problem—we can make the switch." But the associate balked. Being closer to the water puts us farther from the subway, he said. So what did the Dolans want? Unclear. Perhaps only to muddy the picture.

Still, Cross and the Jets were not to be put off. They had another idea. What if money were no object, and you could build a stadium that accommodated three sports: football, hockey, and basketball? In this scenario, the Jets, Knicks, and Rangers would all play in the same facility. Concerts and smaller events would be run out of a new MSG, and the Dolans' MSG group would manage the whole thing—bringing it a handsome new source of revenue.

So eager was Johnson to extract the Jets from being the Giants' tenant in the Meadowlands that in the summer of 2001 he flew to Sardinia, Italy, to meet with Jimmy Dolan, who was racing his seventy-eight-foot yacht *Sagamore* at the Maxi Worlds, to propose creating a company called TriSports to manage the three sports teams. Johnson even raced on the boat for a day. Dolan sounded interested and sent a team of his people to Japan with Cross to visit a stadium that could convert from a soccer field into a basketball court along with a venue for other indoor sports.

No one knew if Jimmy Dolan was really considering any of these proposals or just making nice with the Jets in hopes that the Olympic bid would collapse of its own weight and, with it, the Jets' hopes of relocating to Manhattan. But after New York won the United States Olympic Committee competition to represent our country in 2002, the Dolans must have realized we were not going away. The next spring, Dolan called Bloomberg and said, "You're killing me," as if he hadn't really thought we were serious. Bloomberg responded: "Jimmy, I've been telling you all along. We're going to build this."

In the summer of 2003, after dragging his feet on the joint proposal, Dolan invited Cross and Johnson to meet with him at MSG. He announced that he was bowing out of any discussions of a joint venture and was going to focus on renovating MSG in place because he didn't feel he could count on the No. 7 subway being delivered. According to Cross, he said, "We've looked at it all. We have just concluded it is not for us. If there is anything we can do to help you with your stadium, let us know. Good luck."

Good luck? In fact, Jimmy Dolan was preparing to wage war. As he cheerfully admitted months later on a call-in radio show to a listener who questioned him about his opposition to the stadium, "I am a monopolist." MSG is the only entertainment/sports venue of any significant size in Manhattan, and it is sitting atop great transportation. Jimmy Dolan didn't want to give the competition—even a stadium meant for events up to three times the size of what MSG could host—the slightest shot.

By then, Jimmy Dolan had hired lobbyists already working behind the scenes to sink the stadium, if need be. Lobbyist number one was Patricia Lynch. Lynch had been Sheldon "Shelly" Silver's Press Secretary. When she left with Silver's blessing, she started a lobbying and communications firm on her own. Largely leveraging her connections to him, in just two years Patricia Lynch Associates grew to be the third most active lobbying firm in Albany.

There were always rumors that Lynch and Silver, the pious family man, had an unusually close relationship. When Silver was indicted years later, prosecutors would report that he had two longtime mistresses in Albany. Lynch was identified by many in the press as one of them.

We would later hire Lynch to help us get equally controversial legislation (on congestion pricing) passed in Albany. (If you can't beat 'em, join 'em.) I came to admire her. In reflecting on the stadium battle, she said our biggest mistake was not understanding that Albany would be involved and not putting all our focus on Silver and Joe Bruno, the Majority Leader in the New York Senate.

In addition to Lynch, Dolan had a team of other lobbyists plus an extensive political campaign team doing research, polling, public relations, and media. Her role was not just to handle Silver; her job was to drive public opinion against us to give the legislators cover if they voted no. She and the team were effective. Long before we publicly unveiled the stadium in 2004, they had conducted in-depth polling throughout the New York Metro area. She found that there was no particular groundswell of support for the stadium but that people were essentially neutral to positive. However, they found two themes they could exploit that could turn that lukewarm support into anger and resistance. First, the stadium would bring traffic and congestion; second, and, more importantly, the city and state contributions to the stadium amounted to tax subsidies for a rich team owner. Now, as it happened, in the ten years the Dolans had owned MSG, they had paid no real-estate taxes, which amounted to essentially an $80 million subsidy. But by getting out in front of us, Lynch and her team earned a big advantage in defining the debate.

Bloomberg and I were not in full battle mode yet in 2003, but we were aware the Dolans had objections, and their opposition to the stadium was growing. At the end of 2003, we decided to see if a little diplomacy might work. Bloomberg invited Jimmy and Chuck Dolan to have breakfast with us at Gracie Mansion to see if we could make some sort of a deal. Chuck played the indulgent father who couldn't control his impassioned son. The only thing that would placate Jimmy was if we got rid of the retractable roof and made the stadium open air.

I explained that this was impossible. The biggest problem was that we had secured an agreement with the hotel industry and the hotel workers' union to support an increase in the room tax to help fund an expansion of the "Javits convention corridor." The retractable-roof stadium was essential to making the Javits Center more competitive. Most importantly, we suspected that much of the support for putting a stadium on a valuable piece of land on the West Side of Manhattan would vanish if it were only going to be used ten days a year for football, plus the few concerts that could fill an open-air stadium. Jimmy was angry, and we were unyielding. It ended badly.

We both returned to our corners and began building our armies. The Dolans added to their lobbying team. In addition to Lynch, they brought on the Glover Park Group, a well-respected public strategy group. Glover Park was particularly well connected with the *New York Times,* and, sadly for us, it would prove to be influential with the paper's editorial board. The team was led by Howard Wolfson, an experienced Democratic campaigner who worked against Bloomberg's first reelection campaign in 2005 but then for him in his 2009 campaign, and then joined his City Hall team as Deputy Mayor. He still works for him today.

Although we didn't know it until later, fatefully, they also enlisted former New York Senator Al D'Amato to their team and hired Bruno's son as a lobbyist. We never even thought to bring in outside lobbyists, let alone a former "close associate" of the Speaker, a former Senator, and the son of the Senate Majority Leader. They had put together quite a team of heavyweights with Albany influence. We were outgunned before we even started.

But the truth is, way before the Gracie Mansion breakfast with the Dolans we had already shot ourselves in the head, and we didn't even realize it. As we were negotiating the financing of the stadium early in 2003 we wrestled with a crucial question: How would the state come up with the $300 million the Governor had committed? We were assured that at the end of the day Governor Pataki would find a way to slip a few hundred million dollars through the budget process negotiations.

The real issue, the Governor's point person on the stadium, Adam Barsky, alerted us, was whether the MTA lease of the air rights over the western railyards would require the approval of an obscure board called the Public Authorities Control Board (PACB). Created in 1976 to monitor a plethora of new debt being created by government, the law creating the PACB mandated that eleven statewide public authorities must receive a resolution of approval from PACB prior to entering into any project-related financing. One of the eleven agencies was the MTA. The board was created nobly enough to prevent petty corruption and financial overreaching by unmonitored authorities. But, as in so many cases, its purpose had been perverted. It had become just another way to centralize power.

At that time, the board only had three voters. Guess who? The same big three who ran everything in Albany: the Governor, the Assembly Speaker (Silver), and the Senate Majority Leader (Bruno). And here was the real catch. The approval had to be unanimous. We couldn't just get two out of three. Any one of them could kill the whole thing. Barsky consulted the state's lawyers and came back with the answer: the MTA had the legal power to build the platform without PACB approval. The Governor could force that through the MTA Board, he said.

In retrospect, this is probably where my political naiveté was a massive liability. In advising us to bypass the PACB, did the Governor's staffers really believe this could be accomplished, or were they saying to just go ahead and try it? Did they just say what we wanted to hear—something for which the Governor was famous? There was certainly no piece of paper, no signed agreement, no plan that formally told us we could move forward in this way.

To this day, Barsky insists that no PACB approval was needed. When asked recently, he replied, "Even MTA counsel confirmed to me that they could legally do it without the PACB."

Armed with this opinion from the Governor, I made a bumbling move. As our plans for the Jets stadium, the Javits Center, and the rezoning of Hudson Yards were being firmed up, in late 2003 I decided to make a goodwill tour in Albany to show off the proposals. The response was mostly supportive, but there was some pushback. At least one Assembly member asked in some form, "What if we don't want a stadium on MTA land?" Here I was dumb. I basically said that we did not need the legislature for this; we were just making a courtesy visit. As I would learn, showing disrespect to a legislator (or worse, a group of them), especially one as disempowered as they are in Albany, is never a smart move. We would hear "But you said you didn't need us" repeatedly throughout the next two years as the battle over the stadium intensified.

After we finished the press conference at the Javits Center, I felt soothed. The design and presentation had been so compelling I convinced myself we could overcome the Dolans' objections. But just a few weeks later, in a meeting in City Hall, Barsky dropped a bomb. We would not be able to get around the PACB as he had previously opined. The lawyers had reversed their opinion. I was stunned. Our whole strategy had been predicated on that one assumption.

Even in our state of shock, we began discussing our PACB strategy. Barsky said the Governor could deliver two votes at the PACB (the Governor and Bruno), but we were responsible for delivering Silver. All roads led back to Silver, the very outcome we had tried desperately to avoid.

What had really happened? Years later I learned from Barsky that the Chair of the MTA, real-estate developer Peter Kalikow, appointed by the Governor, had never been enthusiastic about the strategy of avoiding the PACB. He was being pressured by D'Amato, with whom he was close (and who had been retained by the Dolans), to push back on the Governor. Barsky maintains that if the Governor had directly influenced Kalikow, he would have relented, but that the Governor's office had decided "that going the PACB route would be the approach since there wasn't a desire to push the MTA." We had been screwed by the Governor and never really knew it. Albany is a hall of mirrors.

So now we understood what our opponents had understood for two years before us: we were fighting on two fronts. The first and ultimate battle was the war for approval from Silver and Bruno. There would be three men in the room. We had only one on our side so far. The second battle was for the hearts and minds of the public. Our big hope was to build such overwhelming popular support and a broad enough political coalition that Silver and Bruno wouldn't be able to say no regardless of what they really wanted.

At the beginning, Silver's position on the stadium had been unclear. He seemed neutral, open to persuasion. We started off on good terms. When my father passed away in July 2002, he came to the shiva at my house. A minor gesture, perhaps, but a sign of respect. By 2004, the picture had changed. We knew that Silver was our biggest problem on the board of three. At the time of the Javits Center announcement in March 2004, he told the *New York Times* that he had "serious concerns and reservations" about the stadium. Most of his rhetoric focused on whether we were ignoring the rebuilding of Lower Manhattan in our drive to develop the Far West Side.

Of course, we suspected a backstory as well. Not only was it known that Lynch and Silver had a deep personal and professional bond but it was also known that Silver had a special relationship with MSG. He was a passionate New York Rangers hockey fan, and he was often seen attending games. He reportedly got free tickets to Rangers games, and whenever he attended, MSG employees stocked the suite reserved for special guests, Suite 200, with kosher food just for him. A year after the stadium battle had ended, Cablevision, the parent company of MSG, contributed $500,000 to support a ballot initiative advocated by Silver and Bruno that would shift the balance of power in Albany from the Governor to the legislative branch. We didn't know that at the time, of course.

Even though we started way behind, I can say that under the inspired leadership of Matt Higgins, who now worked for the Jets, and Jim Whelan, the experienced political hand I had brought onto our team to "wake up every day obsessed with how we win this thing," we pulled ourselves together and ran an aggressive, two-pronged strategy to influence Silver and Bruno directly and to build a formidable political coalition to pressure them indirectly.

To keep the unions motivated and on our side, I must have done presentations at a dozen meetings of the local branches of the construction trade unions. Some, such as one for the carpenters' local, would draw hundreds of members. They were our biggest boosters, and despite (or maybe because of) the sometimes boisterous and uninhibited nature of the meetings, I really enjoyed them.

We also built deep support in minority communities throughout the city. Early on, I went to Charles Rangel, the powerful US representative who had represented his Harlem district for three decades, and asked what he would need to support our efforts. Rangel was concerned that minority contractors and minority workers get their fair share of the jobs. So we did two things. First, the Jets did a great job in building a Minority- and Women-Owned Business Enterprise plan for contracts for both construction and ongoing maintenance of the stadium. For our part, the Mayor met with Rangel and agreed to create a Commission on Construction Opportunity, in which the city and the trade unions would work together to assure greater access to jobs on all construction projects across the city for minorities, women, and veterans by reserving prized apprentice slots for them and by setting goals for outreach and recruitment. We didn't get it up and running until the fall of 2005, but the promise was enough to get Rangel on our side. He was a frequent presence at rallies and a great spokesperson to the press.

Our team also put the full-court press on city and state politicians outside of Manhattan, many of whose constituents loved the Jets and the jobs that would be created and couldn't care less about traffic on 34th Street. Johnson himself made several trips to court politicians in the Bronx and Queens. He even ate at a White Castle on Webster Avenue. Bloomberg also began a full-court charm offensive on Silver. He attended a Hanukkah ceremony at a Midtown deli, paid a condolence call when the Speaker's brother passed away, and attended the brises (the Jewish circumcision ceremony) for two of Silver's grandsons.

It wasn't all window dressing either. We tried earnestly to listen to Silver's concerns about Lower Manhattan. Bloomberg was willing to roll back commercial taxes downtown and stretch employment credits. He offered five dollars per square foot off the rents of tenants who moved into the Freedom Tower and Seven World Trade Center and was willing to entertain the idea of holding off on extending incentives to developers in Hudson Yards until the Lower Manhattan towers were largely leased.

But Silver would never engage. He was a master of deflection. When my staff would make the ritual pilgrimage to his office, genuflect, and ask what he wanted to help Lower Manhattan, he would look out his window and point to Ground Zero and make some comment about all the lives lost and how we needed to rebuild. But he skillfully avoided any specifics.

Meanwhile, by the end of 2004, the public battle started to get nasty. The Dolans had begun advertising on television, targeting Bloomberg personally. It's hard to know exactly how much they spent—but it must have been tens of millions of dollars. Lynch says they spent $24 million on paid media—television, print, and radio. But that does not include the ads that ran incessantly on MSG's own cable channel or the money spent to support so-called grassroots opposition, such as the Hell's Kitchen/Hudson Yards Alliance, or the money spent on lobbyists such as Lynch. It has been estimated that they spent or benefited from at least $50 million in media or political influence. In addition, Cablevision would not accept the Jets' ads, which led them to hire high-powered litigator David Boies to sue Cablevision on antitrust grounds. The gloves were definitely off.

In 2005, Bloomberg was up for reelection. In light of his later popularity, it is hard to remember how vulnerable he was in 2004 and early 2005. We had started so many things but had few concrete accomplishments to tout. The economy was recovering but still weak. He had raised taxes and imposed the smoking ban, which wasn't popular yet. And, as the countdown to the 2005 mayoral election reached a year, there was a muscular field of Democratic candidates, the strongest of which was Fernando Ferrer, a former Bronx Borough President who had strong ties to the city's large Latino/a community. In February and March 2005, Ferrer, who had not yet clinched his party's nomination, was consistently polling four to eight points ahead of Bloomberg. Ferrer had made opposition to the stadium a centerpiece of his campaign.

As the Dolans launched ever more vitriolic and personal ads, the Mayor's popularity in the polls sank further. The theme the MSG team had identified—the city helping a rich guy (or the 1 percent against the 99 percent)—had indeed resonated with the voters. Many of the ads were not only unsubstantiated but also fabricated, yet they were hurting us nonetheless.

One ad showed sewage pouring into the Hudson River and claimed that this is what the stadium would do. Another ad showed billboards with children who were not able to attend school because public monies were being diverted to a stadium. Another showed Bloomberg as a bobble-head doll just nodding in agreement with anything Johnson wanted. "So here's the choice," the announcer would darkly intone at the end of each ad. "Invest $600 million in neighborhoods, or spend it on a West Side Stadium for the Jets." (In reality, even the Independent Budget Office, a publicly funded agency of the city that provides nonpartisan analysis of city budget issues, opined that the NYSCC would earn a positive return on the city's investment.) The ads weren't their only line of attack. In the winter of 2004–2005, the Dolans filed two lawsuits claiming that our environmental review of the Far West Side was flawed. Both were eventually beaten back, but they were a distraction.

Our strategy was to build so much support for the Olympics and the stadium that Silver couldn't comfortably say no. We wanted to corner him so he would be solely responsible for sinking the Olympic bid. The newspapers in the city were a critical part of that strategy. We had the full support of the *New York Post* and the *New York Daily News*, but the *New York Times* was a completely different story. The *New York Times* was the paper Silver's more active and affluent constituents primarily read and was influential among the members of his caucus. In Manhattan, in local elections, an endorsement from the *New York Times* is like gold.

So few voters even know their elected officials that they tend to look to see whom the *New York Times* is supporting. Conversely, candidates or elected officials are leery of taking positions that contradict those of the paper's editorial board. There were very few issues about which the *New York Times* editors felt more strongly than a stadium on the Far West Side of Manhattan. When the paper of record first editorialized about the proposed West Side Stadium in 1999 in response to Giuliani's State of the City Address, it was slightly positive. By the time we were ready with a preliminary version of the plan four years later, it told a completely different story.

In March 2003, Jay Kriegel, Cross, and I went in to make a presentation to *New York Times* Publisher Arthur Sulzberger Jr., its editorial board, and a group of interested reporters. There must have been twenty people in the cramped conference room at the paper's shabby headquarters on West 43rd Street. We brought a wooden model of the entire Hudson Yards area that showed all of the development that would take place if the investments we were proposing, including the No. 7 subway line extension, the NYSCC, and the expanded convention center, were made. Even before we could launch into our presentation, Sulzberger got up from his chair, walked over to the model, pointed to the NYSCC, and started asking in a dismissive tone questions about the traffic generated by a "football stadium," about why we should dedicate valuable land on the waterfront to a "football stadium." We tried to explain that this was not just a football stadium and that the NYSCC was going to add unique competitive features to a new Javits Center, of which the *New York Times* had been supportive (the editors had never complained about the Javits Center taking up valuable space—seven blocks—along the waterfront), but to no avail. No matter how hard we tried to bring the conversation back to a discussion about the broader plan, the economic impact on the city, and the subway, we could not deter him. Soon enough, most of the others in the room piled on.

Within a week or two, the *New York Times* ran the editorial "Midtown's Final Frontier." After nodding to the big Hudson Yards plan, it then focused on the "multiuse facility," eventually concluding, "No one wants a publicly financed hulk that sits empty most of the time and floods the city with traffic when it is being used." What had happened to the *New York Times'* lukewarm support of the idea between the time Giuliani first made it public in 1999 and 2003? Hard to say. It couldn't have been the building itself—it had only gotten better and more integrated into the Javits Center, the expansion of which the editorial extolled. We hadn't even talked about the financing of it yet.

From that moment, we felt a very different attitude toward the stadium at the *New York Times,* and not just on the editorial page. It was almost as if Sulzberger had given a hunting license to the rest of its staff. The coverage turned decidedly negative, especially by the influential reporter Charles Bagli, who had been so effusive at the USOC meeting in Colorado Springs. I didn't help my cause when he asked about rumors of an upcoming announcement (where we first publicly presented the NYSCC and the Javits Center extension in March 2004) and I misled him. A very stupid move. From that point on our relationship would turn hostile, culminating in his months-long investigation of possible conflicts in my relationship with Stephen Ross, one of the city's leading developers. There was nothing, but that didn't stop the *New York Times* from running it on the front page.

By December 4, 2004, the paper ran the very unusual, page-long editorial "Stop the Stadium in Its Tracks." The editorial board said it supported the Olympic bid and the notion that the Games could be used to boost the city's infrastructure, yet felt we were going about it the wrong way. "To argue that in order to get the Games, the city must use one of its most valuable waterfront sites to build a huge, ugly stadium for eight football games a year turns that rationale backward," the editorial concluded. The negative *New York Times* coverage gave air cover for Silver as we headed into the final months of the stadium battle.

I have a high tolerance for working hard, but as 2005 dawned, I was nearing my break point. In addition to the two major rezonings we were tackling on the West Side, we had dozens of other projects under way, and I was also traveling nearly nonstop to promote our Olympic bid. In the eight weeks after we sent out our bid book to the IOC members in November 2004, I traveled to Dubrovnik, Vienna, Amsterdam, Paris, London, Lausanne, Turin, and Budapest. What I began to find, much to my despair, was that the Dolan campaign at home was beginning to sow seeds of doubt about our bid abroad. Whenever I attended an international or IOC event, reporters and IOC members peppered me with questions about whether we could really get approval for the stadium. I was always positive, but the stress of not really knowing was ripping me up inside.

In February 2005 we faced one of our biggest tests: the IOC had scheduled its Site Evaluation Commission visit. We began preparing like crazy—but the Dolans were watching the calendar as well. They understood that bringing the Olympics to New York was still a very popular idea. It's one thing to kill a stadium for the Jets but entirely another to destroy a city's Olympic dreams—the corner into which we had been trying to paint them. By early 2005, they switched their ad strategy. They were no longer solely attacking the Mayor. They were now also denying the possibility that the city could win the Olympics.

"Don't let them twist the truth," one of their new ads began. "No matter what they say, no matter how hard they push to spend more than a billion tax dollars, it's a football stadium, not an Olympic stadium. That's the truth. Say no to a West Side stadium."

Then on February 4, just two weeks before the IOC site visit to New York, the Dolans made their most diabolical move yet. They surprised us with a completely unsolicited bid of $600 million for the air rights above the MTA railyard, including over the western railyard, where we wanted to build the stadium. The MTA and the Jets had been discussing a $100 million price tag (for just the western railyard).

To insiders, the Dolans' bid was clearly not serious. Their vague proposal claimed that Cablevision would develop a "dynamic, mixed-use community, including a hotel, housing, recreation and entertainment and office space." Beyond that, there were no specifics. The bid estimated the deck would cost $250 million, which might have paid for a part of the deck for a relatively simple (from an engineering perspective) stadium, but we knew from the estimates of the mixed-use community we planned to build over the eastern railyard that it would cost multiples of that to support a series of residential and commercial towers. The extension of the No. 7 subway was the key piece of the puzzle, which would unlock the value of a mixed-use community. The Dolans said nothing about that. But from a public relations standpoint the move was clever. Already resentment simmered within the MTA that the agency was not allowed to put its valuable air rights up for an open bid despite the fact that the city was paying for the $2 billion subway extension. But to the public and to the papers that didn't understand our complex weaving of the many components of our plan compared with Cablevision's cartoonish version, the fight made delicious headlines.

Months later, the MTA would reject the Dolan bid for the empty promise that it was, but in the meantime tremendous damage had been done. That might have thrown me into a tailspin of despair if my staff had not been so incredible. Every time we took a blow, it seemed they bounced back stronger than ever. The IOC visit was no exception.

We planned for the IOC visit as if it were a full military engagement. We had the schedule down to the minute: the IOC Site Evaluation Commission arrived on a Sunday evening at JFK Airport, and we had precisely twenty-seven minutes to get its members to the Plaza Hotel. For people who don't know New York geography or traffic, traveling between those two spots in such time is possible only during rare circumstances such as a Super Bowl or Christmas Eve, when 90 percent of all people stay home. After whisking them through customs, with the help of both the State Department and the Port Authority, our plan was to make it happen without it looking like our government was taking any extraordinary measures to change the way the city normally functioned.

At the appointed time, we took a bus to the airport to greet our guests. Out of the window, I could see that the traffic going in the opposite direction on the Van Wyck Expressway, which cuts north–south connecting the airport and the Long Island Expressway, was bumper to bumper. I glanced at Joe Chan, my City Hall staffer charged with coordinating with our NYC2012 team. He was on the phone sounding frantic. I tried hard to stay calm.

We picked up our guests and, like some magic spell had been cast, the highway moved beautifully. There was a little traffic both in front and in back of us but nothing to stop us from gliding effortlessly into Midtown and then to the hotel. Behind the scenes, however, we were getting help from the traffic control wizards at the New York Police Department, strategically blocking off ramps and letting through only enough cars to maintain the ambience of normality. My apologies to the other drivers that night, but this one was for the city.

That was a glorious moment, and in many ways it set the tone for a visit the team later said felt enchanted. It was February, and there was light snow on the ground. Our headquarters was in the famously elegant Plaza Hotel on Central Park South. By complete coincidence, the artist Christo, famous for draping famous landmarks such as the Reichstag and the Pont-Neuf, had a massive public art installation all through Central Park called "The Gates."

Brilliant, saffron-colored cloth across the seven thousand–plus gates lining the park's pathways could be seen from every window in the plaza. And the enormous crowds who flocked to walk through "The Gates" animated the park with energy and excitement.

Every one of the meetings and events we planned had just the right dusting of pizazz. We took the commission to more than a dozen potential venues—from those that existed to those that needed to be built—in all five boroughs. There was a pep rally at Rockefeller Center on Monday and sports events such as a five-kilometer run through Central Park as well as demonstrations of gymnastics, fencing, judo, field hockey, and other sports throughout the boroughs. Everywhere we went the city's diversity was on display as we hit home our theme: "New York Is the World's Second Home."

We were allowed to entertain the delegates for only one night. Our competing cities gave them dinner with royalty—Queen Elizabeth for London and King Juan Carlos and Queen Sofia for Madrid. (I told reporters who asked how we could compete with that, "We did go to Queens yesterday.") We gave them the full Broadway treatment. Horse-drawn carriages picked them up at the Plaza and took them to a private concert at the brand-new Jazz at Lincoln Center at the Time Warner Center.

Meryl Streep, Barbara Walters, and Olympic gymnast Nadia Comaneci gave short speeches on why New York was special. Comedian Whoopi Goldberg then said: "What's great about my city is that it's a microcosm of the Olympics. We have Asian people making pizza. And Italian people making soul food. You don't see that anywhere else. We are the world. We truly are."

Then jazz legend Wynton Marsalis headlined a musical performance that included Broadway singers, clips of New York–themed movies, and then a dance show "New York: Let the Dreams Begin." At the end, a giant curtain covering the fifty-by-ninety-foot wall of glass behind the stage dropped to reveal a view of Central Park with the Manhattan skyline in the back. A sign of flashing lightbulbs that read "NYC 2012" then descended into view, and gold-colored fireworks lit up Columbus Circle and the night behind it.

Afterward, the crowd was invited to Bloomberg's townhouse to mingle with Matt Damon, Henry Kissinger, and Vera Wang. We served cookies in the shape of the Statue of Liberty, and then Paul Simon performed a mini-concert where all the guests sang along to his globally recognizable tunes. It was a pretty spectacular event start to finish.

The delegates seemed wowed. The IOC team included the World Sailing (the sailing IF) President Paul Henderson, a close friend of Cross's.

Henderson had been to every Olympics since 1964 as a sailor, a coach, or a manager and had led Toronto's unsuccessful 1996 Olympic bid. He told Cross he had never seen such an inspired plan that fully integrated the venues and athletes into a great city. He felt that the athletes' experiences would be amazing.

However, the Dolans' interference in our stadium plans did raise concerns. The press had a field day peppering Kriegel about tension between the Dolans and the Mayor. Kriegel smoothly (if not completely convincingly) glossed over it, insisting we had a "wonderful" and "cooperative" relationship. In fact, the IOC Site Evaluation Commission had visited Madison Square Garden, where the leadership (not including Jimmy Dolan) had been gracious hosts.

But what neither Kriegel, nor I, nor the Mayor could gloss over was the uncertainty planted in the minds of the Site Evaluation Commission members. We were asked about the stadium incessantly at press stops. "We need a stadium," Site Evaluation Commission Chair Nawal El Moutawakel of Morocco concluded simply on her last day in town. All the other bidding cities had stadiums except London—and London had an approved plan for building one.

After the IOC Site Evaluation Commission left, I got back to work, but I was struggling. I was exhausted from travel and overwork. I had begun waking up frequently during the night beginning in mid-2004, and between the lack of sleep at home and the frequent overseas trips, I felt like I was jet-lagged all of the time. What made this period especially difficult was that I could not share my gnawing anxieties with anyone except Kriegel. I felt that, as the leader of the team, I had to hide all my concerns. Any show of weakness, I believed, would undermine everyone else's confidence and energy. My isolation even spread to my home. I withdrew into myself, which Alisa rightfully resented. We both would describe that period as the most difficult in what has otherwise been a wonderful thirty-five-year marriage.

We had entered Harvard at the same time, and I had spotted her on the second day. Back then Harvard had an antiquated custom of requiring a swim test for all incoming freshmen. As I was standing in line by the pool, I spied a tall, thin girl chatting easily with some friends. Even wearing a swim cap and bathed in fluorescent pool light, she still somehow managed to be stunning. It would take six months until I got up the courage to ask her for a date. We went to a local French restaurant and sat and talked for hours. I was instantly in love. I knew that one day I would marry her. Just a year after graduation we were married, and through moves to Chicago and New York, various career decisions, the deaths of my parents, and raising our three great kids, we had been completely supportive of each other. Until that year.

Alisa felt that even when I was home I was not present. I countered, unfairly, that she did not show enough sympathy as I was sinking under the weight of all I was trying to do. Since college, she had been my anchor, and now, for the first time, we were not communicating. I felt very much out on a long limb myself. We even found the time to go to marriage counseling for the first and only time. It didn't help much, but the psychologist did give me a useful trick for falling back to sleep. Flex your feet and count backward by threes from one hundred, she said. We only went about five times and then decided to just wait out the IOC decision, which would come in six months or so.

Meanwhile, the ad attacks on the stadium were now clearly a political liability. On March 3, the *New York Post* ran one of its classic, screaming headlines: "Stadium Dragging Mike Down in the Polls." A new poll showed Bloomberg was now down nearly ten points in a head-to-head race with Ferrer. His approval rating was falling, and his negatives were increasing. "It's all the stadium," political consultant Hank Sheinkopf explained to the *New York Post*. "The stadium has become the catch-basin for all social-class arguments." Bloomberg didn't seem to care, but perhaps because I believed so much in him and the importance of his mayoralty, the polls were making me sick to my stomach.

Bloomberg and I had always had an excellent relationship based on mutual trust and respect. There had always been grumbling among others in the administration that my heart really wasn't in the city or with the Mayor and that I was using his administration to push my own Olympics agenda. Up until this point I could argue in good conscience that everything I had done had the triple benefit of rebuilding the city, helping Bloomberg, and advancing the Olympics vision. That spring it suddenly looked less clear.

Finally, I could no longer hold back my sense of dread. One April morning, I found myself alone with the Mayor in the bullpen. We hadn't once talked about the politics of the stadium and their effect on his reelection prospects, but I felt the responsibility to tackle the elephant in the room.

"Hey, look, as much as I want to win the stadium battle," I said, "it's not worth the price of your losing the election. We can walk away."

At that point, I had worked for him for three years. We would go on to have another decade working closely together. That moment was the only time in those thirteen years that I recall Bloomberg getting angry with me.

His anger is quick and explosive. You can tell because his jaw sets and his eyes narrow in fury. As soon as the words left my mouth, I could see I was in for it. "I don't ever want to hear you say that again," he said in a voice that seemed like a slap. "We got into this together. This is the right thing to do for the city. Let's see it through to the end." I was embarrassed, of course. But he had also just said what I had been wishing to hear. And implicit in his words was that he accepted the risk that fighting for the stadium might cost him the election. It was as if, in his own way, he had given me absolution. I heaved a sigh of relief.

We got some good news as the spring progressed. The National Football League owners awarded the 2010 Super Bowl to the new Jets stadium . . . if it ever got built. There were leaked reports out of IOC headquarters that two cities, Madrid and Moscow, were no longer being considered seriously. We took this as a great sign that New York had vaulted itself up with the clear front-runners, Paris and London.

Our scrappy, hardworking political team led by Higgins and Whelan persuaded a majority on the City Council to sign a letter and to hold a press conference saying it supported the stadium. That contradicted the oft-repeated claim that the stadium lacked political support. Although the Dolans' ads had made the stadium unpopular in more affluent areas of Manhattan below 96th Street, most residents of Upper Manhattan and the other boroughs still wanted it. The team worked overtime to line up support from members of the Senate and Assembly in Albany. Although they never gave us a letter, our staff took weekly roll calls, and we believed we had a majority of support in both of those houses as well.

But it was largely irrelevant. The stadium was never coming up for a public vote. It would be determined by three men in a room. Pataki's was a yes vote. Bruno, we were fairly sure, would not vote no if the other two voted yes. And then there was Silver. My team and I maintained hope, if not optimism, that Silver might eventually vote yes despite his increasingly negative public rhetoric about the stadium. We told ourselves he was just holding out for a higher price. But on the many occasions we tried to engage the Speaker, we met stony silence. On May 1, 2005, the Mayor had to announce that there were delays at Ground Zero because of security concerns. This gave Silver a reason to go on television and complain that our administration was concentrating on the West Side to the detriment of Lower Manhattan. "What about all those promises to rebuild?" he wailed to NY1, the cable news channel that follows city news.

All spring, Silver found excuses for not bringing the stadium to a vote at the PACB. No one in Albany could make anything come up for a vote except Silver and Bruno, and Silver had been dodging that bullet. Clearly, he was hoping someone else but him would make the stadium go away. But by late spring, his final excuses were crumbling.

On June 2, a court threw out the last group of lawsuits seeking to prevent the MTA from selling its air rights to the Jets. So, now, the only thing holding back the stadium deal was the need for approval from the PACB. Under intense pressure, Silver scheduled a vote for Friday, June 3. He then put it off until Monday, in what we perceived on our side as a negotiating tactic. That Friday, Marc Shaw, my fellow Deputy Mayor, who had the closest relationship on our team with Silver and his staff, told me he thought we could get a deal done.

Friday night and Saturday were the Jewish Sabbath, when Silver traditionally disappeared, so we prepared for Saturday night and Sunday as the moments when we would engage in endless back and forth as we haggled out the details with the world's greatest haggler. Instead, there was radio silence.

Sunday, June 5, was the Israeli Day Parade. Bloomberg met Silver for breakfast at the Roosevelt Hotel beforehand. As a last-ditch effort, the Mayor proposed up to $5,000 in tax credits for each employee of any out-of-town company that agreed to locate in Lower Manhattan, along with rent subsidies worth $5.5 million per year for tenants who agreed to go into Seven World Trade Center and the Freedom Tower. Bloomberg and Silver then marched down 5th Avenue together in the parade. Silver said nothing. I waited back in City Hall with my anxious team.

In the early afternoon, Bloomberg and then Silver arrived back at City Hall. He and Bloomberg left the rest of us in the bullpen and went behind closed doors. It seemed like hours before they came out. The sense of dread I felt was overwhelming. For me, it had been eleven years since that soccer game in the Meadowlands. If Silver said no, our Olympic bid was dead. We knew that Silver had scheduled the PACB vote for the next day. What we didn't know was that he had also scheduled a press conference in Albany to coincide with the vote so he could make his own case to the voters.

He had already written the speech he planned to give. "Developing the West Side and ignoring Lower Manhattan. This is what the PACB vote is really about," he would claim in what seemed to me the most cynical possible (and wrong) interpretation of our actions. "The 2012 Summer Games are being used as a shield to hide another goal: to shift the financial and business capital of the world out of Lower Manhattan and over to the West Side."

To this day, we really don't know what motivated Silver. Was it really his concern that the plan for Hudson Yards would compete with Lower Manhattan? (Today both are thriving.) Or was it his relationship with Lynch? Or was it the Dolans' Cablevision, which might have promised to contribute to his power grab against the Governor the next year? Perhaps it was just a matter of political preservation within his district or within his caucus. Perhaps he bore some class-driven grudge against Bloomberg and me. Or maybe he thought we were arrogant to try an end-run around the legislature in Albany, and when that failed, he was determined to teach us (me) a lesson. Probably it was a combination of all of the above.

No matter what, as with the commuter tax and even congestion pricing later, he seemed incapable of grasping citywide issues and having a vision for the future. He was just trapped in his narrow, parochial world. Sunday afternoon, Silver slipped out the side door of City Hall, and Bloomberg came back into the bullpen to deliver the devastating news in his same flat, business-as-usual style. "Well, there is good news and bad," he began. "The good news is that you can build a stadium. The bad news is that it has to be on Ground Zero."

I wasn't laughing, of course. Bloomberg could see that I felt as if the world were coming to an end. He would have none of it. In front of the staff he kept it breezy. He turned to Marc Ricks and Michael Kalt, who had been sitting with me, and told them to shave. "I've used that trick to make it look like I am working hard on weekends."

Then he took me aside and simply said: "What's your Plan B?" Then he left.

CHAPTER SEVENTEEN

BLOOMBERG EXPLAINED

WHO DOES THAT? I had imperiled not only the Olympic bid but also Mike Bloomberg's entire political future. Yet instead of blaming me, or yelling at me, or firing me, any of which would have been understandable, even appropriate, he was calm and ready to follow my lead on the next move. He trusted that I had a next move.

I didn't. But only six frantic days later, we announced a deal with the New York Mets for a new stadium that could also double as an Olympic Stadium, and then just three days after that we inked a deal with the New York Yankees for their own new stadium, with all the needed approvals lined up (which required Bloomberg to go back to the very foe who had defeated the stadium deal), and his poll numbers started to rise again.

The millstone of the stadium had been lifted from his neck, and people saw in our quick recovery resilience and a capacity to rebound. New Yorkers respected Bloomberg, and, in a weird way, the stadium debacle made him more relatable. Everybody has setbacks and disappointments. Here was a guy who didn't dwell on them and just moved forward. It was something New Yorkers could admire. None of that was clear—to me at least—in those first brutal moments. I found his unruffled response unfathomable. As well as I knew him, it wasn't until that point that I understood a core part of his character.

At City Hall we sat side-by-side for six years. We both arrived at work early in the morning. We partnered on projects across the city, working together over weekends and late into the night. When I moved to Bloomberg LP as President of his privately owned business, we continued to talk regularly. Over the years, we grew to be close colleagues and friends. But in the thirteen years I worked for Mike, I probably got an honest glimpse of his true emotional state a handful of times at most.

That was just one of the strange dualities at the heart of his personality. He was emotionally reserved, but when someone needed help, no one had a bigger heart. He was indifferent to public opinion and yet wanted to be the center of attention. He prided himself on the quality of his staff, but he almost never paid us compliments—except in public, when he gave generous praise. He sought changes on a grand scale, supporting projects that would reimagine the cityscape for generations, reframe public health policy for a new century, and galvanize the world behind ameliorating climate change. But I've never seen someone less concerned about his legacy.

Over the years we worked together, I came to realize that normal relationship standards couldn't apply to Mike. The qualities that made him most unusual were also the sources of his greatest strength. Most of us are motivated at least in part by other people. We're on a quest for approval, or we're driven by fear of what other people will think. Maybe we act out of a desire to please others—or ourselves—or to balance our wishes against the needs of those we love. As a result, those desires and fears become limiting factors in our ability to achieve. Mike has no such limitations.

At our core, most of us strive to be happy. We evaluate choices based on whether they are likely to contribute to our happiness, and we make sacrifices accordingly. With Mike, this misses the point. Happiness is not the dimension upon which he evaluates his life. Instead, I believe, what motivates him is making lives better and ultimately saving them—hence his focus on gun control, public health, and climate change. That's where he gets his satisfaction. If you were to ask him what his proudest accomplishment is as Mayor, I'm sure he would say that life expectancy in New York increased by a remarkable three years during his tenure, surpassing the national average for the first time.

Many of us fantasize about the future and live at least partly in our past—revisiting our moments of triumph or greatest mistakes. Mike exists almost exclusively in the present, focusing on what can be accomplished next, working relentlessly to achieve it for however long it takes, and moving on instantly when it is (truly) over. I almost never saw him express pride in his achievements or brood over his few failures. He simply forged ahead.

This practical, task-oriented approach applied to personal improvement as well as politics. After he decided on the campaign trail to learn Spanish at age sixty, he hired two tutors, one of whom came to City Hall when he was Mayor most days and worked with him for an hour a day. He is still taking lessons, undaunted by the challenge of learning a new language and undeterred by his oft-mocked accent, which spawned its own Twitter handle. He set himself a task, and he intends to complete it.

In golf, a sport he took up late in life, he would play every chance he got, frequently lugging around his own bag—sometimes thirty-six holes a day—in a mostly futile attempt to lower his handicap. Even as his rate of improvement leveled off, he remained relentless in his attempt to get better.

When it came to politics, he laid out his intentions clearly and then systematically attempted to execute those ideas regardless of whether the city at large wanted him to. Two of his first official acts as Mayor were to restrict smoking access—a widely reviled act at the time—and raise property taxes. That's more than stepping on the third rail. That's tying yourself to the tracks.

The response was predictable: people hated him. Mike would go to parades and joke that every bar patron he passed gave him the single-finger salute. When asked the typical, inane question about grabbing a beer with the Mayor, New Yorkers didn't just say no. They indicated they would practically bar their doors.

One night at Gracie Mansion, not long after he had gotten the smoking ban passed and the tax increase enacted, we were sitting on the porch overlooking the East River. It was a warm evening, still and quiet, with the city's lights reflected across the water. I ventured a question, even though I was sure I knew the answer: Did the intense hostility bother him? He had given no indication that he cared about anyone's opinion, and I was fully expecting him to blithely blow off the city's collective scorn. Instead, he said quietly, "How could it not?" That was one of the few times I ever saw him lift his guard in a personal way.

Other than that one moment at Gracie Mansion, he projected imperviousness to criticism. Some of that resolve was probably constitutional and some was generational. Stiff upper lips were more common than they are now. He often told the story of how, when his father died (while he was in college), his mother learned how to drive so she could go back to work to support the family. That was him. Don't complain. Just do it. And don't expect lavish praise for doing it.

When Mike talks of his father, he often says, "He worked six or seven days a week until he checked himself into the hospital to die." Those words are hardly sentimental, but he still wears his father's watch daily, fifty-plus years after his death. And, sometimes, when he's asked if he has any regrets, it's that his father didn't live to see his success. I didn't know any of that when my father died just six months into our first term. I flew straight to Detroit without saying good-bye to anyone in the office.

At the funeral, as my brothers and I greeted people in a small room just off the sanctuary, I was stunned to see the Mayor walk in, along with everyone at City Hall to whom I was closest, including Sharon Greenberger and Andy Alper. Mike had identified everyone I cared most about in the administration and helicoptered them (he did the flying himself) from the pad near City Hall to the airport, and then they flew on his plane to Detroit for the service.

When my uncle was diagnosed with ALS, the same disease that killed my father, I felt that I had to do something. I approached Mike. In a rare personal question (more typically, he would perfunctorily ask whenever we got together, "How's your family?" without really caring what the answer was), he asked me what the diagnosis meant for me, and I told him: I had a 50 percent probability of having the genetic mutation that causes ALS. Even if I fell into the positive 50 percent, I had no idea if or when the disease would manifest itself.

He listened carefully, and his face flashed concern for just a moment. Then he asked if there was anything he could do. I told him I was going to start an ALS research organization. He committed $7.5 million on the spot. Three years later, when I told him I wanted to expand the effort, we talked for only a couple of minutes, and he pledged $10 million. The third time I asked, he gave another $10 million without blinking. How to reconcile those two sides? His emotional reserve and his desire to do right for others, especially when they are facing real difficulties?

I trace it back to one of the few achievements I ever heard him speak about with any obvious pride: becoming an Eagle Scout at the unusually young age of twelve. I was a Boy Scout, although never a particularly committed one, never having risen above the middling rank of first class, but I remember the emotional hold the Scout Law had on my early adolescent self. I can still recite it: "A Scout is trustworthy, loyal, helpful, friendly, courteous, kind, obedient, cheerful, thrifty, brave, clean, and reverent."

As I've thought about Mike over the years, I keep coming back to that code. I don't know if it provided a clear organizing structure for his life, but he seems to have internalized it almost completely. So much of what I observed about him over our long relationship reflects that code.

Loyal: I've never known a more loyal person. His loyalty to his staff and friends is legendary—and almost always returned. Some of the most visible and important members of his administration stayed for the entire three terms, almost unheard of given the pressures of the jobs and low pay compared with what those people might have earned elsewhere.

My six years as Deputy Mayor for Economic Development and Rebuilding were the longest anyone served in that job. Many other key figures, including Deputy Mayors Patti Harris, Kevin Sheekey, Cas Holloway, Linda Gibbs, and Dennis Walcott, Corporation Counsel Mike Cardozo, along with Commissioners such as Amanda Burden, Police Commissioner Ray Kelly, Budget Director Mark Page, and Cultural Affairs Commissioner Kate Levin, stayed for Mike's entire twelve years. They knew they were empowered to achieve real change—and he would have their backs as long as they had his. The threshold for losing his trust was extremely high. In fact, as the West Side implosion proved, after he had put his faith in you almost nothing could undermine that confidence. That security and freedom unleashed the staffers' imaginations and creativity.

Perhaps as a result, I can't recall a single unplanned leak coming out of the bullpen, where the top staff sat at City Hall. Part of it was loyalty. But I think people also understood—though it was never explicitly stated—that such a betrayal would constitute a rare fireable offense.

Sometimes his loyalty to others could produce blind spots. As hard charging as he was, he refused to fire anybody. Why? It's difficult not to think it had something to do with his own experience of getting fired and carrying with him a sense that firings can represent management failures, but part of it was also a reluctance to engage in emotional confrontation.

Kind and helpful: Flying to the funeral with all of my friends. But I've seen it in so many other ways. When I got to Bloomberg LP, I was struck by how his company was at its best when people were having their most difficult times. When a loved one was sick, or when an employee died, the company rallied around the employee and his or her family with speed and genuine care, whether that was arranging for people to see the best medical specialists, wherever they were, or paying for expenses. There was never a question. It was as if kindness was institutionalized within the company.

That kindness was rarely evident in a one-on-one situation. Mike isn't a hugger or natural consoler, and he certainly wasn't quick with a compliment.

In my thirteen years working closely with him, I can't ever recall getting a compliment from him when we were in a one-on-one situation. Instead, he talked to other people about me. As a result, every year or so when I worked in City Hall, Peter Grauer, then the CEO of Bloomberg LP, and I would have lunch to share notes on what he had said to each of us about the other one—the only "performance reviews" I ever got in more than a decade.

Sometimes I joked with Mike, asking whether his mother had ever praised him as a child. It was almost as if he didn't even understand the question. But when it came to parceling out credit in public, he wanted everyone to know that his staff did all the hard work. He understood (as few politicians do) that recognition is one of the best ways to reward and motivate people.

When I got to Bloomberg LP, in the first three months I spoke with about five hundred people about the company, either individually or in small groups. Although the company had been doing very well through the financial boom that preceded the financial crisis, I felt there was a deep and growing sense of frustration within the company. I felt, too, that much of the problem was traceable to one person—a particular favorite of Mike's. Grauer and I pleaded with Mike to let him go, but he was resolute. We couldn't fire the man. After hours of arguing, we finally got Mike to agree to transfer him to another office, but he insisted it had to be done with dignity.

Brave: After Mike committed to a path, he didn't waver—no matter the consequences or pressure to relent. The smoking ban, property tax increase, congestion pricing, and stadium were all examples of principled stands he took and stuck with them.

He knew to follow his heart and his internal sense of right and wrong when making decisions, regardless of political or other consequences. He knew to ignore the voices that told him to violate his beliefs or follow the crowd—and in fact, he built his fortune by taking counterintuitive actions.

He started Bloomberg LP in the teeth of the financial stagflation of the early 1980s. During the full-blown recession at the end of the decade, he launched his news operation. If you look at recessions or downturns in the financial markets, each one signaled a time when his company made the greatest leaps forward.

He immediately established an unusual business model: every customer paid the same price, whether buying two terminals or two thousand. The price increased at the rate of inflation every two years—and not more. Everyone told him this was a crazy policy that would alienate customers. He didn't care. He believed that if there was complete consistency with respect to the price, everyone—inside the company and outside—would remain focused on creating a better product. He was absolutely right.

A scheduled price increase came due in the immediate aftermath of the financial crisis in 2009. Every other vendor was slashing its prices. Bloomberg LP raised its prices on schedule. No one protested.

In the first two years after the financial crisis when I was running Bloomberg LP, we increased the number of staff at the company by around two thousand—a 20 percent increase at a time when literally all of our customers were in desperate straits. I didn't even have to persuade Mike. I knew that approach was completely consistent with his beliefs and the history of the company.

It was also the same approach we took in government. If you think of cities as competitive enterprises—vying against other cities for residents, jobs, and resources—it's self-defeating to follow the crowd. Although weighing the risks and evaluating trade-offs, the only way to distinguish yourself is by doing something different. Invest when times are tough, Mike would state, and save when times are good.

When everybody ran to the left, Mike relished dashing right. Part of that approach might have stemmed from his time at Salomon Brothers, where the only way to earn outsized returns was not to follow the crowd but instead to make different decisions than others did.

Still, I believe what enabled him to follow through on these decisions despite the onslaught of naysayers was his ability to distance himself from the emotion of any situation.

Courteous: If you have a meeting with Mike, he'll ask if he can pour you a cup of coffee. If you're on his private plane, he'll ask if he can get you a snack. He has no pretense. In private, he's an unflaggingly hospitable host. And in public, he rarely let fights get personal. As frustrated as he would be in private with Shelly Silver or Governor George Pataki or Joe Bruno, he never took them to task publicly. There were surely strategic reasons for this, but I think he also considered it ungentlemanly. To the press he could be very prickly. But beyond that I am hard-pressed to find examples when he was rude or mean to someone in public (although he could be unsparing in private).

Reverent: Mike is not a religious person, but his reverence manifests itself in principles and in patriotism. Mike is extremely patriotic. His true belief in American values perhaps manifested itself most clearly in the fight over the Ground Zero mosque. In that case, a developer sought to build a $140 million, fifteen-story mosque and community center just a few blocks from where the attacks took place. The proposal drew condemnation from an array of right-wing groups and even some first responders and victims' families. But Mike was steadfast in his support: the US Constitution protects the right to build houses of worship, and it inveighs against discrimination on the grounds of specific religions. The center ultimately failed, but Mike never wavered.

Thrifty: Mike has all the trappings of a billionaire. But it became clear to me that if you scratched the veneer of this multibillionaire, you found a lower-middle-class kid from Medford, Massachusetts. His taste in food is hot dogs and fried chicken. He loves diners. He likes to look nice, but I can't imagine him doing anything other than going to Paul Stuart and buying a bunch of suits at one time and getting it over with (and he takes particular pride in the fact that they last a long time). He only owns two pair of dress shoes. I never sensed that material things actually mattered to him unless they served some other purpose such as convenience (e.g., his planes and helicopter).

Honest/Trustworthy: Since I've known him I cannot remember a single time I ever heard Mike lie to anyone. I don't mean just a big lie. I never heard him tell a white lie or even commit the kind of modest exaggeration (let alone much worse) so common to politicians. That extended to every area of his life, from politics to golf. He would never consider taking a stroke or a mulligan.

When I signed up to join City Hall I didn't know if he would follow through on his promises about his management style or commitment to the Olympic bid. It was a risk. But with the exception of those two early tussles over Commissioner appointments, he was remarkably faithful to commitments he made in our first meeting.

This trait made him an unusual politician. Nearly every official subject to elections tells people what they want to hear. But early on in Mike's tenure as Mayor, after he gave a speech to the Association for a Better New York, he agreed to answer some questions. It must have been around the time his popularity was dropping because of the tax increase and smoking ban, and someone asked whether he felt that he should change his approach. His response: "I am who I am," he said. "I'm sixty-two years old. I'm not going to change now."

If you study his inauguration speech outlining his vision for the city, it was a remarkably accurate blueprint for the next twelve years. He was up front about what he wanted to do, and then he went out and tried to do it. Then he issued public reports roughly every other year grading himself on every promise to ensure that the public and press held him accountable. Few, if any, politicians do that. I think the reason the public perception of him was shaken when he overturned term limits to run for a third term was that he had always said that he wouldn't. There was, as far as I know, never a secret plan to change the law; he simply changed his mind—but that was so rare, it was a shock to a public that took him at his word.

I've always believed that the public developed a deep respect for Mike for a couple of reasons: first, he was effective. Second, he was a different and complex model of a politician. His wealth and lack of political posturing kept people from identifying with him or feeling close. But he was clearly above influence, corruption, or impropriety. Most important, he was totally without guile. He was always himself, invariably straight. He was the rare elected official who said what he intended to do, and then he did it.

That quality had propelled him from a thirty-thousand-vote victory in his first election to a landslide victory of nearly 60 percent in his first reelection in 2005, in a city that was five-to-one Democratic. It also enabled him to sustain approval ratings of around 70 percent or more for about four years in a row.

I think it is what would have made him a great President too. He seriously considered it twice, first in 2007 and then again in 2016. Mike was never shy about the appeal of the job. He often said there were only three jobs he would ever want—Mayor of New York, President of the World Bank, and President of the United States. The three have a couple of things in common—they are among the most visible positions in the world (at least for an American), and they hold the greatest potential for impact.

Both times he just couldn't pull the trigger. Both times he did extensive analysis to determine if a third-party candidate could win. In 2007, he concluded that the probabilities were nearly zero. If they had been merely low—as they were when he began his quest for Mayor in 2001—I believe he would have taken the shot.

In 2016, as it became clear that the level of trust of both Hillary Clinton and Donald Trump, the increasingly likely candidates for their respective party nominations, were at historic lows, and as Mike became more and more disenchanted with their inability to articulate thoughtful and pragmatic solutions to the problems that plagued the nation and the world, he again thought long and hard about running. Although he thought the chances of winning were a bit higher in 2016, he just didn't feel he could risk entering the race and tilting the election to Trump. Still, after the election was over, despite the outcome, I never saw any real hint that he regretted his decision not to run.

Of course, the Boy Scout code doesn't explain everything about Mike. For one thing, he loved being the center of attention. His desire to remain at the center of the action manifested itself when it came to seeking a third term (and returning to the company after vowing to stay away). The prospect of losing that made him incredibly anxious.

We used to talk about this all the time. He was convinced that people would not pay attention to him anymore after he left office. "Don't fool yourself," he told me. "People only want you because of the role that you've had."

I told him that was the craziest thing I had ever heard. He might be the ex-Mayor, but he was still the wealthiest person in New York and gave away half a billion dollars a year. He owned one of the biggest companies in the city. "You think people aren't paying attention to you?" I asked. "You're going to be at the center of whatever you want to be for the rest of your life!" He just didn't believe it.

He also didn't care about long-term legacy. He was almost solely focused on his own lifetime—which he seemed to believe could end imminently or last forever. He has structured his foundation to give away virtually all of his wealth within twenty years after he dies. A hundred years from now, if all goes according to his current plan, there won't be Bloomberg Philanthropies, like there is the Rockefeller Foundation and Ford Foundation, which have survived indefinitely after their founders' deaths.

In 2010, when Bloomberg LP needed more space, and he was sixty-eight years old, I tried to convince him to move to Hudson Yards in part by noting that the developer, Stephen Ross, had offered to name it the Bloomberg Center—essentially dubbing it the city's next Rockefeller Center. He was like all three Rockefellers rolled into one, I argued—the business magnate (John D.), the philanthropist (John D. Jr.), and the politician (Nelson). Now he would have the twenty-first century's version with an entirely new, iconic neighborhood named in his honor, becoming a touchstone for the next generation. Mike couldn't have cared less.

When I pitched a new building in London for our expanding staff there that wouldn't be complete until 2016 or 2017, his response was, "Why do I care about that? I'll be dead by then." I was baffled. How many years did he think he had left? "I don't know," he said. "It's got to be at least twenty-five years from now," I attempted to reassure him. He didn't believe it.

"I'll bet you," I said over the phone sitting at my desk at Bloomberg LP, while he was sitting at his desk in City Hall. As we were talking on the phone, I found an actuarial exam online and started going through a twenty-five-page questionnaire with him that delved into astounding detail on health habits, relationships, life spans of parents, dietary habits, and weight and height and how it had varied over time. I learned more about his personal life sitting there for that half hour going through the questionnaire together than I had in six years sitting by his side at City Hall. When we finished I pressed the button. Sure enough, it predicted he would live until he was ninety-two years old. We went ahead with the building.

I had never intended to end up at Bloomberg LP after leaving City Hall. During the entire six years I was in office, we spoke about his company exactly once, for about an hour, after some large, private equity firms expressed interest in buying it. In a completely out-of-character move, he asked me what I thought his company was worth. He gave me some information about Bloomberg's finances so that I could make an evaluation—a profound expression of trust because that information was a closely guarded secret. After walking through the options, he ultimately decided he didn't want to sell. That was it. We never talked about it again.

When I started at City Hall, I was clear with Mike from the beginning that I would not stay for the full eight years if he won a second term. During the reelection campaign, he asked me if I would stay for an additional two years if we lost the Olympics and he won reelection, given the scale of projects we had set in motion. I readily agreed.

About fifteen months before my six years were up, Mike hadn't mentioned the issue again, so I thought I should remind him. We went out to lunch at a little Vietnamese restaurant near City Hall. It was rare for us to have dinner or lunch, but when I suggested it, he agreed right away. As we sat down, I reminded him of our understanding. "Yeah, yeah, yeah," he said. And that was it. He did not ask about my plans or how he could help. We quickly moved on to other topics, and it didn't come up again.

Nine months went by—it was now six months before I intended to quit—and still he did not say a single word about my leaving. There were no questions about my thoughts on my successor, my plans, the state I expected to leave things in—nothing. I thought perhaps I should remind him. So, I suggested we have lunch again. We returned to the same little restaurant. "I want to remind you again that I'm leaving," I said. "I remember," he said. And that was the end of the discussion.

Four and a half more months went by without another word. Every so often he would hear rumors about things I was considering, and he would make a joke. That was it. Finally, just six weeks before my self-imposed deadline for my departure, as he was sitting in the bullpen, he wheeled his chair around. "Got a second?" he asked. "Sure," I said.

We went up to the tables that overlooked the bullpen, next to the snacks and drinks and microwave. "What would you think about going over and running Bloomberg?" he asked. "What are you talking about?" I said.

We had sat together for six years, literally back to back, and had never discussed the company for more than an hour. I still knew next to nothing about the services it offered. I had never run a large company before. "Why would you want me to do this?" I asked. "I don't know," he said and shrugged. "I just think you'd be good."

I thought about it overnight, and the next morning I told him I accepted—on one condition. "I'm not getting paid one dollar a year anymore," I said. He laughed. We hashed out compensation in fifteen minutes, and the deal was done.

We made the announcement two weeks later. "Now that it's official, what are your expectations?" I asked. His entire fortune was tied up in this company—along with his name and his future. I felt the weight of responsibility he was entrusting to me. "I don't know," he said. "I haven't been there for six years. You go figure it out." I learned later that he'd been talking about my joining the company with its chief financial officer for months. He always played things close to the vest.

Mike always said that when he finished being Mayor he would play golf and then figure out what he wanted to do, although I think he assumed he would devote himself to philanthropy. I had always believed him when he said he would never return to the company. So when he started showing up regularly in the Bloomberg LP offices, I was surprised, although I probably shouldn't have been, given his desire to be in the center of the action. It soon became clear he wanted to come back full time. It was his company. With no hard feelings, I handed the reins back.

On the day I left, on December 31, 2014, I wrote him a heartfelt e-mail about what an honor it had been to be steward of the company on his behalf and expressed the hope we would maintain our friendship for many years to come. I told him I was pleased to be able to stay in the family as a member of the board at Bloomberg Philanthropies and what the experience of being at the company had meant to me. I thanked him for the profound role he had played in my life and offered my deep gratitude. I hoped that I had lived up to his standards at the company and that he found it to be everything he hoped for when he returned. I meant every word.

He wrote back right away, with two lines. "You didn't fuck it up. See you next week."

CHAPTER EIGHTEEN

COMEBACK AND COLLAPSE

ALTHOUGH I GOT the news the afternoon before, word of our defeat at Shelly Silver's hands didn't spread through the NYC2012 office until the next day as he was giving his gloating, righteous speech in Albany. I was totally despondent, especially because, better than anyone else, I knew how dire our situation now was. We had just one month before going to Singapore to make one final presentation with the other candidate cities in front of the International Olympic Committee. This was do or die, and I had no Plan B.

I knew I had to put on a bright face for our staffers. When I arrived at the NYC2012 offices, the mood was somber. Jay Kriegel had been going desk to desk to answer questions and offer consolation. I asked everyone to gather. I could feel eyes turn to me expectantly. It was one of those moments when you intuitively know that leadership is expected and reassurances are needed. Standing at the front of the room, unsure of what to say, I ended up speaking what was in my heart and what I hoped was true. "We are going to do what we've always done," I promised them. "Find a way."

Although we had faced roadblocks before and found solutions, this time I truly had no idea how to move forward. Mike Bloomberg and I had said it in public for so long that I had almost come to believe myself that there was no alternative to the West Side for the stadium.

Fortunately, I was lucky to be surrounded by highly talented and devoted people. They had rescued us from tough situations more than once, and this time they rose to meet the ultimate challenge. Although I am pretty sure I hid the depths of my despair from NYC2012, one of my City Hall staffers, Michael Kalt, was not fooled; he also wasn't humoring me. Monday, as I was consoling the troops, he was already starting to review other options for the stadium, and he was absolutely firm with me: "We can do this."

By Tuesday, Kalt and Andrew Winters, our key Olympic bid planner, had gone back to reevaluate many of the stadium locations rejected before our commitment to the West Side. By the end of that day, they came back to me to announce that we had one option that stood out above all the rest: go back to the Mets and build at Flushing Meadows in Queens.

The irony of Flushing Meadows as a possible location was not lost on me. Many people urged that site on me when we started the Olympic bid. In fact, in our winning presentation to the United States Olympic Committee Board in Colorado Springs in November 2002, we had noted that if we didn't succeed on the West Side, we could always locate the stadium in Flushing. We even included a rendering of a stadium there as an alternative.

We had walked away from Flushing Meadows for two reasons. First, the Mets' owners, the Wilpons, thought they had a sweetheart deal for a new stadium with the Giuliani Administration and weren't interested in the longer Olympic time frame. Second, the previous Summer Olympics in the United States, in Atlanta, had featured a converted baseball stadium, and the IOC had let us know through unofficial channels that it did not like either the sight lines or the cheapness of the temporary stadium. That had been the final straw.

Now, however, the situation was significantly different. After 9/11, with the economy in tatters, Bloomburg had me review the stadium deals Mayor Giuliani had promised both the Mets and the Yankees. Although we had killed those deals, the Wilpons had made serious strides toward envisioning their stadium. They had, for example, drawn up plans for a stadium in masonry that looked like the old Dodgers' home, Ebbets Field, and had even done an environmental impact statement. All this prep work greatly reduced the risk of trouble at the environmental review stage. It meant that if we wanted to try to work something out in Flushing Meadows, we could do it on the accelerated timetable we so desperately required.

There was another plus for Flushing Meadows. The Mets didn't need to acquire any new land. They had stuck to Fred Wilpon's dictum, "Keep it simple." Their plan was to build their new stadium in the parking lot of the old one and then put the parking lot where the old stadium had been. They were keeping to the footprint of their existing site, and no new parkland would have to be taken.

To satisfy the IOC, first the Mets would have to build an Olympic Stadium, part of it temporary. After the Games, they would tear down the temporary sections and finish the permanent baseball stadium. It might not have been ideal, but the IOC wouldn't want New York to drop out of the process. It would have been embarrassing, and it would have taken away some of the drama from the international competition coming up in just a few weeks.

We also had another reason to feel that the IOC might be more favorably inclined to a Flushing Meadows stadium. There was already a cluster of sports venues in the park that the IOC Site Evaluation Commission had visited and loved. Because the new stadium site would be part of that cluster, it already had security, media, and transportation plans in place. So another potentially cumbersome roadblock was removed.

It was almost too good to be true when we reconsidered the stadium in a new light. That raises the fair question of why we didn't just switch our stadium to Flushing Meadows earlier, especially after the Hudson Yards plan was approved in January. The answer is simple. We had made a commitment to Woody Johnson and the Jets, who had invested an enormous amount in the New York Sports and Convention Center. Through the entire battle, it never occurred to us to ask them to switch sites. But, more important, we believed the NYSCC was the best use of the site and thought we would be successful. But now that was no longer an option.

Kalt reached out to the Mets to see if they might be interested in starting all over again. I tried not to get too excited because some significant stumbling blocks were still ahead. For starters, we hadn't had any substantive discussions with the Mets since we killed the Giuliani Administration deals three and a half years before. We were nowhere on structuring a new deal with them. What we did have, though, was a consistent construct we had used with the Jets, the Nets, and even the Yankees, with whom we were much further along in striking a new deal for a stadium. In each of those deals the city would fund only infrastructure costs; the stadium itself had to be financed by the team. For the Mets, a deal that followed that pattern was going to involve a dramatically lower subsidy than the one offered by the previous administration.

Moreover, the Mets would have to agree to design their stadium as an eighty-thousand-seat Olympic Stadium and then convert it into a forty-five-thousand-seat baseball stadium, something they had never considered. Worst of all, if they agreed to this plan, they wouldn't have any place to play in the summer of 2012. The only choice was to play in Yankee Stadium. There was precedent for such collaboration—the Yankees played in Shea Stadium during their own renovation in the 1970s. Yet the Wilpons found this idea so distasteful that they even suggested the Mets play six weeks in a minor league stadium with a capacity of seven thousand instead.

Despite these bitter pills, the Wilpons agreed to swallow our deal whole. Within a couple of days, Winters and the Mets architects worked out a design for a convertible baseball stadium, and the city and state agreed to pay $180 million for infrastructure improvements, including an upgrade to the local subway stop. NYC2012 would foot the entire $100 million bill to convert the stadium (less than it would have cost NYC2012 to convert the West Side Stadium).

Even with a deal with the Mets in hand, there was still a monstrous hill to climb, so my team shifted into an even higher gear. It is wondrous to behold when a group of motivated and talented people are facing an existential crisis. To keep our bid alive by shifting to Flushing Meadows, we needed independent approvals from two powerful sports federations: Fédération Internationale de Football Association, the world soccer governing body, had to approve the field specifications for all Olympic soccer matches (the final game was slated to be held in the Olympic Stadium); and the International Association of Athletics Federations had to give similar approval for track-and-field events. One was in Zurich, the other in Monaco. I immediately dispatched Winters overnight to each to ensure timely ratifications. Kriegel was on the phone with the IOC directly to make sure that we could amend our bid at this late date. He got the IOC's letter of consent signed by June 9, three days after Silver voted us down.

Meanwhile, with the Mets in overdrive mode, Kalt and I had to turn our attention to another issue we had sidelined: a new Yankee Stadium. After Bloomberg and I had shut down the Giuliani deals for the stadiums, both teams had retreated in frustration and disappointment. However, a year later the Yankees had returned. The Bronx Bombers were determined to get a deal. Yankee Stadium was eighty-two years old and literally crumbling beneath them; at one point in 1998, a five-hundred-pound I-beam actually fell and obliterated a seat behind the third-base line.

The Yankees' proposal was relatively complicated in that they wanted to move the entire site to parkland a few hundred yards away. They also wanted more parking in an area that was already highly populated. For the team to get that parkland, the state had to approve the taking of parkland, and the city would have to find new green space to replace it. The Yankees agreed to build their own stadium, but they wanted taxpayer-assisted financing for the parking.

Despite all of these hoops and rings to jump through, we were coming close to a deal by 2004. We agreed that the city would find and build the replacement parkland. We also ended up paying for a portion of a new train station nearby. The state's contribution would be to put money toward the replacement parking. As it turned out, we were able to finance the new parking in a way that made the state's money the only public cash in that part of the deal. The rest of the money came from bonds sold by Lehman Brothers, backed by the projected revenues from the garages themselves.

All nice and neat, but then we put on the brakes. The West Side Stadium battle was beginning to get ugly, and Bloomberg and I had decided we could handle only one stadium battle at the time. The Yankees were furious. Their president, Randy Levine, a former Deputy Mayor for Economic Development under Giuliani, began calling City Hall regularly by the spring of 2005. Occasionally, he would scream into the phone and threaten to move the Yankees to New Jersey. We didn't believe him; George Steinbrenner, the owner of the Yankees, didn't want to move from the Bronx. We had witnessed too many empty threats over the years. Meanwhile, Jerry Speyer, the developer on the project and a Yankee limited partner, would occasionally go over my head and complain directly to Bloomberg that I was being obstructionist.

After we had an agreement with the Mets, we knew we would have to reenergize the discussions about the Yankees deal because the Mets would need a place to play their home games in 2012, and with the Yankee Stadium the only viable alternative, that effectively gave the Yankees a veto over a new stadium for the Mets. So we restarted negotiations with the Yankees, who were all too happy to move forward. And, as it turned out, the terms of the two deals paralleled each other so perfectly that the Yankees' agreement, hammered out over a year or more of negotiations, acted as a template for that of the Mets. In many clauses, we just replaced the name of one team for the other.

So, miraculously enough, we had the plans, we had the teams onboard, we had the IOC and the sports federations' approval, but there was one other piece of business that had to be concluded before we could finalize a deal with the Yankees—the state legislature would have to approve taking parkland to build the new Yankee Stadium and fund a $70 million contribution.

So Bloomberg and I had to go back to the very forces that had just killed the West Side Stadium. If there is one lesson I learned in business that helped me in politics, it is never to hold a grudge. Bloomberg believed this too. We held our noses, were professionals, and went about dealing with Albany just as always.

Silver was more than willing to agree to our proposal because we planned to replace parkland with equivalent or more parkland on the old Yankee Stadium site and because he didn't want to be seen as killing New York's Olympic hopes a second time. He promised us a letter signed by him, Joe Bruno, and Governor George Pataki that the state's $70 million contribution would not have to go before the Public Authorities Control Board.

For me, this was both thrilling and exhausting. The weekend following the stadium defeat, Alisa and I had long planned to attend our twenty-fifth Harvard reunion with our children. Harvard makes a big deal out of the twenty-fifth, and because we were in the same class, our combined group of friends was going to be there. Alisa ended up going up to Cambridge when the reunion started on Thursday. I didn't get there until Friday night, spent the entire day on Saturday on the phone with my team, the Yankees, the Mets, Marc Shaw (the Deputy Mayor conducting negotiations with the state legislature), and Bloomberg. By Saturday evening, we were done. I came back early Sunday morning to make sure everything was ready for a Sunday night announcement, leaving Alisa alone with the kids, as I had done so many times over the previous three and a half years.

Within six days of Silver sending the NYSCC into oblivion, we were ready to announce two new stadiums that had been talked about for years. It is legitimate to question whether this profusion of stadiums was something to celebrate. Municipal sports stadiums have attracted a lot of criticism in recent years, often with good reason. Why should public monies be used to subsidize billionaire team owners and the corporate fat cats who are willing to shell out hundreds of thousands of dollars a year for luxury boxes? Moreover, stadiums typically create few long-term jobs and on their own are not significant economic catalysts.

We believed that in all three cases in which we did stadium or arena deals—the new Yankee and Mets Stadiums and the Barclays Center at Atlantic Yards—our deals proved the exception to the rule. For one thing, we would no longer bear the cost of maintaining the stadiums. The city owned the two existing baseball stadiums and leased them back to the teams. Under these arrangements, the teams were responsible for routine maintenance, but the city was on the hook for significant capital improvements. As the stadiums aged, the burden on the city was growing rapidly. There were constant disputes between the city's Parks Department, which had to pay for the repairs, and the team owners about where the line was to be drawn. Was a flood in the bathroom, for example, caused by someone stuffing too much toilet paper down the loo or the pipe systems being old and corroded? And so on.

In any case, my team calculated that it would cost the city less to invest in new stadiums than to continue repairing the current ones. For example, we estimated that continuing to repair Shea would cost roughly $212 million over the following thirty years. Yankee Stadium was in even worse shape. Under the new deals, the city would own the land and lease it to the teams, who would be responsible for everything else. We would only pay for infrastructure costs outside the stadiums. In effect, we bought our way out of what we calculated would be greater obligations in the future.

Perhaps more important, we never viewed the stadiums in isolation. In the cases of the Yankee and Mets Stadiums (and Atlantic Yards and Hudson Yards as well), the stadiums were just one part of ambitious plans we had to reinvigorate neighborhoods ripe for investment and reinvention. The South Bronx, Flushing, the Far West Side, and Downtown Brooklyn were four of the areas we had targeted for a combination of significant investment and/ or rezoning to make them more attractive, vibrant, mixed-use communities from the beginning of the administration. In all four cases, they were vital parts of our Olympic X plan.

The stadiums were just one piece of a bigger puzzle, and they would help to define the areas but not be ends in and of themselves. In the South Bronx, one of the poorest communities in the city, we invested heavily in thousands of units of affordable housing and unwound a terrible long-term lease for the thirty-one-acre Bronx Terminal Market into which the city had entered with a developer in the 1970s. During the lease, the developer had allowed the site to deteriorate into blight, with the produce market a small shadow of what it had originally been. We helped a new developer step in and convert the vast, aging building into one million square feet of retail space, creating thousands of jobs. Then we connected the Bronx Terminal Market to Yankee Stadium with new parks and rezoned the entire area around Yankee Stadium. In other words, when deciding on the wisdom of using public dollars for funding a stadium, it's all about the broader plan.

On June 6, Silver had killed the West Side Stadium. On June 12, we inked deals with both the Yankees and the Mets. That night Bloomberg and

I marched into the Blue Room at City Hall, packed with reporters, and the Mayor announced on live TV that we had a deal with the Mets that would allow us to go forward with the Olympic bid. It was dramatic and felt glorious. (We held off on announcing the Yankees' deal until three days later. The team wanted its own moment in the sun and did a big press event in the Bronx.)

Unlike the tremendous pushback we got on the West Side Stadium, only minor grumbling could be heard when these stadium deals were announced. The antidevelopment forces were spent. Meanwhile, the stadiums were wildly popular with the public. The week after the West Side Stadium went down in defeat, a Marist College poll showed Bloomberg neck and neck with Fernando Ferrer. Two weeks later, on June 22, the picture had completely changed. A Quinnipiac University poll found that Bloomberg had opened up a double-digit lead over the Democratic field. It also found that his job approval rating was the best in three years and that 61 percent of New Yorkers backed using the Mets Stadium for the Olympics.

An article in the *New York Post* pointed out that Bloomberg had turned his biggest liability into an asset by proving he was neither a whiner nor a quitter. "It's a real New York story. Bloomberg got knocked down. He took his lumps. He got back up and came up with a stadium plan people feel good about. He stole the stadium issue back," a political consultant noted. After that, Bloomberg's poll numbers continued to get stronger and stronger until he finally defeated Ferrer with nearly 60 percent of the vote in November.

Surprisingly, the stadium turnaround was popular not just in New York. Two days after our announcement IOC President Jacques Rogge told the *New York Times* that he was pleased the New York organizers were able to resurrect the bid so quickly. "This shows the quality and dedication of the New York team," Rogge said.

During the third week of June, I traveled to Almeria, Spain, for the Fifteenth Mediterranean Games. I got to experience that new respect in person. Everywhere we went we got congratulations on the new stadium. The IOC members there understood that after a bid is won, not everything goes smoothly. What we had demonstrated, albeit unwillingly, was that as inevitable crises arose, we would have the grit and the bandwidth to handle them. The reception in Spain gave me new hope as we went to Singapore to make our final pitch for the vote. That sense of optimism was buoyed further because shortly before we went to Singapore we got one other big break— Hillary Clinton agreed to join us to help make our case.

That was key because the US bidding model means our city arrived essentially alone for the final vote, whereas each of our competitors looked like it was backed by its entire nation. This manifests itself in who leads the delegation. London brought Prime Minister Tony Blair to Singapore. President Jacques Chirac of France represented Paris. No sitting US president had ever attended an IOC meeting on behalf of its candidate city at an IOC meeting (although President Barack Obama would be the first when he flew to Copenhagen to stump for his hometown Chicago's 2016 bid four years later). Given President George W. Bush's extreme lack of global popularity in 2005, his absence was probably for the best in this case.

But it meant we had to gin up our own political star power. Secretary of State Colin Powell had been very supportive of our bid, but he had other commitments. So did Bill Clinton. Kriegel then reached out to Hillary Clinton through an emissary. She was, after all, the junior senator from New York and, more important, a global superstar from her tenure as First Lady.

Word came back that Clinton was interested, but she needed to be persuaded that we had a good chance so that the long trip wouldn't be a waste of her time. A few days later, I learned from my friend Alex Gilady that she had reached out to his boss, Chair of *NBC Sports* Dick Ebersol, to ask his opinion. This was smart. Ebersol was by far the most influential and plugged-in American with the IOC because of NBC's huge, long-term commitment as its US broadcast partner. Gilady relayed that Ebersol had told Hillary that we had a chance to win and that her presence could meaningfully boost our chances. That Ebersol (and, presumably, Gilady) thought we had a good chance to win was thrilling, made even more so when a few days later Clinton agreed to join us, just two days before we were set to fly to Singapore. It was like a double shot of adrenaline.

The entire NYC2012 team got on a flight to Singapore on a high. Our delegation was more than one hundred strong. We brought dozens of VIPs. Many of the major financial backers of our bid came. The heads of many of New York's labor unions, so supportive of our bid, came and did double duty highlighting the smooth working relationship between the bid and the city's labor movement, which stood in stark contrast with front-runner Paris. Threats of labor strikes were thought to be one of the weaknesses of its bid. Alisa was there, of course, as well as my daughter Ariel and my twin brothers, Andy and Tom.

When we arrived in Singapore, the scene was a five-ring circus. It seemed that everyone associated with the Olympics had descended upon the city.

Meanwhile, it was murderously hot and muggy, so that if you stepped outside you immediately became dripping wet. Everywhere you looked, you saw another city contingent jockeying for position. London brought London taxicabs wrapped in London2012 signs. I wished I had thought of that. All the bidders had their stars. Paris had famed director Luc Besson. London had soccer legend David Beckham. Tony Blair was seemingly ubiquitous, charming everyone.

But our team had The Greatest—Muhammad Ali. Ali was arguably one of the most famous people in the world, and he was an Olympian, having won a gold medal at the 1960 Rome Games at the tender age of eighteen. He was revered in Olympic circles. By 2005, Ali had late-stage Parkinson's and could barely walk, yet when he entered the Ritz Carlton in Singapore, where all the city delegations were housed, it was as if a god had descended to earth. The crowds parted. And then a line of dignitaries and athletes formed to pay homage as he sat on a sofa in the lobby.

In Singapore, we ran two parallel operations. There was a full schedule of events, tours, and briefings for all of our supporters who had come to cheer us on and be part of this hopefully triumphant occasion. Our hospitality team guided, pampered, educated, and kept them feeling special. Meanwhile, our core group focused on the impending IOC vote. So, for me, time in Singapore was spent mostly as it was at other Olympic events, only with much greater urgency, in hotel lobbies and private rooms making the case to members for why they should support us. Also, there were last-minute parties and get-togethers for the final rounds of jockeying.

Two nights before the vote, Bloomberg and I hosted an expensive dinner for the Russian delegation. The purpose was to cement our mutual pledge to vote for each other in the event that one of our bids was voted out in the first round. Because Moscow was thought to be the low city on the totem pole, it was likely this pledge would benefit us. Twelve Russians, including Mayor Yury Luzhkov and the three Russian IOC members, joined Bloomberg, Kriegel, and me and our IOC members. Many toasts over vodka were downed, all in the spirit of Olympic fraternity (and the hope that the other city would bow out first).

Roy Bahat and his team gathered every bit of intelligence and rumor about how IOC members were leaning. We kept our focus on those IOC members we believed most likely to be partial or open to New York's bid. And because voting occurred in several rounds, with a city dropping out each time, we had to strive to be the second or even third choice of members who were committed initially to another city.

I'd like to report that at least some of this was humorous and fun for me, but it wasn't. I was under vise-like stress. The basic mechanics of keeping track of so many moving parts and people was dizzying in itself—like being a host of a huge party at which everyone wants your attention, but you also need to make sure a few special guests are being looked after impeccably. Then we had frequent rehearsals for the presentation. By now, Clinton had arrived. She was invariably gracious, encouraging, and low maintenance. At our rehearsals, she acted as my personal public speaking coach. "More emotion," she urged me.

But it was all made worse by a growing dread. Unbeknownst to most of my staff, even at this very, very late date, the entire bid was in jeopardy, all because of one completely outrageous detail: an unsigned piece of paper. The looming crisis had its origins in the return of Peter Ueberroth as Chair of the USOC in 2004.

From an initial encouraging start, relations with Ueberroth had worsened. We had problems getting him to attend Olympic-related events, which should have been mandatory for the head of the candidate city's National Olympic Committee. His frequent absences began to be noted by members. The powerful Mario Vasquez Raña was holding a meeting of the Pan American Sports Organization in Mexico that spring that I just could not attend. Raña, who liked to show his power, insisted that at least Ueberroth should represent the United States. We practically begged Ueberroth, but he kept evading us. Finally, days before the event, he agreed to go but said no flights suited his schedule and demanded a private plane. We were so desperate that we actually paid $16,000 to accede to his request.

But that wasn't even the worst of it. The IOC has a standard agreement called the Joint Marketing Agreement that delineates the relationship between the candidate city and the NOC (in our case, the USOC) with respect to sponsorship revenues during the four years prior to the Games. All bidding cities are required to sign one. It is a complex agreement, but essentially it describes who will sell sponsorships and how the money will be split between the NOC and the host committee (the entity into which the bid committee morphs when it wins the bid). The IOC is a party to the document because it wants to ensure that the host committee has enough money to successfully put on the Games.

Because the USOC relies on private funding, including sponsorships, to fund its operations, the IOC had historically allowed the USOC to retain a higher percentage of sponsorship revenues than it had other NOCs. But during our negotiations, Ueberroth had proposed a split even more favorable to the USOC. Naturally, we resisted—and the IOC agreed with us. Ueberroth was incensed by the IOC's interference and began stalling on signing at all. The IOC deadline for submission of the Joint Marketing Agreement was in April. It came and went. We had to get an extension. Eventually, Ueberroth caved on the percentage splits, but then the issue became the timing of disbursing the shares. He wanted the USOC to get paid earlier. All spring, Kriegel had been sending new drafts to Ueberroth and his lawyer, and always they came back with a new wrinkle.

Desperate, I went to visit Ueberroth again to ask for some moderation. He wouldn't budge. Instead he railed bitterly about the IOC and even warned that he could pull out of the television and sponsorship agreements, as favorable as they were to the USOC, and have the USOC negotiate its own television and sponsorship deals, and he was confident the USOC would do better alone than as part of the IOC deal. It was madness. We got several more extensions from the IOC and continued to try to persuade Ueberroth to sign, but we had no luck. By the time we had to depart for Singapore, the deal points in contention were minor, but we still didn't have a signed agreement. The IOC made it clear that without a signed Joint Marketing Agreement, it couldn't put forward our candidacy for the vote.

We arrived in Singapore four days before the vote. The very first morning we had breakfast with Ueberroth at his room in the hotel. As always, his wife, Ginny, was present. We had made every change Ueberroth had requested, and as usual he had an excuse. He couldn't sign the document until his lawyer reviewed it. He hadn't bothered to bring this lawyer to Singapore but insisted this lawyer had to evaluate the document in person. So we waited while the USOC's lawyer, Jeff Benz, boarded a plane. This wasn't like flying from San Francisco to Los Angeles. Benz had to get from Colorado Springs to Singapore, two flights and a half a world away! One more day wasted. Up to now, I had been reasonably calm about this, always assuming that we would get it done, but now I was panicking.

Word of our troubles with the USOC was beginning to filter out to the IOC members, with potentially fatal results. Gunilla Lindberg, a respected member from Sweden and a great friend of Charlie Battle, had been very sympathetic to our bid. As we had tallied how we thought members would vote in the first round, we counted her as tentatively supportive. On our second day in Singapore, when she saw Charlie, she had this warning: "You guys have not submitted your marketing agreement, and there is only one of two things we can conclude from that: either Peter Ueberroth doesn't want New York to win, which makes him a lousy partner for you, which is not good for the Olympics, or he does want you to win but still can't get this done, which means, worse, he is a lousy partner for us." It was a devastating indictment.

With forty-eight hours to go until the vote, Olympic Games Executive Director Gilbert Felli, the highest-ranking member of the IOC's permanent staff, informed us that the next day the IOC Executive Board was going to have one final meeting to certify that all of the bids had complied with the IOC's requirements and were eligible for the vote. He firmly explained that our Joint Marketing Agreement had to be signed and delivered to him. If we failed, the IOC would be compelled to announce that our bid was not in compliance, which would effectively doom our chances.

By now Benz had arrived in Singapore, so Peter Ueberroth, Ginny Ueberroth, Benz, Kriegel, and I reassembled in his room. Ueberroth and his wife sat on the bed, and the three of us sat arrayed in chairs at their side. The tension was overwhelming. Benz spoke first, raising technical points so minor I couldn't contain myself. Finally, after months of patience, I blew up. As far as I was concerned, Ueberroth was putting the whole bid at risk to make some empty point. "You can't do this to us!" I screamed. "This is it!" Eleven years of preparation and work were being held up by utterly trivial legal technicalities. Ueberroth was unmoved. All he would say was that we shouldn't yell in front of his wife. Then he threw us out.

The IOC Executive Board met later that day and certified the rest of the bids. Felli told us that the Executive Board was going to meet again the next morning at eight a.m.—the morning of the candidate city presentations and the vote. We had one last chance. The agreement had to be given to him by then, after which the doors would be closed. Meanwhile, Kriegel tried to repair the damage from our disastrous meeting with Ueberroth. The day ended without resolution, although Ueberroth agreed to meet with us at seven a.m. at his hotel.

So the night before I was going to lead our team—New York City—into the Raffles City Convention Center to make our final pitch in front of a global audience, when I needed to be at my most confident, I tossed and turned, unable to sleep, not because I was worried that our presentation wasn't great or that we hadn't done a thorough job of lobbying members (Hillary Clinton, in particular, was a natural diplomat, foreshadowing her success as Secretary of State) but because a single piece of paper hadn't been submitted because our supposed partner and ally, the savior of the Olympic movement, seemed to be indulging in a petty power play.

I got out of bed around six a.m., completely exhausted. Kriegel and I arrived at seven a.m. at Ueberroth's hotel as planned. He was late. He dawdled as long as he could. Finally, he signed at 7:45 a.m. No changes had been made. There had been no point at all to the delay. Kriegel literally ran the document underground through the passageways to the IOC hotel next door, and, huffing and puffing, delivered the Joint Marketing Agreement with minutes to spare.

Just a few hours later, we had to go to the presentation room in the Raffles and make our one-hour presentation. We had, of course, rehearsed like crazy. We also had rakish uniforms designed by Oscar de la Renta. Everyone wore white pants and navy-blue blazers, and then there were scarves and matching ties with patterns of NYC2012 all over them. Later, a local fashion reporter would say we looked like "stewards on the Titanic." But, at the time, we felt pretty stylish.

Our presentation included some overlap with the one we made in Colorado Springs, but we added a steady stream of videos that included as many diverse voices from around New York City as possible: Janet Evans and Bob Beamon explained our venues with backup from a series of videos with athletes from each sport filling in more details, including Sugar Ray Leonard, Magic Johnson, and Serena Williams. The 1964 gold medalist swimmer Donna de Varona covered the seven-year sports marketing program that New York planned on behalf of the forty Olympic sports to boost the development of each international federation.

Bloomberg spoke next and made a plea that subtly referred back to 9/11: "Our city needs these Games in 2012. When I became Mayor four years ago, we didn't know what our future would be. In our city's darkest hour, we asked ourselves, can we recover? New Yorkers stood up then and said, 'Yes, we can recover, we will rebuild, and we must continue to welcome everyone.'"

Clinton's job was to show that the country was behind New York in getting this done. You could have heard a pin drop when she spoke, asserting that New York would have the backing at the highest level of the federal government for security and anything else necessary. She was utterly convincing. We even gave her some backup in video form. Bill Clinton appeared to promote an international peace development program we would pursue if we won the bid. And, in a short clip, President Bush promised the full support of the United States government.

I was the last of the speakers. "After eleven years, I can't describe how it feels to reach this moment," I said. "Give us the chance, and we will make you proud." We ended the presentation with a variation on the video we had used to such great effect as our closing in Colorado Springs two and a half years before. I loved it because it so perfectly conveyed the essence of our bid. It showed the lonely runner carrying an Olympic torch through the streets of the city, gradually joined by thousands of people of every age and ethnic background. It ended with a silhouette of the runner in front of the city's most famous landmark, the Statue of Liberty. Later that day, the *New York Times* would report that our final presentation was "called surprisingly emotional and personal, [and] was almost universally lauded."

At the end of the presentation, we got a rousing round of applause. Then it was time to field questions from the delegates. Those too went well. Most were softballs. Prince Albert of Monaco traditionally asked the first question. He asked whether any more venue changes were planned (no). Sergei Bubka, the legendary Ukrainian pole vaulter, now an IOC member, asked what we were doing to develop interest in track and field in the United States. I pointed to what would be the first permanent track in New York City certified by the IAAF. We were asked whether athletes and officials from countries on the US terrorist watch list would be allowed to travel to New York City (yes).

We were feeling confident—until the very last questioner. It was our old friend, Bloomberg's fellow media mogul from Mexico, Mario Vasquez Raña. He had pledged solidarity with us, his fellow Americans, at our secret meeting in Mexico City. "The Americas must stick together," he had said. Despite this promise, we knew he had a reputation for being completely untrustworthy. So when he rose to ask a question, I was already on edge. Instead of making a query, however, he just lavishly praised our presentation for what seemed like a whole minute. If this had been anyone else, it might have been a good sign. But because of Vasquez Raña's oiliness, Bloomberg and I looked over at each other at the same moment and immediately knew what the other one was thinking: "He isn't supporting us."

After all the cities were finished, we were dismissed to await the voting. Our entire delegation returned to the Ritz-Carlton, and then on large video screens we watched the proceedings continue in the presentation room in the Raffles. IOC rules require a series of votes until one city gets a majority. After each round, the lowest vote-getter is eliminated. At 5:29 p.m., Rogge announced: "The city of Moscow will not participate in the next round." Then, four minutes later, we were shocked to hear: "The City of New York will not participate in the next round."

I was absolutely stunned. It had certainly occurred to me that we would not win, but coming in fourth was beyond my worst expectation. We were universally believed to be in the top three. The picture on the front page of the *New York Times* the next morning would absolutely catch my deer-in-the-headlights confusion. At the press conference afterward, I had to admit, "I don't really know what happened." That barely described how I felt. I felt humiliated, embarrassed, and deeply saddened. I had spent eleven years of my life not just on a failed quest but on a quest that seemed to have failed badly.

When we learned the vote counts, there would be further speculation about what had happened. In the first round, the votes were tightly bunched at 22, 21, 20, 19 (New York), and 15 (Moscow). In the second round we lost, having just 16 votes. We actually had fewer votes in the second round than the first. Per our drunken toasts of kinship, we had expected the Russians and their allies to vote for us in the second round. That should have been at least six votes—three from the Russian IOC members and the others from friendly Eastern European members. We also expected more support from some Latin American and Asian members.

Because of the secret ballot, there is no way to actually know what happened, but later, as we pieced things together, it became clear that a main factor in our second-round exit was Juan Antonio Samaranch, the former President of the IOC. He had been determined to keep his home country, in which his son played a prominent role in Madrid's bid, from being humiliated. He didn't expect to win, but he drew on his personal connections to persuade several members to back Madrid in the second round. After all, most of these IOC members had been appointed by Samaranch, and many felt indebted to him. Asking for their vote only in the early rounds, so as not to embarrass his family, was not a heavy request. This was especially true of the Russians; Samaranch had been Spanish Ambassador to Russia and kept close ties. In fact, in the second round, Madrid actually led all cities in the voting with 32 votes to London's 27 and Paris's 25. In the third round, after many IOC members had apparently fulfilled their commitments to Samaranch, Madrid was eliminated, leaving Paris and London. London won on the fourth vote, in something of a surprise, 54–50.

At the end of the day, we could never really know why we lost. Samaranch. Ueberroth. The USOC. Atlanta. Salt Lake City. Bush and our wars in Iraq and Afghanistan. The West Side Stadium. Who knows?

Later in the evening, Alisa and I went to the party we had planned for our celebration. I really didn't want to go, but knew I had no choice. Both Bloomberg and I got up and told our team how proud we were of all the work and our supporters how grateful we were for their steadfast support. Bloomberg was also gracious as always in defeat and generous to me. I had come to expect that. I would need a lot of support in the months to come. My lucky life had been an almost uninterrupted series of successes, and now I was facing my first major loss (with the exception of my parents' premature deaths)—and on a global scale no less. I was crushed.

CHAPTER NINETEEN

LONG RIDE BACK

BACK IN 2005 the longest nonstop flight in the world was from Singapore to New York—nearly nineteen hours. The day after the NYC2012 defeat, Alisa and I boarded a Singapore Airlines A-340 jet with many members of the NYC2012 team for the trip home. It was an excruciatingly long ride and the start of an even longer journey of reflection and recovery.

As we settled into the flight, I felt numb, exhausted, and disappointed. I was at a loss for what to do next. I was surrounded by many of the people I loved most, some of whom were going through the same feelings I was, and that helped. We were a short-term mutual support society. Hillary Clinton was across the aisle, engrossed in reading a huge pile of wonky-looking briefing materials. I slid into the seat next to her and thanked her again for coming and for being so gracious. She didn't seem to feel even a touch of resentment for having come so far for a failed effort. She grew a little philosophical. She told me that NYC2012 had been a great effort, but that it just wasn't our time to win. She must have intuited my shame at the public nature of the defeat. She offered that she had been through her own painful public moments (quite an understatement) and that things have a way of working out.

Her wisdom would eventually sink in, but I was not ready to hear it. I did recognize that although the loss of a dream is different from the loss of a loved one, I was in a kind of mourning. It wasn't like I had felt when my parents died, but I took a bit of comfort remembering that time did heal the wounds. Still, grief is very powerful; it is not something you control. It is not something you can just put on the back burner because you wish it to be so. It is something you must experience and live with until it lifts of its own accord. It takes time. There is no other way. During the darkness, however, there are little lessons that will finally add up and show you the way to reframe your loss so you can live with it. Clinton had just delivered lesson no. 1.

Touching down in New York that Thursday, July 7, however, I still felt like an enormous failure. The weight of my pain was now showing, and my family was rushing in to provide comfort. In twenty years of flying in and out of New York City, I'd never once been met at the airport by anyone I knew—I had car services for that chore. But this time, my brother Mark had driven down from his home in Hyde Park, about an hour and a half north of the city, to greet us. It was incredibly touching. The significance was not lost on me. With me as his older brother, and particularly an older brother who had helped him through difficult times over the years, here was a moment for Mark to lend me his shoulder for a change and say, "Go on, lean on me."

I had another moment for rumination when we landed in New York. While we were in transit, London had been the subject of a series of coordinated terrorist attacks on the city's public transport system during rush hour. Security is a prime concern in any Olympic bid. It made me wonder if the attacks were planned for the winning city regardless of who won. In planning for the Olympic bid, I had only thought of bringing glory to my adopted home, and the thought that my project might have also attracted a terrorist attack made me shudder.

That weekend, Alisa took me away for a few days of recuperation on Martha's Vineyard, off the Massachusetts coast. The weather was warm and idyllic, the ocean surprisingly warm, the restaurants crowded with vacationers having obviously wonderful times. I was jealous of them, and I couldn't enjoy a minute of it. An optimist by nature, I felt a darkness that I had never felt before. My overwhelming sense of failure was growing. It had now seized control of me. In my head, I was such a public fool that I began to dread going into work. Exhausted and depressed, I spent almost the entire weekend sleeping.

On Monday morning, I willed myself up the steps of City Hall, which had always given me a jolt of excitement as I climbed them. I'm not sure how I expected people to react—maybe with whispers in the halls behind my back or expressions of glee at my defeat—but just the opposite occurred. Instead, as I went about my day nearly everyone had supportive comments like, "What an incredible effort," and "There was nothing else you could have done." That first day back, a few of my staff members took me out to lunch at Odeon, a restaurant near City Hall, to try to cheer me up. They remember my being unbelievably morose. So it didn't help when we walked into the nearly empty restaurant to see Charles Bagli leaving lunch just as we were coming in. It was awkward.

After a couple of days, people stopped commenting, and it appeared that no one seemed to care at all. In fact, it was as if everyone had already forgotten. This led to one of my most important insights: no one cares about you as much as you do. I repeat this all of the time to colleagues and friends, particularly overachievers like me, held back by a fear of failure. When you go through life rarely failing, you build up a fear of loss. For two years after that first conversation with Alex Gilady the very real possibility that we might lose was an ever-present specter trailing me. A part of me dreaded the day when I would stand in Singapore and hear the words "New York City will not participate in the next round of voting" because I was afraid that people would think I was a loser. But when it actually happened everyone quickly moved on to their, and New York's, next adventure.

However, I was still in too much pain over the Olympic loss to fully process it. I remained in an utterly foul mood for weeks. The next week Alisa made plans to get away from New York again, to Jackson Hole, Wyoming, for a long weekend. While we were driving through Grand Teton National Park enjoying the scenery, I got a call from John Cahill, Governor George Pataki's top aide. I liked and respected him—he had brought some degree of order to the chaos then engulfing the World Trade Center site—and he was just doing his job in calling me to discuss one of the never-ending series of problems cropping up in the rebuilding. For no apparent reason, I lost complete control of my temper. I was yelling so hard that I had to get out of the car and walk away.

Thinking back, I was such an ass. But it was another lesson. Relaxing was not going to be the way out of the funk for me. Work was. Before the trip to Singapore, I had committed to Mike Bloomberg that I would stay in City Hall for another two years assuming he won reelection (and we lost the Olympic bid). It was an easy call. I loved working for him, and I certainly had a plethora of projects I wanted to bring to completion.

That promise would turn out to be a saving grace of sorts. About a week after I returned from Singapore, I got a call from my old mentor from Lehman Brothers, Peter Solomon. Peter demanded to know if I was staying on. He was reassured to find out I was. "You don't want to go out on a bad note," he advised. "Get a few more wins under your belt before you begin your next chapter." Fortunately, by the time we got back from Singapore, Bloomberg was still around fifteen points ahead in the polls. But he wasn't taking any chances. He would eventually spend a record $84 million on his reelection. The campaign began in July, and with it we became increasingly confident that he would win in November.

With that in mind and with my determination to recommit myself to City Hall, I decided we needed to do some real planning for the second term. Back in January 2004, I had called for a retreat for all of my staff and the agency heads and their deputies who reported to me. We met for two days at the Staten Island Hilton Gardens (part of our five-borough economic development strategy!) to step back and take a look at our progress. We had already set in motion a lot of big plans, but at that point we hadn't yet taken any of them through a successful approval process. That was the big question we asked ourselves in Staten Island. Could we actually get anything approved?

Just after I got back from Singapore, I told my staff that I wanted to have a second summit—in just three weeks! On short notice, Josh Sirefman, my Chief of Staff, and Marc Ricks, a Senior Policy Advisor, and I pulled together an agenda for the meeting to be held at Gracie Mansion at the end of the month. This time the topic wasn't going to be whether we could get our plans approved but how we could manage the growth that they would, hopefully, create, and then could we get them all built.

The first topic basically boiled down to the question of how we were going to prevent the city from becoming a victim of our own success. Even in the crazy months before the Olympic decision, I insisted that we continue to have our Economic Development Agency Council meetings. At one of the pre-Olympic decision meetings, the City Planning Department brought in Joe Salvo, the head of its Population Division, to make a presentation. Salvo's series of PowerPoint slides told a compelling story: the virtuous cycle of the successful city was taking hold. Crime was down; housing starts, particularly in the outer boroughs, were up; and newcomers were pouring in much faster than people were leaving, at an accelerating rate. The result was that population was growing more quickly than we had anticipated. In fact, he predicted, the city would have a startling 9 million people by 2030 (up from 8.1 million when we took office).

I began obsessing over those extra million people. Early on, I had primarily looked at housing as the constraint on accommodating more people. That is why we had pushed so hard to find land for housing and then to find the money for affordable housing. But as we went through the various rezoning battles, I realized how naive I'd been. Housing was barely the beginning. Think of it this way: we come into a neighborhood and say that we are going to add five thousand residential apartments that can hold roughly fifteen thousand new people. The first thing current residents want to know during the rezoning hearings is whether we will add a school, a park, and a fire station. But even they miss the full picture: the vast range of other services and facilities they take for granted—from the municipal tow pound to stables for police horses—that will also have to be located, expanded, or relocated.

In each of the rezonings we had undertaken—and in the many more we were contemplating—we were beginning to confront what I call the Salt Pile Problem. Every neighborhood needs energy, but no one wants the power plant. Every neighborhood needs garbage pickup, but no one wants to store the sanitation trucks. Every neighborhood demands that its streets be ploughed and salted quickly after a snowstorm, but absolutely no one wants a salt pile, the mound of salt positioned where it can be accessed easily during a storm. This not-in-my-backyard attitude was understandable, of course, but it was also a logistical nightmare. If we wanted timely trash pickup in Brooklyn, we couldn't keep all the trash truck garages in the Bronx.

So a key goal of the Gracie Mansion summit was to have a disciplined, coordinated effort to identify all of the possible locations for the noxious operations nobody wanted in his or her backyard so we could keep growing without causing a host of new problems. We wanted to make sure that these undesirable facilities were distributed fairly across the city for both moral and practical reasons: they needed to be close to neighborhoods to work. Above all, we needed to plan for these mundane, essential, unglamorous services so that they didn't become obstacles choking the city's growth.

The second topic for the summit was to create a mini agency that would handle big building projects from design to ribbon cutting. The trick was that the office would report just to me in the Mayor's office—something that would probably not be popular with my Commissioners. (No one likes to cede power.) So one of the main objectives of the summit was to get the Commissioners to see the organizational issues clearly and lead them to their own conclusion that a centralized office would help them in their efforts.

We started by outlining all sixty projects under way—a stunning number. We pointed out that almost every one had its own strategic plan. Some were city-led, some were state-led, and some were the responsibility of a single agency. As we detailed who was responsible for getting what done, it was clear that many—such as the High Line, the BAM Cultural District, and the waterfront parks in Lower Manhattan and Greenpoint-Williamsburg—split responsibility among several agencies. We added an element of urgency by emphasizing that we had only four more years. (We had no idea then that Bloomberg would eventually overturn term limits and run successfully a third time.) Finally, we outlined clear criteria for when the new office would have jurisdiction—only in projects involving more than one agency where it was ambiguous as to which agency should have the lead.

After hearing this, the Commissioners readily came onboard. By October, Bloomberg signed an executive order creating the Mayor's Office of Capital Projects Development. The role of the office was to oversee project coordination, from soup to nuts, from architectural drawings to successful construction. I knew exactly whom I wanted to be in charge of it: Andrew Winters.

Winters had started with me as an aide to Alex Garvin when we restarted the Olympic bid in 1998. When the planning for NYC2012 was largely complete, he moved over with Garvin to the Lower Manhattan Development Corporation, and then after the selection of the Liebeskind plan, came back to NYC2012. A graduate of the Yale School of Architecture, he proved his competency to me a hundred times over through these trials. He had a unique combination of attributes that made him a perfect fit for the job: he was diplomatic, as witnessed by his performance at Ground Zero, which would enable him to win over the Commissioners; he was an incredible project manager, as I had seen in the miraculous Mets Stadium turnaround, which would be essential in moving complex projects forward; and he had a unique blend of design sense, intellectual curiosity, and construction knowledge combined with a very modest ego.

At its height, the office would have only nine staffers, but I immediately put ten big projects under its purview, including the High Line, Yankee Stadium, and East River waterfront park. The office's impact was felt almost immediately. In the case of the High Line, even though its zoning and funding had been approved in May, almost nothing had been accomplished. This was a high-profile project, so inaction was disconcerting. Right away, Winters went to one of the weekly planning meetings and saw the problem. There were three city agencies involved: the City Planning Department, the Parks Department, and the Economic Development Corporation. In addition, Friends of the High Line was also at the table.

All four groups sent at least three staffers to the meetings, focused on design at this point. After the architects presented designs, each agency would give extensive notes, which often conflicted with those of the others. The meetings lasted six hours. As a result, the architects were frustrated with their inability to present plans that could make everyone happy and left with little idea about how to proceed and process the mounds of contradictory advice they received.

In his first meeting, Winters discovered another problem. The team was currently mired in a debate over whether the High Line should have public restrooms that would be cantilevered up and out over the streets. They might have looked cool, but they added millions and millions of extra dollars to a project already over budget. No one was empowered to make a decision. They had been debating it for months.

Not only did multiple agencies lead to paralysis when it came to decision making but also the issue illuminated still another problem that crops up when multiple agencies work on a project: Who is responsible for paying for it all? In the case of the High Line, the City Planning Department could be particularly demanding when it came to design because it knew it would not have to pay for maintenance and improvements.

Winters immediately killed the bathroom idea. "We're just not doing that," he explained. Then he limited the weekly project meetings to only him, one participant from each agency, and the designer. All notes were prepared by him or his office. He resolved all the discrepancies he could on his own through interagency diplomacy, facilitated by his easygoing, collaborative style. Everyone liked and trusted him.

Those issues he couldn't resolve, he brought to me and I made the call. The weekly High Line meetings quickly shrunk to one hour. Winters was supposed to report to me once a week to resolve conflicts, but it soon became apparent that I agreed with almost every decision he made. We were so in sync that Commissioners soon took him as a proxy for me when he was sitting in on meetings. The same thing grew to be true with state officials. All of this facilitated his ability to get things done so effectively that over the remainder of the Bloomberg Administration my successors and I added many more projects to the Office of Capital Projects Development's portfolio. But perhaps the biggest impact Winters had was in Brooklyn. When we formed the Office of Capital Projects Development, much of our agenda in Brooklyn was stuck.

Coney Island had been through an entire design process for the streetscapes there when it was discovered that the Department of Environmental Protection had a $2 billion, mostly unfunded, infrastructure project that needed to be done below those streets. Brooklyn Bridge Park had a design but no plan for implementation and no clear path toward a governance structure that could implement that plan. The Greenpoint-Williamsburg waterfront parks had dramatic funding problems as well as a demanding community that wanted action.

At the BAM Cultural District, ground hadn't been broken on a single one of the signature projects, and they were spending like drunken sailors on "starchitects." The master plan for the district had passed from Rem Koolhaas and Diller Scofidio + Renfro to Dan Wood of Work Architecture Company. And of the first $100 million the BAM LDC had to spend—the city's $50 million, plus $50 million in still unraised matching funds—roughly 80 percent would be used to build a massive, underground parking garage spanning one or two city blocks. I couldn't fathom why BAM, so close to so much mass transit, would need so much parking. But our team eventually worked through many of the issues, helping to create a new Brooklyn.

At Coney Island, Winters, Josh Sirefman, and many others, including my successors and other agencies of city government, worked with the community to develop a comprehensive but realistic plan to rebuild it, including the renovation of the Brooklyn Aquarium and the public spaces at the boardwalk; a completely rehabilitated subway stop; community amenities, such as a new YMCA; and another Marty Markowitz special, a new five-thousand-seat concert amphitheater. Winters's team took over the rehabilitation of many of the great attractions such as the Parachute Jump, Luna Park, the Steeplechase Plaza, the B&B Carousel, and the amusement district. The projects together helped earn the community's trust to get a 2009 rezoning passed that would permit a sizable amount of new, mixed-income housing to be built. Today, the boardwalk and amusement district are again attracting wildly diverse crowds to the area. More importantly, for the first time in decades we are beginning to see big investments in housing at a wide range of income levels, illustrating our basic approach—eventually, with a smart mix of investments and a plan that earns community trust, even the most neglected area can be brought back to life.

Winters stepped into the Brooklyn Bridge Park mess and helped new President Regina Myer, who had worked for the city, to create a simple phasing and implementation plan that spread out the benefits and ensured the most valuable space was built first. Winters and his staff coordinated with other city agencies working in the area to make sure the various projects in the park could move simultaneously. It is a wonderful thing to build new parks, and the ribbon cuttings are always nice events, but a constant problem in New York is their maintenance. Somehow when inevitably the economic cycle turns negative, maintenance for parks is one of the first budget cuts. As we planned new parks, we tried to get creative in finding permanent sources of funding for them.

The case of Brooklyn Bridge Park is illustrative. When the city and state acquired the piers and created the Brooklyn Bridge Park Development Corporation, we each made a commitment for money to build the park, but there was no provision for operating expenses after the park was built. In addition, it quickly became evident that the park would cost more than we thought to build. The piles that kept up the piers and the edge of the waterfront in Brooklyn were old and rotting and needed to be replaced and repaired en masse and then maintained regularly. The park alone had thirteen thousand timber piles within its borders. We estimated the eventual cost would be several hundred million dollars.

The solution we proposed was to allow some development and some concessions on the park's edges. Then we would capture the city taxes from those buildings and the development rights (in effect, the park would sell the right to build on the designated sites) to pay future costs. For example, one developer wanted to turn an old manufacturing building just to the south of the park at nearby Atlantic Avenue into a luxury condo complex. He asked the city to rezone his building to residential use, which can be a complicated process. Although the boundaries of the park project did not include his building, we proposed including the building in the technical definition of the park—although only on the edge—thus speeding up the process of enabling the developer to convert it to residential use. And then we provided that the future tax revenue and ground rent from the building would be dedicated to park upkeep instead of going into the general city till. We did the same thing with a series of other parcels.

We got sued for our approach. The park purists argued that the sanctity of the park was being invaded by this horrible development. But without the ability to generate that revenue, we probably wouldn't have committed the funds to build the park, thus making their argument pointless. Besides, although the buildings were technically in the confines of the park, mostly for financial reasons, they were only adjacent to it. Through many twists and turns, our scheme was upheld. Based on current forecasts, the five building parcels are estimated to generate $200 million in upfront payments and about $20 million a year thereafter for ongoing maintenance and improvement of the park.

Myer and her team did a magnificent job of building the park, the acceleration of which was made possible when in 2010 Bob Lieber, my successor as Deputy Mayor, engineered the transfer of the state's ownership of Brooklyn Bridge Park and Governor's Island to the city. Having complete control enabled Myer and Leslie Koch, the President and CEO of the Trust for Governor's Island, to move at Bloomberg speed, creating great parks and helping to cement a legacy of parks in New York Harbor.

On the Greenpoint-Williamsburg waterfront, the Office of Capital Projects Development created a phasing plan, established a community liaison, and brought agencies together to build an award-winning new waterfront park, the first in decades.

For the BAM Cultural District, Winters and Cultural Affairs Commissioner Kate Levin decided the city needed to put in more money. The city required as a condition to its pledge of an additional $74 million (on top of the original $50 million already committed) that none of it would go to pay for parking. That meant that above-ground development decisions would not be dictated by the parking grid. In addition, the city took over the development, management, and decision making of the BAM Cultural District. As a result, construction on the Theatre for a New Audience and the Mark Morris Dance Center was able to proceed. Finally, the Arts District was on the move.

Atlantic Yards was more complicated. The lawsuits dragged on long after I left office and almost brought Bruce Ratner down. By 2008, the project had become bogged down, and Ratner said the delays and slumping markets from the 2008 financial meltdown and its aftermath had put the entire project in jeopardy. He had to halt all work within the Atlantic Yards footprint and replace the architect, Frank Gehry, with SHoP Architects, a New York–based firm. To save the project in 2009, Ratner was forced to sell 80 percent of the Nets and 45 percent of the arena to Russian oligarch Mikhail Prokhorov. It wasn't until 2010 that groundbreaking finally began. Eventually, he would sell most of the rest to a Chinese developer.

So, after all that trauma, what were the results? The redesigned Barclays Center opened in 2012 to (mostly) rave architectural reviews, with critics praising its proportions and its fit into the neighborhood. The Brooklyn Nets and the New York Islanders both play there, so Markowitz got not one but two professional teams. And just as predicted, the surrounding area is brimming with great restaurants; nightlife and property values have continued to soar. Thousands of units of desperately needed affordable housing are finally coming online. And how about this for a kicker: the feared terrible traffic congestion never materialized. Whether Ratner and Forest City Ratner will ever make any money on the project, I don't think we will ever know. But Ratner's vision, commitment, and tenacity made this transformative project possible.

When we started planning and pumping city money into Brooklyn, we expected great things. But Brooklyn's renaissance was successful beyond even our wildest dreams. It was a home run. In Downtown Brooklyn, more than $10 billion has been invested in an area that had almost no investment before. Residential development blossomed. By the tenth anniversary of the project, 6,700 new apartments had been constructed, and more than 12,000 more were in the pipeline. Assuming those are built, there will be 35,000 to 45,000 people living in an area that had fewer than 5,000 before. A *New York Times* analysis projected that one-fifth of all apartment rentals coming online in all of New York City would be in Brooklyn's Flatbush corridor. Those new residents attract a vibrant mix of retailers. Most of the infrastructure to make the area more appealing was built, although the park in the middle took a lot longer than we expected.

Although hotel owners took advantage of the rezoning, with forty new hotels opened, the office space was a different story. We projected 4.6 million square feet of office space, but less than half of that has been constructed. Giving developers the option of uses naturally forces them to weigh the economic values of the alternatives, and, despite generous incentives for office space and what we thought was a real need for relatively inexpensive office space in the city, housing was still a more valuable option.

When we passed the Downtown Brooklyn plan, we didn't focus much on affordable housing, largely because we didn't expect the residential demand. In fact, during the first ten years after the plan was approved, only 530 affordable units, or less than 10 percent of all new units, were created. Over time, the Bloomberg and De Blasio Administrations would dedicate more resources to affordable housing in the area, but we quickly learned to tie our rezoning plans and our housing plans together. We would never make that mistake again.

Across Brooklyn employment growth was very strong. According to a report by the state's Comptroller, the number of private-sector jobs in Brooklyn jumped 19.8 percent between 2003 and 2012—or at roughly twice the rate of that of the other boroughs. From 2007 to 2015, Brooklyn (Kings County) had the sixth fastest job growth of any county of over 250,000 people or more in the United States, according to the Bureau of Labor Statistics. And these were jobs Brooklyn could never attract before. Brooklyn is just the kind of place with which cool tech companies want to be associated. It is now home to some very prestigious growth companies such as Vice Media, Etsy, and Kickstarter.

In 2016, the Brooklyn Navy Yard announced that it was undergoing yet another major expansion designed to double its current campus and allow it to employ sixteen thousand people by 2020. At the center of the development is a state-of-the-art, 260,000-square-foot Green Manufacturing Center—an interdisciplinary space designed to support entrepreneurs working in emerging technologies such as robotics and artificial intelligence—right next door to Brooklyn Roasting Company, which offers high-quality, fair-trade, organic coffees. In other words, the Yard is dynamic, sustainable, inventive, and quirky—just the Brooklyn job machine of our dreams.

New housing and jobs attracted young people who wanted to live in the next happening neighborhood. Magazines and other media began proclaiming that Brooklyn was red hot. Brooklyn's population mushroomed. From 2000 to 2010, it grew by 40,000 people, and then 132,000 people over the next five years, making Brooklyn the fastest-growing borough in the city. But the integrated nature of our plan helped Brooklyn be more than a series of high rises; we ensured that it had the culture and the parks that made it attractive to creative types and gave it its own distinct vibe—think artisan food and crafts, offbeat fashion, and cutting-edge film and media. Brooklyn's hipster vibe is so distinct, it is recognized globally.

Tourists who had never heard of Brooklyn ten years ago flock to rebuilt piers in magnificent Brooklyn Bridge Park to ride on the carousel with wooden horses hand-carved in 1922, take in the art installations on the grass beneath the bridge, play sports, or just enjoy the breathtaking views. BabyCenter, the parenting network, notes that the number of newborns named Brooklyn in the United States soared: in 2001 the name was the 172nd most popular for newborn girls; in 2016 it was 33rd.

Whereas many cities once aspired to be the Paris of their region as the Associated Press noted in 2014, now every aspiring neighborhood of artisans wants to be a local Brooklyn. Oakland calls itself the Brooklyn of San Francisco, Glasgow the Brooklyn of the United Kingdom. There is even a Brooklyn of Paris, a gritty suburb where unused warehouses have been taken over by painters and sculptors. Meanwhile, the *New York Times* food section noted that among young Parisians, there is currently no greater praise for cuisine than "très Brooklyn."

Would it have happened without us? That's a fair question. Certainly, good things were happening in Brooklyn. Positive signs were emerging before 9/11. I have asked many of the developers who invested in Brooklyn that question, and the answer was always a resounding no. They say that the commitments the city made, the plans we got approved, and the amenities we packaged into an integrated vision of the borough gave them the confidence to invest. And that confidence snowballed and continues to do so.

And, of course, it wasn't just about economic development. Under Police Commissioner Ray Kelly, crime in Brooklyn during the Bloomberg Administration continued to fall, defying all reasonable expectations. Murders in the borough fell by another 43 percent, and shootings declined by 35 percent. The school system under Joel Klein and then Dennis Walcott improved significantly, offering greater options (219 schools were created in Brooklyn alone) in more neighborhoods. Graduation rates increased in Brooklyn by a third, the largest increase of any borough in the city. The confidence inspired by greater security and better schools—as well as better services pretty much across the board—encouraged many more people to move to and stay in the borough.

And what of the criticism that gentrification forced out poor people? As I discussed in Chapter 6, this is not just a criticism of our efforts in Brooklyn but one leveled at us across the city, often by Bloomberg's successor as mayor, Bill de Blasio. Were we too successful for our own good? In the study I cited there, in May 2016, the New York University Furman Center found that of fifteen gentrifying areas in the city, half were in Brooklyn. But it found that gentrification had done just what we had hoped—it helped to encourage young families and college-educated people to stay in the city. Meanwhile, the report was unable to conclude that significant numbers of lower-income people had been displaced. The one downside was that the overall "rent burden"—that is, the percentage of the money they paid in rent—had gone up.

When you plan for massive transformation, it is hard to calibrate the precise impact. Getting the right balance of supply and demand is hard. That is part of why we thought it was important to have the largest affordable housing program by a city in US history accompanying all of our efforts. It is also important to remember that when we began the planning, the city was on its heels.

When I go to Brooklyn and walk along the Brooklyn Bridge Park with its volleyball courts and marinas, watch a Nets game in a Barclays Center full of screaming fans, walk through Williamsburg or along the boardwalk in Coney Island, or hear Brooklyn praised in Paris or Rio, given the scope of our ambitions, I can't help but feel we got the balance as right as we realistically could have.

CHAPTER TWENTY

REFLECTION AND RECOVERY

WITH ALL THAT came out of the summit—the need for strategic land-use planning and the need to execute on our approved plans—my plate was beginning to refill pretty quickly. But it was becoming pretty clear I was going to need to get much more involved in one more project: Ground Zero. Endless conflicts had mired the rebuilding with no signs of resolution.

Still, even with all of this to occupy and distract me, I was not quite myself. Sometimes, the daily grind distracted from the truth, but then my lingering sadness over the Olympic loss would suddenly resurface. The night of Mike Bloomberg's reelection was one of those times. In November, Bloomberg won a commanding victory. But as I stood by the stage at the Sheraton Midtown, watching the reelected Mayor make his acceptance speech, I felt completely empty. All around me, people were cheering and hugging, and I just could not join them. I had to walk away.

It wasn't just the Olympic loss. My family had a close friend who had recently died and another who was dying. Ruth Sussman, an acting New York Supreme Court Justice, had been an upstairs neighbor in the apartment building we lived in before we moved into our townhouse in the mid-1990s. She also became family when her younger brother Jim married Alisa's only sister, Carolyn. She was our age and died of breast cancer in early September.

That gray autumn became grayer when it was clear that another close friend, Ellen Liebman, was not going to survive her battle with ovarian cancer. Her husband Steve Koch and I had been officemates at Lehman Brothers, but after he moved back to his hometown of Chicago our growing families grew much closer. We each had three children, the same genders and ages. We each named our first child Jacob (coincidentally). We vacationed together dozens of times. Four of our children went to Yale together.

Right before Christmas, Steve called to say Ellen's condition was now critical. I immediately flew out to be by his side. And as it turns out, I was in the room with him and his children when Ellen died. It is hard not to fall into clichés when discussing death, but seeing Ellen lying there with her spirit gone was a profound reminder of how fleeting it all is. In life, neither Ruth nor Ellen was a shrinking violet, as Alisa said. They were energetic, vivacious, and opinionated. To see it all go just like that made me feel very vulnerable and very, very mortal.

Even before Ellen's death, I had decided that I needed to get away and be by myself to reflect on what had happened. I wanted to take a trip alone over New Year's. Alisa agreed, but I could tell she was also a little puzzled and hurt. In my entire life, I had never really been alone, even for a few days. We had been dating or married at that point for nearly thirty years, and since we'd been together I had never spent any time apart other than on business trips or the occasional weekend visiting friends. Every holiday season we went away together. After the brutal previous two years and an especially tough fall after the loss in Singapore, she worried that I was pulling away. It wasn't really that, I explained. I just needed a little solitude to process what the loss meant to me and why it continued to bother me so much. I had hoped that by then I would be through my grief, but it just wasn't happening fast enough.

I wanted to challenge myself physically, at least for a few days. So I decided I would do a quick bike trip in South America. It sounded perfect, I thought. It would be warm, the roads would be good, and I wouldn't be jet-lagged. For at least some of the trip, BlackBerry service—my usual lifeline—would be only intermittent. So on the day after Ellen's funeral in Chicago, on December 29, I flew home with Alisa and the kids, and then the next day I packed my bike and a few things and flew down to Chile. As I left the house, Alisa and I hugged briefly and she whispered simply, "I hope this will be what you need. I love you." As I got into the car to take me to JFK Airport, I uncharacteristically teared up.

I had decided to ride from Osorno, Chile, to Bariloche, Argentina, over three days. The distance wouldn't be too great—just 154 miles—and most of it would be through farmland and then increasingly wooded terrain. That wouldn't be too hard, but in the middle of it would be a climb over the border between the two countries of about 12 miles (20 kilometers) with 5,000 feet of elevation gain. For an experienced biker, it was nothing, but for someone out of shape who hadn't been on a bike in months, I thought it would be a good test. Of what, I wasn't exactly sure. Nearly a day and three flights later, I arrived in Osorno in the midafternoon, changed into my bike clothes in the airport, and cycled out of the airport (with a guy and a van I had hired to trail me at a safe distance!).

That first day was easy as I began pedaling myself back into shape. The route I had selected was flat and boring at first. It was also a highway more crowded with trucks than I had expected. I had preloaded a playlist for the trip on my iPod. As soon as I started out, I pressed play and blasted my specially selected first song. It was "Katmandu" by Bob Seger and the Silver Bullet Band. Its refrain is, "If I ever get out of here, I'm goin' to Katmandu." Before every exam I ever took in college or law school, I played it loudly to the annoyance of my roommates and then later Alisa, air strumming a tennis racket to psych myself up. (Too often, my lack of preparation for the exam wasn't compensated for by the music.) The next song was the Jeff Beck Group's "Going Down," a true classic and my no. 2 psych-up song. Now these two songs, part of my life for so long, seemed to have special relevance to me on this trip. I breezed along, already beginning to unwind. That night, I stayed in a small B&B just off the road, had dinner, and fell asleep immediately. I slept soundly for ten hours, a rare thing for me.

The next morning was New Year's Eve. I woke up early and set off. I knew it would be a hard day. The farmland quickly gave way to rolling hills and then a somewhat steeper climb through the piney forest. By early afternoon, I was already sore and tired. And then it started to get steeper—I would guess about a 7 percent and then at times a 10 percent grade—with an increasing number of switchbacks. I was still on a highway, but the trucks were no longer whizzing by; instead their gears were gnashing. Then I started noticing markings on the road every one hundred meters. I must be, I thought, on the twenty-kilometer climb.

There are two hundred segments of one hundred meters each on a twenty-kilometer climb, and I eagerly awaited each one as a mark of progress. My pace slowed down to twelve kilometers an hour, and then ten, and then eight as the road seemed to get steeper and more twisted. The pine trees grew sparser. At one point, I stopped to rest and to eat a granola bar, and it took me five minutes to get enough momentum to start the climb again. After that, I didn't think I could stop again, but I was pretty sure I didn't have the energy or the strength to make it the rest of the way. But I just kept pushing. I know for the good rider who is reading this that it doesn't sound like much, but for me back then, at that moment, it was grueling. It was the most difficult physical test I had ever attempted.

When I finally crested at the three-hour mark, I stopped and left my bike on the side of the road and walked around the snow-covered peak. The trees were gone, and I could see for what seemed like forever. I was on a crazy adrenaline high. Miracle of miracles, my BlackBerry worked up there! I sent an e-mail to Alisa telling her I made it to the top, and when I didn't hear back from her in a few minutes, I got back on my bike and took off back down the mountain. I felt like some kind of superman, which may explain why speeding down the other side of the mountain at forty-two miles an hour, buffeted by the passing trucks on the curvy road, left me elated rather than terrified. Those three hours did more than make me feel as if I had conquered something big—which is always uplifting. They gave me the time for the reflection I needed. As I struggled up the mountain, I thought a lot about loss.

I remembered Hillary Clinton's words of consolation on the long flight back from Singapore—that things have a way of working out. As I processed the Olympic effort and what it had achieved—for me personally and for New York City—I concluded that she was right. If it hadn't been for the Olympic bid, I wouldn't have met Mike Bloomberg. I wouldn't have become Deputy Mayor of New York, and I wouldn't have had the chance to reshape the city I loved. The High Line, the new stadiums, Hudson Yards, the Brooklyn-Queens waterfront, and so much more flowed, directly or indirectly, from what seemed a failed effort. But I began to understand as I rode those few days that failure is only failure if you define it that way. I had the power to define the experience as a success. That's what I chose to do.

That night, I found myself alone in a hotel outside a small town in Argentina. The symbolism of it being the New Year was not lost on me. That evening, I must have called Alisa and the kids a half dozen times. I still felt the elation of my day's adventure, but I was also coming to the final and most significant insight of my journey. At the core, I am a creature of family and friends. Those relationships are my priority, and they are what make my life whole and worth living. Nothing on the outside could take that away. In the light of Ellen's death, I could see that I needed to do a better job of reaffirming this. I had been difficult, and I vowed to myself to do better. With this, I could feel the weight of my unhappiness lifting.

I'm not going to tell you that I had a transcendent experience. I didn't see God. But that night, Alisa told me that she thought I was probably in the best mood I had been in since the victory in Colorado Springs in 2002. And that is when I knew my recovery was complete. I was ready to go back.

CHAPTER TWENTY-ONE

GROUND ZERO UNSTUCK

I T COULDN'T HAVE come fast enough. Four full years after 9/11, Ground Zero remained a raw gash in Lower Manhattan, an open pit inhabited by a small number of mostly silent, unmoving cranes. The construction of the Freedom Tower and surrounding office buildings had ground to a halt. If pressed, people exclaimed that they wanted to move forward—and quickly—but nothing had happened. There was no construction. No real activity. There were a lot of theories as to why the rebuilding seemed to have stalled and a lot of finger pointing.

I had my own ideas. I had long suspected that Larry Silverstein, the developer who had leased the World Trade Center just six weeks before the attack, did not have the funds to rebuild the site. Almost since I became Deputy Mayor, I had been trying to get a handle on how much money was available for rebuilding—from the federal government, from the Lower Manhattan Development Corporation, from insurance—and how it would be spent. Roy Bahat had tried to generate the best estimate we could about the sources and uses of funds for the rebuilding, but we could never get full cooperation from Silverstein or the Port Authority to do a complete analysis. LMDC was never willing to push them for the information.

Our plan to reshape Lower Manhattan into a true, twenty-first-century, live-work-visit community was showing steady progress, especially with the residential population, which in under four years had grown from just over 20,000 in 2001 to 35,300 in 2005. But on the WTC site, pretty much nothing was going right. The newspapers were getting increasingly agitated, and the Mayor and I watched in horror, our hands tied. We could scream as much as we wanted, but with the state in charge and Governor George Pataki clinging to control, no one had to listen, and they didn't.

Then we saw our chance. In April 2005, Silverstein came to the city and state to request $3.35 billion in tax-free Liberty Bonds granted as part of the federal recovery package. Half of the Liberty Bonds were allocated to the state and half to the city. Silverstein needed more than the state had available. Finally, we had leverage. We told him that to gain our approval to issue the bonds, we needed detailed financial information to make a determination.

It took until September to get the information we needed, but I didn't have confidence that we had the skills in-house to do the kind of sophisticated financial real-estate analysis required, so I reached out to an old friend at Lehman Brothers, Ray Mikulich, who had worked with me on a big refinancing of Rockefeller Center in the mid-1980s. When we reconnected, Lehman Brothers had been vilified in the press for moving its headquarters from Lower Manhattan to Times Square immediately after the terrorist attack and deciding not to come back (unlike American Express, with whom it had shared a building). Mikulich indicated that the firm was eager to do something to help in the recovery. He suggested I talk to one of the senior members of the real-estate investment banking group, Bob Lieber, who had been following the rebuilding efforts closely.

A few days later Lieber and a large team came down to City Hall to meet with me, Andy Alper, and Seth Pinsky, who had joined the Economic Development Corporation just two years before. Pinsky had been part of the talent infusion Alper had recruited into EDC after assuming the helm of that agency. I had only met him a couple of times but loved his obvious smarts, intensity, and passion for New York. He was a native New Yorker whose family had moved to Minneapolis when he was young, and he had always longed to return to New York. He attended Columbia University and, except for studying at Harvard Law School, had been in the city ever since. Law firm work bored him, and after 9/11 he was eager to take a huge pay cut to work for the city.

As the Lehman group assembled in the Committee of the Whole room in City Hall, we laid out our suspicions that there just wasn't going to be enough money to rebuild the site. Still we needed a far more detailed analysis to have the credibility to demonstrate that to ourselves, let alone anyone else. This illustrates an important point about my approach to the issues we dealt with in City Hall. It was never enough to simply make assertions. We held ourselves to a higher standard. We took the time to figure out what the important questions were, did rigorous and dispassionate analysis (bringing in experts, if necessary), and then used that analysis to make arguments—and development policies—that actually addressed the key questions. We then worked hard to translate complex analysis into a story that elected officials, community groups, journalists, and the public could understand.

Lieber understood immediately what we were looking for—a sophisticated, long-term financial model of how much it would cost Silverstein to build each building on the site, the potential sources of those funds, and the costs of infrastructure for the site. Given the complexity of the site, the model would be a monster. "And by the way," I concluded, "would you consider doing the work pro bono?" Lieber laughed but was clearly intrigued. He would have to clear conflicts of interest back at Lehman, he told us, but he promised to get back to us in a couple of days. When we heard from him again it was official: he was in.

We regrouped at City Hall and dumped all of the information we had gathered on him and his team. About three weeks later, the analysis was done. We set up a large screen, brought in a projector in the otherwise technologically barren COW, and awaited Lehman's perspective on the financial forces invisibly but powerfully driving—or restraining—the recovery effort. With the eyes of the Revolutionary War Generals and long-gone Mayors bearing down upon us, we heard the jaw-dropping news. We had worried the situation was dire. The report made it clear: things were much worse.

Lehman projected it would take roughly $7.5 billion to construct the ten million square feet of office space Silverstein claimed the right to rebuild. After a long battle, Silverstein had won only $4.65 billion in insurance payments and had already blown through $1.4 billion for litigation costs, architecture and design fees, fees to himself and his partners, and payments to buy out aggrieved retail leaseholders on the site. That created a nearly $4 billion shortfall. Moreover, Silverstein's estimates for rebuilding did not include his share of infrastructure costs, likely to be another $2 billion. And we had asked for $350 million from the insurance proceeds to go toward rebuilding retail, but Silverstein had offered half. We already knew that he had no tenants for any of the buildings he proposed to build. The market for Class A office space in Lower Manhattan was weak. That meant financing would be difficult, if not impossible.

All of this led Lehman to the conclusion that the most likely scenario was that Silverstein would try to build the buildings one at a time, slowly exhausting his resources. He could use the rents from the completed buildings to get loans for the subsequent ones, but if the rents weren't high enough he would default on his later commitments. Based on existing markets and estimated construction costs, Lehman predicted Silverstein would exhaust all the insurance money and the Liberty Bonds sometime around 2009, but meanwhile he would walk away with hundreds of millions of dollars.

This would also give us another potential problem. Silverstein was asking for the entirety of the remaining Liberty Bonds. He wanted to use two-thirds on the Freedom Tower alone. If we allocated all of them to him and then he defaulted, the valuable Liberty Bonds, which could be used for other buildings in Lower Manhattan, would be lost forever because they expired at the end of 2009.

That meeting was our wake-up call. Our standard for aggressive intervention had been triggered. As a result, we would launch a secret plot to isolate Silverstein from his greatest ally, Governor Pataki (and Sheldon Silver, who was also a total Silverstein loyalist) by colluding with the Governor of New Jersey and the New Jersey side of the Port Authority to ultimately force Silverstein to renegotiate the entire deal. But before all that, we had to explain to ourselves and everyone else with a stake in the rebuilding the depth of the morass.

On the surface, Daniel Libeskind's site plan, which the Governor had chosen in early 2003, seemed to be a deft solution to many pressing and competing interests. It slotted five large skyscrapers into a small space—satisfying the commercial appetites. A modern, fractured, crystalline design and a spire reminiscent of the Statue of Liberty's arm met the civic need for a compelling skyline. And Libeskind had obeyed Governor Pataki's command to leave the footprints of the original towers untouched, enabling a generous memorial plaza upon which "the sun will shine without shadow" each year on the morning of September 11. (I still didn't know what that meant, and, apparently, neither did Libeskind. Later, an architect who was a critic of the plan demonstrated that a tall hotel adjacent to the site would leave a big chunk of Libeskind's "wedge of light" in shadow on anniversaries of 9/11.)

In reality, the selection of Libeskind's master plan, called Memory Foundations, actually resolved nothing. It was a symbolic design that had immediately become strained under the pressures of actual rebuilding. And, as a result, for the next two and a half years, there wasn't much progress.

One problem was that the sixteen acres couldn't contain all of the desires and ambitions for the site: Silverstein wanted his ten million square feet of office space; the Port Authority wanted to add a transportation center and double the retail space to partially compensate for the costs of rebuilding; the city wanted to connect the neighborhoods surrounding the site by reattaching the through-streets that had been cut off when the WTC site had been built; everyone wanted appropriate space for a great memorial and a new cultural facility; and then where was all of the infrastructure, such as bus parking, security, and plants for heating and cooling, going to go?

Although Silverstein had acquiesced to the public design process, he had never believed in it—not one bit. He argued to anyone who would listen that his lease gave him the right to rebuild the way he saw fit. Moreover, he was quite public about the fact that he thought Libeskind was unfit for the task. Libeskind, he argued, not without basis, was a scholarly architect with no actual experience at building tall buildings. He made the same quip repeatedly to drive in the point: "Tell me something. If you needed neurosurgery, would you go to a general practitioner who has never done any kind of operating in his life?"

Ignoring the public competition, he hired David Childs of Skidmore Ownings and Merrill, a deeply experienced architect of more conventional skyscrapers. Silverstein's motives weren't all about experience, really. He wanted bigger buildings than even Libeskind had provided, and he wanted the main Trade Center tower, dubbed the Freedom Tower by Governor Pataki, closer to the transportation center. Childs, who faithfully represented his client's interests, also had contempt for Libeskind's design. He thought the torqued structure was unsound.

Throughout all of 2003 the two architects battled brutally behind the scenes for control. Each relied on his patron for backup, and thus it became a proxy fight between the Governor and Silverstein. In December 2003 at a joint press conference, they revealed a plan that was far more Childs than Libeskind. But meanwhile a year had been wasted. For the most part, Mike Bloomberg and I sat on the sidelines.

Libeskind's master plan also set in motion a stream of complaints from other stakeholders who felt ignored in the public design process. Westfield Corporation, an Australian mall owner and developer that had leased the highly lucrative retail space below the WTC, hated Libeskind's retail design because it provided less and inferior space. It sued within months of the unveiling of Memory Foundations. GMAC, the lending arm of General Motors, from whom Silverstein had borrowed, which technically had the right to approve or disapprove plans might affect its ability to get its funds back, objected that its property rights had been violated. Host Marriott claimed it needed compensation because it owned a hotel on the land Libeskind proposed for the memorial plaza. Eventually, Silverstein and the Port Authority would resolve these claims. But the process wasn't completed until early 2004 and was a drain of precious time and money.

Perhaps the biggest problem was one of governance. No one official or agency was definitively in control of the site. With no one boss, all the powerful interests fought for territory. It was like *Game of Thrones*, New York City style. Lynne Sagalyn, a Columbia University real-estate professor and author of *Power at Ground Zero*, the definitive account of the struggle to rebuild, sums up the problem nicely: "Although Memory Foundations showed that the competing claims of the sacred and the secular could coexist on the site, what it could not do, what none of the other potential design plans could have done either, is solve the two-master problem: the dueling claims of control by the site's public entities and private interests—the Port Authority as landowner with Lower Manhattan Development Corporation as public planning agent and Larry Silverstein as driver of the private profit-making interests."

The Port Authority, which had resented an open design competition for property it owned, showed its passive-aggressiveness by proceeding to secretly design infrastructure under the site without consulting the architects of the buildings on top, undermining their plans. Libeskind's original plan included a transportation center, but instead of hiring him to design it the Port Authority insisted federal regulations demanded that it hire an architect with infrastructure experience. When Santiago Calatrava, the Spanish architect and structural engineer the authority hired in July 2003, unveiled his plan for a grand Transportation Hub for the Port Authority's PATH train, elegantly shaped like a "dove being released from a child's hand," it was originally priced at $2 billion and eventually would rise to nearly $4 billion (although, to be fair, the scope had changed somewhat).

And then there was the memorial itself. To select a memorial, an independent design competition was established. In January 2004, after an international competition that drew 5,201 entries from sixty-two countries, the prestigious jury, which also included a family member of one of the victims, selected a compelling design by an obscure architect who had worked for the New York City Housing Authority, Michael Arad. It was named Reflecting

Absence and called for thirty-foot-deep, stone, square pools where the footprints of the destroyed buildings had been, rimmed by powerful waterfalls. After the addition to the design team of landscape architect Peter Walker, the pools were surrounded by a grove of trees in a parklike setting. I loved the design, but it was going to be very expensive to engineer and build.

During the period between Libeskind's selection in 2003 and our decision to engage Lehman in September 2005, the city—especially First Deputy Mayor Patti Harris—was deeply engaged in the memorial competition, but our main focus was on the site plan. We fiercely defended our demand that the site be properly integrated into the rest of Lower Manhattan, which put us in a three-way war with the Port Authority and Silverstein over the layout of the retail space to be designed into the office buildings. We wanted retail on street level to create a more vibrant street life. The Port Authority wanted to restore the multilevel mall that channeled and trapped commuters, and Silverstein wanted as little ground-level retail as possible because he didn't believe in "sky lobbies."

We kept up the pressure. After our concerns were ignored, we had our own teams do research that demonstrated the city actually retained title to several of the streets required by any master plan. We informed all of the parties of our claim—surely a veiled threat—but we needed any leverage we could find.

Roland Betts, who had run the building design competition for LMDC, was brought back to negotiate some of the thornier differences and develop a new master site plan that would better accommodate all of the demands. He found he was three feet short of the space he needed to build the through-streets the city wanted. We offered to shrink the sidewalks one foot and the street one foot if Silverstein would shrink his building footprints one foot. Silverstein refused—he said it would make the elevators too cramped. But Betts had an architect do the calculations and proved it would only shrink the elevators by an inch. He called Silverstein into his office at Chelsea Piers and illustrated the loss by lining M&Ms against a ruler. "You can't tell me that you won't concede this amount of M&M's out of each building," he reports he told Silverstein, who finally relented. Other difficulties that couldn't be resolved got punted. For example, the Deutsche Bank Building, damaged in the blast, loomed over the site in limbo. As insurers fought about its fate, it remained covered in black netting.

It took until June 2004, more than a year after Libeskind had unveiled Memory Foundations, to come up with a general site plan acceptable to everyone. But even after we had sorted out the streets, the general footprints of the buildings, and the memorial and had conducted a competition for cultural attractions, the rebuilding remained stuck. Famously on July 4, 2004, Governor Pataki, eager to show progress before the Republican National Convention arrived in town in August, insisted that we lay a cornerstone for the building. It was meaningless. A few months later, the oversize stone would be carted away to Long Island.

There were so many possible reasons to be stuck, but during 2003 and 2004, Bloomberg and I kept returning again and again to the money. We didn't think Silverstein had enough. Neither did the Port Authority. We kept our mouths shut because there was one big variable at play: How much insurance money could Silverstein get for the two buildings? By all accounts, Silverstein had underinsured the buildings for the total catastrophe 9/11 caused—after all, 9/11 was unimaginable until it actually happened. But Silverstein had a lot of chutzpah. With his lawyers, he developed the argument that because two different towers were hit by two different planes, 9/11 constituted two insurable acts. Thus Silverstein could claim that his payout should be $7.1 billion instead of $3.55 billion.

Throughout 2003 and 2004, Silverstein pursued this claim in the courts, and he mostly lost. At the end of 2004, he finally resolved his claims with his insurers, agreeing to a recovery of $4.65 billion. It was a large enough increase over the $3.55 billion that his lawyers celebrated. But it still wasn't anything close to the amount needed to rebuild five towers, the "bathtub"—the huge retaining wall under the site that held the Hudson River at bay—and the infrastructure to be contained in it. So, by the end of 2004, it was pretty clear to everyone who followed the rebuilding closely that the terms of the basic agreement between the Port Authority and Silverstein would have to be renegotiated. Except no one acknowledged it.

As 2004 ground into 2005, there were new crises all the time. In April 2004, Goldman Sachs had made a powerful statement by committing to build a massive new headquarters on West Street, just across from the site of the proposed Freedom Tower. On April 4, 2005, the company suspended its plans to build. It didn't just threaten to suspend. Goldman Sachs dismissed its entire architectural and site planning team, took a write-off of $46 million, and began looking for space elsewhere. The company gave several reasons. It was frustrated by the pace of rebuilding Downtown and had lost confidence that the project would be completed in any reasonable time span. It had deep security concerns because of the proposed building's proximity to the Freedom Tower, amplified by what it viewed as a lack of coordination on a security plan.

All of that was compounded by Governor Pataki's insistence that a tunnel be sunk under the West Side Highway to allow easy passage of pedestrians between the WTC site and Battery Park City. We had argued that the tunnel was a huge waste of money and warned that the north mouth of the tunnel would be adjacent to the site of Goldman Sachs's proposed building. Pataki and his Department of Transportation didn't listen to us and charged ahead. Needless to say, Goldman Sachs, which had done a private security analysis of the tunnel, concluded that a bomb detonated near the entrance to the tunnel posed an enormous risk to its building.

The Governor and his staff continued to rebuff Goldman Sachs until the investment bank decided to terminate the agreement. Goldman Sachs was arguably Lower Manhattan's most prestigious tenant. Retaining the firm was an important signal to current and prospective tenants. Losing it would send exactly the opposite signal.

A few days after Goldman Sachs's decision to terminate the deal—and more than a year after Childs and Libeskind had released their compromise design—the New York Police Department finally released its security assessment of the Freedom Tower. The news was bleak. In a public letter, the NYPD said it worried that the Freedom Tower was too close to the roads surrounding it and wanted the building set back considerably. Moreover, it wanted to fortify the base (up to two hundred feet) entirely in steel and concrete. Even I pushed back against Police Commissioner Ray Kelly on this. His unrebuttable response was, "Dan, it is clear that the World Trade Center site, when it is rebuilt, will be the world's number one terrorist target. Do you want to be responsible when people die in the next attack?" Well, no. The entire building had to be redesigned from the base up—at a cost of at least $30 million. Silverstein was furious about the money, and the Governor was furious about the time wasted.

The city, state, Port Authority, and LMDC generally had been very sensitive to the concerns of the families of the victims of 9/11. Support groups were formed, and special viewing and gathering places were created. The families had been included in nearly all of the planning efforts. That was appropriate given the ordeal they had been through. Great efforts had been made to add humanizing cultural aspects to the new towers and the memorial. The LMDC, along with the city and state, had agreed to include two cultural centers at the site. One of them, the International Freedom Center (IFC), was intended as the "intellectual and education[al] complement to the emotional experience of the spiritual memorial." It was meant to be a history of freedom and to give context to the events of 9/11 from a global perspective. And then, abruptly, all of the goodwill vanished.

On June 7, 2005, Debra Burlingame, the sister of one of the pilots whose flight was crashed into the Pentagon, published an op-ed in the *Wall Street Journal*, "The Great Ground Zero Heist." She was on the board of the entity formed to plan and build the memorial but had warned no one of her concerns or intentions. Burlingame was contemptuous of the idea of providing a larger historical context for the events of 9/11 and suggested that some of the more radical members of the IFC Board would promote a "slanted history."

"I fear that this is a freedom center which will not use the word 'patriot' the way our Founding Fathers did," she wrote. She apparently did not see the memorial as the appropriate venue for preaching tolerance, especially if it included the checkered US history of slavery and genocide of Native Americans or explored what might have inspired resentments in the Muslim world. She wanted a more hero-centric center, and she wanted much more space. She set a fire under the families, who quickly split into different factions and ignited a conflagration among New York's tabloid papers, soon one-upping each other with screaming headlines calling for more patriotism. Soon enough, the IFC was dead.

I repeat the dismal tale of these two years not to attempt to provide a comprehensive account of what happened regarding the WTC site (Sagalyn's 901-page account does that very effectively) but instead to simply give some context for the growing sense of alarm Bloomberg and I were feeling. The Governor wanted clear responsibility but couldn't wrangle the various players into place. We knew that the Mayor's office would share in the blame for the lack of progress even though we had limited power. But mostly we worried that leaving a hole where a vibrant economic center of the city had once stood would threaten our recovery. Something had to be done.

After that stunning meeting in September 2005 with Lehman Brothers, it was clear that Silverstein had to be reined in. Although we didn't have the specifics of a plan, we did understand that the only way to make the site work financially was to put more "value" into the system by ensuring that there would be public-sector tenants who would assume some of the space and by splitting the right to rebuild the entire site between Silverstein and the Port Authority, with each getting part of the insurance proceeds and Liberty

Bonds. In effect, the lease would have to be renegotiated—the sooner the better. Bloomberg decided to start using his bully pulpit.

I had shared Lehman's analysis with him. He was not surprised. He had suspected that there wasn't enough of an appetite for office space in Lower Manhattan to support ten million new square feet at top-tier prices, but the depth of the financial hole stunned even him. We agreed that if we denied Silverstein the Liberty Bonds, we needed to prepare the public and explain our position. On October 23, he gave an interview to the *New York Daily News* that the tabloid headlined: "Butt out, Larry. Silverstein must quit WTC site,' says Mike. 'Exclusive: 'Nobody Can Figure Out How' to Make Him Go." A few weeks later, after Bloomberg was reelected in a near landslide, he continued the attack. And it was working. Silverstein was increasingly painted in the press as a greedy developer slowing things down with his intransigence. We began sharing our analysis—which we had boiled down to a twelve-page PowerPoint presentation—with other government officials, especially in the Pataki Administration. There was no evidence Governor Pataki and his team shared our concerns or understood the depth of the looming financial crisis on the site.

None of the rebuilding leaders on the Pataki team had financial backgrounds. At the end of 2004, Pataki loyalist Ken Ringler became Executive Director of the Port Authority. His previous job had been Commissioner of the New York Office of General Services, the state agency responsible for managing buildings, design and construction, procurement, and other support services. Charles Gargano, Vice Chair of the Port Authority and Chair of the state's Economic Development Agency, had been a partner in a construction firm. He liked to be called "Ambassador Gargano" because of his service in the first Bush Administration as the ambassador to Trinidad and Tobago. It was pretty clear that neither focused much on the financial details. They just wanted to build something as quickly as possible to make their boss look good.

But on the New Jersey side of the Port Authority things were changing. New Jersey Governor Jon Corzine had been CEO of Goldman Sachs and a US Senator before being elected Governor in November 2005. His election capped a period of turmoil in the statehouse in Trenton, New Jersey's capital. In the previous five years, New Jersey had had five governors—one resigned to join George W. Bush's administration, one resigned because of a sex scandal, and three were interim governors. The succession of New Jersey

Governors had taken a hands-off approach to the rebuilding, deferring to Governor Pataki. That began to change with Corzine's election.

One of Corzine's early decisions was to retain Anthony Coscia as Port Authority Chair. Coscia had initially been appointed by Governor Jim McGreevey in 2003 and had been kept on by his successors. He was a well-respected corporate and real-estate lawyer and had been Chair of the New Jersey Economic Development Agency. As such, he had been eating the city's lunch by coaxing New York companies across the Hudson River. Coscia also seemed to be one of the most popular people in New Jersey, appointed by Republicans and Democrats alike. And when I met him after he was first appointed, I could see why. There was a striking warmth and genuineness about him. He brought directness to the discussions about Ground Zero that had been lacking. It seemed he just wanted to do the right thing regardless of whether the decision fell on the New Jersey or New York side of the ledger.

Throughout Coscia's first two years as Chair, he was cautious. New Jersey had broader goals for the Port Authority, including procuring $6 billion for a new rail tunnel beneath the Hudson River (which Corzine's successor, Chris Christie, would later kill). It wasn't until May 2005 that Coscia finally directed the Port Authority to ask Silverstein for his in-depth financial plan for rebuilding the towers. Coscia was unhappy enough with the answer presented by Silverstein and his Morgan Stanley bankers that he hired a real-estate advisory firm, Jones Lang LaSalle, to do his own financial analysis.

That analysis told almost the exact same story as our analysis, which alarmed Coscia. That fall, just as Bloomberg was set to go on the offensive, Coscia had a meeting with Silverstein at which he informally offered to trade the right to build some of the ten million square feet of office space for a reduction in Silverstein's rent, set to increase by $18 million in August 2006. According to *New York Times* reporter Deborah Sontag, Silverstein rebuffed him by saying, "You are a very nice young man, and you probably have good things in your future, but you're very naive. Have a nice day."

Governor Pataki was informed of Coscia's concerns around the same time we went to Gargano and Ringler with our financial analysis. Pataki tried to take control of the situation by doing what he often did—setting a false deadline. Without letting us know, he staged a press conference in Long Island in mid-December at which he promised he would go ahead and approve his half of the Liberty Bonds—or $1.67 billion—on the strict condition that

Silverstein agree to work out the Port Authority's concerns about financing and possibly cede one of the buildings within ninety days. The deadline was March 15.

By that point, Coscia and I had realized that we might be allies. In December 2005, we got together for lunch at the Blue Fin restaurant in Midtown. Pinsky and I laid out our financial analysis. We held nothing back. After that, we started meeting regularly at Coscia's Midtown law offices—in part because no one would suspect we were meeting with our New Jersey allies in Manhattan.

Meanwhile, Pinsky and I had been forging a proposal to restructure the deal between Silverstein and the Port Authority. Coscia had a lot of questions as we outlined the plan, but each time Pinsky would come back with detailed responses that allayed Coscia's concerns. We were chipping out a pathway to a better place. Quickly we agreed on a strategy: New York City would forge an alliance with New Jersey to put pressure on Pataki to withhold Liberty Bonds from Silverstein unless he would restructure the deal into something financially feasible. The city, the state, and the federal government would all have parts to play in the deal.

There were five buildings to be built under the agreed-upon master plan for the site. WTC 1 (the Freedom Tower); WTC 2, WTC 3, and WTC 4 (along Church Street); and the former Deutsche Bank Building. Under our proposal, Silverstein had to cede the development of at least two buildings—including the Freedom Tower—to the Port Authority. In return, Silverstein would have to pay ground rent to the authority only for the buildings he was developing. Under the existing deal, he was paying rent on the entire site. He would have the option of developing a third site and pay rent only if he actually developed it.

Whoever developed the fifth building would have the option of building something in addition to office space, such as a hotel or a residential building—both of which were likely to have greater value than office space at that time in the Lower Manhattan market. So if the market for ten million square feet of office space never materialized—as we suspected it wouldn't—there were options. To ensure financing of Silverstein's first building, the city and the Port Authority agreed to rent space at rates *above* then-prevailing market prices. In total, we would agree to take about 40 percent of the space in the building. The state and the federal government would agree to become the first tenants in the Freedom Tower. The Liberty Bonds would be split among the Port Authority and Silverstein. The idea was that construction would be able to proceed on two buildings at the same time, which would demonstrate significant progress at the site, giving confidence to prospective tenants. Assuming that the restoration of the streets and the memorial were moving ahead at the same time, it would be just the jolt Ground Zero needed to finally move forward.

As Coscia and I got into more of the details, we kept returning to the question of how to ensure that Silverstein fulfilled all of his obligations. We didn't want him to build one building (with our leases) and then default on the next one, leaving the Port Authority holding the bag. So, in our proposal we included a requirement that Silverstein be held to aggressive construction deadlines and that there would be terms in the agreement with him that a failure to build the second building would mean that he would lose the first one. This so-called cross-default provision we deemed critical to aligning his interests with those of the public sector. We had Lehman complete a financial analysis of our proposal to demonstrate that each of the buildings could be financed and that there was a high likelihood that the subsequent buildings could be built. Bloomberg, who had stayed engaged in the discussions all along, gave his final blessing to the proposal.

To seal the alliance, Coscia brought me out to Drumthwacket in Princeton, the New Jersey governor's mansion, to meet with Corzine and his Chief Economic Advisor, Gary Rose, to make sure we were all on the same page. The meeting was easy and painless. I had prepared a presentation on the financial situation and our proposed resolution. Corzine and Rose, another former Goldman Sachs partner, peppered us with smart questions about the market for office space Downtown, the proposed rents we suggested the Port Authority and the city pay, the allocation of Liberty Bonds, other alternative structures, and construction costs. We were prepared.

Although as a brand-new Governor, Corzine expressed some concern about the impact that putting pressure on his "partner" in the Port Authority would have on his relationship with Pataki, he never hesitated. Coscia and I walked out of Drumthwacket with his support. For the first time in recent memory, New York City and New Jersey had forged an alliance—all behind the back of the New York Governor. Later, much would be made of the fact that Bloomberg, Corzine, and I had all come out of Wall Street and that we were financial guys. We did all speak the same financial language, and, in this case, the story the numbers told was very clear—without a substantial intervention, Ground Zero wasn't going to be rebuilt.

We started the campaign with a shot across Silverstein's bow by Bloomberg in his State of the City Address in January 2006. In very pointed language, Bloomberg called on Silverstein "to do the right thing" and hand off responsibility for building two towers in exchange for a reduction in the rent he was paying to the Port Authority for the site. Silverstein and his staff claimed that they were absolutely stung by Mike's words. They immediately began a press offensive, claiming that only a private developer—not the government—could be trusted to rebuild efficiently. Government has a bad rap that's easy to exploit. Silverstein said he would have rebuilt already if the government had just handed over the property and the money. It was going to be a tough battle.

We actually needed to fight it on two fronts. Although we were highly sensitive to the public perception of the government forcing a leaseholder to give up part of his legitimately negotiated rights, we knew the public was frustrated with the slow pace of rebuilding. So was pretty much everyone who weighed in on the issue. Our real problem was that the Governor of New York was reluctant to rock the boat and force a renegotiation. I shared our proposal with Pataki's team, who sloughed it off. To put pressure on the Governor, I decided to give an exclusive to Charles Bagli of the *New York Times* despite his negative coverage of our West Side Stadium plans. We shared our analysis and plan with him. He spoke to Coscia, who made it clear that the city and New Jersey were completely in sync. This was an example of how I had learned—often the hard way—that if you are going to function in government—and life, really—you can't afford to hold grudges. Bagli was the preeminent reporter on this subject. I needed him and the *New York Times* to reach the Governor.

On February 6, the *New York Times* ran a story that essentially summed up the findings of the Lehman report and outlined our solution. Bagli reiterated our case: "Mr. Silverstein," he wrote, "could 'walk away from the project' with $565 million in profits, fees and equity, according to the analysis, compiled by a dozen officials at the city's Economic Development Corporation, the Law Department and City Hall. The report notes that Mr. Silverstein has already regained most if not all of the $137 million he and his investors put up when they bought the lease." Bagli also made it clear that New Jersey and New York City were aligned. I doubled down the next day when the *New York Daily News* called to follow up. I was fairly explicit about how our position was hardening. "We are not going to allocate Liberty Bonds today to buildings that are never going to be built," I told the paper.

After that, the Governor's team took our proposal somewhat more seriously, at least on the surface. Throughout February and into March, Ringler led negotiations with Silverstein, but they went nowhere. I'll admit that I can be quite stubborn at times, but Silverstein, even in his seventies, was tough. Laughably, at one point Janno Lieber, Silverstein's point man on the WTC site rebuilding, pulled Coscia aside and told him that we should stop ganging up on Silverstein because he had a weak heart. Coscia almost spurted coffee out of his mouth. "Larry will outlive us all," he retorted.

Silverstein wouldn't concede an inch. The hard-boiled developer was used to—no, enjoyed—scrapping for every dime. Even when a favorable deal was on the table, he would come back and ask for more. I think Silverstein didn't believe he had to compromise in the end either because Pataki had been so accommodating or because Pataki still believed he had all of the cards and could just wait out the city and New Jersey and signaled that to Silverstein. But as the deadline of March 15 arrived, Silverstein miscalculated and overplayed his hand. Every time he sent a new proposal, our team did a financial analysis that showed his taking advantage of the public sector. Even Ringler was getting frustrated. After one more fruitless, late-night negotiating session, perhaps fueled by caffeine, Ringler kicked Silverstein out. He told the press that the Port Authority was tired of Silverstein's "bad faith" counterproposals.

Finally, it seemed, even Pataki had had enough. In a public statement, he said Silverstein had "betrayed the public's trust and that of all New Yorkers. We cannot and will not allow profit margins and financial interests to be put ahead of public interest in expediting the rebuilding of the site of the greatest tragedy on American soil."

Now negotiations had broken down. But Pataki was facing his own deadline—he had committed that ground would be broken on the Freedom Tower by April 2006. It was mid-March. In public, the Governor was bold. He told Silverstein to break ground or "move out of the way." But that was just the public stance. In private, Pataki was much more accomodating. The Port Authority had an impending board meeting on April 1, and Pataki desperately wanted a deal. He began negotiating on the sidelines with Silverstein again, even going as far as to offer him $250 million more to build the Freedom Tower from money set aside from a hike of bridge and tunnel tolls. There was no way we were going to agree to this.

The pressure at this point was unbelievable. In the period after the breakdown of the talks until a compromise was reached six weeks later, the newspapers collectively ran thirty-one editorials decrying the lack of progress. We were all getting hammered, but Silverstein was feeling it the most. We could feel the tide turning our way, and it emboldened us.

Behind the scenes, I used the personal connections I had to Lloyd Goldman, Silverstein's partner in the deal. In fact, Goldman and his sisters, with whom I was close, had put up the money for the original deal with the Port Authority but had stayed largely in the background. We met at a diner for breakfast in the shadows of Silverstein's offices. I told Goldman the city would not let the deal the Governor was negotiating move forward. We would accept only something along the lines of our proposal, in which Silverstein would have to give up control of two buildings in exchange for a reduction in rent and a commitment from the city and the Port Authority to rent space in his building. He listened but was noncommittal, but I'm sure the message he communicated back was helpful in getting Silverstein to understand that we would be dead serious when we made our next move.

Just before the Port Authority's board meeting on March 30, 2006, I decided that it was the moment to play our most important card. That morning in the bullpen, I wheeled around in my chair and rolled the few feet over to Bloomberg's desk. "Now is the time," I said. "If we don't stop them now, Pataki will commit the Port to a terrible deal with Silverstein. The site won't be rebuilt. You have to tell Pataki that you will publicly condemn the deal if he moves it forward."

The value of Bloomberg's opinion was especially high because he was fresh off his commanding reelection victory. Of course, there was also universal respect for his business acumen. Bloomberg, always so gracious to the Governor even when every instinct told him not to be, dialed Gargano. The Mayor was succinct: "It is our deal or we won't support it," he said simply. It was short and brutal, but with Corzine on our side we had him boxed in, and he knew it. Pataki broke.

Over the subsequent three weeks, the public-sector players negotiated among ourselves over the deal we would offer Silverstein. Back and forth we went, but for the first time, because we controlled the numbers, the city played the lead role. Finally, on April 19, Pataki's deadline for laying the cornerstone on the Freedom Tower passed, and the city, the state, and the Port Authority—both sides of it—agreed on a variation of our plan and on an ultimatum.

Under the deal, the Port Authority would take control of the Freedom Tower, using $1.7 billion in tax-free Liberty Bonds and about $970 million in insurance money. Silverstein would be paid to build it. The state would commit some funds toward construction and would secure leases for space in the building. The Port Authority would also get the Deutsche Bank site and would own the retail space on the entire WTC site.

Silverstein would retain the three other office towers, and to ensure that the first one was built, the city and the Port Authority would lease 1.2 million square feet. Silverstein would be held to a rigid construction schedule and would be required to contribute at least $140 million toward the cost of common infrastructure.

Given Silverstein's history of tough negotiating, we decided we had to give him an ultimatum—backed by the unified authority of two states and the city: if Silverstein decided that our plan wasn't acceptable, his only alternative would be to get $50 million in cash plus the Deutsche Bank site, which we valued at $300 million. We didn't want to make it seem to the public or to his allies in government, such as Sheldon Silver, that we were forcing him into a money-losing or unfair deal. Still, it was take it or leave it. We delivered our proposal on a Thursday and gave him until Monday to accept one of the two alternatives. As I told the *New York Times,* "The unified offer from the public sector will ensure full financing and the buildout of the site on an expedited timetable and a deal that's fair to all the parties."

On Monday, the verdict came. Silverstein announced that he would take the offer to reduce his commitment on the site to rebuild the three buildings along Church Street. I can't say I was surprised. His commitment to rebuilding had been so absolute that to sell out for cash and a building site would have been completely contradictory to everything he had said and done over the previous three and a half years. It was also a very fair deal for him. He would be relieved of the requirement to lease the most difficult-to-market buildings—the Freedom Tower and the building that still had to be torn down. Moreover, the Port Authority and the city agreed to lease nearly half of the first building he would construct, which, combined with the insurance proceeds and the Liberty Bonds we would allocate to him, would guarantee that he would have at least one financeable building and most likely two. With the Port Authority committed to developing the Freedom Tower, Silverstein's tower wouldn't stand alone.

There would be enough activity on the site to demonstrate that the site was really, finally, moving forward. The agreement was the event that finally unlocked the Gordian knot at Ground Zero. As Sagalyn wrote in the introduction to her book, "The agreements set forth the most definitive blueprint to date after years of conflict and contention over every piece of the master plan for rebuilding the sixteen acres at Ground Zero. The moment marked a watershed."

Yet, if by the end of April 2006 we had largely pulled the Freedom Tower from the mire, and construction was about to finally start, we were still not in the clear. Ground Zero seemed bound by Murphy's Law; around the time we settled the problems with Silverstein, efforts to move forward on the memorial hit their own roadblocks.

Since the selection of Michael Arad's memorial design, a team of architects and engineers had moved quickly to turn a concept into a detailed plan. Although the concept had been well received, that didn't prevent an eruption of controversies. Perhaps no part of the design was more controversial than how to list the names of the dead. The original proposal was to do it randomly, symbolic of the "haphazard brutality of death." The families of the victims hated it. They wanted to be able to find their loved ones' names. Many wanted to see names grouped together by where they had worked, and some called for arranging the first responders by their police and firefighting ranks. The last idea was detested by others who thought it promoted the idea that some of the dead were more important.

In May 2006, literally days after we had held the press conference with Silverstein to announce the deal to redevelop the site, the contractor chosen for the memorial released a new construction cost estimate of nearly $1 billion—more than double the original estimate. At that price tag, the memorial would be the most expensive public monument ever built in the United States by a factor of five; the most expensive to that point had been the World War II Memorial in Washington, DC, which cost $182 million upon completion in 2004. Bloomberg was outraged and wasn't shy about saying it. In addition, the foundation established by LMDC and chaired by John Whitehead had been so focused on a marvelous design it had barely done any of the fundraising necessary to construct the memorial at the original cost. The foundation agreed to temporarily stop fundraising until a more affordable design could be negotiated.

Eliot Spitzer, then on the campaign trail to be Governor, was having a field day bashing Pataki and everyone else working on Lower Manhattan. "The LMDC—let me be very clear—the LMDC has been an abject failure, and those who were running the LMDC deserve an enormous piece of criticism," he told the press. He wasn't entirely wrong.

At Bloomberg's and my insistence, the LMDC asked Frank Sciame, the well-respected owner of a construction management firm, to do an analysis of the costs and to try to value-engineer the memorial so that the costs could be brought back into the range of the original budget. We instructed Sciame to work on a two-track process. His first priority was to cut costs, but he also had to be respectful of the original design—in particular, to Maya Lin, the renowned designer of the Vietnam War memorial in Washington, DC, who played an influential role on the jury for the memorial design contest. He also had to make sure he was including other stakeholders in the process. If we did not include the families, Arad, and the Port Authority as we went along, we would have a rebellion and an even bigger mess.

Fortunately, Sciame was a natural diplomat because he listened and showed respect, we got surprisingly little pushback when he finally announced his recommended changes in June. Maybe everyone was exhausted by then. He retained the basic design but eliminated many of the frills, overdesign, and overengineering. Mostly, it was good, common sense. In any case, by June, we had a new budget. It was still outrageously high at more than $530 million (it would eventually rise to over $700 million), but we could live with it.

But where was the money going to come from? As part of the Silverstein negotiations, the Port Authority had committed to funding a portion of the costs (although, in typical fashion, the amount would not be precisely documented and would cause conflict for several years to come), and LMDC had committed some, but there were still hundreds of millions of dollars to be raised by the memorial foundation, which had demonstrated little capacity to raise funds.

In the fall of 2006, Patti Harris and I sat down next to the Mayor at his desk in the bullpen and told him that we thought he had to become the Chair of the memorial foundation and raise the money. "It just won't get done without you," we told him. As with so many major decisions in the Bloomberg Administration, after we outlined the issues he said yes. He immediately called Whitehead to offer to take over responsibility for the memorial, and a grateful Whitehead and his board quickly acceded. Once again, the city had stepped in when the project bumped over the guardrails.

Bloomberg, with the help of Harris and a new President and CEO of the National 9/11 Memorial and Museum, Joe Daniels, quickly settled the name controversy, started construction on the memorial largely according to the value-engineered design, raised $350 million from the private sector in addition to $420 million from the public sector for construction, and opened the memorial by the tenth anniversary of the attacks. A museum underneath the memorial plaza opened three years later. By 2016 the museum drew 3.2 million people, and 6.25 million visited the memorial plaza.

In November 2014, the Port Authority opened One World Trade (formerly known as the Freedom Tower), joining the memorial and museum on the site. As of 2017, the building, New York's tallest and biggest with more than three million square feet of rentable space, was more than 70 percent rented, attracting diverse tenants to Lower Manhattan such as Condé Nast, Infosys (a global information services company), and Progenics (a biotech company). The asking price for rent was about seventy dollars per square foot, significantly higher than we had forecast when we renegotiated the deal with Silverstein. Even David Childs's design of One World Trade ultimately charmed me—Governor Pataki turned out to be right. Juxtaposed against the Lower Manhattan skyline, One World Trade rises like an elegant middle finger to the terrorists who tried to humble New York.

By 2017, two of the other three planned buildings were opened or nearly completed. Four World Trade, a 2.5-million-square-foot building designed by Pritzker Prize–winning architect Fumihiko Maki, the building in which the city and Port Authority committed to rent space, became fully occupied in 2017 when Spotify, the streaming music service, leased all of the remaining space. At the time of this writing, Three World Trade, designed by another Pritzker Prize–winning architect, Richard Rogers, was slated to open in 2018. The last of Silverstein's three towers, Two World Trade Center, still awaited the tenants that will make financing the building possible.

Meanwhile, the Oculus, the Port Authority's transportation center, finally opened in March 2016—well behind schedule and way over budget but nevertheless a stunning and soaring addition. Not only does it provide access to the PATH system but also it is connected underground to the Fulton Center, a transit hub serving nine subway lines, all of which make Lower Manhattan easier to reach and navigate. Two million people in New Jersey, Brooklyn, and Manhattan are within twenty minutes of Lower Manhattan.

The site became the focus for a reinvention of all of Lower Manhattan that exceeded even our high expectations. When we took office there were twenty-one thousand residents in the roughly one-square-mile area south of Chambers Street. By 2017, there were sixty-one thousand. Dozens of new residential buildings—not even counting a host of converted office buildings (and residence halls housing college students)—have sprouted throughout the area.

These residents, many of them young, growing families, fill the eighty-four acres of open, green space that ring Lower Manhattan with their strollers and bicycles and weekend football games. They ride through Hudson River Park, picnic in Battery Park staring at the view of the Statue of Liberty, and stroll along the East River Waterfront Park. Pocket parks dot the Lower Manhattan landscape. They are joined by a new influx of tourists. Whereas only seven million people visited in 2007, a decade later more than fourteen million visitors packed attractions such as open-air movie nights and a wide array of cultural institutions, historic sites, and the World Trade Center site. One day they will stream into a new cultural center rising on the WTC site that will be named after Revlon mogul Ronald Perelman. They have also created an exploding market for retail and restaurants. By 2017 there were hundreds of new storefronts and hundreds of restaurants and bars, with more coming. In 2016 alone, seven hotels opened to serve the crowds. In total, there were 6,560 hotel rooms in Lower Manhattan.

With easier commuting options and a greater variety of attractions, the composition of the workforce in the area also changed radically. Before 9/11 financial firms employed 56 percent of all workers in Lower Manhattan. By 2016 that number shrunk to 33 percent. With more commercial diversity came higher rents—the price of office space Downtown climbed to an average of about $60 per square foot. That makes the deal we made for city office space at Four World Trade at $56.50 per square foot look like a reasonable value for the city. Meanwhile, an economic report in 2017 showed that in the five years from 2015 to 2019, the area was set to gain forty thousand jobs, or the most significant employment surge in thirty years. Two-thirds of these jobs are expected to be net new jobs for New York City. Importantly, these jobs will be available to striving New Yorkers without a college degree— 63 percent of the added jobs are expected to employ those with an associate's degree or less.

Yes, Lower Manhattan is thriving, and nearly everything we said we wanted to do in the Mayor's Lower Manhattan Vision speech in December 2002 has actually happened (we couldn't figure out how to get a one-seat ride to JFK Airport, but we tried!). Perhaps even more gratifying is that all of our dreams for the Far West Side have come true too—at the same time Lower Manhattan made progress.

CHAPTER TWENTY-TWO

NEW YORK'S NEW EDGE

SHELDON SILVER'S PESSIMISM that the city couldn't revive two districts—Lower Manhattan and the Far West Side—at the same time was proven quite wrong. The idea that a global capital such as New York—on the path to approaching a population of nine million, where there had been little major development in forty years—couldn't absorb one new commercial center while it was rebuilding another was on its face ridiculous. Not only could both be done—they needed to be done. And the proof is in the results.

When we rezoned Hudson Yards and West Chelsea at the same time in 2005, we hoped that we would create a new edge of New York on the West Side where visitors, residents, and workers would one day be able to walk the more than two miles through new parks extending from Times Square to the Meatpacking District through exciting new neighborhoods filled with new office buildings, apartment towers, cultural institutions, and retail that would become an economic engine for all of New York. It could be the single-most powerful expression of the virtuous cycle at work. It has worked.

By now, the success of the High Line is beyond doubt. In 2016, 7.6 million people visited it, more than visited the Metropolitan Museum of Art or the Statue of Liberty. The 1.45-mile-long park now winds all the way from the Meatpacking District to 34th Street, curving above the cityscape with its gravel and paved paths embedded alongside train tracks and tufts of flowers, as visitors wander through towering groves of trees, past impromptu art performances and sculptures, into covered markets with gourmet food stands, each walk interlaced with original, startling glimpses of the city and the river. By 2013, the High Line was the tenth most Instagrammed site in the world. The public-private partnership we imagined with the Friends of the High Line has worked beautifully. Although the city put up the vast majority of the $152 million for the first two phases of park construction, the $35 million for the third phase was largely paid for with funds raised by FHL. FHL manages—and pays for—the daily operations of the park and has managed to keep the High Line fresh with imaginative programming, public art, and intense focus on operational excellence.

The park's southern end is anchored by the Whitney Museum, which moved from the comfort of the Upper East Side to a neighborhood few would have imagined as the home for a major cultural institution even a decade ago. Its new, gorgeous, Renzo Piano–designed building, on a site that required us to tear down a city-owned building, has sparked an explosion in its attendance figures. Prior to its move, the best-ever annual attendance figure was 372,000. In the first eight months in its new location, the Whitney drew three times that many.

We had staked our investment on the risky idea that the new park would promote development. It paid off. Since the High Line first opened in 2008, West Chelsea has blossomed into one of New York's most appealing neighborhoods. More than 2,500 residential units have been added, with more than 700 additional units under construction at the time of this writing. Meanwhile, the Gallery District has continued to thrive, enjoying the permanent protection from residential encroachment we provided in the rezoning. Today there are more than 350 galleries in the area.

The High Line has had a global impact as well. Within a year or so after the successful opening of the first phase, there were thirty-six "High Lines" under development around the world, many of which, like the 606 in Chicago, have now been completed.

Today, as you saunter north on the High Line, suddenly an angular, glass tower looms ahead, fifty-two stories high. A spur of the High Line passes under an arcade that juts out from the building enabling office workers and visitors to enter the building directly from the park or through an entrance tucked underneath on the street.

This is 10 Hudson Yards, the first of eighteen commercial, residential, retail, cultural, and educational buildings opened, under construction, or slated for construction on or adjacent to the railyards. One developer, the Related Companies, led by Stephen Ross (in partnership with a real-estate company,

Oxford, owned by a Canadian pension fund), is building almost twenty million square feet, which in dollar terms will be the largest single development in US history.

After we completed the Hudson Yards rezoning in 2005 and then later during the process of rezoning the western railyard (where the stadium would have been), the city and the Metropolitan Transportation Authority issued a request for proposals for the right to develop over the railyards. In 2007, it was awarded to one developer, who backed out in April 2008 after the first signs of distress, which would eventually mushroom into the financial crisis of 2008. Even though I had already left City Hall, I immediately called Stephen Ross, the runner-up in the RFP, and told him that he had another chance—by acting quickly he could step into the contract and control the development over the railyards. He did, and for the past nine years he and his partners have relentlessly and creatively moved forward toward completion of the site.

The new company I formed with Google after I left Bloomberg LP—Sidewalk Labs—is headquartered on the twenty-sixth and twenty-seventh floors of 10 Hudson Yards. From my desk, I can look down on the massive construction site. The elegant, glass-enclosed entrance to the completed No. 7 subway line extension is visible, as are the surrounding parks. The platform over the eastern railyard has been built over the tracks of the Long Island Railroad. On top of the platform will be a beautiful five-acre public square and gardens surrounded by three other office towers; a huge retail complex; two residential buildings; a hotel; and The Shed, the cultural institution I have helped to nurse from birth. It will be a uniquely twenty-first-century center for the arts, producing work across the full spectrum of cultural disciplines in a building that will be the most flexible in the world, with the ability to actually move on rails to create a soaring exhibition, event, and performance space.

In the center of the public square will be a new landmark temporarily called the Vessel. Designed by London-based Heatherwick Studios, the Vessel will be 154 interconnecting, copper-colored, steel flights of stairs, creating a mile's worth of pathway rising more than one hundred feet above the public square. Nearly all of this is slated to be completed by late 2018.

The trains are still visible west of 11th Avenue, but construction of the western platform is scheduled to begin in 2018. Eventually resting on it will be six residential buildings, an office building, and a school, all surrounding another eight acres of public gardens. Everything on or adjacent to the railyards will be directly accessible from the High Line. Just as we had hoped, Midtown leapt to the west and West Chelsea burst to the north, creating a new neighborhood in Manhattan's last frontier.

Related Companies estimates that by 2025, when the project is expected to be completely finished, 125,000 people a day will shop, work in, visit, or call the development home, and it will contribute nearly $19 billion annually to New York City's gross domestic product, accounting for an impressive 2.5 percent of the citywide GDP and adding nearly $500 million annually in city taxes.

The rest of the area to the north and east, which we rezoned in 2005, is booming. Taken all together, since the rezoning a total of forty-two buildings in the entire Hudson Yards area have been completed and another twenty-six are under construction. That represents twenty-six million square feet of mixed-use space.

All of the real-estate-related taxes generated out of the entire area are dedicated to paying the debt service on the bonds issued to extend the No. 7 line and build the related parks and other infrastructure. Current estimates are that those real-estate-related taxes will be sufficient to pay all of the interest and principal and then distribute $20 billion to the city over the next thirty years. That's the virtuous cycle at work.

I am often asked if pursuing the stadium on the West Side was a mistake. I still think it was the right thing to do. I don't think the Hudson Yards rezoning, the subway extension, and all of the other investment would have happened if the Olympic catalyst and its strict timetable, which got the rezoning and subway financing done by 2005, hadn't existed—and our rationale for focusing on the West Side was the stadium.

A different question is whether we are better off without the stadium. There I think the answer is more complicated. Although everything now happening on the eastern railyard could have been done with or without the stadium (because it was approved before the stadium was defeated), Related Companies has pursued a strategy of building the commercial space on the eastern railyard first, earning a more modest profit while creating a critical mass of activity and then earning much larger profits on the residential buildings, which are mostly on the western railyard. The company couldn't have pursued that strategy with the stadium. Even I now advocate for moving the Javits Center to Queens and paying for it by capturing the high property values on its existing site. So I am willing to concede that perhaps the best result would have been to switch the stadium to Flushing Meadows after the rezoning was approved in January 2005.

The debate will continue, as it should. But it is happily a debate about whether Hudson Yards would have achieved greater success with or without a stadium. What is not in doubt is the scale of the success: Lower Manhattan and Hudson Yards are thriving.

CHAPTER TWENTY-THREE

PLaNYC: EXTENDING THE VIRTUOUS CYCLE

O N EARTH DAY, April 22, 2007, Mike Bloomberg took the podium beneath the famous twenty-one-thousand-pound model of a blue whale suspended in the cavernous Hall of Ocean Life at the American Museum of Natural History to introduce a whole new way to plan for the urban future: PlaNYC.

Despite its capacious size, the exhibition space was packed to the limit. A jumbotron-like screen projected Bloomberg's image above the more than seven hundred assembled guests as he described our plan to create the world's "first environmentally sustainable twenty-first-century city." The sustainability plan was my last big initiative in City Hall, and it really amounted to the ultimate expression of my philosophy of the virtuous cycle of the successful city.

By mid-2005, after nearly one full term in office for us, the city was clearly on the upswing again after the devastation wrought by 9/11. In fact, we were beginning to feel the strain of that growth. In addition to the problems of locating salt piles and tow pounds, the transit systems and roads were growing more congested, sidewalks were crowded, and housing prices were beginning to rise. Intuitively, it was logical to think that if we didn't manage the growth, we might even choke off the virtuous cycle we had set in motion.

It would take us twenty-one months to figure out how to unpack every element of New York's physical environment and then to develop and finance a 127-point plan that would ensure New York would be able to continue to grow for the next generation—and would demonstrate to ourselves and to other cities around the world how we could make a meaningful contribution to reducing climate change.

Our plan was remarkably ambitious. Even the *New York Times* wrote, "Policy experts said the mayor's agenda, known as PlaNYC, is perhaps his most far-reaching, and its fate could determine whether his administration will be remembered as truly transformative." Ten years later, almost everything we set out to do and more—with one notable exception—has been or is being achieved, with remarkable results.

PlaNYC started with a salt pile—and a presentation that included a projection that New York's population would reach nine million by 2030. Over twenty-one months, hundreds of people worked on the plan, inspired by the opportunity to think about the long-term future of their city. PlaNYC is a perfect example of the extraordinary chain reaction that can take place when a team of city officials is given the rare freedom to focus on the long term, so that a strategy for city services everyone takes for granted but no one actually wants nearby—such as power generation, salt piles for snow and ice, and tow pounds—morphed into a massive plan that covered everything from planting one million new trees to painting roofs with reflective silver, with an overarching goal of reducing carbon emissions produced by New York City by 30 percent.

In my first four years in office I had been so busy helping to get the city back on its feet and pursuing the Olympics that I hadn't thought about the environment at all. In fact, when we met at Gracie Mansion in July 2005 for the summit where I proposed the strategic land-use plan, I couldn't have told you what the word sustainability meant. The UN 1987 Report of the World Commission on Environment and Development defined development as sustainable if it meets the needs of the present without compromising the well-being of future generations. But a series of fortuitous events in the last months of 2005 and early months of 2006 taught me what sustainability really might mean to New York City.

After Bloomberg won reelection in November 2005, he more than doubled the number of agencies, boards, and commissions I oversaw. But the new agencies did not just represent more responsibility—they gave me a very different window into city operations. My new portfolio included the Departments of Buildings, Transportation, and Environmental Protection.

I met with each of my new Commissioners to learn their concerns, their agendas, and their priorities. All of these agencies had particularly vital interactions with the environment. The Transportation and Buildings Departments are the top contributors to New York's carbon footprint, as I would find out later.

I learned that a sustainability task force had been formed in 2004. It had made a hodgepodge of recommendations around land and energy use and solid waste disposal. In addition, the city had numerous programs run out of different agencies focused on brownfields, climate-adaptation studies, and alternative-fuel vehicles. However, little had been implemented.

While I was learning about these early efforts, our strategic land-use plan was moving forward under the direction of Joe Chan and Angela Sung (now Pinsky—she and Seth married in 2011. She had started out as an intern in City Hall and later became my Deputy Chief of Staff). They catalogued every possible source of land owned by the city, other public entities, or the private sector that might make a good home for those hard-to-place uses. In reality, there wasn't a lot. But the project had started to morph beyond that into a greater effort that attempted to gauge the demands of a growing city. Our conversations with Commissioners and their staffs were revealing. When we asked how much new infrastructure we would need to provide power or water or trash collection for a population of nine million, the answer was always, "It depends." That is, the city could either add sanitation or energy plants—or, they suggested, we might just be more efficient and waste less and then be able to make do by upgrading or modifying existing infrastructure.

Chan, Sung, and a young writer and policy analyst who had led our writing efforts on the Olympic bid and whom I brought to City Hall, Sophia Hollander, were fielding and integrating ideas far beyond their original mandate into a sprawling list that covered everything from trees to sewer waste. The agencies were getting excited to think deeply about the consequences and broadly about the city of the future. Two veterans from the City Planning Department, Sandy Hornick and Eric Kober, tackled the project with particular enthusiasm, unleashing ideas bottled up maybe for decades. Before we knew it, our plan for noxious uses, then growth, was evolving into an effort to create a master plan for the physical future of New York. Still, in those early days, we struggled to devise an umbrella to corral these ideas into a coherent whole—all we knew was that they were good, important ideas.

But the concept of sustainability was increasingly creeping into our vocabularies. In early spring of 2006 several things made the link explicit. In March, Ariella Rosenberg (now Maron), a junior staffer in the small energy group at the Economic Development Corporation, asked to come see me. She had recently received a master's degree in city planning from the Massachusetts Institute of Technology. She had studied sustainability plans in other cities, especially London (I was acutely sensitive to anything London did that would make us less competitive because it had just beaten us out for the Olympics). She had been somewhat involved in the development of the strategic land-use plan and saw the connections between what we were doing and what other cities defined as sustainability. She advocated for a comprehensive sustainability plan.

Soon afterward, Nicky Gavron, the Deputy Mayor of London, came to our City Hall. Her ostensible purpose was to ask if New York would join and then host the next meeting of an organization the Mayor of London had recently launched called C20 (now C40) to bring big-city mayors together to share best practices to help curb their carbon footprints. But we spent much of our time discussing London's recently implemented congestion-pricing scheme. Congestion pricing charges a fee to drivers for entering high-traffic areas at peak times. After talking to Bloomberg, we readily agreed to her request to host the meeting. We also quietly began to look at congestion pricing. If London could do it, why couldn't we?

All of this occurred as Al Gore's movie on climate change, *An Inconvenient Truth*, was released in May 2006. It raised the profile of climate change and for us solidified the links between sustainability, the environment, and climate change. That same month, Bloomberg was set to address the League of Conservation Voters. Its Executive Director was the indefatigable Marcia Bystryn, a former Assistant Commissioner of the Sanitation Department, who had introduced recycling in New York City. The organization had been one of the few voices out front on the sustainability issue. Bystryn had even been lobbying the city since 2001 to come up with a plan to address climate change.

Bloomberg's reputation in the environmental community at that point was spotty. He was mostly remembered for suspending, as a cost-saving measure, a large part of the recycling program started by Bystryn. So we decided to use his speech to commit ourselves to some action. When Bloomberg addressed the gathering on May 18 he promised to create a new office whose goal "will be nothing short of formalizing policies of sustainability as integral to the future growth and development of our city."

After we had made an admittedly vague promise, we had to deliver. Our strategic land-use plan had evolved into a monster, involving dozens of city agencies. I realized we were going to have to develop a plan that had many of the characteristics of, well, the Olympic plan. It had to tell a compelling and coherent story about the city and its challenges and how we were going to meet them, it had to be specific enough to give it credibility, and it needed someone to lead it who could drive it forward with relentless zeal.

My then Chief of Staff, Marc Ricks, recommended a former colleague from McKinsey & Company, Rohit "Rit" Aggarwala. He certainly had the intellectual heft: he had a PhD in US history from Columbia (and had done his thesis on how New York had outpaced Philadelphia to become the leading US metropolis at the turn of the nineteenth century!) as well as an MBA in finance. He had been a management consultant, which gave him extensive experience managing large, complex projects. He had even worked at the Federal Railroad Administration, all of which led me to believe that he would understand how to turn a diverse set of ideas into a coherent plan with achievable tasks.

Aggarwala came into City Hall and met with me, Josh Sirefman, and Jeff Kay, who headed the Mayor's Office of Operations and had been in charge of relations with the state legislature for the city's Office of Management and Budget. Aggarwala was intrigued, but, as is his nature, a bit skeptical. At our first interview, he questioned whether we would be willing to tackle the really tough issues even if they were unpopular. He raised congestion pricing. We had been secretly studying the idea for a couple of months. When he brought it up, I blurted out, "We are already crunching the numbers!" He signed on.

He quickly recruited a team. Maron was first to join, then Laurie Kerr, who came up with many of the best ideas in the plan, and Amy Chester, who helped organize outreach efforts. We added outside resources. McKinsey helped us to organize the many work streams that needed to be consolidated. As with NYC2012, we created an advisory board that would help guide us in the development of a plan and would help us gain political and scientific acceptance of the decisions we made and the plans we crafted. We looked for leaders who represented a broad cross section of the constituencies—environmental, labor, business and real estate, and political—we thought would be necessary to get our plans embraced.

In the end, our Sustainability Advisory Board had seventeen members, including Ed Ott, Executive Director of the New York City Central Labor Council, an umbrella group of New York's labor unions; James Gennaro,

Chair of the City Council's Committee on Environmental Protection; City Council Speaker Christine Quinn; Steve Spinola, President of the Real Estate Board of New York; representatives of five environmental groups, including Bystryn and Andy Darrell, New York Regional Director of the Environmental Defense Fund; Kathy Wylde, CEO of the Partnership for New York City to represent the city's business leadership (Wylde was also, not coincidentally, a ferocious advocate for congestion pricing); and representatives of environmental justice organizations, foundations, and other private-sector interests. We even included Bob Yaro from the Regional Plan Association, who had been fiercely opposed to the stadium. (Hold no grudges!) In short, it was an all-star group that represented the many sides of the diverse set of issues we thought we would have to address.

Bloomberg dropped in on the first meeting of the Sustainability Advisory Board to show his support. In his remarks, he touched on the uniqueness of the board. He noted how rare it was that often-opposing constituencies gather to help shape policy rather than criticize it. Throughout the fall, the full advisory board met once every three weeks with the participating city agencies. In between, subgroups focused on eight specific areas: energy efficiency and green buildings, energy supply and distribution, transportation, green infrastructure, land use and brownfields, waste management, water, and climate-change adaptation.

The staff, with its consultants and advisors, worked hard to ground everything in data, science, and financial analysis. For each idea that came up in one of the meetings, we got the facts and attempted to understand the impact, the likelihood of success, and the costs of implementing it, especially if it required large public investment or mandates on the private sector. Early on, we agreed that we wouldn't consider innovations we didn't believe would be practical, either technologically or financially, within the foreseeable future. That eliminated a lot of discussion about theory.

To give focus to our deliberations, we articulated a single goal that could be reached at a date certain for each aspect of the physical environment.

Eventually the board members resolved to develop ten goals that fell into six broad buckets: land (housing, brownfields, open space), water (water quality, the reliability of the water network), transportation (congestion, "state of good repair"), energy, air quality, and climate change. The target date they established was 2030.

The goals were specific and bold and bear repeating here:

1. Create homes for almost a million more New Yorkers while making housing more affordable and sustainable.
2. Ensure that all New Yorkers live within a ten-minute walk of a park.
3. Clean up all contaminated land in New York City.
4. Open 90 percent of our waterways for recreation by reducing water pollution and preserving our natural areas.
5. Develop critical backup systems for our aging water network to ensure long-term reliability.
6. Improve travel times by adding transit capacity for millions more residents, visitors, and workers.
7. Reach a full "state of good repair" on New York City's roads, subways, and rails for the first time in history.
8. Provide cleaner, more reliable power for every New Yorker by upgrading our energy infrastructure.
9. Achieve the cleanest air quality of any big city in the United States.
10. Reduce our global warming emissions by 30 percent.

Starting with a certain date forced us to demonstrate how the package of initiatives addressing that goal would add up to achieving it. Take the goal of a 30 percent reduction in the city's carbon emissions by 2030. Because climate change cuts across nearly all of the other issues, it is the most complicated. For almost everything—across all of the goals—we evaluated, we did a calculation of its impact on reaching the carbon reduction goal. Of course, we had to start with a baseline, so we did an inventory of carbon emissions generated by the city. We discovered that almost 75 percent of the city's emissions came from the heating, cooling, powering, and lighting of buildings. The other 25 percent came from transportation and waste.

Many other cities had put in regulations demanding that future buildings be carbon neutral, which sounds very progressive. We quickly realized that we couldn't just focus on new buildings. In fact, even if every building completed in New York after 2005 were carbon neutral—something no building had achieved at the time—we wouldn't reach our reduction goal by 2030. So we realized our focus should be on making older buildings more energy efficient. (Many other cities have since followed our example and put new emphasis on old buildings.)

Of course, getting a building owner to fix something that already exists and is making money is a much bigger imposition than just creating regulations that will affect future builders. That's why we had to be sensitive about costs. And that's why we wanted to work with an advisory board to craft our initiatives—we needed to constantly be reminded of how our actions would play out in the real world.

Ultimately, for every initiative we considered, we framed it in terms of growth: Could we accommodate more people and still pass the test of sustainability, meeting the needs of the present without compromising the well-being of future generations?

Before Thanksgiving 2006 we had a pretty good idea of how we intended to meet the ten goals and were close to being able to announce a plan. But I was beginning to have a different set of concerns. I was acutely aware that I had been the force behind the failed Olympic bid. Although I already deeply believed that the Olympic effort had proven itself a valuable catalyst to getting things done—and I had confidence that Bloomberg felt the same—I knew there would be skepticism—within City Hall and outside—of another Doctoroff master plan.

So, I asked for advice on how to roll out the plan from the two sharpest political and communications minds in the Bloomberg Administration— Kevin Sheekey and Ed Skyler. By this time, Skyler was Deputy Mayor of Operations, but in Bloomberg's first term he had been Press Secretary and Communications Director. Sheekey had also been promoted to Deputy Mayor in the second term and oversaw, among other things, Intergovernmental Affairs. He was the person Bloomberg trusted most for political judgment. I also looped in Kay, because of his thoughtfulness about the strange ways of Albany. The advice from Sheekey, Skyler, and Kay was clear: wait. Roll the plan out in two stages. First announce the purpose and the goals and then give the public, the politicians, and the constituencies with a vested interest a chance to weigh in. Then, after a reasonable time, announce the plan. That way, they advised, people would feel some ownership of the plan. Maybe I had learned something over the past five years—I listened.

The first effort to engage the public was a speech the Mayor gave at the Queens Museum of Art on December 12, 2006. Before the speech, we decided we had to give the plan a name and snappy graphics. Doug Bernstein came up with PlaNYC (which prompted a big debate: Is it Plan-Y-C or Plan-N-Y-C? It is actually the former).

The speech reminded New Yorkers how far we had come in just five years and remade the case for future growth: "The engine driving New York's future is growth—growth that's evident all around us. . . . This growth could bring incredible benefits: billions of dollars of new economic activity will be generated by new jobs, residents, and visitors." He asserted as fact that New York was on a path to grow to nine million people and asked New Yorkers whether they could imagine their already crowded city with another million people—as many as Boston and Miami had combined. Then he switched the focus to ask what the city would be like when we added another million people and how its citizens would experience the effects of climate change—unpredictable weather patterns and longer, hotter summers. He summarized the ten goals and called for a citywide conversation about them with the objective of releasing a plan over the next several months.

It had already been more than a year since we started on the strategic land-use plan. The team was exhausted from the late nights and Sunday City Hall meetings. But now things intensified dramatically, particularly after we picked Earth Day—five months from then—for release of PlaNYC. The following Sunday we stuffed 1.3 million brochures outlining the opportunities and challenges of growth and our ten goals (in both English and Spanish) in newspapers, under front doors, and in apartment building lobbies across the city urging citizens to visit our website and submit their own ideas.

All seventeen members of our Sustainability Advisory Board voluntarily endorsed all the goals and allowed us to list their names. We had made clear that they would have no such obligation, so this was a big stamp of approval. Our announcement in the papers and on the flyers worked as well as we might have hoped. More than three thousand suggestions came pouring in. My favorite comment was a suggestion that we find a way to harness the energy produced by the subway turnstiles. Over the next four months, in all five boroughs, our team gave dozens of presentations to and hosted town hall meetings with community groups, public officials, and planning groups.

The public input gave some important feedback. Green roofs are a good example. They use plantings like grass and gardens as natural insulation for the building below. In theory, they absorb water and reflect sunlight, keeping the space below cool. Although our team loved the concept, we had discounted them because they didn't pass our "most-bang-for-the-buck" test. We concluded that in most cases, because of weight and drainage problems, rooftop gardens were too costly. Instead, we opted to include a proposal for property owners to paint their roofs with white or silver paint, a relatively cheap option that reflects sunlight and can reduce cooling bills by 25 percent.

Still, the public loved green rooftops. At nearly every town hall or public forum someone would ask about them. Everyone liked them for their non-quantifiable benefits, such as the psychological respite they offered to a concrete city or, perhaps, the chance to plant a favorite flower or shrub. Because of that feedback, the plan eventually included green roof tax abatements. (However, our first impulse was correct. After a few years, the city found that the cost for roof gardens was still too high, and uptake on the abatement was low, and therefore, the abatements were allowed to expire.)

Much more of our time in the four months from the speech at the Queens Museum of Art to that on Earth Day was spent putting the plan together. The major lesson from NYC2012 was that the key to gaining support for a big plan is to back up a strong vision with substance. We were going to detail exactly what we planned to do and when, who was going to do it, how much it was going to cost, and what we expected to achieve. The ideas were going to be clearly explained and humanized so that every New Yorker could read the plan and understand its implications for his or her own life—not always easy when writing about complicated energy systems, the science of carbon emissions, or the technicalities behind brownfield remediation. The ideas could be brilliant—but if no one cared or realized their significance, the plan would be doomed to the dustbin that holds grand, meaningless planning documents from cities the world over. If we were going to make people care and state our plans clearly without hedging or hiding behind impressive, vague promises, we had to be confident we could deliver. That meant it all had to add up.

The first step was to finally agree on the initiatives that we had to include and then painstakingly translate them so that they could resonate with a broad audience. In the end there were 127 initiatives, detailed in a 155-page book now taught in universities around the world. Hollander, a journalist who had written for the *New York Times* before joining the Olympic bid, studied the city's previous master plan from 1969, written by famous author William H. Whyte. That text was startling in its literary ambition and vivid description of the city. Now, Hollander—a third-generation native New Yorker who had penned the speeches, brochures, and website—set out to write a love letter to the city that integrated real neighborhood reporting; traced the history of the city's systems; and, in the spirit of Whyte's manifesto, offered a sometimes brutally honest accounting of what had gone wrong in New York's approach to date. Most importantly, it outlined our vision for how New York could make growth work for us rather than against us.

The plan was remarkable for its scope. Mirroring the planning process, it was structured around the ten goals. For each one, there were between seven and twenty-one separate initiatives—each one laid out in detail—designed to add up to the achievement of the ten goals by 2030.

For example, to meet the goal of enabling every New Yorker to live within a ten-minute walk of a park, we said we would open schoolyards across the city as public playgrounds (they were typically closed after school hours); make high-quality competition fields available for more hours; complete eight "destination" parks planned in the days of Robert Moses and never finished; convert asphalt into multiturf fields; maximize time on existing turf fields by installing lights for evening use; create a new, or enhance an existing, public plaza in every community; and expand the city's Greenstreets program.

We also helped to define the Department of Parks' plan to plant one million new trees across the city (a beloved goal achieved by 2017). These weren't just vague aspirations. Each was backed with detail. For example, for the plan to open school playgrounds, we identified the 290 schoolyards that could be opened, what kind of improvements would be required for each, how many children they would be able to serve, and therefore how their availability would help us to get to our goal. We applied the same standard to nearly all of the initiatives.

We committed 10 percent of the city's annual energy bill to fund energy-saving investments in city operations; we proposed mandates, challenges, and incentives to reduce demand among the city's largest energy consumers; we detailed how to expand and improve access to the city's ferry, biking, and mass transit networks, including initiating Bus Rapid Transit routes; we proposed a set of enhancements to the city's water network, including new filtration and disinfectant plans and backup programs for aging infrastructure; we introduced green infrastructure plans to reduce the stress on our overburdened combined sewer system; we outlined new requirements or incentives to reduce emissions by fleets of taxis, black cars, and others; and we proposed launching a citywide strategic planning process for climate change adaptation. And these were just a handful of the initiatives.

A key factor in our debates over which initiatives to include always involved an analysis of the relative contribution toward achieving our goals and the relative costs. For each one, we provided a detailed estimate of the capital and operating expenses. It would all add up to nearly $2 billion, including $800 million to retrofit the city's own buildings to make them more energy efficient. On that one, we did the analysis and concluded that it would have a payback of seven or eight years, better than the cost of the city's capital.

In other cases, the math was not as clear-cut, but we concluded the indirect benefit was compelling. When we were debating the $400 million plan to plant a million trees, we were able to demonstrate that the average payback on a tree was about nine times its cost, largely from increased property values, reduced runoff, and the energy savings from the temperature of the city as a result of the increased tree canopy. The agencies, my staff, and the advisory board had all worked on this without knowing if it could ever be funded.

After we had a pretty firm sense of what we would propose and how much it would cost, it was time to present it to Mark Page, the Budget Director. He grimaced through the entire thing. We argued that investing in sustainability would pay back not only in terms of the item-by-item analysis we had done but also in promoting the virtuous cycle. A healthier, more convenient, more environmentally forward city would attract more people, who would pay more taxes, which we would invest back into the city, perpetuating the cycle. From that perspective, we weren't spending money—we were making money.

Page wasn't completely sold when I started the process of laying everything out for the Mayor. He had been engaged throughout the development of the plan but hadn't seen everything put together. It took Aggarwala and me three meetings to walk him through how we planned to meet the ten goals, including the costs and expected returns. Bloomberg couldn't have been more supportive. He hesitated on only one: congestion pricing. He was right to be skeptical. We knew it was going to be the lightning rod of the entire plan, and it was going to have to be approved in Albany.

Our proposal called for imposing (with some exceptions) an eight-dollar charge on car trips (trucks would pay more) into the congestion zone, which we defined as Manhattan below 86th Street during peak hours. At every border crossing there would be cameras to detect the license plates of cars and other vehicles coming in, which would be charged automatically. We knew this would be particularly sensitive for the relatively small number of residents and businesses who lived and operated outside of the zone who regularly came into Lower or Midtown Manhattan (and, therefore, their elected representatives), so we proposed that all of the revenues, which we estimated to eventually climb to nearly $1 billion annually, be plowed back into enhancing the mass transit system, especially in Upper Manhattan and the other boroughs. Despite enormous investments over the previous quarter century in the mass transit system, it was still woefully underfunded.

Getting around the city in 2007 was horrible. The evidence was overwhelming that it was going to be the single-biggest factor in choking off our potential to grow in the coming twenty-five years. Aggarwala, the Department of Transportation (now led by Commissioner Janette Sadik-Khan, whom Bloomberg and I had recently hired to execute on our PlaNYC transportation agenda), and our outside consultants produced maps of expected capacity on every road, bridge, tunnel, subway, and train line into Manhattan by 2030, assuming a population growing to nine million. They coded each route: green, yellow, red, and dark red, with dark red representing a disaster. By 2030 nearly all of the routes were dark red.

We spent a lot of time with our counterparts in London, who were eager for us to follow their lead. In 2003, London began charging drivers extra for being on the most trafficked streets in the peak hours. When Mayor Ken Livingstone introduced congestion pricing, he was vilified by opponents who charged essentially that the plan would have ruinous effects on business by discouraging people from coming into the center of the city. The *Telegraph* actually called him London's "deadliest enemy." He persevered anyway and placed what amounted to a ten-dollar tax on cars that entered the heart of London during peak hours.

By 2005, it was already clear that congestion pricing was a great success. Traffic delays in London plunged by 30 percent; road speeds increased by 19 percent; the feared drop in retail spending never materialized; and, best of all, in just two years, London raised more than $360 million and funneled it all back into expansion and improvements of mass transportation. As a plus, air quality also improved.

New York's business community was solidly behind importing the program. Wylde had persuasively told National Public Radio in a November 2005 interview: "New York is competitive for business not because we have low costs—we have high costs—but because people think they can get things done faster and better in New York. That's productivity. And we want to make sure, since our prime competitor in today's world in many respects is London, that we don't miss a beat." Back then, Bloomberg's response was, "Congestion pricing is not something that we're talking about."

That was 2005. By the spring of 2007, the Mayor was more open to it. When Aggarwala and I first began presenting the idea to him formally just a month or so before our planned Earth Day unveiling, he was skeptical, but he heard us out. He found London's experience persuasive. He was somewhat heartened by the business community's support of the idea. In addition, our entire Sustainability Advisory Board had endorsed congestion pricing, and it included the Speaker of the City Council and the Chair of the Committee on Environmental Protection. He was taken aback by our projections of congestion in 2030. I think he thought that our proposal to reinvest all of the proceeds from the charge into enhanced mass transit would help address the political issues.

Still, I didn't exactly have credibility with my colleagues in City Hall when it came to predicting how Albany would react to . . . anything. The pushback in the bullpen was pretty fierce. Some high-level political staffers would whisper to Aggarwala behind my back and say, "You are going to break the Bloomberg Administration."

Bloomberg treated congestion pricing as he did other potentially divisive and hard-to-sell ideas: he sat through briefings from us and probed for the holes in our arguments. It was never about politics. But still he needed to be convinced. The Wednesday before Earth Day Aggarwala called me anxiously as he was getting out of the subway. We needed to go to the printers on Friday. "Do we have a decision yet?" he asked. I told him not to worry. Bloomberg agreed the next morning. And after he was in, he was all in. He would be a fearsome advocate for the plan.

The report went to the printers, and we began a highly choreographed three-day rollout in advance of Bloomberg's speech at the Museum of Natural History. The plan was so complicated and intricate that we felt we needed to explain ourselves ahead of time. First, we briefed the *New York Times*. Then, Aggarwala led a three-hour, embargoed briefing with the rest of the press. We also briefed key members of the City Council. To strike quickly, within a week of the announcement we intended to submit our budget request to the City Council. Learning from my huge stadium faux pas, Kay and I even briefed Sheldon Silver's top aide.

We asked all of the elected officials to withhold comment on the plan until we had rolled it out. We wanted the break because we knew we had an unusually strong, deep coalition behind PlaNYC, including strange bedfellows such as labor unions and environmentalists, who would provide political air cover. Amazingly, everyone honored our request—except Anthony Weiner, who held a press conference in Times Square on the day before the unveiling of the plan and attacked it.

Bloomberg started his Earth Day speech by quoting a plaque just outside the Hall of Ocean Life. It was, he said, stamped with a Kenyan proverb: "The earth was not given to you by your parents, it was loaned to you by your children." That was the very definition of sustainability that had guided us for the past year. He then made the case for action, saying, "Let's face up to the fact that our population growth is putting our city on a collision course with the environment, which itself is growing more unstable and uncertain. Let's recognize that many of the gains we have made in the quality of our air, water, and land will be lost if we don't act." He described the key elements of the plan and made the case for congestion pricing and then closed by returning to the Kenyan proverb: "We can return this city to our children. And it will be stronger, healthier, cleaner, greener, and greater than ever."

Mike got a several-minute standing ovation. There were multiple roars and crescendos. The biggest ovation came when he asked, "If we don't act, who will?" I was proud and should have been on cloud nine, but instead I felt distant. I knew I wouldn't be there to see this plan through to the end—in fact, I knew I was going to be leaving City Hall at the end of the year.

But old habits die hard. The next morning, while Aggarwala was on his way to work, after perhaps his first night of relaxation in a year, he received an e-mail from me that read: "Rit, now that you have had some time to relax, we should start thinking about implementation." I was joking, but not entirely. After all, the next morning there were only 983 days to go, and the countdown clock Bloomberg had installed in the bullpen was there to prove it (it would be reset when he won his third term). So we began rolling out our new programs on an almost weekly basis.

Within months of the announcement, we had turned scores of once-barren concrete schoolyards into new playgrounds open to the public during nonschool hours. We had launched a "carbon challenge" to encourage private-sector companies to match the city's promise to reduce emissions by 30 percent by 2017. Bloomberg signed an executive order requiring the city to invest 10 percent of its energy bill to fund greenhouse-gas-emission-reduction projects. Within six months, the city launched more than 90 percent of the initiatives.

Every year, the Bloomberg Administration published a progress report on PlaNYC. The one for 2013, Mike's last year in office, is compelling. Thanks to Aggarwala, the Office of Long-Term Planning and Sustainability, and the hundreds of city employees at more than a dozen agencies, nearly all of the initiatives were well under way or completed.

At the time Bloomberg left office, greenhouse gas emissions dropped 19 percent in just six and a half years. The city adopted a Greener, Greater Buildings Plan; a Clean Heat Program; the Million Trees Program; a Green Infrastructure Plan; and the nation's first municipal brownfields cleanup program. New York also spent billions to protect and enhance the water system. Under Sadik-Khan, bike lanes were expanded, streets were pedestrianized, and bike share and bus rapid transit were introduced.

PlaNYC continued to evolve as the needs of the city changed. The administration expanded its focus on resiliency, which took on dramatically greater urgency in the wake of Superstorm Sandy. Seth Pinsky and Marc Ricks led the development of a PlaNYC-like resiliency plan called A Stronger, More Resilient New York that detailed hundreds of strategies to enable the city to adapt to climate change. Mayor de Blasio has continued the work, and the Office of Long-Term Planning and Sustainability has grown, but he changed the name from PlaNYC to OneNYC.

But there was one major initiative that conspicuously never happened: congestion pricing died in Albany. We had wanted to get congestion-pricing legislation enacted before the legislative session ended in Albany in late June, just two months after the announcement of PlaNYC. We thought we had learned our lesson from the stadium loss and did everything right. The City Council passed a resolution in support of congestion pricing. We briefed leaders in Albany before announcing the plan. After Earth Day, we sent teams of representatives from City Hall and the agencies up to the state capital armed with tailored briefings for each New York City–based legislator, detailing for him or her how many constituents commuted into Manhattan for work by car (almost none) and what specific mass transit improvements we were proposing for their districts (a lot).

Bloomberg wined and dined legislators at Gracie Mansion. We convinced the George W. Bush Administration to give us $354 million in grants to pay for the implementation of the congestion-pricing program—a powerful incentive to adopt it. We developed a powerful coalition of business, labor, environmental, and community organizations in support of the plan. Our allies at the Environmental Defense Fund and the Partnership for New York City paid for television advertising to support the measure. We were completely aligned with newly elected Governor Eliot Spitzer, who could not have been a more forceful advocate for the cause (although the rocky relations with the legislature he quickly developed with his steamrolling approach probably didn't help). We even hired the very capable Pat Lynch as our lobbyist.

In the end, it all came down to Silver again. The playbook he employed on the stadium came down off the shelf, and he began his process of obfuscation and evasiveness. Silver offered all sorts of reasons for why the congestion plan had to be "studied more" before the legislature could move forward. He argued that the cameras we would use to enforce the plan might impinge on privacy. He protested that the charge might be increased down the road. In July, at a special session of the legislature, he did what he did best. He delayed. The best we could do to forestall defeat was to get him to agree to "study" the issue and then take it up again in the next legislative session the following year.

By then, I had already left City Hall. But in April 2008, a congestion-pricing bill was introduced in the state Senate. The Assembly, which Shelly led, didn't follow suit. In fact, he announced that the congestion-pricing bill "will not be on the floor of the Assembly." It was dead without even a vote. As I said, Albany is a hall of mirrors.

But I know that sooner or later the combined pressures from the need to control congestion and to find a way to fund desperately required mass transit modernization will force New York to adopt some version of the plan, whether that is in the form of tolls on bridges or a congestion-pricing charge like the one we proposed.

I will cheer on whoever picks up the baton to get that done, and I will take great comfort in the fact that Silver won't be able to block it, even from the comfort of Suite 200.

EPILOGUE

WE MANAGED TO keep my resignation a secret almost up to the moment the Mayor announced it. At the meeting just before the hastily arranged press conference, only one person, then Chief of Staff Jim Whelan, knew what I was about to say. By then, my immediate team had grown from the original six with whom I had started to more than three dozen because the number of agencies, boards, and commissions I managed had grown from fifteen to thirty-five.

After they settled in, as I looked around the room, I became wistful, sad even. I had hired everyone in the room. A quick scan of the faces reminded me of all of the battles we had been through together. We had become a closeknit family, and I was about to tell them I was leaving. I decided that the only way was just to dive in. I told them how proud I was of what we had accomplished together and how we had done things that would change New York for the next century or more. I told them how much I loved my job, but that I was afraid I was growing a little cynical, and it was good to leave before that took hold.

I paused and looked up. Several members of the team were sniffling or in tears. I explained that I had sworn not to tell anyone what I was going to do next, but they would find out shortly when the Mayor held a press conference. An hour or so later, we gathered in the Blue Room in front of the media. Mike Bloomberg was brief:

> Peter Grauer, the Chairman of Bloomberg LP, and a friend of Dan's for twenty years, has hired Dan to be the new President of Bloomberg LP. I don't think there is any person in the world better for that job. Dan, I just hope they give you a pay raise!

Let me just say in closing that we are going to miss Dan very much. I'm not one to lavish praise, but today I want to tip my hat to someone who has given his all, and his all is as good as it gets.

Dan, I have done everything I could to try to keep you here, so it is sort of a bittersweet moment for us, but you really have made an enormous difference in this city, and on behalf of 8.2 million people, I just want to say thank you.

We then took questions. In response to one question, even Bloomberg appeared to choke up when he said, "He has been a true partner, a trusted friend, and the architect of the most sweeping transformation of New York since the days of Robert Moses."

An accompanying press release listed the highlights from the six years we'd worked together: our economic development team had initiated 289 separate major projects and initiatives that we expected to culminate in the creation of 130 million square feet of commercial and residential space, three new sports arenas or stadiums, a new subway line, 2,400 acres of parks, the regeneration of more than sixty miles of waterfront, and an affordable housing plan for a half million New Yorkers. With all of that, we expected to displace only four hundred residents. The economy had recovered much faster than anyone expected after the 9/11 destruction, including the creation of more than a hundred thousand jobs, accelerated by the creation of a climate in which businesses wanted to locate and people wanted to work. Maybe most important, PlaNYC had set the stage to accommodate the growth of the city for the following twenty-five years in a truly sustainable way.

As we were announcing my departure in the Blue Room, my assistant, Marla Pardee, attached the press release to a note from me and sent it to several hundred people in New York with whom I had worked closely, thanking them for their help and telling them of my plans. In return, I got an outpouring of appreciation. My favorite response, though, was from the man who would later spell tap with two p's in a tweet. Our future forty-fifth President scanned my note to him and sent it back. On it he had written in a thick felt-tip pen, "Great job!!" Then, down below, where a sentence mistakenly ended with a small typo (I think two periods), he circled the error and added an exclamation point next to it.

The *New York Daily News* and the *New York Post* were very positive. The *Daily News'* coverage called me "brilliant" but "imperious," but on the editorial side the headline ran: "Well Done, Dan." The *Post* called me "Prince of the City" and acknowledged in its good-bye editorial, "Even when Doctoroff didn't succeed—such as [with] the West Side Stadium/New York Jets complex or bringing the 2012 Olympics here—it certainly wasn't for lack of vision or effort. And Doctoroff, who knew that New York City is all about big goals and big projects, succeeded far more often than not. The city will benefit from his vision and hard work for decades to come."

In its front-page coverage the next day, the *New York Times* concluded that my impact on the city "has been decidedly mixed." The paper began its story with a strongly skeptical tone: "As Mr. Doctoroff ends his tenure as the longest-serving deputy mayor for economic development, much of his agenda remains unrealized, despite his many achievements." Only now, a decade after I left City Hall, is it possible to test that rather sour judgment. The fact is that virtually everything we set in motion has been completed or is well under way. At one point, some of my former staffers and I went back to our list of 289 initiatives and counted how many would never be done. It was a handful (the Olympics and the stadium being the most obvious).

Some of that must be attributed to the Mayor's third term. The continuity he provided gave my successors as Deputy Mayor, Bob Lieber and Bob Steel, and the Commissioners of the agencies, four more years to push our agenda forward. Only seventy-eight rezonings were done or in process when I left, but Amanda Burden remained in her post as Chair of the City Planning Commission for all twelve years of the Bloomberg Administration and eventually completed 140, rezoning a remarkable 40 percent of the city. We were only 40 percent of the way through the New Housing Marketplace Plan when I stepped down, but Shaun Donovan, Rafael Cestero, and Mat Wambua, who rose from Policy Advisor on my staff to Commissioner of the Department of Housing Preservation and Development in four years, ensured that the plan was completed despite the financial crisis of 2008.

Rit Aggarwala built the Office of Long-Term Planning and Sustainability into a globally emulated department and then not only executed almost all of the 127 initiatives (other than congestion pricing—which will come back someday!) but also expanded the brief to focus even more on buildings and resiliency. Janette Sadik-Khan took some of the rough ideas for transportation that we outlined in PlaNYC and turned New York into a world leader on how to creatively rethink how we can use the streets as public space. I might have seeded the germ of an idea of a new campus on Governors Island, but then Seth Pinsky, who became the head of the Economic Development Corporation just a few years after working with me on the restructuring of the World Trade Center site deal, and Bob Steel led the effort to redefine it and make it relevant for a moment when New York could effectively compete for high-tech jobs and then flawlessly executed on making Cornell Tech on Roosevelt Island a reality. Andrew Winters and his team at the Office of Capital Planning and Development did exactly what I had hoped—they just made stuff happen.

Despite the criticisms, the economic revitalization that took place in New York City during Bloomberg's tenure as Mayor is impossible to deny. A city that was devastated just three and a half months before he took office gleamed when he left City Hall. New York has been rebuilt, and not just Ground Zero but all five boroughs. The city has more people, more jobs, more housing, and more visitors than ever before. And that has continued—and even accelerated—in the years since Bloomberg left office.

The purpose of this book is to show how we engineered a comeback that no one thought possible and made New York greater than ever. Although the city's situation is clearly unique, I think the four critical elements that enabled our success are universal.

THE CATALYST

THE NATURAL STATE of a city is to do nothing. Getting things done is hard. Serving in government isn't like being in the private sector. You have to be patient because there is a process for everything. There are so many constituencies that have valid, vested interests in the process. At the same time, you have to act with a sense of urgency at all times, or everything will die of its own weight given how complicated it is to get things done. So, how do you generate that sense of urgency? You need a catalyst.

For us, the first catalyst was 9/11. On the day of the tragedy, Mayor Rudy Giuliani told the world of New Yorkers' spirit and vowed to rebuild the city and make it better than ever. New Yorkers, aided by people from around the world, took the challenge of 9/11 truly to heart. Bloomberg echoed that mandate in his inauguration speech just three and a half months later.

To some extent, the city had confidence that it could be successful because it had a history of rallying when times were their bleakest. Team Bloomberg entered office with little experience. But tragedy provided a common sense of purpose.

Other cities can capitalize on different catalysts. In my hometown, Detroit, the catalyst to the regeneration beginning to emerge has been financial catastrophe. Detroit was forced into the country's largest-ever municipal bankruptcy, but that has given it the opportunity to restructure its finances and to elect new leadership.

It doesn't require a calamity to provide the catalyst. Leaders with courage and vision ought to be able to stimulate great progress and take big swings even when there's no particular crisis or public demand. PlaNYC was created out of nothing more than increased awareness of climate change brought on by Al Gore and others and a conviction among city officials that New York's virtuous cycle could choke on its own growth. There was no public cry to re-think every element of New York's physical condition. Bloomberg made it his cause, and a dedicated team of public servants and interested citizens banded together to tell a compelling story and then develop a plan.

Although 9/11 might have been the initial catalyst for many of the initia-tives I led, the Olympic bid gave us the deadlines to actually get things done. In many ways, that was my original insight in thinking about an Olympic bid. Hosting the Olympics—or even bidding for them—could be the spur to getting things done that otherwise would have been politically unfeasible or financially impossible. After watching what had happened in Tokyo, Bar-celona, Atlanta, and other Olympic host cities, I saw that the Olympics was one of the few things that ever occurred in a city's life on a deadline. The fact that we were able to get the Hudson Yards, West Chelsea, Downtown Brook-lyn, and Greenpoint-Williamsburg plans developed and approved (let alone the Yankees and Mets Stadium deals done) in the three short years before the International Olympic Committee decision in 2005 demonstrates the value of having or creating deadlines.

THE PHILOSOPHY

A CATALYST—A BRUTALLY tough one such as 9/11, say, or an effort to attract the Olympics, that helps a city to focus on deadlines or timing—is meaning-less without a guiding philosophy.

The Bloomberg Administration had a philosophy—not one based in tribal politics but in our economic understanding of how cities thrived. We believed in growth. Growth is not only good but also *essential* for a city's continued or renewed success. The alternative is stagnation and decline in the quality of life.

All of the areas we redeveloped, the neighborhoods we reinvigorated, and the jobs we helped to create had an impact on the city's bottom line.

The simplest and most dramatic metric is the growth of the city's operating budget—from around $42 billion in fiscal year 2003 to $70 billion in fiscal year 2014. So, what's the big deal about an extra $28 billion? That might seem like an obvious question, but it's not. There are lots of ways for government to spend $28 billion.

Our strategy, year after year, was to invest these additional funds right back into the city—into safety, education, health, transportation, housing, social services, cultural institutions, parks, sanitation, and the environment—the things that improve quality of life. Over Bloomberg's three terms (from fiscal year 2003 to fiscal year 2014), growth in spending across the agencies responsible for those aspects of quality of life increased by 54 percent. We believed our mission was to improve the lives of New Yorkers—of all income levels, in every community, and of every race and ethnicity.

Our experience in New York provides compelling evidence that growth is not a zero-sum game. The increase in tax revenues was overwhelmingly from a growing economy, not new taxes. For progressives, those revenues enabled a significant expansion of the educational system, a significant increase in the amount spent on transportation, a major investment in addressing social issues such as homeless services, and a dramatic expansion of parks around the city. At the same time, those revenues enabled New York City to pay for skyrocketing pensions and health-care costs for city workers (which grew by $8 billion over the same period), costs that can hobble US cities that fail to grow.

All of these initiatives improved quality of life for everybody. It's not the 1 percent who benefit most when the city can still afford to pay for pensions. It's not the 1 percent who benefit most when spending per pupil increases by thousands of dollars in the public schools. The simple fact remains: the best way to provide these services is to pay for them.

As we continued to reinvest back into the factors that make New York great, we began to experience what I have referred to as the virtuous cycle of the successful city. Not only did residents and visitors benefit but also the city's magnetic strength grew, attracting even more residents, businesses, and tourists into our orbit. And they came bearing gifts: additional revenues for the city, which we would then reinvest—perpetuating the cycle once more. So, to be a progressive city, we must be a prosperous city. And we can't be a prosperous city unless we are a growing city.

Believing in growth is only half the battle. Critical to engineering that growth is a robust partnership with the private sector. Our view of government was to do whatever we could to make the private sector work effectively—in short, to be a helpful partner. The goal should not be a government that never intervenes, as some free-market extremists would prefer. Nor should the goal be a government that crowds out and demonizes the private sector. The model we established in the Bloomberg Administration can be replicated throughout the world, and its ideological underpinnings formed a "third way" between laissez-faire and a nanny state. In short, we offered a well-managed, activist government that viewed its role as an able partner of the private sector as well as the protector of the common good.

When Bloomberg took office, parts of the city had been largely untouched since the city's darkest days in the 1970s. Some of them weren't that far from a functional market economy—they just needed a boost to get there. And with carefully considered investment to help them reach a tipping point, many of those neighborhoods are now among the city's hottest and fastest growing, repopulating every day with new residents, restaurants, businesses, community facilities, and other amenities lacking for decades. As that has occurred, those new residents and businesses generated the revenues to raise our sights and invest in more neighborhoods. Virtuous cycle.

No private company could have extended the No. 7 line. But businesses, the tens of thousands of New Yorkers who work for them, and many of the 8.6 million residents (and climbing) who will be the beneficiaries of the $20 billion in net new real-estate-related taxes created as a result of that money will greatly benefit from its existence.

No private company could have created the High Line. But millions of New Yorkers benefit from its beauty every year, as do small businesses that benefit from the tourists it attracts, and all New Yorkers benefit from the revenues generated by the development that came from saving the High Line and its associated rezoning. Smart investment to prime the virtuous cycle is critically important.

New York is a remarkably compassionate city. It believes in helping those in need, making the city more affordable, and providing the tools for people to capitalize on opportunity. As a lifelong, progressive Democrat, I completely subscribe to that ideal. But all of that requires money. We should never forget how quickly the virtuous cycle can go into reverse and how disastrous the consequences can be. That will happen when we cease to be business friendly and when we think about spending money before we make it.

Did we allocate the fruits of growth fairly and appropriately? Despite the overall gains made during Bloomberg's tenure as Mayor, and despite the massive investments we made in communities across the city, inequality grew (although no more than it did nationally), and it is clear that the cost of living increased for too many during a period when incomes, especially for the middle class, were flatlining. Certainly, as I discussed in Chapter 6, we could have done more to respond to the growing pressure faster, but I think it is fair to say that we reestablished the principle that affordable housing is a key obligation of the city and then developed the new programs and policies necessary to meet that obligation in a twenty-first-century context.

A PLAN

A CATALYST AND a philosophy only have value if there's a plan in place to capitalize on them. A leader makes decisions based on the thoughtful calculation of investment and return. Where are you going to get the biggest bang for the buck not just in terms of dollars but in maximum quality of life for the most people? The Bloomberg Administration brought to government a more methodical, disciplined approach to thinking about those kinds of investments and the ultimate returns. We also brought a countercyclical orientation to it, too. Yes, there are political considerations. But at the end of the day, improving the city is the smartest political move—it will attract more people, who will lead to more growth and increase the marginal revenues on that growth. Virtuous cycle.

When the Bloomberg Administration came into office, we were brutally frank with ourselves—and with the citizens and businesses and interest groups—about New York's strengths and weaknesses. We brought big groups together to talk honestly about what really was good about the city, what was bad, and how we could successfully compete with other cities around the world. We carefully went through every industry and said, "Here are the things we can compete for, and here are the things we can't." Without sentimentality, we cut off all subsidies for those that didn't have a realistic future in the city.

The city does not exist in a vacuum. There are able competitors for businesses throughout the world. And the single-biggest liability for New York is that costs in New York are high. Cost of living. Construction costs. Taxes. And yet we also have great strengths, most notably the one that the Japanese banker pointed out—no matter who you are, no matter what you look like, New Yorkers assume that you belong. Our status as the most open city in the world gives us the ability to attract people from anywhere, to have them feel at home—to be, in many ways, the world's second home.

So we had to be honest about our global and national competition and build our plans around those industries for which we could successfully compete and those places that would supply the space we would need to do that. For decades, nostalgia for the glory days of manufacturing—an industry that stood very little chance of ever recovering its previous heights—held us back from developing some of the most valuable real estate in the world.

As New York proved over the past fifteen years, there are many areas in which the city could build its job base with smart focus, building on its real strengths rather than nostalgia and wishful thinking (in the case of manufacturing) or the equally dangerous mistake of assuming that what's working today will work tomorrow (in the case of finance jobs, which were booming in 2001 but could not be relied on to shoulder the city's tax base as much in the future). Industries such as tourism, film and television production, higher education, life sciences, and, most recently, technology had to be attracted to maintain the tax revenues the city would need to continue to grow and to meet future obligations.

We came into office with a physical plan that recognized New York would have to adjust to the transformation in the economy. The entire idea behind the Olympic X plan was that huge swaths of land across the city were underused.

Since 1961, Hudson Yards was an area on the Far West Side of Manhattan zoned for manufacturing. It was filled with vacant lots, parking lots, auto body shops, and warehouses at the very moment it was increasingly clear that our inventory of office space was becoming out of date and that the city would need to accommodate a growing population. It was irresistible. The same logic applied in our efforts to create other mixed-use districts around the city, including in Downtown Brooklyn, Long Island City, Harlem, Flushing, Coney Island, and Jamaica, Queens. Each case required a very targeted, specific approach to finding the right balance between meeting the community's needs and developing a plan that met the city's broader strategic needs.

As conditions changed, or as we learned more (often from our mistakes or from simply listening better), we adapted. We didn't initially have a housing plan. When we better understood the relationship between growth and housing—for all New Yorkers—we developed a record-breaking plan. As the growth of the city accelerated, we expanded it and added new tools and approaches. As we began to feel that we were risking choking on our growth and stunting our future capacity to grow, we stepped back and analyzed every aspect of the physical environment to identify the barriers to growth over the long term and developed PlaNYC.

Did we always get it right? Did we always adapt fast enough? Unfortunately not. But I think we got it mostly right. And the fact that we were guided by a plan—which we were willing to change when conditions warranted—gave us the confidence to move forward boldly and swiftly.

EXECUTION

GETTING STUFF DONE in government is hard. It doesn't matter how strong the catalyst, how consistent the philosophy, or how sound the plan. As Mayor Giuliani told me when I first presented the idea of bringing the Olympics to New York, there are always going to be haters. With everything we did, at every step of the way, people and groups opposed what we wanted to do—constituencies that had competing visions for the city, for their neighborhoods, and for their lives. And that didn't even count the people in government, our own or those at the state or federal levels.

Governing is about accomplishing things. Over the years I've thought a lot about whether a magic formula enabled us to be so successful. I think, more than anything else, it comes down to four things: people, alignment and communications, money, and storytelling. It always starts at the top. On so many things, it came back to Mike Bloomberg's philosophy of management. First, pick good people. He didn't care what party you came from, or who your friends were, or even if you voted for him (not that he bothered to ask), just whether you would be the best at what he asked you to do.

When he picked people, he just wanted to make sure that they were in sync strategically, and then he let them do their thing, supporting them with resources and encouragement and taking the flak when necessary. He did that with me (and other senior members of our administration), and I like to think I did that with the people who worked for me, and so on down the line. That style of management breeds extraordinary loyalty and empowerment, which is why the Bloomberg team enjoyed such remarkable stability and creativity, particularly important in government, in which everything is so complicated and often takes years to complete.

But the people have to work together as a team. They have to communicate effectively. Here again, Bloomberg set the tone. When on the first day of the Bloomberg Administration I walked into the bullpen in City Hall and found that my "office" was going to be a five-foot-long desk separated from my neighbors by a six-inch-high divider, I was aghast. Within hours, I began to appreciate the benefits. Could it have been easier to make sure that we were on the same page, or to get a decision, or to just talk through an issue, than simply wheeling around in my chair and asking the Mayor? Other than with my own small staff, however, I didn't have the luxury of my direct reports being in the same room.

In the seams of the bureaucracy, big or small plans don't usually fail because of bad faith or even disagreements among the parties. Most often, different parts of the bureaucracy simply have different priorities, funding sources, or resource constraints. There has to be a mechanism to quickly identify the gaps and resolve them. The structure of our administration, which gave Deputy Mayors authority over nearly all of the agencies necessary to get things done within their domains, worked beautifully. For example, to get a major rezoning planned and approved, nearly all of the Commissioners of the agencies key to getting the plan done—Housing, Economic Development, City Planning, Transportation, and Environmental Protection—reported to me. If a dispute arose, I could bring them together and make the decision. Our Economic Development Agency Council meetings, shared strategic plans, multiagency summits, and constant day-to-day interaction, driven by the super-competent staff of Senior Policy Advisors in City Hall, facilitated the alignment and communications to move things forward at uncommon speed.

We did manage to get our plans developed and approved in record time. Hudson Yards was three years from start to approval. Greenpoint-Williamsburg was about the same. Downtown Brooklyn was less. PlaNYC, all 127 points of it, went from initial conception to fully fleshed out and funded in twenty-one months. With each effort we got a little bit better at listening, a little bit better at reflecting community input, and a little bit better at adjusting the plans without compromising their integrity and coherence.

In many of the cases where we had big plans, we had to be very creative in the ways we found the money to get them done, especially at the beginning of the Bloomberg Administration. The fact that several of us—especially the Mayor, who would ultimately make the decisions—had financial backgrounds was a huge benefit in coming up with creative solutions to difficult financial challenges. There had never been a tax increment financing in New York before we created the biggest one in history to extend the No. 7 line. We managed to figure out how to gain leverage from a sleepy housing finance agency because we knew how to read a financial institution's balance sheet and income statement. To expand the use of inclusionary zoning or to develop a mechanism to transfer air rights so that we could win the support of all thirty-eight owners of property under the High Line, we needed to understand how the private sector was going to be financially incentivized and develop policies and programs accordingly.

More than that, though, we brought from the private sector a disciplined approach to thinking about investment and return. That didn't mean every issue could be reduced to a simple formula where the dollars invested would be compared to the tax revenues returned, but thinking about decisions using a thoughtful investment framework helped to convince ourselves and others, especially the minders of the budget, that our plans weren't going to be a drain on the city's financial position. It also enabled us to see investments we made—in neighborhoods, in facilities, or in broad initiatives such as sustainability—in a much broader context, including whether we were helping to stimulate the virtuous cycle.

No matter how compelling the plans, you still have to sell them to the many constituents—inside the administration, the City Council, other levels of government, community groups, labor unions, the business community, the media, and many others—that have a vested interest in the outcome. Perhaps the single-most important lesson I learned from the Olympic bid was the importance of storytelling. Without a compelling narrative that articulates the problem and the opportunity, the process of selling a complex idea is much harder. But the story has to be backed up with real substance. There is no possible way a guy no one knew could have sold the business community, a skeptical Mayor, local elected officials, and others on the crazy notion that New York ought to host the Olympics if I hadn't spent eighteen months researching every impact of the event on a host city *and* presented a vision of how it could be done in New York. We never would have untied the Gordian knot at Ground Zero had we not taken the time to develop a detailed model of the likely financial outcomes at the site and then made them understandable. PlaNYC was only successful because we did the work to justify every one of the 127 initiatives, lay them out in detail, and then wrap them in an elegant and honest narrative that everyone could appreciate.

There are no shortcuts to getting big things done.

TECHNOLOGY

THERE IS A fifth element I think is going to be critically important to the next generation of cities; they will have to learn to integrate digital technology into their physical environments. I have little doubt that when one of my successors writes a book about New York's—or any other city's—next comeback twenty-five years from now, a key element of that story will be how the city managed to harness the set of digital technologies pervading our personal and work lives to meaningfully improve its quality of life.

When it became clear Bloomberg wanted to be more involved at Bloomberg LP, it became equally clear that though I would still be the president, I would become his de facto deputy, so I decided to step aside. At fifty-six, I didn't want to be his Deputy Mayor again. So, I invited him out to dinner and let him know that despite my love of the company, and my love and admiration for him, I had decided to leave. As I told him, I thought I saw three emotions flash across his face—guilt (he had always pledged not to come back, and I had relied on that promise), sadness (he had always enjoyed our working together and thought I had been a successful steward of his company), and relief (he wasn't going to have to worry about tiptoeing around me at the company). Not that he actually said any of this.

Just as we had when he surprised me and asked me to move over to Bloomberg LP when I was preparing to leave City Hall, we worked out the details of the transition in a matter of minutes. He was incredibly generous and asked me to join the board of Bloomberg Philanthropies, his foundation, on which I still sit. We remain close friends.

Still, I had to figure out what I wanted to do next. I had closely followed the developing "smart cities" movement and thought that given the combination of my two previous careers—running a city and a technology-driven data and analytics company—I might be uniquely suited to play a role in fulfilling the promise offered by an emerging set of digital technologies such as ubiquitous connectivity, sensing (including GPS, cameras, computer vision, specialty sensors, and the Internet of Things), social networks (which, because of our capacity to share, our opinions enable us to trust a wider circle of people, places, and things), advanced computing power (such as artificial intelligence and machine learning), and new design and fabrication technologies (robotics and 3-D printing) to improve urban life.

I had gotten a taste of the potential of this through my efforts as the founding Chair of The Shed, the cultural institution at Hudson Yards. Early on we decided we wanted to put a cultural institution at the very heart of the new West Side to generate energy that would radiate through the entire area. We set aside perhaps the prime site in the entire area—at the intersection of Hudson Yards and West Chelsea along three hundred feet of the High

Line—for a to-be-determined institution. We had no idea what it should be. We just knew that it had to be something never done before in New York, which isn't easy in a city with 1,200 cultural institutions.

After we completed the rezonings, we began convening groups of leaders in New York's cultural world to try to come up with some ideas. Eventually, we had an insight: the Internet was beginning to rearrange the cultural ecosystem. Artists were undertaking an unprecedented number of cross-disciplinary collaborations, shattering traditional silos that persist in most institutions. Artists and institutions were able to reach their audiences directly, giving them global reach like never before, drawing in new sources of funding. And yet there wasn't a single facility in the world flexible or connected enough to be able to capitalize on these forces. The Shed, the world's most connected and flexible cultural building, designed by Liz Diller and David Rockwell, will be the first twenty-first-century cultural building when it opens in April 2019.

After I left Bloomberg LP, I began applying this newfound appreciation for urban technology. The first thing I did after I announced I was leaving the company was to team up with my friends at Related Companies to acquire the troubled parent of Citi Bike, the bike-share franchise Janette Sadik-Khan had willed into existence (it also managed bike-share systems around the United States, Canada, and Australia). Bike sharing capitalizes on digital technology by enabling riders to share a common asset more easily and less expensively than they otherwise would be able to do. Our group acquired the company and, under the leadership of Jay Walder, former Chair and CEO of the Metropolitan Transportation Authority, began the process of upgrading management, technology, and the digital customer experience, turning it into a beloved, vital part of the transportation infrastructure in New York City. It costs the city nothing.

Around the same time, Eric Schmidt, Executive Chair of Google, approached me. He told me that Larry Page, the CEO and cofounder of Google, shared my view that the combination of digital technologies would help bring about a revolution in urban life as profound as the three previous technological revolutions that have largely defined the modern city, which were the steam engine, the electric grid, and the automobile.

So we established a new company, Sidewalk Labs, to attempt to accelerate the process of integrating these digital technologies into cities. We didn't delude ourselves into thinking that this would be obvious or easy. Cities are big, complex, and messy places. Urbanists and technologists speak almost completely different languages. But Page and I believe cities don't have time to wait. The greatest periods of economic growth and productivity have always occurred when we integrate innovation into the physical environment.

The foundation of this new digitally enabled world is connecting everyone. That's why the first thing we did at Sidewalk Labs was to form a company to install LinkNYC, six thousand kiosks that offer free high-speed broadband throughout the five boroughs, in a city where three million people don't have access today.

But the potential for these new technologies is breathtaking. Take just one: self-driving cars. As they are adopted, almost everything in a city will begin to change. Assuming they are shared, consumers will see huge transportation cost savings. Up to 30 percent of land in a city used for parking and separated roadways can be reclaimed for more parks, pedestrian paths, and bike lanes, which mean more active lifestyles and potentially significant health-care savings over time. Safe streets mean busy parents can feel confident that their children will be able to walk home from school alone, saving them precious time. Better access to open space and less need for on-site storage as a result of cheap, autonomous delivery mean residents won't need as much living space, which will reduce housing costs.

That's just one innovation. We are exploring others across infrastructure, buildings, health care, and even governance. Our hope is that when cities adopt these and many other technologies, the impact will be as profound as they were for the three previous urban technology revolutions.

Central Park. The Brooklyn Bridge. The subway system. Lincoln Center. New York is a city of big leaps that have taken it in new and thrilling directions. I like to think that when generations from now people compile their lists of New York's big leaps, the Bloomberg years will be recognized for our five-borough strategy to accommodate the growth so essential to improving the quality of life of New Yorkers in the twenty-first century.

In government, the easiest thing to do is nothing, especially in a loud and active democracy in which the media blast their megaphones. It's easier to do nothing because every single plan, no matter how small, no matter how popular, will have someone on the other side. In a city such as New York, where that volume is naturally amplified both by the personalities of its citizens and by virtue of its being the media capital of the country, what might be small, manageable opposition elsewhere quickly can seem like an entrenched, well-armed foe.

A successful urban leader must be willing to endure a sizable contingent of doubters. He or she needs not only the political skill to convert doubters into believers and skeptics into cheerleaders but also the political will to move forward even when it becomes evident that there is no clear path to approval. Unless leadership is willing to take some shots both from dissenters and from the media, great innovations are impossible.

One of the most fascinating elements of the Bloomberg era was the way in which his tenure confounded conventional political wisdom. Conventional wisdom holds that the most likeable person usually wins. Bloomberg was never a beloved "have a beer with" Mayor, and he didn't try to fake it. But his enduring popularity (even today 70 percent of New Yorkers have a favorable opinion of him as Mayor) proves something few political leaders have the courage to believe—voters don't have to love you. What they have to do is respect you. They have to trust you. Eventually they accept you and your personality for whatever it is.

Yes, you have to listen, you have to be responsive, and you have to understand that you work for the very people who are calling you names in the press. But at some point someone has to say yes. And even though it is uncomfortable and sometimes agonizing to see your good name and the tremendous hours you and your staff have put into trying to better the city described unkindly by those who oppose your projects, it's incumbent upon a leader to keep his or her eye on the vision that will emerge after the project is built.

Government can work. That's what the New York comeback after September 11 demonstrates. Sure there were advantages on which we capitalized. But mostly, our experience is one from which any city—or maybe even state or nation—can learn. Fearless vision and leadership; nonideological policies grounded in hard truths, facts, and analysis; and great people organized, inspired, and unleashed to work together to help improve lives. That's the timeless recipe for taking big leaps forward.

That's also a recipe for looking beyond today's cynicism and disillusionment to imagine brighter days tomorrow when together we successfully overcome the challenges confronting us.

ACKNOWLEDGMENTS

I was a reluctant New Yorker. I was also a reluctant writer. I never expected to write about my experiences helping New York to recover from 9/11, or anything else. The process of getting to this point has been a fairly long one, but it has been made much more enjoyable because of the many people who helped me to do it.

If there is one single thing about which I am most proud it is the teams that I was fortunate to assemble at NYC2012 and then in City Hall. I was truly blessed (not a word I use lightly) to work with the most dedicated, hard-working, creative, and resourceful people imaginable. The NYC2012 crew originally came together when the idea was little more than a glint of an idea in an unknown investor's eye and yet they had faith that together we could develop a vision that would help to change to face of New York. They were led by Jay Kriegel, who despite his initial reluctance ("that's the stupidest fucking idea I've ever heard!") leapt into the quest with extreme Kriegel zeal, indefatigability, and refusal to accept anything other than excellence in every single thing we said, did, or produced (he applied that same standard to this book, which is infinitely better than it otherwise would have been because of his intense review). Beyond the professional tutoring he has given me for past two decades, I can say without hesitation that I have learned more from Jay about how to be a good person than anyone, perhaps excluding my parents whom I idolized.

My great fortune building great teams continued in City Hall. When I accepted Mike Bloomberg's offer to become Deputy Mayor, Jay advised me that if I wanted to be a successful public servant I should try to be proactive 30 percent of the time and just deal with the day-to-day business of government the other 70 percent. This was one of the few instances when I ignored him: I tried to be proactive the vast majority of the time, as our 289 separate initiatives attest. The only reason we were able to do so much was because I got extraordinary leverage from my staff, starting with my four chiefs-of-staff. Sharon Greenberger set the tone of collegiality and collaboration among our City Hall and agency colleagues and developed much of the strategy that guided us. As I noted in the book, hiring her was the smartest move I made. To this day, she offers me always on-point counsel and unwavering friendship. Josh Sirefman, Marc Ricks, and Jim Whelan followed Sharon, and each couldn't have been more perfect for the time that they sat in the seat next to me in our tiny cubicle in the bullpen. Each led a team of Senior Policy Advisors, who were the real reason we managed to accomplish so much. I haven't been able to mention all of them by name any more than I could detail each of the couple of hundred initiatives they led—the book would have become an encyclopedia—but they were essential to the range of accomplishments. Angela Sun, though, deserves special mention because she was not only a star in City Hall who worked on a whole range of things—including ridding New York City of Off-Track Betting, developing the strategy to enhance New York's competitive position in financial services, and rezoning Jamaica, Queens—but when I left to run Bloomberg LP, she agreed to come with me as my chief-of-staff and stayed for all seven years I was there. I couldn't have had a more skilled or loyal partner.

It is one thing to get a lot done, it is another to get it all down and then fashion it into a book. For that, I have also been able to depend on a wonderful team. Ken Kurson helped me to develop the proposal for the book, which my agent Flip Brophy then sold. But it was Leslie Kaufman, who for many years was a reporter for *The New York Times*, who pried the recollections out of me (not easy after ten to fifteen years) and about the seventy other people she interviewed and who exhaustively researched documents, clips, and books written about our time in government. She crafted first drafts and then we went back and forth, debating narrative arc, style, and words. Having never done this before, I can't compare it with other experiences, but I can say that I loved working with Leslie. We had fun together and learned an enormous amount from each other.

Once we had a good second or third draft, I turned to Sophia Hollander to edit the whole book. Sophia had written the massive bid book that we submitted to the International Olympic Committee and then the elegant and comprehensive PlaNYC book. There are few people in whom I have greater confidence, as a writer and as a person. After she left government, she became a reporter for the *Wall Street Journal.* Fortunately for me, she left there just as I was getting close to completion on *Greater Than Ever.* She offered to review the whole book. Its structure and clarity have benefitted enormously from her skill.

My assistant, Marla Pardee, was there through the entire Olympic effort and my time at City Hall—and we continue to work together today. In fact, we have been a team for a quarter of a century. She has a magical ability to recall every person I know and every meeting I have had, which has been of incalculable value in putting this account together.

As we raced to the finish line, colleagues at Sidewalk Labs Carrie Denning, Megan Wald, Robie Evangelista, and Madelyn Fried helped to find photos, make sure the map was accurate, and do final proofing.

There are hundreds and hundreds of facts in the book. My daughter, Ariel, researched every single one of them with relish and an ability to uncover obscure information that wowed her already awestruck father. Ariel is a screenwriter, who sold her first series idea to a network just days after she finished her work with me. I only wish she lived in New York with her brother and sister, Jacob and Jenna, both of whom read drafts of the book and were especially effective at puncturing any hints of overinflated ego.

Our work making sure that the book is accurate was helped by the many people who reviewed all or part of it, especially Frank Barry, Sharon Greenberger, Alex Garvin, Amy Stanton, Andrew Kimball, Andrew Winters, Andy Alper, Josh Sirefman, Jerilyn Perine, Rafael Cestero, Roy Bahat, Lynne Sagalyn, George Fertitta, Vishaan Chakrabarti, Jim Whelan, Jay Cross, Marc Ricks, Joe Chan, Michael Kalt, Angela Sung, Seth Pinsky, Anthony Coscia, Rit Aggarwala, and Ariella Maron. What is so amazing is that we are all still so close.

For the entire process from proposal to publishing, I am completely indebted to Clive Priddle of PublicAffairs. He bought one idea and then encouraged me to redo it to make it my story but one that would have relevance to others. He was right, of course, just as he was on every other point that he raised and every word, sentence, or chapter that he edited. He also pushed me to meet his deadlines, which I did with more modest success. I am completely indebted to him for his confidence in me—and for his patience. Melissa Raymond demonstrated even greater patience with me as we neared the finish line, and Kristina Fazzalaro was a resourceful and tenacious publicist.

While this book is my story, in a very real sense it is the story of Mike Bloomberg's leadership. Mike hates compliments—maybe as much as he hates giving them—so I will let it go that I can't begin to describe how grateful I am for his friendship and the opportunities he gave me.

Finally, I want to acknowledge my family. My parents, Martin and Allene Doctoroff, died too young, and every morning I look at a picture of them and wish they had been able to go on my New York journey with me. They encouraged their four sons to support each other, and Mark, Tom, and Andy have always been there for me.

Alisa and I came to New York never expecting to stay. Two years max, we said. We definitely never saw ourselves as the immigrants that E. B. White described as "generating as much heat as Consolidated Edison" with great New York dreams. And yet, very gradually, we forged a life as real New Yorkers and were inspired by the people we met and the city itself to do more, achieve more, and ultimately give back more. While I was pursuing my Olympic dreams and then overwhelmed in City Hall, Alisa was guiding Jacob, Ariel, and Jenna through their teen years, helping them to become the remarkable people that they are, all the while crafting a career for herself in Jewish communal life. She ultimately became the Chairman and President of UJA-Federation, the largest local philanthropy in the world. Throughout it all, her support, encouragement, and love have been unwavering. When we first started dating, I used to tell her—ironically quoting Lou Gehrig's farewell speech—that I was "the luckiest man on the face of this earth." Forty years later, I feel exactly the same way.

INDEX

Daniel L. Doctoroff is the founder and chief executive officer of Sidewalk Labs, an Alphabet company that was formed to accelerate the intersection of digital technology into urban environments. Prior to launching Sidewalk Labs, he was CEO and president of Bloomberg LP, the leading provider of financial news and information. From 2002 to 2008, he was New York City's deputy mayor for economic development and rebuilding. Outside of work, he serves on the boards of the University of Chicago, World Resources Institute, the United States Olympic Committee, Bloomberg Philanthropies, and Human Rights First. He is a founder of Target ALS, an initiative to streamline discovery of new approaches to treating ALS (also known as Lou Gehrig's disease), and a founder and chair of The Shed, New York's newest cultural institution. He lives in New York City with his wife, Alisa. They have three grown children: Jacob, Ariel, and Jenna.

PublicAffairs is a publishing house founded in 1997. It is a tribute to the standards, values, and flair of three persons who have served as mentors to countless reporters, writers, editors, and book people of all kinds, including me.

I. F. STONE, proprietor of *I. F. Stone's Weekly*, combined a commitment to the First Amendment with entrepreneurial zeal and reporting skill and became one of the great independent journalists in American history. At the age of eighty, Izzy published *The Trial of Socrates*, which was a national bestseller. He wrote the book after he taught himself ancient Greek.

BENJAMIN C. BRADLEE was for nearly thirty years the charismatic editorial leader of *The Washington Post*. It was Ben who gave the *Post* the range and courage to pursue such historic issues as Watergate. He supported his reporters with a tenacity that made them fearless and it is no accident that so many became authors of influential, best-selling books.

ROBERT L. BERNSTEIN, the chief executive of Random House for more than a quarter century, guided one of the nation's premier publishing houses. Bob was personally responsible for many books of political dissent and argument that challenged tyranny around the globe. He is also the founder and longtime chair of Human Rights Watch, one of the most respected human rights organizations in the world.

·　　·　　·

For fifty years, the banner of Public Affairs Press was carried by its owner Morris B. Schnapper, who published Gandhi, Nasser, Toynbee, Truman, and about 1,500 other authors. In 1983, Schnapper was described by *The Washington Post* as "a redoubtable gadfly." His legacy will endure in the books to come.

Peter Osnos, *Founder*